THE
UNITED STATES
IN THE
TWENTIETH CENTURY

CULTURE

CONTRIBUTORS TO THIS VOLUME

Ian Bell, Department of American Studies, University of Keele

Kate Bowles, Department of English, University of Wollongong

Helen Dennis, Department of English, University of Warwick

Andrew Goodwin, Department of Communication, University of San Francisco

Allan Lloyd Smith, School of English and American Studies, University of East Anglia

Richard Maltby, School of English and American Studies, University of Exeter

Phil Melling, American Studies, University College of Swansea

Jeremy Mitchell, Faculty of Social Sciences, The Open University

John Pearson, Bechtel International Center, Stanford University

Matthew Roudané, Department of English, Georgia State University

Douglas Tallack, Department of American and Canadian Studies, The University of Nottingham

Kenneth Thompson, Faculty of Social Sciences, The Open University

John Wilson, Department of Sociology, Duke University

Cover

Central Park, New York

Photo: United States Travel & Tourism Administration

THE UNITED STATES IN THE TWENTIETH CENTURY

CULTURE

Edited by Jeremy Mitchell
and Richard Maidment

Hodder & Stoughton

in association with

The Open University

This text forms part of an Open University Second Level Course D214 *The United States in the Twentieth Century*. If you would like a copy of *Studying with the Open University*, please write to the Central Enquiry Service, PO Box 200, The Open University, Walton Hall, Milton Keynes MK7 6YZ, United Kingdom.

Cataloguing in Publication Data is available from the British Library.

ISBN 0 340 59687 2

First published 1994

Impression number   10 9   8   7   6   5   4   3   2   1
Year   1998   1997   1996   1995   1994   1993

Edited, designed and typeset by the Open University.

Printed in Great Britain for the educational publishing division of Hodder Headline Plc, Mill Road, Dunton Green, Sevenoaks, Kent TN13 2YA by Thomson Litho Ltd, East Kilbride.

7067C/D214 Book 1

CONTENTS

PREFACE

The five volumes in this series are part of an Open University, Faculty of Social Sciences course *The United States in the Twentieth Century*. In many respects the course has been a new venture — it is the first time that the Open University has entered the field of American Studies and it did so at a time when resources were not abundant. So the development of this course is due, in no small part, to the enthusiasm and support of many colleagues in the Faculty of Social Sciences. There are too many people to thank individually, but my appreciation must be recorded for some of them.

The United States in the Twentieth Century would not have been made without my academic colleagues, Anthony McGrew, Jeremy Mitchell and Grahame Thompson. Their role was central to the conception and planning of the course and their presence made the production of it an intellectually stimulating as well as an enjoyable experience. Mike Dawson, the Course Manager, took all the tension out of a process that is normally fraught and difficult. His calm efficiency, common sense and good humour got the rest of us through the production process with few anxieties. Jeremy Cooper of the BBC not only ensured that the course has an excellent audio-visual component, but made a very important contribution to its overall development. The Course Team owes a substantial debt to the editorial work of Stephen Clift and Tom Hunter who did all that was asked of them plus a great deal more. The designs for the covers, and indeed for the entire course, by Sarah Crompton were immediately and enthusiastically welcomed by everybody. David Wilson of the Book Trade Department was always available and his advice was both appreciated and heeded. Our colleagues in Project Control and in the Operations Division of the university were unfailingly supportive and helpful. However, none of these books would have seen the light of day without Anne Hunt who, along with her colleagues Mary Dicker and Carole Kershaw, typed successive drafts of the manuscripts of all five volumes without complaint and with remarkable accuracy and speed.

These books owe an enormous debt to our Americanist colleagues in institutions other than the Open University. This series has drawn on their scholarship and expertise, and above all on their generosity in being willing to participate in this project. The Course Team owes a particular debt to Professor David Adams, Director of the David Bruce Centre at the University of Keele, the external assessor of *The United States in the Twentieth Century*. His tough advice and wise counsel assisted us greatly. We incurred a similar obligation to Professor Ian Bell, also of the University of Keele, who helped us far beyond the call of duty. Doctor Ronald Clifton, who has done so much for American Studies in Britain, was enormously helpful and supportive in making sure this course came to fruition.

Finally there were moments when it might have been easier for Margaret Kiloh, the Dean of the Faculty of Social Sciences, to have been less than enthusiastic about *The United States in the Twentieth Century* but her support never wavered.

Richard Maidment, Course Chair
Milton Keynes, December 1993

We would like to thank all the contributors, we could not have produced this book without their unstinting co-operation. We would like to record our gratitude, in particular, to Professor Ian Bell of the University of Keele, who gave us the benefit of his scholarly advice and immeasurably improved this volume. His judgement was, as always, acute and critical while remaining very supportive. Norma Sherratt made several shrewd observations and saved us from numerous pitfalls. Paul Smith worked hard and to great effect over the illustrations. Finally we would like to thank all our colleagues on the Course Team of *The United States in the Twentieth Century*.

Jeremy Mitchell and Richard Maidment
Milton Keynes, December 1993

THE CONSTRUCTIONS OF AMERICAN CULTURE: AN OVERVIEW

Ian Bell ★

America is about beginnings, about newness, about continual self-creation, and American cultural forms are permeated with inquiries about origins, about lines of ancestry, about invention. And if a 'culture' is to be broadly defined as the whole way of life of a nation, a coalescence of economic, political, social and aesthetic conditions and beliefs, then, as the following chapters will show, *American* culture is always to be viewed as hetero-geneous rather than homogeneous: the process of America's understanding of itself during the twentieth century is, more than anything, a recognition of the tensions between unity and diversity. In part, this is as a result of the necessarily contradictory nature of American ideology, as Allan Lloyd Smith will demonstrate, the strain between the founding and continuing promise of individualism, self-reliance and liberty from the Declaration of Indepen-dence and the Constitution in the late eighteenth century, and the practices of twentieth-century society. In Chapter 10 Lloyd Smith provides a useful summary of these contradictions:

> Although these beliefs have persisted in American life ... the actu-ality is (and always was) rather different. Bureaucratic control, stra-tegic manipulation of advantage, the development of monopoly and the subversion of regulative structures have been another 'American Way'. So among the features of the majority culture we have to acknowledge a capacity for living with the contradiction between the apparent and the actual processes of the society. In the twentieth century, scientific management, bureaucratic government, philo-sophical pragmatism, and vast, integrated structures of financial control have often underpinned the slogans of independence, indi-vidualism and the free market that continue to dominate public dis-course in the United States.

What is perhaps most extraordinary about these contradictions is the very persistence of that founding promise, the continuing attraction held out by the visions of anti-statism, populism and egalitarianism which themselves go such a long way towards enabling American culture to *live through* the tensions outlined by Lloyd Smith, to envisage itself as engaged continually in strategies of resistance and re-invention.

1 OPPOSITION AND CREATION

The twentieth century arrived in America early, around the middle of the nineteenth century. We see this arrival not only in the rapidity of developments in technology and business practices, but in the modernity of American artistic forms. It is no exaggeration to suggest that the modern novel and the modern poem both begin to take shape in the works of novelists such as Herman Melville and poets such as Walt Whitman during the 1850s, and that with James McNeill Whistler in the 1870s we witness a substantial contribution to modern painting. All three forms have in common an oppositional stance that more than anything is the principal feature not only of the more visible avant-garde in the twentieth century, but of the widespread sense of living within a world that is alterable. This oppositional stance is well exemplified in the attitudes towards language and meaning that we discover in one of the major novels of the earlier period, Melville's *Moby Dick* (1851), the story of Captain Ahab's fanatical search for vengeance on the white whale responsible for the loss of his leg.

Melville's modernist concern here is with the ways in which meaning is not to be derived from the simple, single, non-problematic relation of word to its object, of signified to signifier, but from the paradoxes and contradictions of that relation — meaning is produced by the multiplicity of a word's reference rather than by its singularity. The thrust of the novel is to display the falseness of any fixed 'centre' of significance, the imprisoning system which inhibits the full articulation of meaning. Moby Dick, the white whale itself, for example, is not to be confined by any single definition, however sophisticated, but it is to be understood by the variety of definitions available to the free-play of society itself: Ahab's error is to adopt one definition as a totality of truth, for the purposes of revenge on the whale, to the exclusion of all others — a form of linguistic dictatorship. Melville's work supplants such dictatorship with a grammar of the new republic where meaning is available only through a community of readings. Here, the lesson pursued by twentieth-century descendants is that language is partial and provisory: its function is to deny the fixedness, the tyranny of established value. Text after text, from Nathaniel Hawthorne's novels and tales of the 1840s and 1850s to the fictions of Don De Lillo in the 1980s, propose an insistently indeterminate world that is shadowy, fantastic, evasive — a world that ceaselessly questions the apparent givens of organized society. The 'counter-culture' of the 'Beat' generation of the 1950s and 1960s, writers such as Jack Kerouac, William Burroughs, and Allen Ginsberg, recapitulates the resistances of the mid-nineteenth century, resistances which continued to refuse the institutional tyrannies which occasioned the novelty of the new nation in the first place. It is precisely in the free-play of its linguistic endeavours that we discover the cultural determinants of American literature in both centuries: it is not merely anecdotal to relate that, on meeting Ginsberg in 1985, I was struck by his ability to recite great tracts of Melville's poetry with extraordinary accuracy. When Whitman wrote in *An American Primer* during the early 1850s of American's 'appetite' for 'unhemmed latitude, coarseness, live epithets, expletives, words of opprobrium, resistance,' he was establishing a manifesto for much of the literature which follows, maintaining a view of language which 'seldomer tells a thing than suggests or necessitates it' (Whitman, 1969, p.21). Words, which are always given a specifically constructive role in American thought (seen, literally, as builders), thus operate against the conventions of mimesis and verisimilitude: a linguistic strategy which 'suggests' rather than 'tells' inevitably resists also standardizations of perception and undermines a fixed literalness of representation by principles of indirection and variousness. To resist the tyranny of fixed words and fixed meanings is to resist the tyranny of institutions.

To be 'American' has always involved the creation of new space — geographically, politically, and aesthetically — to be 'American' is thus always to enter into acts of opposition, acts which depend upon a continual process of re-invention, of beginning again. In a sense that is both real and metaphorical (and America is where such divisions are far from clear-cut: Richard Brautigan's novel of 1967, *Trout Fishing in America*, has 'America' as 'often only a place in the mind'), 'America' is invented by strokes of the pen in the Declaration of Independence of 1776 (composed, in the main, by Thomas Jefferson) and in the Constitution of 1787. Chronologically, twentieth-century America begins again by further re-inventions, by re-asking questions about what it means to be 'American'. In 1924, the Johnson Immigration Act (which, following on from the Dawes Act of 1887, granted full citizenship to the Indian population) reflected what a recent critic, Walter Benn Michaels, has called 'the newly official interest in everybody's ancestors' (Michaels, 1990, p.221) and brought to the fore the questions about diversity and assimilation which always characterize the notion of 'America'. The novelist Willa Cather wrote, in 1923, of her up-bringing in Nebraska, an account which may serve to exemplify the changing conditions of the new century:

> The county in which I grew up, in the south-central part of the State, was typical. On Sunday we could drive to a Norwegian church and listen to a sermon in that language, or to a Danish or a Swedish church. We could go to the French Catholic settlement in the next county and hear a sermon in French, or into the Bohemian township and hear one in Czech, or we could go to church with the German Lutherans.
>
> (quoted in Lee, 1989, p.33)

Cather's choice of sites of religion to make her point is especially instructive: as Kenneth Thompson will show in the first chapter, following Seymour Martin Lipset, American individualism is 'strengthened by its special religious character', dissenting and congregational — a 'voluntary religion' which fosters 'egalitarian, individualistic, and populist values which are anti-élitist'. And Thompson demonstrates clearly how the extent of religious schisms and sectarian diversification has allowed religion to play 'a central role in creating and perpetuating ethnic divisions through language, traditions, organization and patterns of interaction.' In the face of such diversity we find what is perhaps the most characteristic feature of 'America' — the sense that 'America' itself is America's most fundamental invention in its constructions of homogeneity against the realities of an inescapably pluralist society. We see these constructions in virtually every aspect of American cultural expression, from the consensus-led manœuvrings of the political parties to the cohesive gestures of domestic life, as Allan Lloyd Smith notes: 'those endless and indistinguishable Holiday Inns, Howard Johnsons or Crown Motels; the preference for McDonald's or Burger King hamburgers, expressed through consumer choice; the apparent sameness of television programming, even across 30 channels.'

The question about diversity and unity, difference and assimilation, particularly as it applies to matters of ethnicity and of the genealogy of what is 'America', is arguably the hall-mark of twentieth-century American cultural debate. Kenneth Thompson will argue that, during the first half of the century, the emphasis lay upon the hegemony of unity 'through the assimilation of ethnic groups into a common culture — Americanization', while since the 1960s there has been a shift to 'a view which celebrates cultural diversity, subcultural pluralism and ethnic differences'. It is certainly true that the century is ending as it began by questioning the nation's identity, and that, as the chapters by Phil Melling on the novel and John Pearson on rock 'n' roll will show, White Anglo-Saxon Protestant (WASP) dominance is being challenged from the margins of American society in the shapes of the increasing prominence currently afforded to Chicano or Chinese-American literature, for example, and of the African-American resources of popular music. Nevertheless, it is important to recognize that cultural pluralism was already much in evidence during the 1920s and 1930s not only as an object for establishment suspicion but, in the models provided by Native American life, recognized as a powerful antidote to what was seen as an atomized and commercialized society. The terms in which that antidote is articulated are themselves instructive for an important strand of Americanness — the allied notions of harmony and process.

The Dawes Act strove to contain Native Americans (the current definition of the Indian population) within the hegemony of white Anglo-American conformity, and depended upon the need to fragment communal consciousness: Theodore Roosevelt, in his 1901 State of the Union message, saw the Act as a 'mighty pulverising engine to break up the tribal mass'. But the ascendancy of interest amongst intellectuals in the 1920s and 1930s in the possibilities of cultural pluralism occasioned a revaluation of Native American life which admired rather than felt threatened by the collectivity of its harmony. This revaluation presented a different way of looking at the individualist tenets of American thought: as David Murray has noticed most recently, Native American life understood the ideal society as one which was based not so much on 'voluntarist individualism' as on 'the values of conservative institutions and heritages as supportive and creative of personality'. The organicist approach which underwrites this view found its official voice in the Meriam Report of 1928 and in the thinking of figures such as John Collier (an active supporter of Native American groups during the

1920s who was to become Commissioner of Indian Affairs in 1934) for whom the harmony of Native American culture presented an example, in Murray's words, of 'how to survive by community rather than be destroyed by individualistic competition'. Collier's autobiography found in the combination of 'earth loyalties and human loyalties' a revised notion of individualism which saw Native Americans as possessing 'the fundamental secret of human life — the secret of building great personality through the instrumentality of social institutions' (Murray, 1982, pp.11–15).

As Kenneth Thompson's discussion of *Habits of the Heart: Individualism and Commitment in American Life* will show, this form of communitarianism took on more urgent force in the 1980s as a reaction against right-wing individualism. Thompson distinguishes between 'expressive individualism' which integrates individuals into a larger 'civic' or national community and 'Americanization', involving conformity to WASP values, which produces alienated individuals with no communal identity. Tellingly, he concludes that it is by leaving behind 'Americanization' that ethnic members become 'American'. Nowhere is the story of this process so well told as in the present challenge to male, white, imperialist dominance by novels, poems, and, to a lesser degree, films from the margins of society — from women and ethnic writers. Against the discourse of WASP adventurousness and renewal emerges a literature which seeks to undermine WASP history by personal testimony, immediate experience, the oral transmission of values, ethnic genealogy and ancestral lore.

In Chapter 2 Phil Melling provides an excellent summary of the challenge when he argues that 'the ethnic American is no longer the silent, passive witness of history. The current mission in ethnic literature is to reinstate the memories of an ancestral tradition and to unburden those tribal "ghosts" whose lives and stories lack recognition.' Within the literary and historical interventions of writers such as Alice Walker, Toni Morrison, Maxine Hong Kingston, or Sandra Cisneros, we see also a revised notion of how ethnic identity (be it Native, African, Chinese, or Hispanic American) reconstructs a connected strand of what 'American' means — the notion of process, of *becoming* American. Again, this strand holds as true for the beginning of the century as for its end. Essays on American writing during the 1920s by the novelist D.H. Lawrence established what he called 'the aboriginal life of the continent' as the proper concern for American history and its role in establishing national identity (Lawrence, 1936a, pp.90–1), and a work of 1925 by the poet William Carlos Williams, *In the American Grain*, attempted to excavate the authentic language of that identity (Williams, 1971, p.5). Lawrence's review of Williams's book was sensitive to the newly figured 'spirit of place' in Williams's enterprise, and argued for American history as essentially a history of 'Americanization', a history of the 'continuity' between 'the murdered Red America and the seething White America'.

This new history is above all a history of process rather than achievement, 'a glimpse of what the vast America *wants men to be*, instead of another strident assertion of what men have made, do make, will make, can make, out of the murdered territories of the New World.' Within this scheme of things,

'A man, in America, can only *begin* to be American', as Lawrence recognizes the 'spirit of place' as part of the process of creating and becoming at a time when 'All America is now going hundred per cent American' (Lawrence, 1936b, pp.92–3). The communitarianism that Collier had identified in Native American culture tended to see the harmony which made it possible in terms of organic process, an interaction between 'earth loyalties' and 'human loyalties' (assumed in part by the 'spirit of place' advanced by Lawrence and Williams), but other thinkers in the early period of the century understood process as a more factitious affair, more available to social alterability.

One of the best examples of this latter line, and rather more in tune with the constructionist element within American thought that is evident from the eighteenth century onwards (as we have discovered in Jefferson, Melville and Whitman), is to be found in an important essay by the philosopher John Dewey in 1934, 'The Need for a Philosophy of Education'. In seeking to find out 'what education really *is*', Dewey argues:

> In the first place, it is a process of development, of growth. And it is the process and not merely the result that is important. A truly healthy person is not something fixed and completed. He is a person whose processes and activities go on in such a way that he will continue to be healthy.

> (Dewey, 1964, p.4)

So although the educator must use results 'that have already been accomplished', he or she cannot make them 'his final and complete standard' — and like the artist, 'he has the problem of creating something that is not the exact duplicate of anything that has been wrought and achieved previously' on the premise that 'existing likes and powers are to be treated as possibilities, as starting-points' (ibid., pp.7–8). And the end of this constructionist process of education is parallel to the kind of collectivity Collier discerned in Native American culture and urged later by *Habits of the Heart* in the 1980s: 'A society of free individuals in which all, through their own work, contribute to the liberation and enrichment of the lives of others, is the only environment in which any individual can really grow normally to his full stature' (ibid., p.12). Also parallel is the enemy against which all three position themselves: a fragmented and manipulative society — in Dewey's words, 'the spirit of inhumanity bred by economic competition and exploitation' breeding 'the demon of prejudice, isolation and hatred' that is to be contested by 'a common effort to rebuild the spirit of common understanding, of mutual sympathy and goodwill among all peoples and races' (ibid., pp.13–14). This constructionist process of becoming powerfully underwrites every area of American ideology: in Chapter 8, for example, John Wilson will use sport as a lens for not only reflecting dominating notions of patriotism and individualism and their antitheses within the inequalities and divisions in American society (in terms of gender, race, and class), but also as a vivid expression of the principle that so many Americans become Americans and are not born to the status.

Perhaps the most instructive contradiction within American culture lies in this idea of 'becoming' in that it dramatizes America's urge for homogeneity whilst recognizing a potency of resource at the edges of organized society, the very sites which homogeneity seeks to repress and appropriate. Here, we are talking not only about the extent to which homogeneity disguises a range of divisions (Allan Lloyd Smith's view of Thornton Wilder's *Our Town* as concerned with a nostalgic mystification of social fracture is an exemplary exposure of such disguise), but about what is, in significant areas, America's manipulation of this contradiction. We can see this manipulation in rock 'n' roll music, for example, a genre which belongs, as John Pearson will demonstrate in Chapter 7, to 'the continuing tradition of American popular music that is always looking to find ways of having white musicians translate black musical styles into commercial success', and which displays, after 1945, 'music coming in from the margins of America'.

2 MODERNITY AND POSTMODERNITY

I hope by now it is apparent that America, uniquely, is to be characterized as being aware of itself as America. Its self-consciousness is there from the very start, in the establishing of a written Constitution which constructs the idea of America: and, historically, the Constitution is not only a made artefact, immediate in the national memory, but is alert to itself as continually to be remade — interpreted and reinterpreted as a measure of America's continual sense of the construction of its own process of becoming. America's self-consciousness of its own construction plays a large part in creating America as the site which, more than any other national culture (because of the rapidity and success in its development of a capitalist economy), displays so vividly *the* great shift of twentieth-century thought from modernism to postmodernism. The shift which occurs, roughly, in the post-1945 period, may be generally graphed as a move from a sense of cultural forms as engaged with a wider society to a sense where such engagement is disavowed. Single definitions of the terms 'modernism' and 'postmodernism' are not only impossible but are not meaningful. This is particularly true of 'modernism' which, as the variousness of usage in subsequent chapters will show (in their wielding of not only 'modernism', but 'modern' and 'modernist'), is heterogeneous rather than homogeneous, and we need to avoid the reductiveness which imposes a speciously unifying grid over a complex and complicated cultural situation — other than allowing that it is used for purposes that are both social *and* aesthetic. As you read this overview and the following chapters you will pick up a cluster of definitions which, while far from being tidy, will generate a 'vortex' (the painter Wyndham Lewis's term for modernism) of understanding (the best guides to the subject remain Bergonzi, 1970; Bradbury and McFarlane, 1976; Faulkner, 1977). The most visible manifestation of the shift from modernism to postmodernism may be found in those areas of American culture which are most closely allied to the world of the new technology and the new corporations which structure twentieth-century life — such as architecture, TV and film.

The Chicago architect Louis Sullivan provides a good example of the modernist strain. As Douglas Tallack will show in Chapter 9, Sullivan's modernism was both technical (allying form with function) and ideological (allying building and society). It is the skyscraper that is the characteristic donation of American architecture, and for Sullivan 'the tall building was intimately connected with a democratic American society' where 'the skyscraper could be conceived organically, rather than merely stylistically, and in the context of the social organism'. By contrast, with the shift to postmodernist perception, after the Second World War, the skyscraper becomes an 'isolated block'. Tallack provides a good summary of the new shape: 'Modernist tenets of technical practice were harnessed by corporate capital and stripped of their social ideology to perpetuate the narrow, wholly individualistic vision of the skyscraper ... The symbols of a triumphant new world were the sleek skyscrapers, free to rise in the absence of strong planning initiatives and laws.' Dissociated style replaces the intimacy of form and function within an increasingly commodified culture where, following the arguments of the contemporary French philosopher who has attended closely to the effects of commodity and consumer culture in America, Jean Baudrillard, the apparently solid world is being replaced by images of its solidity — the 'natural' is replaced by the idea of naturalness, and the authenticity of 'person' is replaced by the performative, calculated and calculating notion of personality (Baudrillard, 1975, Chap.2). In a postmodern world, we live in the design of a designed world at the behest of a consumerism where objects are always filtered by other media and where our looking becomes voyeuristic — the films of David Lynch or the photographs of Cindy Sherman provide appropriate examples. American culture is one that depends upon theatricality, performance, and spectacle — acting and, above all, voyeuristic perception are its characteristic postmodernist functions, as Matthew Roudané tells us in Chapter 6: 'from elections to executions, from World Series to world summit meetings, America is a culture that loves to watch the watchers watching the watchers watch'.

Design and display are the principal features of postmodernity, and their effects are wide-ranging: as Allan Lloyd Smith observes, the 'explanatory structures' of modernism are replaced by 'fragmentation, the end of theory, a loss of historical or spatial orientation, of originality and the self' and what emerges are practices of 'collage, intertextuality and pastiche'. Here, aesthetic production has been integrated into commodity production to create 'the culture of the image or the *simulacrum*' and in the paintings of Andy Warhol or Roy Lichtenstein, for example, we see clearly how objects or people are presentable only as, or through, the layers of other forms of representation (cartoons, advertisements, Hollywood filters). The postmodernist world is, then, a world of surface visibly estranged from solidity (mirroring the accuracy of Marx's earlier prediction, 'all that is solid melts into air'), and Lloyd Smith provides a good summary:

> contemporary culture repudiates the older models of significant *depth* (of the inside versus the outside; of essence against appearance; the Freudian models of latent and manifest elements of con-

sciousness and of repression; the existential modes of authenticity and inauthenticity; and finally, even the opposition between signifier and signified, the sign for something and the thing itself). Depth is replaced by multiple surfaces and a sense of 'intertextuality', the positioning of one text (or piece of writing, image or speech act) in relation to others.

The earlier part of the century had already displayed signs of this condition, but the difference from full-blown postmodernity is itself instructive for the postmodern condition. It was during the 1920s that the consumer culture (the economic foundation of postmodernity) began to manifest itself most clearly in America, and the drastic shift from the period of abundance in the 1920s to the Depression of the 1930s enabled the American novel to witness with especial clarity the effects of consumption. Phil Melling sums up the novel of the 1930s as testifying to a world where 'Reality is displaced by a neon image; illusions have become so vivid and persuasive that people are committed to living within them', and he notes of the decade's characteristic California fiction that on a landscape of decaying scenery, writers like Horace McCoy, Nathanael West and James Cain show the way the high hopes of a westward movement collapse on the Pacific shore in the vacant glare of a sunlight that gilds the cheapest artefacts of a transient American technology. These comments would seem very close to the argument advanced in Chapter 4 by Richard Maltby and Kate Bowles on Hollywood's postmodernist role in a mature capitalist economy, that 'The illusion has become real, and the more real it becomes, the more desperately they want it.' But the difference lies precisely in the fact that, during the 1930s, despite the coerciveness of consumerism, the distinction between 'reality' and 'image' could be sustained with some confidence, whereas in the contemporary period, the distinction is not only not so easily discernible but is virtually meaningless. The condition of postmodernism lies not in a confusion between 'reality' and 'image' but in the new reality of image itself. Maltby and Bowles go on to argue that 'This is not to suggest that the illusion has been mistaken for the object it represents, but that the illusion (the painting, the movie) has acquired enormous material significance in its own right.' The new real of postmodernism is exactly the simulacrum, the image/illusion deprived of any matrix within an objective world. This is what the novelist Norman Mailer means by saying 'Reality is no longer realistic', what enables a character in Truman Capote's *In Cold Blood* (1966) to refer to 'a real place. Like out of a movie', and what prompts Kurt Vonnegut's observation on Americans in *Breakfast of Champions* (1973): 'They are doing their best to live like people invented in story books. This was the reason Americans shot each other so often. It was a convenient literary device for ending short stories and books.'

There is, of course, playfulness in Vonnegut's statement, a playfulness to which I shall return shortly on behalf of the alternative positions allowed by contemporary debates about gender, but here I want to stress that in defining postmodernism, we are not talking simply about the ways it is somehow recognizable as belonging 'out there' as estranged from our personal experience. Its most awkward aspect lies in its profoundly unsettling capacity for an intimate invasion of human life — of our bodies, our emotions, and our desires. Maltby and Bowles are right in acknowledging Hollywood's integration with consumer culture in exactly these terms: 'Hollywood's most profound significance lies in its ability to turn pleasure into a product we can buy in the entertainment supermarket: capitalism at its finest.' One of the best definitions of this invasion that I know of is given in Christopher Lasch's *The Culture of Narcissism*. Lasch describes what he calls the 'new narcissist' as the male who is 'haunted not by guilt but by anxiety', doubting 'even the reality of his own existence' and forfeiting 'the security of group loyalties' out of a sense of rivalry with others. The condition of narcissism is fractured by contradictions: sexual liberation brings little sexual peace; a distrust of competition fails to alleviate a demand for approval; the extolling of co-operation conceals deeply antisocial impulses where an advertised respect for rules is announced in the belief that they do not apply to oneself. Finally, the narcissist is endlessly acquisitive, but his acquisitions are not accumulated against the future — they are prey to the impulse of immediate gratification, leaving him in a 'state of restless, perpetually unsatisfied desire' (Lasch, 1978, p.xvi).

Lasch's narcissistic man of postmodernity is a necessary descendant of the paranoid man who signalled the closing phases of modernism in film and literature where Maltby and Bowles discern 'the principal, standardizing story-line of heterosexual romance' as concealing a growing uncertainty, during the Depression and the 1940s, about the status of masculinity. The shifts from male power to female authority in John Steinbeck's chronicle of dust-bowl emigration, *The Grapes of Wrath*, of 1939 (and turned into an interestingly contrastive film by John Ford in the same year) marks the onset in mainstream fiction and cinema of prevailing oscillations in gender relations. It is in the area of gender that we might begin to trace an alternative reading of postmodernity, a reading which, while acknowledging the dominating force of the *simulacrum*, recognizes ways in which such dominance may be turned to more positive ends.

3 NEW LIBERATIONS

Historically, postmodernism coincides with a sustained development of the movement for female liberation and, more latterly, for gay liberation, both of which have found their most expressive home in America. Here, we need to be interested not so much in renewed possibilities for issues such as equal opportunities and a redressing of power relations (urgent as these are) as in the ways these movements (particularly the gay movement) oblige us to rethink the nature of gender itself. I have suggested the intimacy of postmodernism's invasion of the world of body and desire, and it is exactly here that gender plays the principal role. Gender is additionally pertinent to the preoccupations of this essay because it throws into vivid relief the prevailing American ideology of resistance — of a willingness to see the world in constructionist rather than essentialist terms. The debate about gender forces us to see ideas about the masculine, the feminine, and the gay not so much as biological or psychological givens, but as a matter of social manufacture. The disclosure, some years ago, that Rock Hudson, an epitome of Hollywood maleness, was gay, is a good example of the new recognitions we need to confront. Much recent gender theory has shown the inadequacies of essentialism in the face of sexual pluralism and how the social constructions of image, the presiding feature of postmodernism, more effectively approaches the issues of desire and sexuality within the gender paradigm. The idea of play is central here in that it indicates a controlling flexibility of attitude whereby cultural constructs of gender may be questioned and deconstructed. In part it re-invokes the playfulness of the absurdist American novel in the 1960s and early 1970s (Ken Kesey, Kurt Vonnegut, Joseph Heller, James Purdy, Richard Brautigan, for example) which used the techniques of the ridiculous, the burlesque, the theatrical and black comedy, to effect a critique of what it saw as a dehumanizing technological and bureaucratic America. The playfulness of these writers indicated a knowingness about postmodernity, a fluency and confidence in turning the features of the enemy against the enemy which became increasingly difficult to maintain as postmodernity entered its most intrusive phase during the mid and late 1970s and the 1980s.

Playfulness within the current debates about gender achieves more than this reinvocation. It shows signs of being a technique that is equally as strategic as it was in the pens of the earlier absurdists. The test case is Madonna — the performer who has spent the bulk of her professional life cultivating herself as *the* great postmodernist icon. By taking advantage of all the equipment of postmodernism, the world of the voyeuristic image, she has turned her often bewildering manipulation of styles (from 1930s decadence, Hollywood glamour, peep-show exhibitionist, and underground pornographer) into the stylistics of style itself by dissolving a whole series of conventions about being female and being gay. And she achieves these turns by availing herself of the design of a designed world, by foregrounding the exposure of her (often deeply intimate) self as the performance of exposure. She uses the image(s) to know the image(s): when Warren Beatty observes in the video *Truth or Dare* (otherwise known as *In Bed with Madonna*) that 'living' for Madonna has no meaning except on camera, he intends an opposition between an imagined 'real' self and a performer which is strongly questioned by the whole thrust of a video aiming to demonstrate exactly the weakness of such essentialist assumptions. In *Truth or Dare* and in her book *Sex*, Madonna displays display itself as the knowing construction of the self, an acting out of the variousness of female sexualities not only to assert its alterability, but to foreground the conditions of its production. Madonna's playfulness is an indication that, thoroughly within the tenets of American ideology, postmodernist techniques are becoming knowingly self-conscious again, moving beyond the prison-house of images to enable genuine rethinking about the conditions of its manufacture, revitalizing the recognition that constructed worlds are always available for reconstruction.

REFERENCES

Baudrillard, J. (1975) *The Mirror of Production*, Poster, M. (trans.), St. Louis, Telos Press.

Bellah, R.N., Madsen, R., Sullivan, W.M., Swidler, A. and Tipton, S.M. (1985) *Habits of the Heart: Individualism and Commitment in American Life*, Berkeley, University of California Press.

Bergonzi, B. (ed.) (1970) *Sphere History of Literature in the English Language, vol.7: The Twentieth Century*, London, Barrie & Jenkins/Sphere.

Bradbury, M. and McFarlane, J. (eds) (1976) *Modernism 1890–1930*, Harmondsworth, Penguin.

Brautigan, R. (1970) *Trout Fishing in America*, London, Jonathan Cape (first published in the US in 1967).

Capote, T. (1966) *In Cold Blood*, New York, Random House.

Dewey, J. (1964) 'The need for a philosophy of education' in Archambault, R.D. (ed.) *John Dewey on Education: Selected Writings*, New York, Random House.

Faulkner, P. (1977) *Modernism*, London, Methuen.

Lasch, C. (1978) *The Culture of Narcissism: American Life in an Age of Diminishing Expectations*, New York, Norton.

Lawrence, D.H. (1936a) 'America, listen to your own' in MacDonald, E.D. (ed.).

Lawrence, D.H. (1936b) 'American heroes' in MacDonald, E.D. (ed.).

Lee, H. (1989) *Willa Cather, a Life Saved Up*, London, Virago.

MacDonald, E.D. (ed.) (1936) *Phoenix*, London, Heinemann.

Madonna (1992) *In Bed with Madonna*, London, Secker & Warburg.

Madonna (1992) *Sex*, London, Secker & Warburg.

Melville, H. (1961) *Moby Dick*, New York, New American Library.

Michaels, W.B. (1990) 'The vanishing American', *American Literary History*, vol.II.2, pp.220–41.

Murray, D. (1982) *Modern Indians. Native Americans in the Twentieth Century*, BAAS Pamphlets in American Studies, no.8, South Shields, British Association for American Studies.

Steinbeck, J. (1939) *The Grapes of Wrath*, London, Heinemann.

Vonnegut, K. (1973) *Breakfast of Champions*, London, Jonathan Cape.

Whitman, W. (1969) 'An American primer' in Murphy, F. (ed.) *Walt Whitman*, Penguin Critical Anthologies series, Harmondsworth, Penguin.

Williams, W.C. (1971) *In the American Grain*, Harmondsworth, Penguin.

IDENTITY AND BELIEF

Kenneth Thompson ★

This chapter tackles the question of 'American-ness': ideas and ideals about what is distinctive about America and whether it is exceptional. This raises the further question about whether there is a single national culture, into which all Americans are assimilated, or a plurality of different cultures that coexist or conflict. These questions will be treated through a discussion of the role of religion and values, and of ethnicity and other bases of identity in an increasingly complex society.

We begin with a discussion of the notion of American exceptionalism, which dates back to the founding of America and to even earlier utopian ideas. It is closely bound up with certain religious ideals and values, despite the secular basis of the republican state. Religion, in turn, plays an important role in the formation of ethnic group identities and in mediating between these and the larger society.

We then turn to the issue of unity versus diversity and the balance between these two tendencies in different periods of American history, particularly from the late nineteenth century, when mass immigration became a serious issue. Can America be said to have assimilated all its different groups into a common culture, like a 'melting-pot'? Or is it more like a 'mosaic' or 'salad bowl' in which different ethnic cultures remain separate to varying degrees?

In conclusion, we will ask whether global trends in the late twentieth century may be presenting new challenges to America.

1 AMERICAN EXCEPTIONALISM

The term 'American exceptionalism' derives from Alexis de Tocqueville's *Democracy in America* (1835), although the idea itself is even older. It has been argued that the question of American identity and the meaning of America itself is complicated by the fact that the 'idea of America' preceded its discovery by European settlers. As early as 1519, some European intellectuals had begun to refer to America as a futuristic idea, partly fantasy and partly reality. It served to symbolize at one and the same time, both the absence of negative aspects of European culture and an emblem of an idealized version of what might be — a Utopia (Vaughan, 1991, p.444). Although, subsequently, as American social problems multiplied, it came to represent dystopia as much as Utopia.

American exceptionalism, therefore, rested to a large degree on an ideological conception of what America was different from, specifically, in the first instance, Europe. This ideological conception, it will be argued, frames many of the subsequent debates about communal and personal identity in the US down to the present day. Debates about social and political problems frequently take the form of, or give rise to, debates about moral identity. As Richard Hofstadter noted, 'it has been our fate as a nation not to have ideologies but to be one' (quoted in Kazín, 1989). And, according to Seymour Martin Lipset:

> The United States is organized around an ideology which includes a set of dogmas about the nature of a good society. Americanism, as different people have pointed out, is an 'ism' or ideology in the same way that communism or fascism or liberalism are isms ... That ideology can be subsumed under four words: anti-statism, individualism, populism, and egalitarianism.

> (Lipset, 1991, p.16)

Lipset, like many other commentators, points out that the ideological streak in the American experience has been strengthened by its special religious character. He notes that Edmund Burke, at the time of the struggle for American independence, in explaining to the House of Commons that Americans were culturally different and not simply transplanted Englishmen, particularly emphasized religion. Burke called Americans the Protestants of Protestantism, the Dissenters of Dissent (Burke, 1904, pp.180–1). Historically, many of the early Americans adhered to sects and groups that were regarded in England as Dissenters and Nonconformists, voluntary associations rather than state churches. The sociologist Max Weber, in *The Protestant Ethic and the Spirit of Capitalism* (1935), identified these sectarian beliefs as the most conducive to the kind of rational, competitive, individualistic behaviour which encourages entrepreneurial success. The American religious ethic has been described as functional not just for a bourgeois economy, but also, as Tocqueville noted, for a liberal polity. Since most of the sects are congregational, not hierarchical, they have fostered egalitarian, individualistic, and populist values which are anti-élitist (Lipset, 1991, p.19). The emphasis on voluntary association in America has impressed foreign observers as diverse as Tocqueville, Weber, and the Italian Marxist Antonio Gramsci, who have identified it as a distinctive American trait that is linked to the uniquely American system of 'voluntary religion'. No other modern society has consistently maintained such a high level of commitment to a multitude of voluntary religious associations, which provide a focus of communal and personal identity. There is some dispute about how exceptional America is among economically advanced societies with respect to the level of religious belief (contradictory comparative statistics are given by Greeley, 1991, and Wald, 1987). However, there can be no disputing the exceptional character of the variety of voluntary religious associations and the importance of this for understanding the nature of 'ideological community' and identity in America.

One aspect of American exceptionalism in this respect is its moralistic and utopian character:

> the emphasis on Americanism as a political ideology has led to a utopian orientation among American liberals and conservatives. Both seek to extend the 'good society'. But the religious traditions of Protestant 'dissent' have called on Americans to be moralistic, to follow their conscience with an unequivocal emphasis not to be found in countries whose predominant denominations have evolved from state churches. The dissenters are 'the original source both of the close intermingling of religion and politics that (has) characterized subsequent American history and of the moral passion that has powered the engines of political change in America ... Americans are utopian moralists who press hard to institutionalize virtue, to destroy evil people, and to eliminate wicked institutions and practices. They tend to view social and political dramas as morality plays, as battles between God and the devil, so that compromise is virtually unthinkable.'

> (Lipset, 1991, pp.21–2, quoting Huntington, 1981, p.154)

Huntington goes so far as to suggest that Americans give their nation and its ideological creed 'many of the attributes of a church' (Huntington, 1981, pp.158–9). Whilst Robert Bellah maintains that, overarching the different sectarian varieties of belief, America has a national 'civil religion', which has provided 'a religious dimension of the whole fabric of American life, including the political sphere'. America has frequently been described in biblical terms as the new Israel: 'Europe is Egypt; America the promised land. God led his people to establish a new sort of social order that shall be a light unto all nations' (Bellah, 1970, p.175; Wald, 1987, pp.48–55). Of course, this moralistic tendency can be both divisive as well as integrative for America. In periods of crisis, such as the Vietnam War, good and evil were located on different sides of the conflict by various groups. For some evangelical Protestant groups it was the Communist regimes of North Vietnam and its allies that incarnated evil; for more liberal religious groups it was the US military-industrial complex that needed to be denounced as the seat of evil. Divisions of political opinion are normal in all pluralist societies, but some observers maintain that, unlike societies which had more of a majority church tradition (whether Catholic or Protestant), America has more of a 'utopian' approach to foreign affairs rather than seeing itself as merely defending national interests (Kennan, 1966). In order to understand this ideological tendency in America it is necessary to look more closely at American religious and ethnic history.

SUMMARY

The idea of American exceptionalism rested on an ideological conception of what America was different from, specifically, in the first instance, Europe.

The ideological streak has been strengthened by American religious character, with Americans showing a high level of commitment to a multitude of voluntary religious associations — a system which has fostered egalitarian, individualistic and populist values.

One aspect of American exceptionalism, therefore, is its moralistic and utopian character.

Some sociologists, such as Bellah, argue that there is a national 'civil religion' overarching the different sectarian varieties of belief, which gives America a moral character and a sacred mission. This may be a source of national integration, but it can also be divisive.

2 RELIGIOUS AND ETHNIC IDENTITY

Religion has always been one of the most important sources of personal and communal identity for Americans. There are many indicators of this. Americans give more money and donate more time to religious bodies and religiously associated organizations than to all other voluntary associations put together (Gallup, 1982, reported in Bellah *et al.*, 1985). Some 40 per cent of Americans attend religious services at least once a week and religious membership is around 60 per cent of the total population. Perhaps more exceptional than the relatively high level of religious adherence in America is the promiscuous tendency to schism and sectarian diversification, which is euphemistically referred to as 'religious pluralism'. This is sometimes explained as an outcome of the ideology of individualism. Certainly, religious individualism goes very deep in the US. Even in the earliest period, when some states tried to maintain a religious establishment, such as seventeenth-century Massachusetts, a personal experience of salvation was often a prerequisite for acceptance as a church member. Later, through the peculiarly American phenomenon of revivalism, the emphasis on personal experience tended to override all efforts at church discipline and already, in the eighteenth century, religious bodies had to compete in a consumers' market and grew or declined depending on their adaptation to changing patterns of individual taste (Bellah *et al.*, 1985, p.233). In its extreme form, this individualism found expression in statements such as Thomas Jefferson's 'I am a sect myself'.

However, this individualism and pluralism is not random, but socially patterned and stratified:

> Under American conditions, religious pluralism has not produced a purely random assortment of religious bodies. Certain fairly determinate principles of differentiation — ethnic, regional, class — have operated to produce an intelligible pattern of social differentiation among religious groups, even though there remains much fluidity.

> (Bellah *et al.*, 1985, p.225)

Seems to be a difference between 'many non-confor
sects,' → strength
'American Ideolo
tenets of . . . . .

true religions
pluralism, base
upon ethnic differences.

This raises a number of questions. First, how does the pattern of differentiation of religious groups correspond to other bases of social differentiation, such as ethnicity, region and class? Secondly, is it possible for there to be a common national culture and ideology, characterized by such values as individualism, egalitarianism and populism, and at the same time a highly differentiated and pluralistic pattern of religious associations? Finally, what problems has this created for individuals, groups and the nation as a result of social changes during the twentieth century?

The classic sociological portrayal of the apparently socially-integrative functions of religion in twentieth-century America is the snapshot of a single community presented by Robert and Helen Lynd in their book *Middletown* (1929) and their follow-up study *Middletown in Transition* (1937). What is particularly interesting about this study, based on Muncie, Indiana, is the fact that reviewers seemed eager to accept this as a faithful portrayal of America itself. A *New York Times* reviewer spoke of their chosen small city as the whole nation writ small: 'Despite some local and sectional peculiarities, Middletown is the country in miniature, almost the world in miniature' (quoted in Marty, 1991, p.17). Although the Lynds are said to have 'set out to prove how secular small-town America had become' (ibid., p.18), they ended up by showing the reverse to be the case: religion served to sacralize the secular social order. Many Middletowners, particularly those from the middle classes, were enmeshed in a web of affiliations and 'spiritual' activities, ranging from formal religious organizations to the Rotary and other service clubs that provided sources of religious loyalty and zeal. The authors concluded that: 'civic loyalty, "magic Middletown", as a religion, appears to be the greatest power for some Middletown citizens'. Some Muncie/ Middletown business people, they said, even classified the church itself among their civic responsibilities. The Lynds made a thesis of this and showed how the local church connected with the nation: 'National patriotism is civic pride writ large'. Even the small Catholic and tiny Jewish communities in largely Protestant Middletown appeared to the Lynds to be doing pretty much the same as the Protestants — helping people to fuse religious and civic loyalties on the local level with the national culture.

This view contrasted with that of a foreign observer, André Siegfried's *America Comes of Age* (1927), which opened with the question: 'Will America remain Protestant and Anglo-Saxon?' It continued with the statement: 'The essential characteristic of the post-war period in the United States is the nervous reaction of the original American stock against an insidious subjugation by foreign blood' (Siegfried, 1927, pp.1–3).

Beneath the surface harmony of Middletown America there were forces that seemed to threaten disintegration. The nineteenth-century open-door immigration policy had brought in millions of immigrants who were not of European Protestant stock. This threatened disintegration of the Protestant dominance and the thin veneer of local civic unity. The result was a rise in aggressively ideological movements promoting '100 per cent Americanism'. The Lynds themselves described the revival of the Ku-Klux-Klan in the early 1920s as coming upon Middletown like a tornado, stirring up thousands in Indiana into a frenzy of activity and threatening disintegration. It is esti-

17

mated that 3,500 Middletowners joined the Klan, their fears stirred by the Klan's claims of threats to their culture from the influx of 'undesirables' — Catholics, Jews and black people. It might seem paradoxical that the apparently harmonious and 'normal' order of Middletown could so easily feel threatened by such small elements of diversity. The explanation lies in a combination of the economic factor — fear of unemployment and lower wages as a result of cheaper immigrant labour — and the cultural factor of ethnic and religious differences that can appear as 'alien' threats to the cultural unity of community and identity. The closely related phenomena of ethnicity and religion have the potential to act either as a 'social cement' or as a source of divisiveness.

An ethnic group 'consists of those who conceive of themselves as being alike by virtue of their common ancestry, real or fictitious, and who are so regarded by others' (Shibutani and Kwan, 1965, p.47). And ethnic identity can entail feelings of:

1   community — through neighbourhood, peer-group and leisure-time pursuits;

2   association — participation in work, educational and charitable organizations dominated by people of a common ancestry;

3   tribalism — a sense of peoplehood and common origin, a feeling of primordial ties; and

4   common religion.

(Wilson, 1978, p.309)

(It should be noted, however, that the definition of what constitutes an ethnic group is highly controversial. There are different views about whether it should include shared attributes such as language, geographic origin, and even biological characteristics such as skin colour or facial features.)

Religion has tended to play a central role in creating and perpetuating ethnic divisions through language, traditions, organization and patterns of interaction. 'The survival of ethnic identities seems to be only meaningful in the context of the survival of religious identities. Religion provides an essential mediation between the ethnic group and the larger culture of the modern world.' (Bellah, 1975, p.108.) However, the question at issue for America has always been whether the mediation would serve to integrate the diverse ethnic groups into a common national culture, or promote ethnic segregation and even conflict. The answer depends on a number of variable factors, such as the amount and source of immigration, economic opportunities, residential distribution, and cultural agencies such as churches, education and the mass media.

SUMMARY

Religion and ethnic identity have been closely related throughout American history. The differentiation of religious groups tends to correspond to other bases of social differentiation, such as ethnicity, region and class.

At the local level, especially in towns such as Middletown, religious and civic loyalties seemed to mesh together and formed the basis of national patriotism.

The surface harmony of Middletown America threatened to disintegrate when the Anglo-Protestant cultural dominance seemed to be threatened by mass immigration. This led to the revival of the Ku-Klux-Klan promoting '100 per cent Americanism' in the 1920s.

3   MELTING-POT OR MOSAIC?

The issue of unity versus diversity has been central to discussions of America throughout its history, but the balance between the two has varied from one period to another. For the first 60 years of the twentieth century the emphasis was on processes which were thought to produce unity through the assimilation of ethnic groups into a common culture — Americanization. Since the 1960s there has been a shift of emphasis to a view which celebrates cultural diversity, subcultural pluralism and ethnic differences — 'more like a mosaic and less like a can of mixed paint' (Menand, 1992, p.3). We will begin by reviewing some of the earlier discussions emphasizing processes of assimilation, before turning to the recent debates about ethnic pluralism and whether America now has a 'postmodern', fragmented culture that resembles a mosaic.

The periodic revivals of the Ku-Klux-Klan and other '100 per cent American' movements serve to illustrate this central dilemma in American history: how to reconcile the need for national unity with ethnic diversity. In 1782, a Frenchman, Hector St. Jean de Crèvecoeur, wrote: 'What then is the American, this new man? ... Here [in America] individuals of all nations are melted into a new race of man, whose labours and posterity will one day cause great changes in the world' (Crèvecoeur, 1957, p.39).

This idealistic notion of America as a 'melting-pot' has influenced later conceptions of how the various cultures comprising the American people have adapted and interacted. However, the reality of intergroup relations appears to have been somewhat different from the ideal of the melting-pot. Some would maintain that it is more realistically described as Anglo-domination or Anglo-conformity. This is not surprising because the first substantial European migration to America was that of the English between 1607 and 1660, and this established the English character of American institutions, language and culture. Later ethnic groups were forced to adapt to the economic, legal and political traditions that the English had brought with them. The idea of the 'melting-pot' arose in the context of the situation in the middle colonies (New York, New Jersey, Pennsylvania, Delaware), which contained substantial settlements of Germans, Dutch, Scots-Irish, Scots, Swedes, and French Huguenots. These diverse ethnic groups were not immediately inclined to accede to the pressure to assimilate by conforming to the established Anglo culture. In Pennsylvania, for example, Germans insisted on maintaining their own language, churches, and culture, which generated some of the earliest recorded antagonism among European ethnic groups in America. Benjamin Franklin openly expressed the widely held fears of the 'Germanization' of Pennsylvania:

> Why should the *Palatine Boors* (Germans) be suffered to swarm into our Settlements, and by herding together, establish their Language and Manners, to the exclusion of ours? Why should *Pennsylvania*, founded by the *English*, become a Colony of *Aliens*, who will shortly be so numerous as to Germanize us instead of our Anglifying them … ?
>
> (quoted in Dinnerstein and Reimers, 1975, p.7)

This fear, and the dilemma it represents, continues in various forms at the end of the twentieth century, particularly in areas with large numbers of immigrants, such as California. People in the areas most affected often express fears about being swamped by an 'alien' immigrant culture, even though they may pay lip-service to the idea of America reflected in Emma Lazarus's classic poem, 'Give me your tired, your poor, your huddled masses yearning to breathe free … '.

Like Anglo-conformity, the ultimate objective of the melting-pot policy is a society without ethnic differences, but in this case without the cultural tradition of any particular group being considered superior. In the 1950s, when immigration declined and the first-generation immigrants of the pre-1920 era seemed to have been assimilated, a new version of the melting-pot theory was put forward. It suggested that the once sharp distinctions between ethnic groups, such as those represented by the combination of common ancestry and common religion, were being eroded. Although church attendance was booming, interest in and knowledge of specific church doctrines was declining. The suggested explanation for this took the form of a modified version of the melting-pot theory.

According to Herberg, the three major faiths — Protestantism, Catholicism and Judaism — had become the principal sources of American self-identification, more important for that purpose than either class or ethnicity *persistence* (Herberg, 1960). He maintained that they were three different cultural manifestations of the same fundamental unity. They represented a common subscription to a dominant set of values that he and others labelled the 'American Way of Life'. These included a positive evaluation of religion itself, a faith in the democratic system, a belief in progress, and a sense of national mission. The implication of Herberg's melting-pot theory was that ethnicity was on the decline in the 1950s. However, this was the period when the Cold War was beginning and there were pressures to strengthen Americanism and to root out 'unAmerican activities'. In that respect it resembled the 1920s when the Ku-Klux-Klan stirred up fears of alien influences produced by immigration. The revival of ethnic consciousness from the 1960s onwards suggests that Herberg's melting-pot thesis may have had its relevance limited to the 1950s.

There were many criticisms of the Herberg version of the melting-pot thesis and its claim that ethnic identification was becoming less important. Some critics argued that, whilst ethnic groups might be *acculturated* through learning the English language, they were not necessarily becoming *assimilated* in the sense of worshipping with other ethnic groups, marrying them, or tolerating them in the same neighbourhood (the evidence against Herberg's thesis was reviewed in Wilson, 1978). Since the 1960s the debate about ethnicity has changed its focus from discussions about whether the older, European immigrant groups were becoming assimilated and ethnicity dying out, to discussions about whether the wheel has turned full circle with the century ending as it began: the US again becoming a nation of immigrants and being transformed in the process as individuals search for and identify with their ethnic roots. The question at issue is how best to describe what is taking place: melting-pot, mosaic, balkanization, or hybridization?

3.1   IMMIGRATION AND ASSIMILATION

Oscar Handlin's famous portrait of America as an immigrant society, *The Uprooted* (1951), opened with the lines 'Once I thought to write a history of the immigrants in America. Then I discovered that the immigrants were American history.' Two decades later in a postscript to the second edition, he wrote that immigration was already 'a dimly remote memory, generations away, which had influenced the past but appeared unlikely to count for much in the present or future' and that ethnicity in the 1950s had seemed 'a fading phenomenon, a quaint part of the national heritage, but one likely to diminish steadily in practical importance' (Handlin, 1973, pp.274–5). The difference at the end of the twentieth century is that the millions of new immigrants (legal and illegal) hail not from Europe but from Asia and Latin America. The cultural processes involved are being described not by the term 'melting-pot', but rather 'hybridization' or a 'mosaic maze'.

> The American ethnic mosaic is being fundamentally altered; ethnicity itself is being redefined, its new images reified in the popular media and reflected in myriad and often surprising ways. Immigrants from a score of nationalities are told that they are all 'Hispanics', while far more diverse groups — from India and Laos, China and the Philippines — are lumped together as 'Asians'. There are foreign-born mayors of large American cities, first-generation millionaires who speak broken English, a proliferation of sweatshops exploiting immigrant labour in an expanding informal economy, and new myths that purport to 'explain' the success or failure of different ethnic groups. Along 'Callo Ocho' in Miami's Little Havana, shops post signs to reassure potential customers that they'll find 'English spoken here', while Koreatown retailers in Los Angeles display 'Se habla español' signs next to their own Hangul script, a businesslike acknowledgement that the largest Mexican and Salvadoran communities in the world outside Mexico and El Salvador are located there. In Brooklyn, along Brighton Beach Avenue ('Little Odessa'), signs written in Cyrillic letters by new Soviet immigrants have replaced old English and

Yiddish signs. In Houston, the auxiliary bishop is a Cuban-born Jesuit who speaks fluent Vietnamese — an overflow of 6,000 faithful attended his recent ordination, and he addressed them in three languages — and the best Cuban café is run by Koreans.

(Rumbaut, 1991, p.209)

This may not correspond to the old idea of a melting-pot, but is it more accurately described as 'hybridization' or 'mosaic'? The idea of hybrid identities and cultures has been introduced in recent discussions of processes of 'globalization'. It is argued that the late twentieth century is experiencing a tremendous increase in globalization: processes, operating on a global scale, which cut across national boundaries, integrating and connecting communities and organizations in new space–time combinations. These processes, most strikingly illustrated by developments in electronic communication and rapid transport, as well as the transplantation of cultures and populations, are said to be undermining strong identifications with nation-state culture and strengthening other cultural ties and identities 'above' and 'below' that level. An example of an identity 'above' or broader than that of the nation-state might be that of the 'West' or 'Islam'. The strengthening of local identities can be seen in the defensive reaction of those members of the dominant ethnic group who feel threatened by the growth or persistence of minority group cultures. The reaction may be less violent and crude than earlier racist movements, such as the Ku-Klux-Klan, but it has been described as a form of 'cultural racism'. This is sometimes matched by a strategic retreat to defensive identities among minority communities, which may take the form of re-identification with cultures of origin; the construction of counter-ethnicities; or the revival of cultural traditionalism, religious fundamentalism and political separatism. Another possible response to globalization, particularly the process of global transfers of population from the Third World, is the production of new, hybrid cultural identities. Many immigrants retain strong cultural links with their places of origin, but neither seek a return to the past nor find it desirable or possible to totally assimilate to the dominant host culture. Salman Rushdie offered a defence of this 'hybridity' in defending his novel *The Satanic Verses*, by suggesting that migrants like himself had to learn to inhabit at least two identities, to speak two cultural languages, to translate and negotiate between them, without giving themselves totally to one or the other.

A different possibility is put forward by some cultural theorists who argue that the trend towards global interdependence is leading to the break-down of *all* strong cultural identities. This is said to be producing a fragmentation of cultural codes, a multiplicity of styles, with an emphasis on the ephemeral, the impermanent, and on difference and cultural pluralism which has been described as a postmodern 'mosaic'. According to this view, the main sources of identity are not the strong nation-state cultures characteristic of modernity, but the fleeting and multiple consumer and mass media styles of late-modernity or 'postmodernity'. However, this notion of the reduction of cultures and cultural identities to consumer and mass media styles does not do justice to the persistence of ethnic cultures and identities in US society.

The strength of any ethnic identity depends on the degree to which it is supported by other cultural and structural factors of a positive or negative sort. There is no doubt that some revivals of ethnic culture, particularly for economically successful, predominantly middle-class groups, may be the result of a positive desire for cultural enrichment after having overcome earlier negative discrimination. This may be the case, for example, for American Jews, particularly as a result of the stimulation gained from cross-fertilization with Israeli culture and institutions. As Jews have moved up the social ladder, taking full advantage of educational and economic opportunities, they have dispersed across the nation to cities like Los Angeles and Miami and into the suburbs, leaving behind their older compact Jewish neighbourhoods with their informal associational networks that provided secular alternatives to the synagogue. The synagogue has again become the primary communal institution in the new suburban settlements, modelled on the synagogue of the 1920s, but enlarged to meet more varied social and cultural requirements.

By contrast, African-Americans have experienced the strongest combination of negative factors that have blocked and reinforced their ethnic identity. Rather than being viewed as simply another ethnic group attempting to struggle up the ladder to take their place in American society, they have always been viewed as a 'problem'. Tocqueville forecast that white and black people would never live in harmony in America, and even Abraham Lincoln entertained the idea of removing African-Americans from the society altogether, persuading Congress to pass legislation subsidizing the voluntary emigration of ex-slaves to the Caribbean (Steinberg, 1981, p.177). It was only as a result of the upheaval of the Civil Rights movement and the 'long hot summers' of ghetto rebellion in the 1960s that a concerted effort was made to reduce discrimination in jobs, education and housing. The Civil Rights laws of 1964 were followed by President Lyndon Johnson's War on Poverty in the late 1960s; educational disadvantages were addressed through attempts to desegregate schools and the Head Start programme was launched to help disadvantaged children overcome educational deprivation associated with poverty; the Office of Civil Rights and the Equal Opportunity Commission were established, the latter to oversee implementation of Title VII, which outlawed discrimination in employment; and an open-housing bill was passed. In the 1970s and 1980s the economic and political tide turned against these efforts and by the end of the 1980s a National Academy of Science study was noting that while white people were increasingly supportive of the 'principles' of racial equality, they offered 'substantially less support for policies intended to implement principles of racial equality' and continued to shun sustained and close contacts with black people (Jaynes and Williams, 1989, p.117).

Some social scientists have argued that the 'race problem' would only be solved when whites softened their racist attitudes towards blacks and were willing to associate with them more closely in residential, social and workplace settings. Since the 1950s, there have been periodic attitude surveys of the racial attitudes of white people by the National Opinion Research Center (and subsequently Gallup and the Institute for Social Research at the University of Michigan). Based on these surveys it is possible to construct a 'social distance scale', measuring the preparedness to associate with black people, which tends to indicate a liberalization of white attitudes over the decades. However, other researchers have continued to document widespread discriminatory *behaviour* in housing, education and work-place.

Other scholars have rejected this 'individual prejudice' approach in favour of more 'structural' explanations for the position of African-Americans. Some versions suggest that black people lag behind white ethnics because the latter settled earlier in the urban northeast and Midwest than Southern blacks — a 'Blacks-as-the-last-of-the-immigrants' theory (Glazer, 1971). Another version of this, put forward by Thomas Sowell, argues that the rural background of the black ethnic group left them lacking the values of the work ethic (Sowell, 1981); a strange argument in view of the strong Protestant religious culture of African-Americans. However, Sowell's economic rank ordering of ethnic groups, based on family income, has prompted commentators to explore some of the structural factors that might account for the differences in upward mobility between ethnic groups. Sowell found wide variations between white ethnic groups, from 103 for Irish-Americans to 172 for Jewish-Americans, and between non-white groups, with 60 for Native Americans and 132 for Japanese-Americans (see Table 1.1).

As Landry (1991) points out, although Sowell's index makes it clear that ethnic groups have experienced different degrees of success 'in scaling the economic ladder', it is evident that, with the exception of Japanese- and Chinese-Americans, all groups with a family income above the mean are white. If we leave aside distinctions between ethnic groups and concentrate on the ratio of black-to-white average earnings, we find that they widened even further between 1970 and 1990; according to figures supplied by the US Department of Commerce (Darity and Myers, 1992).

3.2 NATIVE AMERICANS AND ETHNICITY

Nowhere is the issue of ethnic identity versus cultural assimilation and blocked upward mobility more acute than among the groups of Native Americans (or, as they were traditionally labelled American 'Indians'). For a long time they were not considered to be part of American society, but occupied an almost 'alien' status. An early and bizarre example of this 'alien'

Table 1.1 Average family income for US ethnic groups (average = 100)

Jewish	172	Total US	100
Japanese	132	Filipino	99
Polish	115	West Indian	94
Chinese	112	Mexican	76
Italian	112	Puerto Rican	63
Anglo-Saxon	107	African-American	62
German	107	Native American	60
Irish	103		

(Source: Sowell, 1981, p.5)

categorization occurred when the California Supreme Court ruled in *People v. Hall* (1854) that Chinese should be considered 'Indian'(!) and denied the political rights accorded to whites (*The Harvard Encyclopedia of American Ethnic Groups*, 1980). During the early years of contact between European settlers and the aboriginal people of America the term 'nation' was used for those land-controlling groups that had enough internal cohesion to oppose white people or make treaties with them. 'A nation was made up of Indians who spoke a common language or set of mutually intelligible dialects and maintained a common set of customs. Such units were regarded by whites as similar to those that were recognized in Europe as nations' (ibid., p.64). During the nineteenth century, however, the term 'tribe' began to be applied to these units, with some of the European imperialist connotations of inferiority, as in Rudyard Kipling's phrase 'a lesser breed without the law'. In the twentieth century Native Americans rejected this term and insisted on using the term 'nation', even though the Bureau for Indian Affairs continued to refer to them as tribes. Social scientists gained some support for the term 'ethnic groups', but this too has been contested as being weaker than 'nation' or 'race' with regard to the claim to collective identity and rights or as ignoring racial discrimination.

The problems of terminology are not just superficial as they point to deeper conflicts over cultural and political identity, as well as shifts in policies and attitudes. It is difficult to discuss the position of Native Americans without coming up against the legends and myths which surround them, due in no small measure to the ways in which they have been portrayed in Hollywood films during the twentieth century. Despite the fact that before white people arrived most Native American groups were in stable communities of farmers and fishermen, not nomadic hunters, the most influential stereotype derived from the newly-migrated Plains Indians (Siouan speakers from the Great Lakes and northern Mississippi valley) who, when equipped with European horses, guns and metal knives, found they could subsist almost wholly from hunting the buffalo. It was the image of these Plains Indians, and the Apaches who had migrated south from Canada, that gave rise to the fabled Indian in the feathered head-dress, the scalp-collecting warrior horseman.

Another stereotype is that of a vanishing race who could not adapt. It is certainly the case that disease, forced removal, and massacre drastically reduced their numbers, particularly in the nineteenth century. However, this has reversed in the twentieth century and by the census of 1970 their total number of 791,839 in the US was not far from some estimates of their numbers when the white settlers first arrived. Nor is it the case that they have lost their sense of distinctive identity. Despite the government policy of forced cultural assimilation, imposed through the Bureau of Indian Affairs from the 1880s until they were granted citizenship in 1924, Native Americans did not identify with white American culture:

> Rather they identified themselves more intensely as Indians and developed symbols of their identity in the form of religious beliefs, music, dance, selected items of dress, like headbands and moccasins, particular ceremonies, and their own heroes and heroines, many of

whom were admired because they fought for Indian independence
... This vital process has counterbalanced the extensive replacement
of cultural elements in Indian life and blocked their absorption by
the dominant society.

(*The Harvard Encyclopedia of American Ethnic Groups*, 1980, p.64)

In this period of forced assimilation dating from the 1880s Native American
leadership often took the form of religious prophecy, telling of promised
lands where the old ways could be renewed without white domination.
Some of these messages spread like wildfire, as in the case of the Ghost
Dance, spread by the Messiah of the Paiutes in Nevada, Wovoka (c. 1856–
1932). It was this religion and its power to stir up Native Americans that
frightened the whites into the massacre at Wounded Knee, South Dakota,
which became a burning symbol for both Native Americans and white people for many years. The peyote cult and other visionary religions became
permanent and remained distinctive features of the Native American church.

The fact that a majority of Native Americans continued to speak an Indian
language, despite the determined efforts of the Bureau of Indian Affairs to
stamp them out through formal schooling for many years, is a testimony to
their determination to resist absorption. Similarly, although the missionaries
had persistently sought to replace native religions with Christianity, in many
Native American communities in the 1960s there developed a 'cultural
nationalism', which included a return to traditional religious and spiritual
concerns, rearticulated with other cultural elements in order to assert a separatist 'ethnic' identity entitled to equal recognition and rights. The final
irony came in 1978, when leaders and activists actually mobilized against an
initiative in the US Senate to abolish the Bureau of Indian Affairs, despite
Native Americans' long antagonism to it. The Bureau symbolized the fact
that Native Americans had legal recognition as a 'national' group with a
collective identity and rights; this represented a difference in philosophy
from the traditional American ideology which recognized only individual
citizens and their rights as individuals. In contrast with more pluralist states,
such as Switzerland, the US has maintained an individualistic political structure, never giving political recognition to any ethnic group: except the only
group that pre-dates the Anglo-Saxon founders, the Native Americans.

SUMMARY

The central dilemma for America has been how to reconcile the need for
national unity with ethnic diversity. The balance between the two has
varied from one period to another, depending on a variety of factors. For
much of its history the emphasis in America has been on the assimilation
of different groups into a dominant Anglo-culture — a process referred
to as 'Americanization'. The idealistic idea of the 'melting-pot' interprets
this process as the blending of different ethnic groups into a new, shared,
American culture and identity, without the cultural tradition of any particular group being superior.

In the 1950s it was thought that ethnic differences were declining. Herberg reconciled this idea and the concurrent strength of religious adherence by developing a modified version of the melting-pot theory which saw the three major faiths of Protestantism, Catholicism and Judaism, as representing a common subscription to a dominant set of values that he and others labelled the 'American Way of Life'.

Since the 1960s there has been a revival of interest in ethnicity and support for the idea of America as a collection of separate ethnic groups — more like a mosaic than a melting-pot. However, there are several different predictions about possible trends, ranging from those which see global trends of greater population mobility, particularly from the Third World to the First World, creating hybrid cultural identities, to those which suggest that global interdependence is leading to the break-down of all strong cultural identities.

Studies of minority ethnic groups that have focused on problems of 'racial discrimination' show that the degree of separateness or assimilation varies between groups. The revival of ethnic culture among some groups, such as the relatively economically successful Jewish- and Italian-Americans, may be the result of a positive desire for cultural enrichment after having overcome earlier negative discrimination. Other groups, such as African-Americans and Native Americans, have a long and continuous experience of negative discrimination that has reinforced their sense of ethnic identity.

4 E PLURIBUS UNUM?

In the 1960s and 1970s an increasing number of critics suggested that the American slogan *e pluribus unum* (many made one) represented more of an ideological slogan than a statement of established fact. Some writers also began to raise similar doubts about the assimilation of different ethnic groups. The recurrent issue of unity versus diversity has taken various forms, including dilemmas of Americanization versus ethnic pluralism, and civil religion versus religious particularism. According to those who stress ethnic diversity, Americanization 'was really WASPification' (dominance by White Anglo-Saxon Protestants) in the words of the American Catholic writer Michael Novak (quoted in Gleason, 1980, p.57). Another critic, Harold Cruse, stated: 'America is a nation that lies about who and what it is. It is a nation of minorities ruled by a minority of one — it thinks and acts as if it were a nation of white Anglo-Saxon Protestants' (ibid.).

Ethnic revival since the 1960s has been explained as dialectically related to the weakening of the plausibility of the ideological element in American identity. The decade from 1965 to 1974 witnessed a succession of movements and events that called into question the claim that America actually incorporated a set of values in its institutions that were consonant with the ideologically defined 'American Way of Life'. The ideological version of American identity was undermined by the evidence of racial and sexual discrimination, the Vietnam War, the Watergate scandal, political assassinations, business corruption, crime and violence. Although much attention was given to the reaction in the form of youth counter-cultures, probably of more fundamental significance was the ethnic revival. By remembering and reviving their ethnic identities, people could dissociate themselves from responsibility for the defects of the American system and establish a claim against those they held responsible — usually defined as the WASP establishment.

In the following decade, from the late 1970s through the 1980s, there was a reaction against the counter-cultures and the policies of 'affirmative discrimination' in favour of minority group interests. The 'Moral Majority', religious fundamentalists and various New Right movements reasserted what they claimed were the traditional values of America and the 'American Way of Life'. The mainline Protestant denominations, such as Methodists, Presbyterians and Episcopalians, which had been at the centre of much of the social criticism of the previous decade, now found themselves losing ground. According to the religious historian, Martin Marty, they failed to exploit the hunger for personal experience, a desire for authority in the face of relativism and chaos, and the pull of organizations that provide personal identity and social location (Marty, 1985). The Roman Catholic church tried to take over the task of articulating a social vision with a communitarian rather than individualistic emphasis. However, when the National Conference of Catholic Bishops issued a pastoral letter on the economy in 1986 that appeared to be critical of the Reagan Administration's free market economic policies, they were accused of espousing 'un-American' values (*Congressional Record*, 22 December 1986, p.78). It was suggested that the Catholic church's social teaching was medieval and European, with an 'organicist-communitarian' framework (society is like a body in which all the parts are dependent on each other), rather than individualist-libertarian and therefore American. Conservative lay critics within the church, such as William Simon and Michael Novak, put their criticism differently: the bishops had focused on justice at the expense of the more distinctively American value — liberty (*New York Times*, 29 November 1986).

Symptomatic of the shift towards a reassertion of Americanism in the 1980s was the fact that former advocates of ethnic pluralism in the 1970s, such as Novak and Jewish intellectuals associated with the American Jewish Committee-sponsored *Commentary* magazine, forged new alliances with the conservative evangelical-moralist leadership. Civil religion, for its part, became more conservative and nationalist, and this led to profound ideological disputes between theological progressives and theological orthodox which cut across denominational lines, whether Protestant, Catholic or Jewish. In the two decades following the Second World War, empirical investigations such as the 1958 Detroit Area Survey, published under the title *The Religious Factor* (Lenski, 1961), had found that large differences still existed between Protestants, Catholics and Jews in their view of the world. The religious factor had a marked effect in shaping people's views of morality, the role of the family and attitudes to various aspects of the American Dream. By contrast, a large-scale Religion and Power Survey in 1987 found that the main division, which cut across denominational lines, was between theological orthodox and theological progressives. A majority of the orthodox, Protestant, Catholic and Jewish, said the US was 'a force for good in the world', whereas progressives were more inclined to say the US was 'a force for evil' or at best 'neutral'. Similar divisions occurred on all the moral issues and values covered by the surveys (Hunter and Rice, 1991).

The conclusion of the authors of this survey of religious attitudes, in the volume *America at Century's End* (Wolfe, 1991), underlines the moralistic and utopian character of American exceptionalism, and its capacity to divide some groups as it unites others. The grounds for division derive from the different religious and secular sources of American ideology:

> What *unites* the orthodox and progressives *across* tradition and *divides* the orthodox and the progressives *within* tradition are different formulations of moral authority. Whereas the orthodox side of the cultural divide is guided by conceptions of a transcendent source of moral authority, the progressive formulation grants that authority to what could be called 'self-grounded rational discourse'. These opposing conceptions of moral authority are at the heart of most of the political and ideological disagreements in American public discourse — including the debates over abortion, legitimate sexuality, the nature of the family, the moral content of education, Church/State law, the meaning of the First Amendment free speech liberties, and so on and on. We are dealing with more than 'religion', strictly defined. ... They no longer revolve around specific doctrinal issues or styles of religious practice and organization; they revolve around fundamental assumptions about value, purpose, truth, freedom, and collective identity.

(Hunter and Rice, 1991, p.331)

The senior author of this survey, James Davison Hunter, made clear the serious nature of the growing split over fundamental American values when he gave his subsequent book the title *Culture Wars: the Struggle to Define America* (1991). It was not just intellectuals and activists who were divided about 'what America is really all about', according to his case studies of 'stories from the front'; ordinary people in their daily lives were shown to be caught up in the 'culture wars' because the conflict had an impact on virtually all of the major institutions of American society. In the case of the *family* the conflict was not just over critical issues of reproduction and abortion, but on a wide range of other issues such as the limits (if any) of legitimate sexuality, the public and private role of women, questions of child-raising, and even the definition of what constitutes a family in the first place. The cultural conflict is also concerned with the structure and content of public *education*, of how and what American children should learn. The same divisions affect the content of the popular *media*, from the films that are shown to the television shows that are aired, the books that are read and the art that is exhibited. Hunter claims that these divisions are not just a normal feature of a pluralist society where people hold different opinions and agree to differ, nor are they confined to the public discourse of intellectual élites. His argument is that the fundamental division between orthodox and progressive values impacts on the private culture that guides and makes sense of everyday life. People who follow the orthodox tendency in American culture have a fundamental commitment to *an external, definable, and transcendent authority* (e.g. the final authority of scripture, the church, natural law, etc.). This tendency is increasingly polarized, according to Hunter, against a cultural progressivism defined by *a tendency to resymbolize historic faiths according to the prevailing assumptions of contemporary life* and marked by a spirit of rationalism and subjectivism. Although it might seem that modern society favours the more pluralistic approach of progressivism, which is strongly entrenched in the intellectual élites of cities such as Washington, New York, Boston, Chicago, Los Angeles and San Francisco, the 'culture wars' of the 1980s showed that orthodox pressure groups could gain widespread support among the middle and working classes, particularly in small towns and rural areas, and effectively lobby on issues such as abortion, pornography, homosexuality, and the content of educational curricula and the mass media.

Another version of the idea of a fundamental division over the values that give America its exceptional character appeared in 1985. In that year Robert Bellah and a group of distinguished colleagues published *Habits of the Heart: Individualism and Commitment in American Life*, a study of contemporary American culture and values that became one of the best-selling and most debated books of the decade. There can be no doubt that the book's topicality derived from its criticisms of the neo-Liberal version of individualism described as 'utilitarian individualism', which had been reasserted in the 1980s.

> Utilitarian individualism views society as arising from a contract that individuals enter into only in order to advance their self-interest. According to Locke, society is necessary because of the prior existence of property, the protection of which is the reason individuals contractually enter society. Utilitarianism has an affinity to a basically economic understanding of human existence.
>
> (Bellah *et al.*, 1985, p.336)

This version of individualism is contrasted with that of 'expressive individualism', which arose in opposition to 'utilitarian individualism':

> Expressive individualism holds that each person has a unique core of feeling and intuition that should unfold or be expressed if individuality is to be realized. This core, though unique, is not necessarily alien to other persons or to nature. Under certain conditions, the expressive individualist may find it possible through intuitive feeling to 'merge' with other persons, with nature, or with the cosmos as a whole. Expressive individualism is related to the phenomenon of romanticism in eighteenth- and nineteenth-century

European and American culture. In the twentieth century, it shows affinities with the culture of psychotherapy and New Age Religions.

(Bellah *et al.*, 1985, p.335)

Bellah and his colleagues adopt Tocqueville's term 'habits of the heart' to refer to the 'sum of moral and intellectual dispositions' that are shared by members of a society and give the nation its particular character. Tocqueville warned that one aspect of American character — what he was one of the first to call 'individualism' — might eventually isolate Americans from one another and thereby undermine the conditions of freedom. The Bellah team focused their attention on the values of the middle class, on the grounds that the middle class has so dominated American culture that neither a genuinely working-class culture nor a genuinely upper-class culture has fully appeared. They quote a sociological study of class and kinship in America by Schneider and Smith (1973), who define the middle class as a 'broad but not undifferentiated category which includes those who have certain attitudes, aspirations and expectations toward status mobility, and who shape their actions accordingly' (quoted in Bellah *et al.*, 1985, p.148). Status mobility depends on advanced education and competence in specialized occupations. Middle-class Americans are said to find it essential to develop a highly competitive and calculative attitude in educational, occupational and other spheres of life, in order to achieve 'success' and upward mobility and an egoistic self-fulfilment. However, according to Bellah *et al.* there are limits to the satisfaction to be gained from this utilitarian individualism, and the 'empty self' seeks to 'reconnect' with others through commitment to a 'community of memory'. There are ethnic and racial communities of memory, each with its own story ('constitutive narrative') and heroes and heroines; similarly, religious communities have strong narratives, ritual re-enactments and saintly exemplars. Neighbourhoods, localities and regions can be communities, but they are weakened if there is a high level of mobility and self-sufficient individualism; such communities are described as degenerating into mere 'lifestyle enclaves'.

Perhaps it is because *Habits of the Heart* takes its biographical case studies from the American middle classes that it finds little space to discuss ethnic communities, despite the importance it attaches to them as communities of memory. It tends to accept Schneider and Smith's argument from the early 1970s 'that it is in the lower class that ethnicity, as a specific pattern of cultural life, survives in America, and that as individuals enter the middle class, ethnicity loses distinctive social content even when it is symbolically emphasized' (quoted in Bellah *et al.*, 1985, pp.151–2). Bellah *et al.* add that the point is not that lower- and upper-class Americans are not individualistic, but rather that their individualism is embedded in specific patterns of relationship and solidarity that mitigate the tendency toward an empty self and empty relationships in middle-class life. However, the book does provide one case study of middle-class ethnic reattachment, which illustrates how ethnic diversity and conflict can have positive results:

Angelo Donatello, a successful small businessman who has become a civic leader in a suburb of Boston, tells how a reluctant concern for the ethnic heritage rooted in his family finally led him into public life:

> One of the important things that got me into politics was that I was a confused individual. I came from a real old-fashioned Italian family in East Boston. We spoke both languages at home, but I was more Americanized than my brothers or sisters, so to speak. We were forgetting our heritage — that meant becoming more free, more liberal, being able to express myself differently. Thirteen or fourteen years ago, there was a group of people in town who talked about forming a chapter of the Sons of Italy. I would not have been one of the first ones to propose such a thing. My wife was Irish — I was one of the first ones in my family to marry out. But I went to these meetings. Before I had gotten into this I had forgotten my heritage.

What catalysed Angelo's involvement was the unexpected appearance of prejudice when the group tried to buy a piece of land for the Sons of Italy hall. In fighting the opposition, which seemed to focus on the belief that Italians are drunken and rowdy, Angelo became involved with the town government. Remembering his heritage involved accepting his origins, including painful memories of prejudice and discrimination that his earlier efforts at 'Americanization' had attempted to deny. The experience of ethnic prejudice helped Angelo see that there is more to life than leaving behind the past, becoming successful on his own, and expressing himself freely. But as he became more involved with the community he had tried to forget — more active, that is, in the Sons of Italy — he also became more involved with his town. Elected a selectman, he saw it as his duty to represent not only Italian-Americans, but also the welfare of the town as a whole. Abandoning one kind of individualism, he was led toward a civic individualism that entailed care for the affairs of his community in both the narrower and wider senses. While leaving behind 'Americanization', he became American.

(Bellah *et al.*, 1985, pp.157–8)

Habits of the Heart is replete with optimistic examples of middle-class Americans finding a new sense of communal commitment through various forms of expressive individualism involving shared activities that are not undertaken in the interests of the self at the expense of commitments to others — the prime examples are involvements in religious and civic activities. However, there is little consideration of the negative separatist effects of a heightened sense of difference, such as when ethnicity, discrimination and residential separation are combined, as in the case of groups such as African-Americans, Native Americans and Hispanic-Americans.

The authors of *Habits of the Heart* are firmly in the camp of 'communitarianism' in reaction against the right-wing 'individualism' that was dominant in the 1980s. Expressive individualism is regarded as a good thing and is thought to integrate individuals into a larger 'civic' or national community.

Whilst, in contrast, 'Americanization', involving conformity to WASP values, is thought to produce alienated individuals with no communal identity.

SUMMARY

The decade from 1965 to 1974 saw a succession of crises for American values and the claims of the slogan *e pluribus unum*. There was a revival of interest in ethnic and other cultural differences.

In the 1980s there was a reaction in the form of a reassertion of the conservative version of the 'American Way of Life' and its traditional values.

This, in turn, has been met by a response from those who claim that it distorts the true meaning of American values, such as individualism. Bellah *et al.*, in *Habits of the Heart*, take seriously Tocqueville's warning that individualism might eventually isolate Americans from one another and undermine the conditions of freedom, unless it takes the form of 'expressive individualism'. They find hopeful signs of expressive individualism giving rise to a new sense of communal commitment in a variety of religious, ethnic and civic involvements. However, it is difficult to judge how significant their findings are because they draw all their examples from certain middle-class strata.

[handwritten margin note: Ethnic recognition not assimilation?]

5 CONCLUSION

Is America exceptional? Has it succeeded in making the many into one (*e pluribus unum*), not just at the level of the lowest common denominator of culture (e.g. common language), but by raising them up to the level of its ideological conception of American exceptionalism?

American exceptionalism was said to have rested to a large degree on an ideological conception of what America was different from, specifically, in the first instance, Europe. Equality was one of the realized values that was believed to distinguish it from Europe. But, as we have seen, some ethnic groups, such as African-Americans and Native Americans, have not received equality of treatment and have reacted by accentuating their separate ethnic identities. In some respects their situation and attitudes have resembled those of immigrants to Europe from former colonies, who possess what Salman Rushdie has referred to as a 'hybrid' identity.

There has been greater success in assimilating different ethnic groups at the level of popular culture, such as sport and entertainment (as discussed in other chapters of this book). However, even here there is a danger of ethnic stereotyping and cultural condescension. African-Americans have been identified with jazz, dance and physical prowess at sports, but not with more intellectual pursuits. W.E.B. Du Bois expressed pride in his African-American heritage: 'there is no true American music but the old-sweet melodies of the Negro slave; the American fairy-tales and folklore are Indian and African; and, all in all, we black men seem the sole oasis of simple faith and reverence in a dusty desert of dollars and smartness' (quoted in Holt, 1980, p.21). But he also wrote of the double-consciousness and split identity of African-Americans, who always had the 'sense of looking at one's self through the eyes of others' and the malaise of 'measuring one's soul by the tape of a world that looks on in amused contempt and pity' (ibid.). Du Bois's ultimate resolution of his divergent national identities involved seeking asylum in Ghana in 1960; others such as black Muslims sought a similar separation or searched for their roots through the study of black history, literature and culture. Even more economically successful and predominantly middle-class groups, such as Jewish-Americans and Italian-Americans, who have gained some wider recognition for their contributions to high culture, still suffer from popular culture stereotypes such as the Jewish comedian and the Italian mafioso. Such groups have been helped in reconciling their American and ethnic identities by their religious organizations which have been successful in adapting to the status of voluntary associations within a denominational framework. This once contrasted with the situation in European states where there was a dominant religious body, but it is less exceptional now that most states are secularized.

Where America is exceptional is not so much with regard to its values, which are largely those of the European Enlightenment, but in the sheer scale of immigration that it has absorbed. By the 1980s the US had admitted two-thirds of all legal immigrants world-wide (the numbers of recent illegal immigrants to America and other countries are more difficult to calculate). Other countries, such as Australia, may have a higher proportion of immigrants, but the US has for a long time had the largest total immigrant population in the world. Until 1890 the overwhelming number of immigrants came from northwest Europe, supplemented by some labourers from China and Japan. After 1890 a much larger 'new' immigration from southern and eastern Europe arrived, with authorized immigration reaching a peak of 8.8 million during 1901 to 1910. The backlash from the Ku-Klux-Klan and other '100 per cent American' movements led to the passing of restrictive immigration laws in 1921 and 1924, limiting the annual flow to 150,000 for eastern hemisphere countries and setting national-origins quotas that barred Asians and allocated 82 per cent of all visas to north-western Europeans, 16 per cent to south-eastern Europeans and 2 per cent to all others. No restrictions were set on western hemisphere countries at the insistence of American growers, on the understanding that these labourers could be deported *en masse* when no longer needed (as happened during the 1930s and during Operation Wetback in the mid-1950s). The McCarran–Walters Act of 1952 retained the national-origins quota system, with slight changes, and it lasted until the Hart–Celler Act of 1965 abolished quotas. By the end of the 1980s more than 80 per cent of total legal immigration originated in Asia and Latin America. Eight countries accounted for more than half of all legal immigration since 1975: Mexico, the Philippines, Vietnam, South Korea, China, India, Cuba, and the Dominican Republic. Mexico and the Philippines alone sent 20 per cent of all legal immigrants, and of the 3 million illegal immigrants who qualified for legalization under an amnesty in 1989, 2 million were Mexicans. Furthermore, there is evidence of increasing spatial concentration, with California accounting for 29 per cent of all immigrants in 1987–9 and 54 per cent of all illegals applying for amnesty (Rumbaut, 1991).

This recent Third World migration to America has affected the terms of the debate about whether America is best imagined in terms of the 'melting-pot' model of acculturation-cum-assimilation or the 'salad bowl' model celebrating cultural pluralism. It has been suggested that neither of these models adequately represents the experiences and perspectives of these Third World immigrants.

> Because both models posit the nation-state as the significant context for determining the immigrant identity formation, ignoring the forms of domination existing between host and sending societies, neither model adequately captures the transnational aspect of the culture and politics that third-world immigrants are creating in their present-day diasporas ... in debating the future of American national identity we need to reckon with the 'transnational' interests and identities of these new immigrants, for they are important in internationalizing the racial categories, the politics, and the public culture of American society.
>
> (Sutton, 1992, p.231)

Rather than becoming hyphenated Americans, it is argued, some of these recent immigrants — Asians, Caribbeans and Latinos — operate with a dual-place identity. This is facilitated in ethnic groups, such as Caribbeans and Latinos, by the geographic closeness of their 'homelands' and is encouraged by an 'ideology of return'. In a case study of Caribbeans in New York (Sutton, 1992) it was found that there was a great deal of back-and-forth visiting, facilitated by cheap airfares, and dual-place identity was kept alive by the internationalizing of social ties of family and extended kin, such as the culturally approved practice of sending children to be cared for by female kin or close friends. There was also a continuity of Caribbean traditions and resistance to the imposition of the dominant US cultural forms through the transfer to New York of Afro-Caribbean religions such as voodoo and Santeria — a Yoruba-derived Afro-Cuban religion that attracts considerable numbers of Hispanics, black Americans, and some West Indians, as well as many college-educated, second generation Caribbeans interested in African culture. Many of these people view themselves as living in a diaspora: of being related to diverse groups of people dispersed over different parts of the world and to whom they are connected by 'ancestral' ties and shared experiences of belonging to a subordinate-oppressed-outsider group, alongside other such groups.

Clearly, it is not only America that is affected by these diaspora cultures and dual-identities brought about by increased flows of people and capital between the Third World and First World. They are a function of globalization processes. However, the implications for America are striking for two reasons: the scale of its immigration, and the moralistic and utopian character of American ideology. The challenges have taken many forms in recent years, such as the struggles and controversies over bilingual education in public schools, the problems experienced in stemming illegal immigration at the Mexican–US border, the conflicts over the core curricula taught in schools, and the concern over the failure of public schools to stem the drop-out of Hispanics and black people and to integrate them into the national culture. America, like other Western nation-states with increasing Third World immigrant populations, may have to accept that it cannot construct a culturally unified 'imagined community'. Increasing globalization involves coming to terms with a transnationalized multiculturalism that operates within as well as across permeable borders. American exceptionalism, resting on a clear ideological conception of what America was different from, is becoming ever more difficult to sustain.

SUMMARY

We have examined the question of whether America is exceptional from a number of angles: its values, the role of religion and ethnicity, the assimilation of immigrants, and balance between cultural unity and diversity at different times.

Although American values may not be exceptional in themselves, there are several features of American culture that are exceptional, at least in degree. For example, the scale and variety of religious involvements is exceptional, as is the sheer size of the immigration America has experienced.

The religious and ethnic pluralism, which has persisted despite periodic conflicts and pressures in favour of homogenization (particularly WASPification), may help to explain many of the other areas of American culture: literature, music, sport, etc.

Contemporary global trends, such as mass immigration from the Third World and the internationalizing of social, cultural and communication links, pose new challenges.

REFERENCES

Bellah, R.N. (1970) *Beyond Belief*, New York, Harper & Row.

Bellah, R.N. (1975) *The Broken Covenant: American Civil Religion in Time of Trial*, New York, Seabury Press.

Bellah, R.N., Madsen, R., Sullivan, W.M., Swidler, A. and Tipton, S.M. (1985) *Habits of the Heart: Individualism and Commitment in American Life*, Berkeley, University of California Press.

Burke, E. (1904) *Selected Works*, Oxford, Clarendon Press.

Crèvecoeur, H. St. J. de (1957) *Letters From an American Farmer*, New York, E.P. Dutton (first published in 1782).

Darity, W.A. and Myers, S.L. (1992) 'Racial earnings inequality into the 21st century' in *The State of Black America 1992*, Washington DC, National Urban League, pp.119–40.

Dinnerstein, L. and Reimers, D.M. (1975) *Ethnic Americans: a History of Immigration and Assimilation*, New York, Harper & Row.

Glazer, N. (1971) 'Blacks and ethnic groups: the difference and the political difference it makes', *Social Problems*, vol.18, Spring, pp.441–61.

Gleason, P. (1980) 'American identity and Americanization' in *The Harvard Encyclopedia of American Ethnic Groups*, pp.31–58.

Greeley, A.M. (1991) 'American exceptionalism: the religious phenomenon' in Shafer, B.E. (ed.), pp.94–115.

Handlin, O. (1973) *The Uprooted*, Boston, Little, Brown (first published in 1951).

The Harvard Encyclopedia of American Ethnic Groups (1980), Thernstrom, S. (ed.), New Haven, Harvard University Press.

Herberg, W. (1960) *Protestant, Catholic, Jew*, New York, Doubleday.

Holt, T.C. (1980) 'Afro-Americans' in *The Harvard Encyclopedia of American Ethnic Groups*, pp.5–23.

Hunter, J.D. (1991) *Culture Wars: the Struggle to Define America*, New York, Basic Books.

Hunter, J.D. and Rice, J.S. (1991) 'Unlikely alliances: the changing contours of American religious faith' in Wolfe, A. (ed.), pp.318–31.

Huntington, S. (1981) *American Politics: the Promise of Disharmony*, Cambridge, Mass., The Belknap Press of Harvard University Press.

Jaynes, G.D. and Williams, R.M. (eds) (1989) *A Common Destiny: Blacks and American Society*, Washington DC, National Academy Press.

Kazín, M. (1989) 'The Right's unsung prophet', *The Nation*, 20 February, no.248, p.242.

Kennan, G. (1966) *Realities of American Foreign Policy*, New York, Norton.

Landry, B. (1991) 'The enduring dilemma of race in America' in Wolfe, A. (ed.), pp.185–207.

Lenski, G. (1961) *The Religious Factor: a Sociological Study of Religion's Impact on Politics, Economics and Family Life*, New York, Doubleday.

Lipset, S.M. (1991) 'American exceptionalism reaffirmed' in Shafer, B.E. (ed.), pp.1–45.

Marty, M.E. (1985) 'Transpositions: American religion in the 1980s', *Annals of the American Academy of Political and Social Science*, no.480, pp.11–23.

Marty, M.E. (1991) *Modern American Religion, vol.2: The Noise of Conflict 1919–1941*, Chicago, University of Chicago Press.

Menand, L. (1992) 'Being an American: how America is becoming less, not more, diverse', *Times Literary Supplement*, 30 October, pp.3–4.

Rumbaut, R.G. (1991) 'Passages to America: perspectives on the new immigration' in Wolfe, A. (ed.), pp.208–44.

Schneider, D.M. and Smith, R.T. (1973) *Class Differences and Sex Roles in American Kinship and Family Structure*, Englewood Cliffs, Prentice-Hall.

Shafer, B.E. (ed.) (1991) *Is America Different?*, Oxford, Clarendon Press.

Shibutani, T. and Kwan, K. (1965) *Ethnic Stratification: a Comparative Approach*, London, Macmillan.

Siegfried, A. (1927) *America Comes of Age*, Hemming, H.H. and Hemming, D. (trans.), New York, Harcourt & Brace.

Sowell, T. (1981) *Ethnic America: a History*, New York, Basic Books.

Steinberg, S. (1981) *The Ethnic Myth*, Boston, Beacon Press.

Sutton, C.R. (1992) 'Transnational identities and cultures: Caribbean immigrants in the United States' in D'Innocenzo, M. and Sirefman, J.P. (eds) *Immigration and Ethnicity: American Society — 'Melting Pot' or 'Salad Bowl'?*, Westport, Greenwood Press, pp.231–42.

Vaughan, L.J. (1991) 'Cosmopolitanism, ethnicity and American identity: Randolph Bourne's "trans-national America"', *Journal of American Studies*, vol.25, no.3, pp.443–59.

Wald, K.D. (1987) *Religion and Politics in the United States*, New York, St. Martin's Press.

Wilson, J. (1978) *Religion in American Society*, Englewood Cliffs, Prentice-Hall.

Wolfe, A. (ed.) (1991) *America at Century's End*, Berkeley, University of California Press.

FURTHER READING

See Bellah *et al.* (1985), Shafer (1991) and Wolfe (1991) in the references.

D'Innocenzo, M. and Sirefman, J.P. (eds) (1992) *Immigration and Ethnicity: American Society — 'Melting Pot' or 'Salad Bowl'?*, Westport, Greenwood Press.

THE AMERICAN NOVEL

Phil Melling ★

1 HISTORY, MEMORY AND THE AMERICAN ADAM

The American novel, we are told, has always struggled to break free from the binding conventions of history and locality preferring instead the more abstract realm of 'existential and metaphysical speculation' (Claridge, 1990, p.9). Alexis de Tocqueville predicted as much in *Democracy in America* and much of our liberal post-war criticism has tended to confirm the validity of the thesis.

In his discussion of the role of democracy in American letters Richard Chase, in *The American Novel and its Tradition*, considers the emergence of the romance form — with its reliance on myth, melodrama and idyll — as the logical outcome of the absence of class and old-world manners in post-revolutionary America. In romance writing, says Chase, disorder and contra-diction as well as a fascination with extremes of conduct and irreconcilable ideas are an indication of the anguish and insecurity of New World modern-ism — its crisis of expansion, its positive attempt to seek out alternative modes of expression in a society that lacked the mediating influence of class and tradition.

In another of the great foundation works of modern American studies, Henry Nash Smith's *Virgin Land*, the question of what is an 'American' and what are 'the defining characteristics of American society', is answered by a writer who argues the case for dynamic renewal. History, he says, is a pro-cess governed by an act of re-invention. He puts it thus:

> one of the most persistent generalizations concerning American life and character is the notion that our society has been shaped by the pull of a vacant continent drawing population westward through the passes of the Alleghenies, across the Mississippi Valley, over the high plains and mountains of the Far West to the Pacific Coast.

> (Smith, 1950, p.3)

This thesis is nothing if not controversial. There are many, for example, who would argue that the American continent in the act of being 'shaped' was far from 'vacant' of indigenous people. Nor would they agree that those who were indigenous were swept away and culturally redefined in the 'pull' westward — or, if relocated, necessarily uprooted themselves in a voluntary celebration of the 'vacant'. Those who would offer this criticism — and one thinks, for example, of the Native American novelist Louise Erdrich or the Mexican-American borderlands poet Gloria Anzaldúa — would doubtless react with similar hostility to the arguments put forward by R.W.B. Lewis in that other, classic, pre-1960s treatise on American studies, *The American Adam*.

What Lewis offers us in *The American Adam* is an investigation 'of the authentic American' and how that American appeared in the New World 'as a figure of heroic innocence and vast potentialities, poised at the start of a new history'. The link provided by Lewis between authenticity, Adamic rebirth and an unblemished, virginal America confirms the importance of a legendary figure in American life. We have met him before in the guise of Andrew the Hebridean, the eighteenth-century 'born again' Protestant in Hector St. Jean de Crèvecoeur's *Letters From an American Farmer*. In Lewis's *The American Adam*, Andrew the Hebridean stands once more at the epicentre of American cultural and mythic experience. He is, says Lewis, 'an individual emancipated from history, happily bereft of ancestry, untouched by the usual inheritance of family and race; an individual standing alone, self-reliant and self-propelling, ready to confront whatever awaited him with the aid of his own unique and inherent resources ... fundamentally innocent.' (Lewis, 1955, p.5.)

In waving a dismissive goodbye to what the African-American novelist, Toni Morrison, refers to as the 'vital' presence of an ethnic memory (Morrison, 1989, p.14), Lewis endorses the Protestant mythology of errand and rebirth and retrieves the idea of an exceptional American, a positive and 'radically new personality'. He removes the blemishes of history from this personality, the burden of guilt transmitted to the hero from previous disputes. In so doing he is unwilling to acknowledge the survival of an alternative version of American history, a version that is defined by ethnic genealogy and ancestral lore and the ancient heritage of pre-colonial life.

If the American Adam is 'innocent' because he is dominant then, presumably, as long as he remains dominant he can be exonerated from the consequence of his actions, especially if those actions can be explained as Adamic, as having occurred, in other words, as a necessary reaction to those who profess an alternative faith and identity. In making the mythological American authentic and 'unique' and in specifying that connection on the basis of adaptability and innocence, Lewis willingly discounts the Americanness of those who wish to retain their traditional ethnic or old-world allegiances. By definition, such allegiances are contaminated by history: they are compromised by the convictions of class and the static conventions of race and community. In Leslie Fiedler's *Love and Death in the American Novel* the compelling quality of the American Adam is the urge to disavow 'civilization', to escape the restrictions of the domestic family and the responsibilities of history. Ihab Hassan describes this urge, as 'radical innocence'.

SUMMARY

The US is regarded by many critics as the ultimate experiment in modernism. It is seen as the birthplace of the American Adam, a spiritual Protestant who embodies the dynamism of a new democracy and the invigorating potential of the frontier West.

It is argued that the US is not beset by the same historical problems that afflict other countries. In a place where the opportunity to escape history is unprecedented, the American writer is said to be fascinated by the potential for individual expression and the apparent urge to disavow civilization.

2   THE CITY AS THE NEW FRONTIER

For nineteenth-century American writers the frontier West is the traditional location for the act of separation or statement of disavowal. In the twentieth-century novel, however, the locus of change becomes the city and for those who subscribe to the notion of renewal the Adamic personality is frequently found in an urban or metropolitan location.

In the detective and gangster novels of the 1920s and 1930s, the Adamic individual is discovered not in the villages or farms, but in the alleys and mean streets of cities like Los Angeles, Chicago and New York. In the work of Raymond Chandler and Dashiell Hammett detectives like Philip Marlowe and Sam Spade are descendants of a frontier archetype first developed by Western writers like Owen Wister and Zane Grey. In the petrified forests of Southern California they live according to a vanishing code of voluntary individualism, picaresque shrewdness, justice and celibacy. Leslie Fiedler describes the early American private eye not as 'the dandy turned sleuth' but as 'the cowboy adapted to life on the city streets, the embodiment of innocence moving untouched through universal guilt ... the honest proletarian, illuminating by contrast the decadent society of the rich' (Fiedler, 1967, p.489). The detective–gangster novel of the inter-war period is an 'urban-pastoral', says George Grella, because the central character insists on sharing the basic individualism of the cowboy in a society where conformity to rules and traditions is the price for security (Grella, 1968, p.187). Like the nineteenth-century backwoodsman, part of the mobster's appeal lies in his refusal to acknowledge the priority of social regulations. Like the backwoodsman he is admired because he is untutored, proud of his ignorance, responsive and instinctive. He too lives by a code and a gun and inhabits a lower, and fundamentally more corporeal, level of existence. His violence, glamour and excitement exert their strongest pull on the voyeur who does not know first hand the world of crime and corruption.

The idea of an urban frontier in American society derives, as R.A. Burchell suggests, from the immediate post-Civil War period when disgruntled farmers, as a result of the failure of the Homestead Act of 1862, abandoned their farms and sought employment in the American city. From the 1870s onward the transfer of the frontier metaphor from the world of the garden to the world of industry has much to do with the extraordinary expansion of a capitalist economy centred on the city and the construction of a mass-consumption culture. As a result of these nationalizing tendencies the insularity of the rural, small-town culture of America was seriously disturbed. These 'island communities', as Robert Wiebe describes them, with their sense of permanence and intimacy and binding tradition, were rapidly undermined by the impact of an industrial system which sought to rationalize the differing regional identities of the United States within a mass, consumer economy. Capitalism, says Douglas Tallack, allowed individuals to see beyond their own community, to make rational predictions concerning their future and to take advantage of a rapidly expanding communications network and the upward social mobility which that network offered. The idea that the small-town community was effectively sovereign and retained the 'capacity to manage [its] own affairs within its [own] boundaries', was seriously questioned as capitalist markets began to erode ideological and cultural allegiances and to regulate local and national markets (Wiebe, 1967, p.44).

The appeal of the mass-consumption economy and the liberating effect which the new technologies exerted on the traditional, pre-modern communities of New England and the Midwest, is, says Tallack, a 'phenomenon with which all twentieth century writers and artists' have 'had to contend'. For many novelists the capitalist market, together with the 'sheer ... range of possibilities' offered by mass communications gave an obvious boost to the Adamic ideas of renewal and rebirth (Tallack, 1991, p.10). It breathed new life into areas of the country calcified by tradition and provinciality. In the city, as Guy Szuberla has noticed, a new association began to develop between an industrial landscape and a sublime garden. In the minds of Naturalist writers a link was established between nature and technology, one that received much of its inspiration from the work of architects like Daniel Hudson Burnham and Frederick Law Olmstead at the Columbia Exposition in Chicago in 1893.

SUMMARY

In the nineteenth and twentieth century the idea of the frontier as an urban rather than a rural location enters the American novel. In the gangster and detective novel the backwoodsman is now an urban cowboy who has adapted himself to life on the city streets.

The city increasingly intervenes in the life of rural communities. It restructures the village and small-town culture of America. It offers new and, some would say, exciting opportunities to insular communities. It breathes new life into regions whose Adamic convictions have atrophied.

3   IMAGES OF WOMEN IN THE MODERN CITY NOVEL

One of the concerns of novelists at the turn of the century is the effect of a capitalist economy on the role of women. To what extent, they ask, will women be able to avail themselves of the new opportunities for upward social mobility, and in what ways will this new class and/or geographic mobility transform a woman's expectations both in society and in the home?

In Stephen Crane's *Maggie* (1893) and Frank Norris's *The Octopus* (1901) the answer we get is not reassuring. In the increasingly combative and amoral city young women drift into prostitution under the pressure to survive socially and economically. Crane's Maggie and Norris's Minna Hooven fail to recognize the Darwinian conditions of conflict and competition and the naturalistic laws which regulate social relationships, economic transactions and the politics of the market-place. For such women the city is hellish and depraved; it is home to the Bowery, Rum Alley and the brothel; it is a place of sub-human violence where women fall from grace without the support of a community or the help of an advising parent or friend.

In *Sister Carrie*, a novel first published in 1900, we are given an entirely different picture. Dreiser's Carrie Meeber enters Chicago aware of the illusions that can cause her downfall and yet willing to be assimilated by an urban process, a moving principle of amoral energy that can bring significant change to her status. As Dreiser's Midwestern madonna, Carrie leaves her home in Columbia City, Indiana at 18 years of age and heads out for the bright lights of Chicago, a city which, by the turn of the century, had a population of over 1 million. Carrie is encouraged by the opportunism of the city, the twin energies of 'westering' and 'urbanizing' that are attracting not only immigrants from Europe but farmers and villagers on western homesteads struggling to survive under a burden of 'recurrent agricultural depression, mechanization, and mortgages' (Bradbury, 1983, p.1). Carrie participates in a new process of history, one that overwhelms not only the past but past world-views and forms of education. Again and again we see her sitting in a rocking chair as darkness gathers, gazing out at the city 'where the lights were reflected on wet pavements'. Carrie's sensibility is shaped by the new technologies of illumination. As the restaurants and hotels of the city kindle into life and the marquees of the theatres blaze with 'incandescent fire' her appetite for the art and spectacle of Chicago is whetted. The decisive moment in her early life comes when she performs her first role in the Elks Club play. Here she proves herself intuitively aware of the need to represent the magic and novelty of an urban landscape, to incorporate within her performance the principle of self-advertisement and social display. As Carrie enters she is already moving 'with a steady grace, born of inspiration'. We are told that 'she dawned upon the audience, handsome and proud, shifting, with the necessity of the situation, to a cold, white, helpless object' (Dreiser, 1970, p.135). Carrie shifts into the role of advertised object in the play just as she does during her time in Chicago with Hurstwood and Drouet, her two lovers. The need for an accommodating performance — to transform the body into a yearned-for object, a commodity — is learnt by observing the city and its night-life: the lamp-lit residences, the gilded shops, the illuminated restaurants, the brilliant play of reflected light on the bottles of liquor where Hurstwood works at Fitzgerald's & Moy. As Carrie professionalizes her identity in Chicago she is able to discover her independence and an ability to alter relationships with those who see her as a trophy or possession. Yet in spite of this she is never happy and as she sits in her opulent suite in the Waldorf at the end of the novel, in possession of all the things her heart has ever desired, she is immensely bored.

The transformation of the body into a display object, a thing of spectacle, becomes, for certain kinds of women, an important route to self-dramatization. If Carrie is aware of this particular route so too is Undine Spragg in Edith Wharton's *The Custom of the Country*, a novel which chronicles the aspirations of another young, material girl from middle America — one who, at the turn of the century, seeks recognition in the high societies of New York and Europe. Edmund Wilson describes Undine as 'the prototype in fiction of the "gold digger", of the international cocktail bitch' (Wilson, 1929, p.202). The observation conceals a genuine dilemma for a woman of intelligence like Undine, one who is obliged to expend her entrepreneurial talents in pursuit of partners and fictitious business. Undine recognizes, in the words of Charlotte Perkins Gilman, that a woman's survival in society and her 'economic profit comes through the power of sexual attraction' (Gilman, 1966, p.3). Newly arrived in New York from Apex, Indiana, Undine, like Carrie, is acutely aware of the comings and goings on the New York stage; indeed, much of her early social education takes place at the theatre. With her fiancé, Ralph Marvell, she attends the début of a fashionable actress in a play that attracts 'a large audience'. Aware of her charisma as a display object, and of the relationship between crowds and power, Undine enters her stall in the theatre exactly on cue. With the audience assembled she pauses for a moment in order to allow Ralph 'to remove her cloak' from her shoulders. The audience responds with a nod of approval at the timeliness of this act of commodification. Undine overhears a woman remark, 'There she is — the one in white, with the lovely back', and a man answer: 'Gad! where did he find anything as good as that?' Always willing to use her body as a resource for social control Undine turns and offers 'a smile of possessorship to Ralph'. Aware of the desire she has evoked in others — not least of all in Ralph — Undine experiences 'a last refinement of pleasure as might have come to some warrior Queen borne in triumph by captive princes, and reading in the eyes of one the passion he dared not speak' (Wharton, 1989, p.61).

In the theatres and salons of New York Undine works to overthrow patriarchal authority by exploiting a capitalist economy of desire and the idea that marital partners are useful additions to one's business empire. On the commodities market Undine is regarded by those who trade in female stock as a good investment, a woman whose capital will increase in value in a 'Stock Exchange' society. Such speculation, as it turns out, is not well-founded. In marriage Undine is a bitter disappointment to those who trade with her. With Ralph Marvell she is self-made and combative, and if economically dependent on her husband, she is never socially subservient to him. The tension is played out brilliantly by Wharton who shows Undine, in her travels through class, continent and marriage, as a casual scatterer of wreckage. A conspicuous consumer, Undine is willing to display the wealth and power of the men she marries (Ralph Marvell, Raymond de Chelles and, finally, Elmer Moffatt). But she is also a surrogate entrepreneur — a child of the manufacturing and industrial forces of America, who fights to establish her identity in a competitive market. Although willing to trade with the highest bidder she does not, in any way, grant her partners the right to take-over or to economic control.

Undine's restlessness and her urge to acquire and spend other people's money is compulsive. In her marriage to the aristocratic Catholic, Raymond de Chelles, she ventures out beyond the decorous society of Washington Square and wanders into Europe. There she mounts an attack on the genteel civility and parochial culture of old world France. Neither Ralph Marvell in Washington Square nor Raymond de Chelles in his chateau at Saint-Désert are able to counter her aggressive materialism or her assault on cultural continuity. They suffer, like F. Scott Fitzgerald's Dick Diver, the fate of men who live on the wrong side of history, 'the exact furthermost evolution of a class', the remnant of a type exposed and destroyed by industrial manufacture and new age morality (Bigsby, 1971, p.143).

SUMMARY

Women are casualties and beneficiaries of big city America. Prostitution features strongly in the Naturalist novel at the turn of the century. In the immoral and amoral city women are seen not only as victims. They are also liberated individuals capable of undermining masculine authority through resourceful and aggressive behaviour.

Women are also advertisers. They are imprisoned by their bodies and the way men view them as sexual and economic objects. They are not sufficiently liberated to be able to compete with men on an equal footing in politics or business.

4   THE PROVINCES

Not so George F. Babbitt, the spiritual descendant of Undine Spragg and the central character in Sinclair Lewis's best-selling novel, *Babbitt*. *Babbitt* is dedicated to Edith Wharton and again we witness not only the democratization of class in America but also the transformation that has taken place in the Midwest under the impact of a 'fast-intruding', urban, industrial economy. Like the salesman, Babbitt, the inhabitants of Zenith are, in part, the product of a new consumer tribalism, one in which 'the tastes of the crowd', as George E. Mowry puts it, have become 'an increasingly important determinant, first in popular culture and later in political and economical institutions' (Mowry, 1963, p.1). Babbitt and his fellow citizens possess the raw, untutored energy of the newly liberated; they live on the surface of life with a brashness and confidence that has been conferred upon them by the speculative tendencies of post-war America. Like Undine Spragg and Elmer Moffatt they embody 'the chaos of indiscriminate appetites' which, in Wharton's analysis, comprises the 'modern tendencies' (Wharton, 1989, p.vii).

The chaos is epitomized best by Babbitt himself, a man who is both a purveyor of consumption and one of the consumed: 'the facsimile of an adult', 'a clown beating a bass drum'. What Babbitt admires most in Zenith is the immediately agreeable and novel surface, the 'poetry of industrialism', the architecture of the new. When Lewis says that Babbitt is 'conscious of the loveliness of Zenith' we see a mind that is utterly enthralled by new forms of industry and industrial production: 'Factories producing condensed milk, paper boxes, lighting-fixtures, motor-cars. Then the business centre, the thickening darting traffic, the crammed trams unloading, and high doorways of marble and polished granite. It was big — and Babbitt respected bigness in anything; in mountains, jewels, muscles, wealth or words.' (Lewis, 1926, p.390.)

If Zenith is inflationary then words are one of its worst extravagances. Speculative tendencies reduce language to a throwaway product, a currency minted for the immediate, a vocabulary designed to match the accelerated moment of history through which the Midwest is passing. Here is Babbitt penning an advert about the Zeeco car in which, as he puts it, he decides to stick 'to the straight poetic'.

> The long white trail is calling — calling — and it's over the hills and far away for every man or woman that has red blood in his veins and on his lips the ancient song of the buccaneers. It's away with dull drudging, and a fig for care. Speed — glorious Speed — it's more than just a moment's exhilaration — it's Life for you and me! This great new truth the makers of the Zeeco Car have considered as much as price and style. It's fleet as the antelope, smooth as the glide of a swallow, yet powerful as the charge of a bull-elephant. Class breathes in every line. Listen, brother! You'll never know what the high art of hiking is till you TRY LIFE'S ZIPPINGEST ZEST — THE ZEECO!
>
> (Lewis, 1926, p.123)

The currency of hyperbole can not entirely disguise the insecurity that regions like the Midwest experience in the early twentieth century. Whatever its surface idealism Zenith remains a peculiar amalgam of the ancient and modern, a place of bravado and insecurity, of old fears and new faiths. This is a town invaded by the styles and values of the metropolis, yet one in whose imagination their still lingers a lost sense of community, a barely articulated craving for the old moral values of a Gemeinschaft culture. Zenith is outwardly buoyant but inwardly suspicious. If the 'Regular Guys' like Babbitt are busy creating a new civilization, then 'the Standardised American Citizen' must still be protected from the 'long-haired gentry who call themselves "liberals" and "radicals" and "non partisan" and "intelligentsia"' (Lewis, 1926, p.180). Although Zenith is willing to allow itself to be seduced by the appeal of urban commodities it still retains a profound suspicion of imported ideas. The benefits of a mass production, consumer economy may be acceptable but not the new idealisms of the left. Whatever impact the city has made in the l920s, anti-intellectualism retains its appeal in small-town America.

The problem worsens in Sherwood Anderson's *Winesburg, Ohio* (1919), a collection of stories about a small, Midwestern town struggling to understand the new consumer rhetoric of the age. The community of Winesburg is deeply traumatized, its voice and vocabulary painfully inadequate as a method of defence against a new commercial culture. Winesburg is a town whose history is on the point of breaking up, one which cannot cope with the combative tactics and interventionist presence of the secular city. The problem is explained to us in the story 'Godliness'.

> Books, badly imagined and written though they may be in the hurry of our times, are in every household, magazines circulate by the millions of copies, newspapers are everywhere. In our day a farmer standing by the stove in the store in his village has his mind filled to overflowing with the words of other men. The newspapers and the magazines have pumped him full. Much of the old brutal ignorance that had in it also a kind of beautiful childlike innocence is gone forever. The farmer by the stove is brother to the men of the cities, and if you listen you will find him talking as glibly and as senselessly as the best city man of us all.
>
> (Anderson, 1966, pp.70–1)

In the buried, provincial communities of the Midwest, says Anderson, the stability and 'brutal ignorance' of an old American language has been replaced by the soundbites of the city. The loss of the old words and the old ways of using them is the fault of strangers who, in the words of John Dos Passos, have made the language 'slimy and foul'. One of these strangers, a travelling salesman selling substitutes for collar buttons, appears in the story 'Queer'. He visits a store owned by Elmer and Ebenezer Cowley and uses a sales pitch that relies on an 'eager patter of words'. Elmer and Ebenezer, 'afraid' of the assault to which they are subjected, pull a gun on the glib-talking traveller. As they throw him out of the store words fail at the crucial moment and Ebenezer appears at a loss to explain what he is doing with the weapon. Ambiguity gives way to paralysis, language pulls away from its referential base and collapses into vagueness. '"We don't want any collar fasteners here." An idea came to him. "Mind, I'm not making any threat", he added. "I don't say I'll shoot. Maybe I just took this gun out of the case to look at it. But you better get out. Yes sir, I'll say that."' (Anderson, 1966, p.193.)

Brian Way describes *Winesburg, Ohio* as Sherwood Anderson's 'great book of loneliness', a mood which derives from 'the atmosphere of transition' through which this community is passing (Way, 1971, pp.107, 109). It derives also from a loss of confidence in traditional narrative and the inability of a local vernacular to combat, what Wing Biddlebaum calls, 'the roaring of the voices'. Anderson is exposing a culture, therefore, that has lost its balance, its historical poise. And for those who attempt to regain it, like the book's central character George Willard, the only available solution, it appears, is to leave home. The artist's capacity for growth, demonstrated by Willard's ability to listen to others and to accept without fear a principle of uncertainty, can only be fulfilled, says Anderson, if Willard avoids the suffocating rhetoric of 'the grotesques', those who petition him with their tortured messages of retaliation.

SUMMARY

In the small towns of the Midwest, enormous changes take place in the early years of the twentieth century. Small communities appear overwhelmed by the new mass culture of the cities. Yet, whatever the level of surface idealism, there is still an underlying tension that distinguishes the Midwest from metropolitan America. The region remains suspicious of imported ideas. It is not consistent in its views. It may react aggressively in defence of the old ways. Or it may crave a lost sense of community, while still accepting the benefits of commercialism.

5 YOU CAN'T GO HOME AGAIN: AMERICA'S MOST FORBIDDING PROVERB

The train that takes George Willard, Carrie Meeber and Undine Spragg away from the Midwest to their 'future life in the city', reverberates throughout the American novel of the twentieth century. Its echoes are particularly distinctive in the American novel of the 1920s and 1930s. In John Dos Passos's trilogy *USA*, for example, no one dies in the place they are born in. According to Leo Gurko, 'rootlessness' has become, for Dos Passos, 'the prime aspect' of American civilization with the whole country on the move, shuttling from state to state, from city to city in a restless urge to escape the past. By *The Big Money*, the final novel in the trilogy, we have fully entered the world of automation; the sophisticated touring car, the newly invented plane, the plush Pullman, the Cunard liner. The rhythm of the machine becomes the primal beat of the people. As Gurko puts it: 'Dos Passos is the great roadmaster of American fiction. His figures rack up more mileage than any since Smollet. They are constantly, incessantly on the go' (Gurko, 1968, p.51). In *USA* the escape from history deteriorates into an indiscriminate yearning for sensation. For characters like Joe Williams and Fenian McCreary the home has all but disappeared or is left behind. According to F.R. Karl:

> The wife, love? — there is not time. Lust is preferable because it is
> faster. The child in the family? — he is too small to count unless he

rebels and moves out. A man's profession? — is usually a step toward something else, or work to which he is not committed. Relaxation is impossible. The road-train, river, ocean — consumes all energy; the quest to escape self becomes a national mystique.

(Karl, 1968, p.203)

In many of the novels and autobiographies of the 1930s the attempt to escape unemployment and the Depression expresses itself in a dream of re-invention. On an imaginary frontier California becomes the symbol of a second chance in the New World while Hollywood offers, what Lewis Mumford terms, a 'Utopia of Escape', a desert island rather than a reconstructed social system. With its sunshine and oranges, youth and fertility, optimism and progress, Hollywood seems a refreshing contrast to the industrial blight and freezing climate of the East and North. ALL ROADS LEAD TO HOLLYWOOD flashes the neon sign in Horace McCoy's *I Should Have Stayed Home*. For McCoy's Midwestern émigré hero, Ralph Carston, Los Angeles is 'the most terrifying town in the world'. It is also a place of 'miracles' where 'today you are broke and unknown and tomorrow you are rich and famous'. Reality is displaced by a neon image; illusions have become so vivid and persuasive that people are committed to living within them. 'Hollywood … is where I belong, this is my destiny' murmurs Carston, a personal conviction which has its roots in the belief that America was fated to realize its 'manifest destiny' and extend across the continent from the Atlantic to the Pacific (McCoy, 1966, pp.1, 68). The faith is misplaced. Unwilling to acknowledge that the democracy of the frontier has been replaced by an oligarchy of big business, that the fluidity of the West has been succeeded by the standardization of Main Street, the peripatetic Adam, in the California novel of the 1930s, makes a solitary hegira to nowhere. On a landscape of decaying scenery, writers like Horace McCoy, Nathanael West and James Cain show the way the high hopes of those who head west succumb to frustration and punitive violence. In a painting offered by the central character, Tod Hackett, in *The Day of the Locust*, this violence culminates in the ritualized riot of 'The Burning of Los Angeles'.

If a dream of apocalypse is a way of making it new in America — of setting fire to the city before rebuilding it — the riots which took place in South-Central Los Angeles in 1992 appear to provide us with an intriguing and chilling confirmation of Tod Hackett's vision. These riots and the earlier Watts Riots of 1965 can be seen, says Joan Didion, as a vindication of the dream of apocalypse.

> The city burning is Los Angeles's deepest image of itself … and at the time of the 1965 Watts Riots what struck the imagination most indelibly were the fires. For days one could drive the Harbor Freeway and see the city on fire, just as we had always known it would be in the end.

(Didion, 1974, p.179)

Much of Didion's writing on California (*Slouching Towards Bethlehem* and *Play It As It Lays*, in particular) is a stylish testimony to the breakdown of history. For those who emigrate to California, violence is 'casual' and endemic, an inevitable consequence of the 'sloughing off' of history (Didion, 1974, pp.19–21). In her work, the road and freeways of California are the routes we take to a longed-for amnesia, an escape from the past, a yearning for death in the heart of the city which accompanies a desire to be 'born again'.

SUMMARY

Those who migrate to the city are often confused by what they encounter. The search for renewal can easily deteriorate into frenetic activity and incessant travel. In the Hollywood novel the idea of renewing oneself on a make-believe frontier appeals as a core, historic duty. California becomes popular as a destination for those who wish to escape the Depression. The desire to escape is often frustrated. Southern California acquires a reputation as volatile and apocalyptic.

6   THE CITY AS SPECTACLE

This idea of California as a place of abandonment, self invention and enigmatic hallucination, is repeated — perhaps somewhat fancifully at times — in numerous novels of the twentieth century: Alison Lurie's *The Nowhere City*, Thomas Pynchon's *The Crying of Lot 49*, John Rechy's *City of Night*, and Raymond Chandler's *Farewell my Lovely*, *The High Window* and *The Little Sister*. In these texts we see the city as a spectacle lacking in both substance and rationality, the illuminated projection of a mythic ideal, a place in which light and neon anaesthetize the traveller. In a city like Los Angeles, says Claus Oldenburg, the most primary form of experience simply involves 'sitting in a car and watching letters silhouetted against the sky' (Clarke, 1988, p.131). The prevalence of neon signs and forms, what Tom Wolfe calls 'electrographic architecture', underscores the visual character of the city, the sense of continuous flow and process that technology creates (Wolfe, 1969, p.380). In Joan Didion's *Play It As It Lays* the freeway on which Maria Wyeth travels as she weaves her way through the suburbs of Los Angeles generates the same feeling of entry and momentum as the train does for Carrie Meeber at the opening of *Sister Carrie*. Like Carrie, Maria is exhilarated by the signs of the city and the kinetic energy which those signs generate.

> She drove it as a riverman runs a river, every day more attuned to its currents, its deceptions, and just as a riverman feels the pull of the rapids in the lull between sleeping and waking, so Maria lay at night in the still of Beverly Hills and saw the great signs soar overhead at seventy miles an hour, Normandie 1/4 Vermont 3/4 Harbor Fwy 1.

> (Didion, 1973, p.16)

Guy Debord defines the spectacle of modernist technology as 'the material reconstruction of the religious illusion' (Debord, 1970, para.36). The power of 'illusion' that technology can generate is also acknowledged in a story published by F. Scott Fitzgerald in 1922, *The Diamond as Big as the Ritz*. In the western village of Fish the religious ideal is no longer associated with Christianity and has been replaced by a devotion to technology. Each evening at seven o'clock at the station depot The Twelve Men of Fish gather silently in prayer to witness the arrival of the Transcontinental Express from Chicago. The 'observation of this ... preposterous phenomenon', says Fitzgerald, has 'become a sort of cult among the men of Fish' for whom religion has atrophied into voyeurism and technology has taken over from the worship of the Virgin (Fitzgerald, 1965, p.96). The twelve disciples are empty-headed dreamers. The presence of a vital mechanism is sufficient to inspire within them 'a dim, anaemic wonder' of obedience. Such is the power of the miraculous dynamo that the men of Fish are transformed into a secular and passive congregation of witnesses. They feel compelled, as Henry Adams puts it, by an 'inherited instinct' that teaches 'the natural expression of man before silent and infinite force' (Bradbury, 1983, pp.20–1).

The question of how to equate an historical and religious impulse with the acquisition and display of material objects remains a central concern for F. Scott Fitzgerald. In *The Great Gatsby*, Jay Gatsby is presented to us as a child of the new forces at work in modern America. Like the self-conscious author of the novel, Nick Carraway, he is a devotee of the new, a man whose sense of wonder expends itself on a vision of consumption and a poetics of colour: hydroplanes, yellow Rolls Royces, gold bath taps, pink suits, silver ties, imported silk and linen shirts and a woman whose voice is redolent with the sound of money. For Nick Carraway the acquisition of 'gorgeous' products is an affirmation of Gatsby's 'romantic readiness', his 'heightened sensitivity to the promises of life' that the products of consumption are able to convey (Fitzgerald, 1953, p.2). Yet Carraway's narrative, which itself is seduced by the power of urban spectacle and the spectacle of urban wealth, is not always consistent. As the member of an enterprise culture Gatsby is all things to all people — gangster, bootlegger, holy man, fool, a child of humble origins who is 'born again' in the redemptive fire of American capitalism, a westerner who travels east in order to display his wealth and purchases. Gatsby's house reminds Nick of the World's Fair, a city on a hill lit up to look like a Hollywood film set for the benefit of New York's leisure and advertising classes. The house is visually appealing but is also synonymous with obstructed vision, loss of memory, and a feeling of 'oblivion' that overwhelms the visitors to Gatsby's parties (ibid., p.107). The problem of amnesia is endemic in the novel. It is not only Gatsby that cannot accurately remember or corroborate his own past; neither can Nick Carraway, a narrator who does little, if anything, to disentangle the actual from the imaginary, the substantive experience from the merely intriguing. Nick allows himself to wander between material and mythic explanations of history, often deliberately confusing the two in order to construct a best-selling novel about a man whose links with sports and the underworld would have made him instantly recognizable to readers of tabloid journalism in the

1920s. In the 'supersensual universe' of the city Gatsby is a glamorous, if flawed, American Adam. Through him the link is established between the capacity for wonder and the celebration of technology, between pastoral idealism and the methods of modern commercial advertising.

SUMMARY

Cities are places of spectacle which exhilarate and beguile the onlooker. Technology is a primary source of beguilement and illusion. So too are the products of mass culture which the cities are awash with. Some of the most famous American novels illustrate the seductive effect of consumerism on the mind of the American provincial.

7 THE END OF HISTORY

The conflict between those who see technology as the agent of renewal and those who see it as a source of breakdown in a secular age has been the basis of a considerable tension in American thought since the Civil War. Much of this tension is documented in Leo Marx's study of American cultural thought, *The Machine in the Garden*. In this book Marx charts the 'profound contradictions' of 'value' and 'meaning' that result from the 'unbelievably rapid industrialization' of the 'rustic and in large part wild landscape' of the United States in the nineteenth century (Marx, 1967, p.343). He shows us, in particular, how the pulling apart of history and culture by the forces of industrialization dominates one of the great works of modern American autobiography, *The Education of Henry Adams*. Henry Adams's *The Education* was privately printed and written in the third person. It chronicles the effect which industrial manufacture and mechanical motion have begun to exert on the American mind in the immediate post-Civil War period — an age of brash, entrepreneurial capitalism that was to produce 4,000 millionaires by the early 1890s. Technology in the form of railroads, steamboats and the telegraph appears to have separated Adams from his eighteenth-century patrician upbringing. The new education to which he is exposed is one of violence and the contradiction of past and present values.

For Adams a new version of America is unfolding with its accelerating forces, expanding markets and new transportation and communications systems. Adams feels overwhelmed by the prospect of a new education in which the traditional notions of culture and intellect and the feminine or sensual principle of history — one which expresses an intrinsic relationship between feeling and power — has been removed. His pessimism about the direction of history is intensified on a visit he makes to the Great Exposition in Paris in 1900. Here he finds himself, as he says, 'lying in the Gallery of Machines ... his historical neck broken by the sudden eruption of forces totally new'. As he stares in wonder at the new industrial, 40-foot dynamo, he is possessed by an impulse to pray to the new 'occult mechanism', the same feeling of devotion and wonder experienced by the Christians in the presence of the Virgin. In this new kingdom of 'force' the machine represents not only a sublimated sexual and religious vitality, but also domination and violence. It represents the onset of 'an industrialised society that threatens, as no previous society has threatened, to destroy the creative power embedded in the Virgin' (Bradbury, 1983, pp.20–1).

If twentieth-century American writers are intrigued by the power of technology they are also deeply suspicious of it. The possibility, as Adams puts it, that 'Man has mounted science and is now run away' is of great concern for the American novelist, especially in the early years of the twentieth century. Such feelings intensify during the First World War when the impact of rampant industrialization appears to offer convincing proof that the writer is witnessing a new condition of modernity, a world of the future, an experimental landscape on the other side of some essential line drawn across experience. Those who survive that experience and come to maturity because of it see themselves as the bearers of a special kind of knowledge that an older generation does not possess. As Paul Fussell tells us, the political and military leaders of the First World War were wholly unaware of the impact of the forces they were able to unleash. 'The Great War', he says, 'took place in what was, compared with ours, a static world, where the values appeared stable and where the meanings of abstractions seemed permanent and reliable' (Fussell, 1975, p.21).

In the years between 1912 and 1917, says Henry F. May, a complete cultural revolution took place. The central tenets of nineteenth-century civilization — the certainty of moral values, the inevitability of progress and the importance of traditional literary culture — lost much of their relevance. This change in traditional values can be attributed to the First World War which brought about, in May's words, 'the end of American innocence'.

In *A Farewell to Arms* Frederic Henry points to the damaging limitations of provincial innocence. In the following, celebrated passage he considers the inadequacy of established military belief and the precarious nature of the emotional rhetoric on which that belief so often depended: 'I was always embarrassed by the words sacred, glorious, and sacrifice and the expression in vain … Abstract words such as glory, honor, courage, or hallow were obscene beside the concrete names of villages, the numbers of roads, the names of rivers, the numbers of regiments and the dates.' (Hemingway, 1969, pp.184–5.)

The First World War undermined the value of service as an ethical ideal on the battlefield. Instead of the fire of war there appeared the mud of the trench, instead of the hero there were only the faceless masses butchering each other with none of those personal tests of bravery and courage celebrated in the epics. In such a war the individual soldier was capable of very little. He could advance, retreat, spectate, desert or suffer the consequence of random action. Most of the time he might wait, bored, or, if unlucky, be hit unexpectedly by a chance fragment from a long-distance shell. In Hemingway's novels there is rarely significant description of the man that fights or is actively engaged in a battle that effectively tests his strength and courage. In the technological slaughterhouse of the First World War there are no traditional heroes and the individual has been reduced by the military mind to an object fit only for butchering. Machines have made the individual's chance of survival both irrational and unfathomable. They have destroyed the relevance of absolute values and his ability to predict the outcome of events.

SUMMARY

Technology destroys as much as it beguiles. The need to educate one-self in the new industrial processes separates the individual from the traditions of history. The First World War is one of those processes. American novelists see it as a slaughterhouse which erodes vitality and undermines traditional manners and faiths.

The idea that war is the ultimate purpose of technology is an enduring metaphor in twentieth-century fiction. Those who are fascinated with calculation and scientific precision — managers, militarists, scientists, engineers — are regularly seen as the evil geniuses of our age.

8   ETHNICITY AND THE CITY

Since the 1960s there has been a tendency among writers who represent the interests of indigenous communities — Chicanos and Native Americans, for example — to regard the city as a centre for cultural assimilation. Often located on land from which the indigenous American was evicted, the city is historically associated with loss, displacement and denial, as well as a buried, supernatural power that can still undo the colonizing race. Those who seek to recover that power and reclaim the buried, instinctual energies of the past invoke the spirit of the absent ancestor. By conjuring up the spirit of history the city's authority to control the memory of those whose lands it once usurped is fundamentally challenged. In the poem *New Orleans*, the Creek Indian, Joy Harjo, is led to the Mississippi River where her 'spirit' can catch the 'voices' of the 'ancestors' buried deep 'beneath the currents, their stories ... made of memory'. The sedimentary past deposits rich silt, a silt of history which is dredged from the depths by the chants and incantations of the poet. In a city of 'magic stones' and memories the modern-day experience of adventure in New Orleans amounts to so much tourist traffic, the trivial pursuits of pleasure craft on the river. The city of commerce, says Harjo, is helpless to suppress the tide of memory, the-river-as-creek that bides its time in 'the undercurrent' of the Mississippi (*The Heath Anthology of American Literature*, 1990, pp.2546–7).

To those who are members of a traditional culture, says the Mexican-American journalist Richard Rodriguez, the promise of adaptation and change in the modern American city, is 'colourless' and 'odourless'. The promise relies upon a 'conventional', immigrant myth of 'amnesia' in which the ethnic American leaves 'behind several time zones' and his 'names for things' and accepts the 'assumption' that his heritage no longer has any meaning. Rodriguez continues:

> The theme of America is discontinuity. America's national faith is Protestant. Americans believe in conversion, in Pauline rebirth. You can escape your father's eyes. You can escape your father's sins. You can escape your father. You can — you should — earn more money than your old man. You can escape history. All that the past had in store for you should be dissolved.

> (Rodriguez, 1990, p.212)

If the thesis of dissolution is the melting-pot, its historical home is the American city. This text, popularized in the early twentieth century by the playwright Israel Zangwill, argues that America is God's divine crucible and the city a melting-pot in which the ethnic components of those who come there can be melted down into something approaching Anglo conformity. The idea does not find favour, however, with the cultural spokesmen of America's indigenous communities. Native American writers, for example, regard the city as a place constructed not for them but for others. They point to what John Winthrop said in 1630, on board the Arbella: 'We shall find that the God of Israel is among us, when ten of us shall make us a praise and glory, that men shall say of succeeding plantations; the Lord make it like that of New England: for we must consider that we shall be as a City on a Hill, the eyes of all people are upon us'. For the Native American the 'us' and 'we' in Winthrop's assembly are the people of Anglo-Saxon attitudes, those whose duty it is to revise and reinvent the aboriginal environment of the colonies in the light of His metropolitan instruction. The city is for those who are obligated to cultivate the wilderness and transform the unregenerate into a fitting resident of a City on a Hill, a place administered by members of His congregation.

SUMMARY

Minority groups are politicized in the 1960s and become more militant. In recent years ethnic protest is most vociferous when it focuses attention on the loss of physical territory and culture to white, Anglo-Saxon, Protestant America.

Ethnic writers dissociate themselves from the Adamic myths of amnesia and renewal. Native Americans, in particular, dispute the authority of the city and the notion of a melting-pot where ethnic differences are supposed to boil down.

9 RECOVERY OF LANGUAGE AND LAND

For the Native American novelist Louise Erdrich it is the memory of land, and of lost land in particular, that gives shape and meaning to political and cultural narratives of resistance. In her fiction the search to recover a geographical identity is linked with the preservation of land, the values of the wilderness and the narrative voice of those who live in it. In *Tracks* (1988), Erdrich's second novel, the desire 'to win back control of ones own territory' (Said, 1990, p.77), drives Fleur Pillager and her father Nanapush to resist the lumber companies of North Dakota who buy up reservation land in order to build fishing lodges. In responding to the loss of his allotment Nanapush is the ancient nonconformist who dares speak out against capitalist intervention and the policy of acquiring land 'for profit'. His narrative relives a history of constant struggle: the loss and decimation of the Chippewa tribe through sickness, the disappearance of the buffalo and the haemorrhaging of land to the mining and lumber interests. In spite of that loss his narrative acts like an incantation, a chant of rescue for his granddaughter, Lulu Pillager. The narrative which recalls Lulu's life as a child and her rescue from the government school calls out to her not to forget in later life the family's struggle to survive the loss of its ancient lands. What Nanapush gives Lulu is the 'love medicine' of history, the authentic story of the family's attempt to retain control of Pillager land and the woods and lakes which are continually under threat.

> My girl, I saw the passing of times you will never know. I guided the last buffalo hunt. I saw the last bear shot. I trapped the last beaver with a pelt of more than two years' growth. I spoke aloud the words of the government treaty, and refused to sign the settlement papers that would take away our woods and lake. I axed the last birch that was older than I, and I saved the last Pillager.
>
> (Erdrich, 1988, p.2)

Edward Said describes the style of writing as 'cartographic', the intention being, he says, to search out 'a new territoriality' based on the need for 'assertions, recoveries and identifications'. Resistance literature, says Said, expresses a mood of anti-imperialism for it is rooted in the 'pressing need for the recovery of the land' that has been usurped by the colonizing power. As Said puts it:

> If there is anything that radically distinguishes the imagination of anti-imperialism it is the primacy of the geographical in it ... For the native, the history of his or her colonial servitude is inaugurated by the loss to an outsider of the local place, whose concrete geographical identity must thereafter be searched for and somehow restored.
>
> (Said, 1990, p.77)

The anti-imperialist imagination is prominent in modern Chicano literature. In the works of Gloria Anzaldúa, Rudolfo Anaya, Thomas Rivera, Ron Arias and Ronaldo Hinojosa the Chicano is no longer a figure of marginal importance in the American novel, nor is he or she a bit-player in American history, the child-like object of patronizing sentiment often encountered in American cinema. The Chicano is a member of a border culture (los atravesados), a 'mongrel', 'mulatto', or 'hybrid' American who inherits the traditions of two, discrete worlds that have come together and formed 'a third country' in the American southwest. Said describes this border region as having 'a third nature', one which 'derives historically and abductively from the deprivations' of history, and especially the loss of language and land (Said, 1990, p.79).

The lives of people in this 'third country' are wonderfully evoked by Ronaldo Hinojosa in the novels *Klail City, Dear Rafe*, and *Rites and Witnesses*. Hinojosa gives us a complex, dynastic and mythological account of a people whose genealogy can be traced back over hundreds of years on both sides of the Rio Grande river. This territory, acquired from Mexico by the US after the Mexican–American War of 1846 and the Treaty of Guadalupe Hidalgo in l848, is symbolically repossessed and ancestralized in Hinojosa's fiction. In the histories, biographies, and oral narratives of those who live in Hinojosa's fictional Belken County, we see a way of life and a folklore that has tenaciously survived the depredations of the melting-pot and the economic and social discrimination waged by the Texas Anglos and their urban, corporate, power base in the city. Hinojosa's language of resistance is picaresque and his novels, many of which are written in Spanish, wholly or bilingually, seek to restore the language of the region — a language which was systematically eradicated by the US government in the years after Guadalupe Hidalgo — to its pre-eminent position in the Chicano text. The identification of language and land as reference points for Chicano culture allows the writer to locate, if not to retrieve, the space or territory that was once usurped by an occupying power 'under the aegis', as Said puts it, 'of the metropolitan center' (Said, 1990, p.78). In *Klail City* the past is chewed over in the cantina, the Acquí me Quedo Bar, the name of which, translated into English is, 'Here I stay' — thereby providing a symbolic assertion of the Chicano's right to language and land. Loss of land and loss of language, is, of necessity, the starting point for Chicano resistance. The act of reclaiming the novel as the cultural property of those who have been dispossessed can be seen as a way of overturning history: an attempt to repossess space by actively evicting a gringo culture from the territory of the text. By manipulating the use of English, Hinojosa is able to subvert, at will, a language whose history is one of oppression. By choosing to write in Spanish or English, and by employing a combination of the two in various syntactical forms — a frequently employed device called 'code switching' — the Chicano writer can illustrate the richness of his or her multicultural heritage and transform the language into a political tool, an expression of what Said calls: 'decolonised identity'.

SUMMARY

Chicano writers preserve the idea that language and land give shape and meaning to political and cultural narratives of resistance. Chicano writing is anti-imperialist for it insists on the need to retrieve what is lost to the colonizing power.

Novels written in Spanish are an affirmation of faith in the need to evict a gringo culture from the territory of the text. The novel in Spanish is symbolic property for the Chicano people, a sacred territory which the writer retrieves from an interventionist culture.

Native American writers also emphasize the need to recover a lost identity. They rediscover ancestral memories and the narrative wisdom of those whose voice the canon (the general criterion) has attempted to bury.

10 THE CITY IN ETHNIC HISTORY: AFRICAN AND JEWISH-AMERICANS

It would be wrong to conclude that all ethnic American writers and communities are suspicious and resentful of the city's authority. While Native Americans were the tragic victims of the rush to create a settled, urban environment, other ethnic groups in the US entered the city of their own volition, precisely because they wished to escape the persecution and racism endemic in the countryside. Ethnic attitudes toward the city, therefore, cannot be regarded as consistent, either between differing ethnic communities or, for that matter (depending on the circumstances surrounding the act of migration to the city), within the same community. For example, Jewish writers tend not to exhibit the same antipathy toward the city as Chicanos while African-American novelists, like Toni Morrison or Walter Mosley, have a different perspective to that of black historians like Alain Locke. The city is not always The Great Wrong Place for ethnic communities, especially so for Chinese, Japanese, African or Jewish-Americans. These communities lost whatever land they owned (if not their memory of rural ownership), prior to their arrival on the shores of America and tend not to share the same hostility as indigenous cultures whose land the city was often built on. Black people who travelled north between 1910 and 1920 in the Great Migration from the American South to cities like Chicago, Philadelphia, Detroit and New York, did so to escape unemployment and widespread racism in the South, while the Jews who poured into New York from 1880 to 1920 in order to escape the pogroms of Eastern Europe responded to the lure of American enterprise and mobility. 'We were the children and grandchildren of the last great tribal migration of our species on this planet', says the Jewish-American novelist Chaim Potok, 'the east–west wandering of the frightened, the persecuted, the hungry, the poor, the seekers after new wealth and power' (Potok, 1981, p.162).

In the work of Jewish novelists from Michael Gold to Saul Bellow and from Henry Roth to Bernard Malamud, the city is drama, a contested space of immigrant streets, diverse languages and ethnic groups, each of which competes for a foothold. In the Jewish novel the city is the very fountain of multicultural life, a place of congestion and poverty, sweat shops and laundries, stock yards and junk yards, hoodlums and politicians and a unique location in which to discover the broad sweep of twentieth-century experience. It is a place where one experiences the struggle to break away from the world of the fathers; to construct — not always successfully — the necessary bridge between being a Jew and being an American; a place in which to acquaint oneself, as Saul Bellow's Augie March puts it, with the 'lessons and theories of power'. The journey through this border region is never easy or clear cut; it involves an experience, as Norman Mailer puts it, where 'ones emotions are forever locked in the chains of ambivalence — the expression of an emotion forever releasing its opposite ... ' (quoted in Goldman, 1975, p.317).

In Chicago Augie March finds himself with the children of immigrants from every part of Chicago aspiring to be American, learning to acquire 'power' by way of wealth and social manipulation. Augie resists the lure of materialism but Charlie Citrine, in Bellow's novel, *Humboldt's Gift*, wonders whether the challenge of culture is worth the effort:

> For could a poem pick you up in Chicago and land you in New York two hours later? Or could it compute a space shot? It had no such powers. And interest was where power was ... It was not Humboldt, it was the U.S.A. that was making its point: Fellow Americans, listen. If you abandon materialism and the normal pursuits of life you wind up at Bellevue like this poor kook.
>
> (Bellow, 1975, p.169)

The cost of being a Jew in America, of joining a community and a tradition of suffering, is accepted as necessary by the young Italian Frankie Alpine in Bernard Malamud's *The Assistant*. Alpine gradually becomes more like the elderly Jewish storekeeper he has robbed. At the novel's conclusion he is painfully circumcised in order to mark his conversion to Judaism. But the event is shrouded in ambiguity. The reader is unsure if Alpine has commenced a journey toward redemption or whether he is heading toward another dead end, a willing victim of the bondage of Judaism rather than a man in search of freedom.

In Jewish-American fiction the city can be loved or loathed but it cannot be avoided. 'My parents hated all this', says Michael Gold of the slums he grew up in. 'But it was America, one had to accept it' (Gold, 1984, p.30). For Chaim Potok New York was the stuff of fiction, a place of violent confrontation between the culture of the family, the Semitic past, and the tidal energies of a turbulent city which immersed him as a youth:

> The Bronx of the Thirties and Forties was my Mississippi River Valley ... And alone, on a concrete and asphalt Mississippi, I journeyed repeatedly through the crowded sidewalks and paved-over back-

yards, the hallways of the brick apartment houses, the hushed public libraries, dark movie houses, candy stores, grocery stores,
Chinese laundries, Italian shoe-repair shops, the neighborhoods of
Irish, Italian, blacks, Poles — journeys impelled by eager curiosity
and a hunger to discover my sense of self, my place in the tumult of
the world. I was an urban sailor on the raft of my own two feet.

(Potok, 1981, p.161)

The imagery of tidal flow and cultural immersion is developed by Alain
Locke in *The New Negro* in 1925, a book which explains the Great Migration
of black people from the rural South as a great opportunity, an act filled
with 'oceanic stimulus' and 'visionary excitement' (Mulvey, 1990, p.95). In
The New Negro Locke utilizes the eighteenth-century mythology of Hector St.
Jean de Crèvecoeur to describe the impact of the modern city on the arriv-
ing migrant. He sees the Negro embarking upon a new chapter of history,
one in which a new black person will come into being, re-forged in the
smithies of industrial America.

Locke's vision of a New Negro, a black Adam, is disputed in two fundamental ways by other African-American writers. In his great novel of
Harlem, *Invisible Man*, Ralph Ellison negates the exuberance and positivism
of Locke's New Negro by showing us a migrant who travels unseen in a
world that is lacking in hope or renewal and is blind to colour. The problem
faced by Ellison's protagonist is, as the elderly pianist Toledo puts it in
August Wilson's play *Ma Rainey's Black Bottom*: 'We done sold ourselves to
the white man in order to be like him' (quoted in DeVries, 1989, p.53).

In Toni Morrison's work the city does indeed offer hope but only in terms of
an encounter with Africa — the ancestral past that black people carry with
them wherever they go. Better to be born-again historically, she says, than
embrace a mythology of denial and amnesia. The New World city, she continues, merely encourages black people to suppress the memory of slavery
and the absent ancestor of Africa: the memorial parent who has no identity,
no accredited role in the white man's city or in his novels. James Baldwin
agrees. 'The motion of the white people in this country', he says, 'has been
— and it is a terrifying thing to say this, but it is time to face it — a furious
attempt to get away from the niggers' (Baldwin, 1981, p.135).

In the 1900s the 'niggers' in America came close to the centres of power,
migrating north in unprecedented numbers and causing a furious racial
backlash in cities like New York. The act of migration, says Morrison, enabled the black population to recommunalize and rehistoricize itself in urban
'village' enclaves like Harlem. Here, the oral heritage of the South and the
surviving memory of Africa took root on the streets in a communal folklore,
an idiom that expressed awareness and concern for those left voiceless in
the past. In black culture, says Morrison, the city is a 'wholesome' and
'loved' place when 'neighbourhood links are secure' and the memory of history is made available in the presence or form of an ancestor. In Harlem in
the 1920s, says Morrison, the city was a village. Although 'the hospitals,
schools, and buildings' black people lived in, 'were not founded nor con-

structed by their own people', she says; 'the relationships [were] clannish because there [was] joy and protection in the clan' (Morrison, 1981, p.38).

The playwright August Wilson also experienced similar feelings of 'joy and protection' on the streets of Pittsburgh where he lived his youth. In the bars, brothels and work-places, Wilson claims to have searched out the company of 'old' men, those who had refused to abandon — in the words of Toni Morrison — the 'traditional role of advisor' and preferred to retain a 'strong connection to the past' (Morrison, 1981, p.40). The city streets for Wilson were an acceptable venue on which to discover the cumulative history of the American South as well as African culture. The banter of street corner gossip provided him with a rich loam that nourished the roots of his creativity. In plays such as *Fences, Ma Rainey,* and *Joe Turner's Come and Gone,* Wilson relies heavily on the use of a black oral tradition that has survived — through various migrations — the loss of the American South and the African village. What he attempts to recover, in the words of the novelist John Wideman, is a 'lost experience' whose 'primal authenticity' rests in 'a language of immediate, sensual, intimate reciprocity, of communal and self-definition'. Whether spoken, sung, chanted or played, this language makes contact, says Wideman, 'with the old ways, the ancestral spirits that animated Afro-American prayers, music and motion' (Wideman, 1989, pp.46–7). As Claude Purdy, who staged Wilson's play *Fences* in Rochester, NY, puts it: 'it is writing based on centuries of "hearing"' (quoted in DeVries, 1989, p.52).

Of particular interest to writers like Morrison and Wilson are the linkages that exist in black culture between musical and oral forms of expression and the way in which the city as village connects with Africa in a theatre of the streets. In charting the route toward self-definition black writers have repeatedly turned to jazz as a story that relates the journey from Africa. Moreover, they see jazz as a form that enables the modern performer to connect himself to the gossip of the tribe through improvisation.

In the l920s African-American art, and jazz especially, exerted an enormous influence on the construction of American culture. For the poet Langston Hughes, blues and jazz were authentic sources of buried history in the black community. Jazz was an art form which relied, as black society itself did, on a 'subtle' combination of 'improvisation and fixed form'. For Ralph Ellison, jazz functioned 'as an image of the individual Negro's relationship to his community', an art form 'embedded in a shared experience', an act of 'collaboration' rather than a simple 'social anodyne' (quoted in Bigsby and Thompson, 1981, p.164). (This idea is also restated in Wilson's *Ma Rainey's Black Bottom* set in Chicago in l927, in which the power of the blues to sustain communal bonds and permit individual ebullience is powerfully evoked.) In his essays *Shadow and Act,* Ellison describes how the jazz musicians of his youth inspired him to explore the idea of an aesthetic of resistance in musical form, 'an idea of human versatility and possibility which went against the barbs or over the palings of almost every fence which those who controlled social and political power had erected to restrict our roles in the life of the country' (quoted in Tanner, 1971, p.50). In her most recent novel *Jazz,* Toni Morrison acknowledges her immense debt to black music. Jazz, she says, 'does what art is supposed to do', it acknowledges its social obligations, its interdependencies. 'This is how I want my work to be', she says, 'a private thing for public consumption'. In *Jazz*, Morrison deals with concepts of structure and improvisation that find their expression in musical form. Her novel focuses on the lives of those who moved north after slavery. It sees in the new-found freedoms of Southern black people a creativity that expresses itself in the 'jazz gesture', in urban experimentation and ideas of uncertainty (quoted in Bigsby, 1992).

SUMMARY

For many ethnic communities the city is not a centre of disinheritance. Jewish-American and African-American writers describe the intense emotion the city generates and the complex responses it elicits from different ethnic communities.

For black people the Great Migration north between 1910 and 1920 is an effort to escape unemployment and racism in the Southern states. The city it is said, will create a New Negro.

Jewish communities are established by those who escape the pogroms of Eastern Europe. Jewish novelists describe their upbringing in America's cities as intense and memorable.

The city is the place where Jewish and black people are able to recommunalize and rehistoricize themselves. It is a place of opportunity, ancestral memory and linguistic vitality, of tradition and experimentation.

11 RACE AND THE PROBLEM OF IDENTITY

If African-Americans have come a long way culturally and geographically from the white slave master, they have 'never lost touch', says John Wideman, 'with the old ways'. The 'time' they spent 'on the cross' has given their work a particular resilience, a self-confidence that was lacking in southern WASP culture (Wideman, 1989, p.47). Whereas Morrison celebrates the arrival of the ancestor in Harlem, Ike McCaslin, in William Faulkner's *Go Down Moses*, sees the city as a melting-pot where 'Chinese and African and Aryan and Jew, all breed and spawn together until no man has time to say which one is which nor cares' (Faulkner, 1973, p.364). The need which is often expressed in Faulkner's fiction to inhibit migration to the 'worldly and even foreign city' (Faulkner, 1964, p.74) and to preserve ethnic purity in a rigid system of codes and signs demands that each person be identified according to a system of class and racial stereotypes. The legacy of slavery, what Robert Penn Warren defines as 'the particular Southern curse', expresses itself in Faulkner's Yoknapatawpha County as an insular obsession with territoriality and racial coding, a fear of foreignness and ethnic indeterminacy. Faulkner's work is awash with precariously positioned half castes such as Joe Christmas and his father in *Light in August*, alleged 'white niggers' who threaten the South with the nightmare prospect of racial confusion and multicultural mix-up. In a world devoted to knowing not only who a person is but also what a person is, we see in Faulkner's fiction a psychotic need that each be identified (on the basis of race and blood) as a Snopes, a Sartoris, a Mexican, a Jew.

The contemporary debate of who speaks for whom, in what language and on what issues, derives, in part, from the need that writers of colour now have to subvert the pre-emptive identities given to them in the past. In the contemporary ethnic novel there is a strong emphasis on credentialism and authenticity, on the need to ensure that literature is ethnographically specific and politically correct. There is a demand that those whose fictions have traditionally underpinned the canon are investigated critically by those whose communities were excluded from the canon and that only those who authenticate what they say by their membership of an interest group can be deemed to provide legitimate commentary on matters of race. We are, it is said, what we are taught, and since much of what we have been taught is incorrect we are now obliged to expose it. Culture, it is argued, has become no more than a tool for its white, Anglo-Saxon, Protestant beneficiaries; a hierarchical instrument of control for those who endorse 'a history of oppression, imperialism and male dominated achievement'.

This is obviously a controversial view of American literature but it is one that is shared, to a large extent, by black intellectuals like Henry Louis Gates and black novelists like Alice Walker, writers for whom a literary canon — that which is chosen in the curriculum as the intellectual heritage of educated Americans — is essentially Eurocentric and reflects an 'aesthetic and political order in which no women and people of colour' have made any worthwhile appearance (quoted in Wood, 1990). Instead of representing the interests of black people or Hispanics or Asian-Americans the canon, it is said, is a mask of convenience worn by those who seek to protect the economic integrity of the dominant culture. Thus the schoolteacher who abuses his pupils in Morrison's *Beloved*, is villainous not just because he is the white slave master of the ironically named 'Sweet Home', but because he is supposed to teach and educate. He is a symbol not just of slavery, but of institutionalized slavery, which has robbed black people of their freedom and their culture.

In recent years ethnic writers have responded vigorously to Toni Morrison's charge that the US has been badly served, as a pluralist society, by multicultural texts. Ethnic issues, it is often claimed, have been under-represented or misrepresented in the American novel. In order to correct this, ethnic writers now insist that there is no such thing as a disinterested language of culture, and that testimony and witness are among the central concerns of contemporary art. Only those whose work has the mark of authenticity on it, the approved credentials of race and class, the sign of immersion that certificates the work and renders it true and distinctive, can replace, what the Nigerian writer Chinua Achebe describes, as the 'short, garbled, despised history' of Third World people (Killam, 1973, p.7). It is this belief in an ethnographically correct representation of culture that sustains the Chicano novelist Sandra Cisneros when she says of her upbringing in Chicago: 'You knew some things growing up in your communities that heads of state are never going to see. And once you've seen it, you can't unknow it … What you know at a very early age gives you empathy and compassion.' Behind this argument lies the belief that you cannot articulate what you do not understand, nor can you convey an experience that you have not actively shared with others, especially so if you are the product of a community which has been 'denied achievement'.

Contemporary writers of colour, says Toni Morrison, 'are the subjects of [their] own narrative, witnesses to and participants in [their own] experience' (Morrison, 1989, p.9). Personal testimony, the act of bearing witness, can no longer be thought of as a disability. 'When I was eleven years old in Chicago', says Sandra Cisneros, 'teachers thought if you were poor and Mexican you didn't have anything to say. Now I think that what I was put on the planet for was to tell these stories because if I don't write them, they're not going to get the stories right.' (Cisneros, 1991.) In order to correct the errors of a badly transcribed history, Maxine Hong Kingston describes her intention in *The Woman Warrior* as that of a 'daring talker of the tribe'. The need to record history through personal testimony is best appreciated, she says, by those who belong to minority communities. 'I liked the Negro students (Black ghosts) best', she announces, 'because they talked the loudest and talked to me because I was a daring talker too' (Hong Kingston, 1981, pp.149–50).

Like Hong Kingston the ethnic American is no longer the silent, passive witness of history. The current mission in ethnic literature is to reinstate the memories of an ancestral tradition and to unburden those tribal 'ghosts' whose lives and stories lack recognition. In the act of recovering the unassimilated past 'silences are being broken', says Morrison, and 'lost things have been found'. In the process of 'disentangling received knowledge from the apparatus of control' ethnic American writers are 'resolved to write themselves into, or back into, an America which hitherto had written them out of its record'. These new 'self-inscriptions' says A. Robert Lee, are 'defiant' and 'exhilarating' and 'contribute' what can only be regarded as a helix of largely 'missed vocabularies in the nation's overall identity' (Lee, 1991, p.9).

SUMMARY

A large number of ethnic writers argue the need to identify the ethnic heritage of America and to correct whatever mistakes have been made on the subject of race.

Writers of colour, in particular, insist on the need for authenticity. Ethnographic correctness, it is argued, is a way of avoiding the mistakes of the past. Writers are asked to testify and bear witness to what they have experienced. Since America has become a multicultural society it is no longer obliged to honour the memory of the American Adam.

12   CONCLUSION

There are few twentieth-century novelists who have not struggled to identify the essential character of the American city and the extent to which the
American metropolis has imposed its culture and ideas on the rest of us. In
American literature the city evokes a range of feelings: wonder, revulsion,
wholesomeness, love. For Henry Adams the city of 1900 was 'supersensual'
and those who wished to enter it were obliged to accept their role as 'the
child of new forces' in a born-again world. One hundred years and Adams's
ideas still remain fashionable with contemporary commentators. For the
journalist Simon Hoggart the American city is stylish and exceptional, yet
perpetually committed to reinvention and 'possibility' (Hoggart, 1989). For
Jean Baudrillard New York and Los Angeles contain, as he puts it, 'something of the dawning of the universe' (Baudrillard, 1988). For Todd Gitlin,
Alan Fair and Douglas Tallack the city is no longer territorial or neighbourly
but a vast consumer community whose surface objects and novel events sig-
nify 'a rejection of history', a fundamental depthlessness which makes 'commitment and communality difficult to achieve' (Tallack, 1991, pp.319–20,
322).

Yet, as Chaim Potok puts it: 'Different cities boil within each of us' (Potok,
1981, p.167). For Studs Terkel the danger of seeing our lives as depthless
reflections in the window of mass culture and bricolage fashion (the pairing
together of unlikely combinations) becomes all too apparent when we look
at the riots in South-Central Los Angeles in the summer of 1992. Black people felt frustrated, says Terkel; in a city of 'endless summer' they felt abandoned and forgotten. The American obsession with an exceptional
landscape, says Terkel, has created a nation of grasping consumers; one that
is politically 'docile' and 'obedient and obeisant to power'. Lack of racial
memory, he continues, represents a failure of moral imagination and will
and it derives principally from a diminishing 'sense of history' (Jacobson,
1992).

Against such an uncompromising view we must balance the work of contemporary essayists and fiction writers like Hisaye Yamamoto, Walter Mosley or even Toni Morrison. In texts such as *Seventeen Syllables*, *Devil in a Blue
Dress* and *Jazz* the city becomes the repository of history, the place where
ethnic Americans can once again renew their tribal affiliations with the village. Where recent postmodernists are inclined to relinquish their history —
or, like Paul de Man, seek to bury it because it is embarrassing — ethnic
writers retrieve the autobiographical past in the unacknowledged and marginal communities. Their allegiance to the neighbourhood is a gesture of
defiance in a world of surface and superficiality.

REFERENCES

Adams, H. (1931) *The Education of Henry Adams*, New York, Random House.

Anderson, S. (1966) *Winesburg, Ohio*, New York, Viking.

Baldwin, J. (1981) 'The language of the streets' in Jaye, M.C. and Watts, A.C. (eds).

Baudrillard, J. (1988) 'How the West was lost', *Guardian*, 21 October, p.27.

Bellow, S. (1975) *Humboldt's Gift*, New York, Viking.

Bigsby, C.W.E. (1971) 'The two identities of F. Scott Fitzgerald' in Bradbury, M. (ed.).

Bigsby, C.W.E. (1992) 'Jazz queen', *The Independent on Sunday*, 26 April, p.29.

Bigsby, C.W.E. and Thompson, R. (1981) 'The Black experience' in Bradbury M. and Temperley, H. (eds) *Introduction to American Studies*, London, Longman.

Bradbury, M. (ed.) (1971) *The American Novel and the Nineteen Twenties*, London, Edward Arnold.

Bradbury, M. (1983) *The Modern American Novel*, Oxford, Oxford University Press.

Chase, R. (1957) *The American Novel and its Tradition*, New York, Doubleday.

Cisneros, S. (1991) 'From the Barrio to the Brownstone', *Los Angeles Times*, 7 May, Sections FI, F7.

Claridge, H. (1990) 'Writing on the margin: E.L. Doctorow and American history' in Clarke, G. (ed.) *The New American Writing: Essays on American Literature Since 1970*, London, St. Martin's Press.

Clarke, G. (1988) '"The Great Wrong Place": Los Angeles as urban milieu' in *The American City: Literary and Cultural Perspectives*, London, Vision Press.

Debord, G. (1970) *The Society of Spectacle*, Detroit, Black and Red Unauthorized Translation.

DeVries, H. (1989) 'The drama of August Wilson', *Dialogue*, vol.1, no.83, pp.48–56.

Didion, J. (1973) *Play It As It Lays*, Harmondsworth, Penguin.

Didion, J. (1974) *Slouching Towards Bethlehem*, Harmondsworth, Penguin.

Dreiser, T. (1970) *Sister Carrie*, New York, W.W. Norton.

Erdrich, L. (1988) *Tracks*, London, Picador.

Faulkner, W. (1964) *Absalom, Absalom!*, New York, The Modern Library.

Faulkner, W. (1973) *Go Down Moses*, New York, Vintage.

Fiedler, L. (1967) *Love and Death in the American Novel*, London, Paladin.

Fitzgerald, F. Scott (1953) *The Great Gatsby*, New York, Charles Scribner & Sons.

Fitzgerald, F. Scott (1965) *The Diamond as Big as the Ritz and Other Stories*, Harmondsworth, Penguin.

Fussell, P. (1975) *The Great War and Modern Memory*, New York, Oxford University Press.

Gilman, C.P.E. (1966) *Women and Economics: a Study of the Economic Relations Between Men and Women as a Factor in Social Evolution*, Boston, Harper.

Gold, M. (1984) *Jews Without Money*, New York, Carroll & Graf.

Goldman, A. (1975) 'A remnant to escape: the American writer and the minority group' in Cunliffe, M. (ed.) *American Literature Since 1900*, London, Sphere.

Grella, G. (1968) 'The gangster novel: urban pastoral' in Madden, D. (ed.) *Tough Guy Writers of the Thirties*, Carbondale, Southern Illinois University Press.

Gurko, L. (1968) 'Dos Passos' *USA*: a 1930s' spectacular' in Madden, D. (ed.) *Proletarian Writers of the Thirties*, Carbondale, Southern Illinois University Press.

Harjo, J. (1990) 'New Orleans' in *The Heath Anthology of American Literature, vol.2*.

The Heath Anthology of American Literature, vol.2 (1990), Lauter, P. (ed.), Lexington, D.C. Heath & Co.

Hemingway, E. (1969) *A Farewell to Arms*, New York, Charles Scribner & Sons.

Hinojosa, R. (1987) *Klail City*, Houston, Arte Publico Press.

Hoggart, S. (1989) 'America: where the future is always at home', *Observer Review*, 10 December, p.34.

Hong Kingston, M. (1981) *The Woman Warrior*, London, Picador.

Jacobson, K. (1992) 'The Studs you like', *Weekend Guardian*, 9–10 May, p.14.

Jaye, M.C. and Watts, A.C. (eds) (1981) *Literature and the American Urban Experience*, Manchester, Manchester University Press.

Karl, F.R. (1968) 'Picaresque and the American experience', *Yale Review*, Winter.

Killam, G.D. (ed.) (1973) *African Writers on African Writing*, London, Heinemann.

Lee, R. (1991) 'Ethnic America: the non–European voice', *The British-American*, vol.3, no.1, June.

Lewis, R.W.B. (1955) *The American Adam*, Chicago, University of Chicago Press.

Lewis, S. (1926) *Babbitt*, London, Jonathan Cape.

McCoy, H. (1966) *I Should Have Stayed Home*, Harmondsworth, Penguin.

Marx, L. (1967) *The Machine in the Garden: Technology and the Pastoral Ideal in America*, New York, Oxford University Press.

May, H.F. (1960) *The End of American Innocence*, London, Jonathan Cape.

Morrison, T. (1981) 'City limits, village values: concepts of the neighbourhood in black fiction' in Jaye, M.C. and Watts, A.C. (eds).

Morrison, T. (1989) 'Unspeakable things unspoken: the Afro-American presence in American literature', *Michigan Quarterly Review*, vol.28, Winter.

Mowry, G.E. (ed.) (1963) *The Twenties: Fords, Flappers and Fanatics*, Englewood Cliffs, Prentice-Hall.

Mulvey, C. (1990) 'Harlem entrance and initiation' in Boelhower, W. (ed.) *The Future of American Modernism: Ethnic Writing Between the Wars*, Amsterdam, VU University Press.

Potok, C. (1981) 'Culture confrontation in urban America: a writer's beginnings' in Jaye, M.C. and Watts, A.C. (eds).

Rodriguez, R. (1990) 'Night and day' in *Frontiers*, London, BBC Books.

Said, E. (1990) 'Yeats and decolonization' in *Nationalism, Colonialism and Literature*, Minneapolis, University of Minnesota Press.

Smith, H.N. (1950) *Virgin Land*, New York, Random House.

Tallack, D. (1991) *Twentieth-Century America: the Intellectual Cultural Context*, London, Longman.

Tanner, T. (1971) *City of Words: American Fiction 1950–1970*, London, Jonathan Cape.

Way, B. (1971) 'Sherwood Anderson' in Bradbury, M. (ed.).

Wharton, E. (1989) *The Custom of the Country*, New York, New American Library.

Wideman, J. (1989) 'The magic of the word', *Dialogue*, vol.1, no.83, pp.46–8.

Wiebe, R. (1967) *The Search for Order, 1880–1920*, New York, Macmillan.

Wilson, E. (1929) *The Wound and the Bow: Seven Studies in Literature*, Boston, Houghton Mifflin.

Wolfe, T. (1969) 'Electrograph architecture', *Architectural Design*, July.

Wood, J. (1990) 'Farewell! A long farewell to all my greatness', *Review Guardian*, 13 December, p.23.

FURTHER READING

Conrad, P. (1984) *The Art of the City: Views and Versions of New York*, New York, Oxford University Press.

Godden, R. (1990) *Fictions of Capital*, Cambridge, Cambridge University Press.

Mumford, L. (1968) *The Urban Prospect*, London, Secker & Warburg.

Susman, W. (1985) *Culture as History*, New York, Pantheon.

★ ★

GENDER IN AMERICAN LITERATURE AND CULTURE

Helen Dennis ★

> One is not born, but rather becomes a woman.
>
> (Simone de Beauvoir, *The Second Sex*, 1953)

> One is one's body from the start, and only thereafter becomes one's gender. The movement from sex to gender is internal to embodied life, a sculpting of the original body into a cultural form.
>
> (Judith Butler, 1987)

A particular area of concern to contemporary American writers is that of gender, its relation to sexuality but also its relation to society. Gender roles have come under increasing scrutiny in the United States since 1945, and inevitably the debate has been at times highly emotional as well as political. In this chapter I shall outline briefly the trends of feminist thought around the issue of gender in American culture, and then look at a few representative texts where gender is a major theme and preoccupation. I shall also briefly indicate the ways in which, in the wake of the women's movement which re-emerged in the late 1960s (often called second-wave feminism), not only 'femininity' but also 'masculinity' is currently being problematized, and no longer accepted as 'God-given'. I shall focus my argument on the following texts: Betty Friedan, *The Feminine Mystique* (1963); Sylvia Plath, *The Bell Jar* (1963); Marge Piercy, *Braided Lives* (1982); Toni Morrison, *Beloved* (1987); and Robert Bly, *Iron John* (1991).

1 'MAN'/'WOMEN', SEX/GENDER: THE LOP-SIDED POLARITIES

> Here [in the US] as in France and elsewhere, despite changes in educational technique and with comparatively few exceptions, the vast majority of girls are still more or less explicitly directed towards predatory coquetry and consequent masculine support in marriage or otherwise as a prime aim in life, in contrast to boys, who are commonly schooled in violence and initiative and urged towards a life of productive activity.
>
> (Beauvoir, 1972, p.9, translator's preface)

Thus the American translator of Simone de Beauvoir's *The Second Sex* (*Le Deuxième Sexe*), writing from Smith College in 1953, argued for the relevance to American society in the 1950s of a French existentialist analysis of 'the problems of women' (Beauvoir, 1972, p.31). Together with Betty Friedan's *The Feminine Mystique*, published a decade later, her work could be said to signal the second wave of feminism in the US. Their work has remained a focus and a catalyst for feminist debate; and one can see how they have been followed by two different, possibly contradictory strands in American feminism.

Beauvoir's text was predominantly a work of analysis, not a solution to the problem. If anything she advocated the emergence of a gender-free society, an erasure of unequal sexual difference. However, within American culture an alternative type of feminism emerged which has been very vocal since the 1960s, a feminism which emphasizes difference, which seeks cultural representatiŏns of difference, but which also attempts to rewrite the relative value of the feminine and to alter the relative power structures in favour of a female or 'matriarchal' system of values. This type of feminism has called itself radical feminism, or gynocentric feminism, and is also termed essentialist feminism usually by its critics and detractors. Its exponents include, Elizabeth Gould Davis, Mary Daly, Dorothy Dinnerstein, Susan Griffin and Adrienne Rich, and its influence on other women writers has been far-reaching. All these writers have focused on enhanced, energized representations of female experience, on re-visioning patriarchal myths in matriarchal modes, on revaluing woman-centred identity, including the promotion of a cultural continuum which rejects compulsory heterosexuality and advocates lesbian existence as the preferred solution. Radical feminism is characterized by an interest in myth and the visionary as well as by a revisionist imagination, and is essentialist in that it ultimately bases female cultural identity on the biological accident of being born a female body.

On the other hand, socialist feminists and constructionists have followed Beauvoir's famous dictum: 'One is not born, but rather becomes a woman' (ibid., p.295). They have drawn attention to the artificiality of gender, to the way it is a cultural formation not a natural consequence of biology, to the ways in which gendered identity is constructed in response to social, economic and political pressures as well as to psychological and cultural configurations.

Friedan's *The Feminine Mystique* (1963) heralded the most recent revival of the women's movement, and demonstrated that it was not enough to have won the vote, and to have won civil and legal equality. She realized that there was still a pervasive oppression which blocked women from fulfilling their potential, and that equal rights were useless when cultural pressures blocked women from taking full advantage of them. In particular her surveys of women college students and of suburban housewives suggested that women internalized their own oppression, and were in effect agents of patriarchy working against themselves, and that the result of this was a widespread frustration, depression and low self-esteem, which she identified as the 'problem that has no name'.

Of particular relevance to both Sylvia Plath and Marge Piercy is Friedan's chapter on women college students in the 1950s. A series of interviews reveal that at the time when 'more American women than ever before were going to college' the prevailing ethos was not to appear interested in intellectual pursuits, but to patiently sit through it. College women were suppressing personal ambition, they were not interested in having a serious career. They were preparing themselves to be full-time wives and mothers, living their lives vicariously through their husbands and children.

In other words the reason why young women went to college in the 1950s was to catch a husband who would provide a good home. Young women were sadly misusing their educational opportunities because of the strength of the feminine mystique. Interestingly Friedan conducted her original set of interviews at her own college, Smith College, in 1956, the year after Plath left Smith College to study in the UK at Cambridge. Part of Plath's tragedy, clearly delineated in her *Journals* (1982), is that she was absorbed by the feminine mystique. She put a lot of intellectual and imaginative energy into planning who would be the best husband for her to catch; and she seemed to believe that by making the right choice of husband she could have a happy, fulfilled life in which housework, motherhood, marital love and her writing would be held in perpetual harmony.

Friedan's answer to the 'problem that has no name' is the appropriate use of education leading to true individual growth.

> If woman's needs are not recognised by herself or others in our culture, she is forced to seek identity and self-esteem in the only channels open to her: the pursuit of sexual fulfilment, motherhood, and the possession of material things. And, chained to these pursuits, she is stunted at a lower level of living, blocked from the realization of her higher human needs.
>
> (Friedan, 1963, p.274)

Growth is normal to humanity. Psychology in the past taught patients to 'adjust' to a society that denies individual growth. This critique of psychology, and in particular its impact on women patients in the post-Second World War years is the framing device of Piercy's powerful science fiction, *Woman on the Edge of Time* (1979).

Friedan interviewed suburban housewives, high school girls and other college students; and made extensive use of the evidence of women's magazines to graphically chart the crisis women in America were facing in the 1950s. She defined the 'problem that has no name' as an identity crisis which female college students had to face, and which if they did not face would reappear later in their life. It arose from the social constructs of femininity in the 1950s, and the gender roles which American society found acceptable for women, which were focused on marriage, mothering and domesticity. A woman's identity was supposed to be grounded in her husband and her family, not in her own self-fulfilment through a satisfying career. Women were not expected to enter the job market seriously, or to be in competition with men; it was considered unfeminine. As Friedan says:

It is my thesis that the core of the problem for women today is not sexual but a problem of identity — a stunting or evasion of growth that is perpetuated by the feminine mystique. It is my thesis that as the Victorian culture did not permit women to accept or gratify their basic sexual need, our culture does not permit women to accept or gratify their basic needs to grow and fulfil their potentialities as human beings, a need which is not solely defined by their sexual role.

(Friedan, 1963, p.68)

Despite the radical ground-breaking nature of Friedan's work she is also to some extent guilty of subscribing to the feminine mystique herself. She believed that it had been mistaken for women to stunt their intellectual and psychological growth in order to catch a husband through pleasing femininity: that a woman who grew to autonomous independence, emotionally and psychologically, and who found intellectual satisfaction in a demanding job would actually make a better mother, and that marriages with such a woman tended to be more stable and happier. So Friedan's solution was increased educational opportunities for mature women, and more individuals juggling opportunities to achieve happiness.

This led to the formation of the National Organization of Women (NOW) in the mid-1960s; which Shulamith Firestone describes thus:

Often called the NAACP [National Association for the Advancement of Colored People] of the woman's movement (and indeed, because it too is full of older professionals — career women who have 'made it' — it is similarly attacked by the younger liberation groups for its 'careerism'), NOW concentrates on the more superficial symptoms of sexism — legal inequities, employment discrimination, and the like.

(Firestone, 1979, p.389)

Despite its fundamental conservatism, its lack of an analysis of the underlying forces that cause sexism, and its tendency to put the responsibility for the solution to the 'problem that has no name' in the hands of individual middle-class women who should develop good careers for themselves, *The Feminine Mystique* had a powerful effect on women at the time; it spoke directly to their problems and to their previously unnamed sense of dis-ease, in a lucid prose style which is still strongly compelling 30 years on. Its extensive review of the symptoms of the feminine malaise is still useful, even if one believes that underlying causes need to be analysed and put right, rather than attention paid to superficial symptoms.

Certainly a reading of Friedan will lead to a more informed reading of, for example, Piercy's *Braided Lives*. It will demonstrate the way in which characters are both 'individuals' and also representative types; and that character is formed by social pressures. Society writes our lives for us, rather than we as individuals write society.

Another 'seminal' feminist text, first published in 1970, is Firestone's *The Dialectic of Sex: the Case for Feminist Revolution*. Firestone is a type of radical feminist who draws on the traditions of historical feminism, but who also uses the analysis of Marx, Engels and Freud, in order to critique the perpetuation of unequal power relations, both in economic and social organization and also in individual psychology. She attempts a thorough analysis of the causes of oppression; but rejects the solutions of the left, because she believes that sex oppression is more fundamental than class oppression. She suggests that the family structure as we know it both at micro and macro level has built in power imbalances, so that a complete revolution in social organization is necessary. Unlike Friedan, who sees education as the solution, Firestone sees the schooling system as one of the major perpetrators of oppression.

Firestone not only believes in the break-up of the nuclear family structure through revolutionary tactics, she also believes that women cannot be liberated unless and until they transcend their biological destiny — which had been the sticking point in the past. She suggests that feminists should espouse technology: and that in a utopian future, people of whatever gender could have babies — through *in vitro* fertilization and incubation — when they wanted them. In *Woman on the Edge of Time* Piercy applies this idea in a utopian vision of the future. In this respect Firestone and Piercy are closer to the socialist feminists, who believe in political struggle and change, rather than the radical feminists who sometimes seek *power* precisely in woman's biological role as a mother. In fact, motherhood as source of power is perhaps the most difficult thing for American feminists to give up.

SUMMARY

Radical feminism embraces the dark, the other of patriarchal culture and re-values it, often by coining neologisms, playing with etymologies and (re)inventing matriarchal mythologies and women-centred 'herstories'. It has worked through direct action, through communal ritual and primarily by harnessing women's imaginations to envision alternatives to the status quo which it perceives as a deadly patriarchy.

The work of the socialist feminist is to expound an analysis of the social, economic, and political forces which effect the transformation of male into the concept 'man', female into the concept 'woman', and often to instigate appropriate social and political change when such concepts advantage one social sex above another.

After the conservatism of the 1950s, both these strands of feminism emerged in the 1960s, although arguably radical feminism has been more vocal in American cultural productions.

2 'THE WOMAN IS PERFECTED': PLATH'S PRESCIENCE

Sylvia Plath was born in 1932, and achieved adulthood in the 1950s, the decade of reaction, when 'Rosie the Riveter' returned to the suburbs and 'hubby' did his best to become 'one-dimensional man'. It was a time of increasing conservatism, of the McCarthy trials, of the Cold War and of women's magazines busily telling housewives how to achieve perfection in domestic skills. Plath attended Smith College from 1950 and graduated with distinction in June 1955. She committed suicide in February 1963, just a few weeks after publication of *The Bell Jar*. In that novel, a highly symbolic, post-modernist text, Plath registered the condition of post-war women, the dis-ease that many of them felt. In her 'stream of consciousness' style, she described the malaise that Friedan was to call the 'problem that has no name'. Friedan's work and Plath's novel were published in the same year; both testified to the ground-swell of emotion in women against the con-straints of the gender role ascribed to them in the 1950s. As Friedan said: 'We can no longer ignore the voice within women that says: "I want some-thing more than my husband and my children and my home"' (Friedan, 1963, p.29).

In Plath's *The Bell Jar*, the protagonist Esther Greenwood (in one of her fan-tasies 'Ee Gee', following in the footsteps of Jay Cee, her editor: 'E.g.' an example to other young ladies in a similar situation), sits in bed recovering from a bout of severe food poisoning, following a lunch at the *Ladies Day*, a women's magazine specializing in colour illustrations of recipes, and reflects on her relationship with her 'boyfriend' Buddy Willard. The general situ-ation and incidents follow closely the pattern of Plath's relationship to Dick Norton, which Plath recorded and mused over in her *Journals* at the time. In fact her journal entries about her boyfriends are quite remarkable. Plath in attempting to reconcile the conflicting roles of perfect wife, mother and suc-cessful writer considers boyfriends from the point of view of their contri-bution to the balancing act and to social acceptability. The problem Plath addresses in her *Journals* is how to be a perfect wife and mother, to fulfil the feminine role society expects of her; and then how to reconcile this with her ambition to be a successful writer. Her anxiety is that she will be a failure at either or both: to fail at the former would incur social opprobrium; to fail at the latter would be to disappoint herself.

So as she recovers from the ptomaine in the crabmeat, the poison at the heart of the glossy picture of domestic excellence, Esther reads a story from a book sent by *Ladies Day*.

> I flipped through one story after another until finally I came to a story about a fig-tree.
>
> This fig-tree grew on a green lawn between the house of a Jewish man and a convent, and the Jewish man and a beautiful dark nun kept meeting at the tree to pick up the ripe figs, until one day they saw an egg hatching in a bird's nest on a branch of the tree, and as they watched the little bird peck its way out of the egg, they

touched the backs of their hands together, and then the nun didn't come out to pick figs with the Jewish man any more but a mean-faced Catholic kitchen-maid came to pick them instead and counted up the figs the man picked after they were both through to be sure he hadn't picked any more than she had, and the man was furious.

I though it was a lovely story, especially the part about the fig-tree in winter under the snow and then the fig-tree in spring with all the green fruit. I felt sorry when I came to the last page. I wanted to crawl in between those black lines of print the way you crawl through a fence, and go to sleep under that beautiful big green fig-tree.

It seemed to me that Buddy Willard and I were like that Jewish man and that nun, although of course we weren't Jewish or Catholic but Unitarian. We had met together under our own imaginary fig-tree, and what we had seen wasn't a bird coming out of an egg but a baby coming out of a woman, and then something awful happened and we went our separate ways.

(Plath, 1982a, p.57)

Plath's technique here is superb. The material for her novel is largely auto-biographical, and yet she achieves an incisive objectivity, which distances herself as author from the voice of the first person narrator. The writing is witty and scathingly humorous, at the expense of Esther as much as Buddy. Esther is naïve, Plath is not. Plath dissects her female protagonist as scientifically as Buddy and his friends dissect the cadaver at medical school.

The story is presented as a parable, full of Biblical and symbolic resonances. The fig-tree is traditionally a symbol of fertility, one need only consider the shape of the fruits and the plenitude of seeds. Rather than the fruit of the tree of knowledge of good and evil, the fig is the fruit of the tree of knowledge of sexuality and desire. Rather than the fall from innocence and grace, this Adam and Eve learn that sexual desire and celebration of fecundity cannot be permitted to continue if other religious morals and social mores are contravened. Symbolically it also suggests that although man and woman can come together for a moment to delight in procreation, social forces will tend to separate them shortly thereafter, since it is an illusory escape from the normal constraints of social existence.

The story is romantic, and Plath subtly sends up the romanticism of it, with the beautiful dark nun picking the ripe figs as a compound image of woman as pure virgin and woman as passionate temptress, contrasted with the 'mean-faced Catholic kitchen-maid' whose attitude to the figs is that of the utilitarian housekeeper. She also associates its romanticism with an escapism that could be suicidal or self-annihilating: 'I wanted to crawl in between those black lines of print the way you crawl through a fence, and go to sleep under that beautiful big green fig-tree.' (Later in the novel the description of her first suicide attempt involves crawling into a small space under the house, close to the earth and putting logs back in place across the hole.)

Despite the similarities to Plath's own situation and actions Plath undercuts her first person narrator. Esther compares herself and Buddy to the Jewish nun and the man, but Plath then deflates the comparison making Esther seem faintly ridiculous: 'It seemed to me that Buddy Willard and I were like that Jewish man and that nun, although of course we weren't Jewish or Catholic but Unitarian.' Yet in an extended passage of recollection, Esther/ Plath describes with analytic precision the pressures on young American women and men to play the dating game according to the unwritten rules that appear like the strait-jacket of conventional behaviour, uncomfortable to be inside, but well-nigh impossible to escape.

In the ensuing narrative of their relationship, Esther accuses Buddy Willard of being a hypocrite. The hypocrisy she resents is sexual hypocrisy, arising from the double standards which apply to men and women. She has to keep herself pure and virginal, he has to pretend he is pure and virginal although he has had an affair with a waitress all summer. 'What I couldn't stand was Buddy's pretending I was so sexy and he was so pure, when all the time he'd been having an affair with that tarty waitress and must have felt like laughing in my face' (Plath, 1982a, pp.73–4).

But Plath's narrative makes it clear, although Esther's recollection does not admit this, that Esther is as much a hypocrite as Buddy. She is under pressure to conform to the social norm, or be accused of being unfeminine and find herself ostracized by her fellow students. She covertly seeks advice:

> Back at college I started asking a senior here and a senior there what they would do if a boy they knew suddenly told them he'd slept thirty times with some slutty waitress one summer, smack in the middle of knowing them. But these seniors said most boys were like that and you couldn't honestly accuse them of anything until you were at least pinned or engaged to be married.
>
> (Plath, 1982a, p.73)

Esther's predicament is that she wants to be accepted by her college peer group, which means that she should appear to be marking time until she gets engaged to be married; but in conflict with this social pressure to conform is her desire to read avidly, to study and to become a writer. Her solution is as hypocritical as Buddy's: when she hears that he has TB she lets it be known that they are practically engaged: 'I simply told everyone that Buddy had TB and we were practically engaged, and when I stayed in to study on Saturday nights they were extremely kind to me because they thought I was so brave, working the way I did just to hide a broken heart' (ibid., p.76).

Esther's sarcasm directed at her fellow students and her situation (at Smith College) is strong, Plath's sarcasm directed at Esther, her former self and at Middle American society in the mid-1950s is even stronger.

Betty Friedan attended the same college as Plath ten years earlier, and experienced much of the same predicament as Plath, which she describes as a crisis in woman's identity:

I remember the stillness of a spring afternoon on the Smith campus in 1942, when I came to a frightening dead end in my own vision of the future. A few days earlier, I had received a notice that I had won a graduate fellowship. During the congratulations, underneath my excitement, I felt a strange uneasiness; there was a question I did not want to think about.

'Is this really what I want to be?' The question shut me off, cold and alone, from the girls talking and studying on the sunny hillside behind the college house. I thought I was going to be a psychologist. But I wasn't sure, what did I want to be? I felt the future closing in — and I could not see myself in it at all. I had come at seventeen from a Midwestern town, an unsure girl; the wide horizons of the world and the life of the mind had been opened to me. I had begun to know who I was and what I wanted to do. I could not go back now. But the time had come to make my own future, to take the deciding step, and I suddenly did not know what I wanted to be.

I took the fellowship, but the next spring, under the alien California sun of another campus, the question came again, and I could not put it out of my mind. I had won another fellowship that would have committed me to research for my doctorate, to a career as professional psychologist. 'Is this really what I want to be?' The decision now truly terrified me. I lived in a terror of indecision for days, unable to think of anything else.

The question was not important, I told myself. No question was important to me that year but love. We walked in the Berkeley hills and a boy said: 'Nothing can come of this, between us. I'll never win a fellowship like yours.' Did I think I would be choosing, irrevocably, the cold loneliness of that afternoon if I went on? I gave up the fellowship, in relief. But for years afterwards I could not read a word of the science that once I had thought of as my future life's work; the reminder of its loss was too painful.

I never could explain, hardly knew myself, why I gave up this career. I lived in the present, working on newspapers with no particular plan. I married, had children, lived according to the feminine mystique as a suburban housewife. But still the question haunted me. I could sense no purpose in my life, I could find no peace, until I finally faced it and worked out my own answer.

(Friedan, 1963, pp.61–2)

Friedan made the choice, took the decision to conform, even if she could not explain at the time the social conditioning that informed that choice. Plath, and her first person narrator, found the decision more difficult, indeed quite debilitating.

I started adding up all the things I couldn't do. I began with cooking. My grandmother and my mother were such good cooks that I

left everything to them. They were always trying to teach me one
dish or another, but I would just look on and say, 'Yes, yes, I see',
while the instructions slid through my head like water, and then I'd
always spoil what I did so nobody would ask me to do it again. ...

I didn't know shorthand either. This meant I couldn't get a good job
after college. My mother kept telling me nobody wanted a plain
English major. But an English major who knew shorthand was
something else again. Everybody would want her. She would be in
demand among all the up-and-coming young men and she would
transcribe letter after thrilling letter.

The trouble was, I hated the idea of serving men in any way. I
wanted to dictate my own thrilling letters. Besides, those little shorthand symbols in the book my mother showed me seemed just as
bad as let t equal time and let s equal total distance.

My list grew longer. ... The one thing I was good at was winning
scholarships and prizes, and that era was coming to an end. ... I
saw my life branching out before me like the green fig-tree in the
story.

From the tip of every branch, like a fat purple fig, a wonderful
future beckoned and winked. One fig was a husband and a happy
home and children, and another fig was a famous poet and another
fig was a brilliant professor, and another fig was Ee Gee, the amaz-
ing editor, and another fig was Europe and Africa and South America, and another fig was Constantin and Socrates and Attila and a
pack of lovers with queer names and off-beat professions, and
another fig was an Olympic lady crew champion, and beyond and
above these figs were many more figs I couldn't quite make out.

I saw myself sitting in the crotch of this fig-tree, starving to death,
just because I couldn't make up my mind which of the figs I would
choose. I wanted each and every one of them, but choosing one
meant losing all the rest, and, as I sat there, unable to decide, the
figs began to wrinkle and go black, and, one by one, they plopped
to the ground at my feet.

(Plath, 1982a, pp.78–80)

Plath's literary imagination achieves an analysis comparable to Friedan's
exposition as social scientist. She transforms the story of the Catholic nun,
Jewish man and fig-tree, which is essentially a patriarchal story of thwarted
romantic love, where women are identified as either attractive but unob-
tainable or as the unattractive upholder of patriarchal values, into a symbolic image of the female identity crisis. First she lists her attainments, or
lack of them, recording as she does so the part her mother and grandmother
play as agents of patriarchy, pressurizing her to social conformity,
'educating' her in what are acceptable values and aspirations for young
women. Then comes the transformation of the original story into an image
which could appear surreal. Indeed it would be easy to read this as an indi-

cation of the neurotic breakdown into 'madness' which ensues, without taking account of gender as a factor. Read as symptomatic of neurosis, Esther Greenwood merely appears bizarrely eccentric and out of touch with 'normality'. Read as an analysis of the effects of gender roles on women, it describes schematically the impossible choice young women were forced to make. The nature of the female identity crisis is that there is no way out except by maiming the self, by figuratively speaking lopping off one of the branches. A man can choose a career and a home and family, in fact the one enhances the other. A woman can choose one or the other or remain in irresolute conflict. But, as Friedan argued, to choose one only deferred the crisis to later; a better solution had to be found to allow women to achieve full maturity and self definition.

Despite her breakdown and first attempt at suicide, Plath continued to try to do both; at a cost which was eventually to prove too high.

SUMMARY

Plath was one writer who registered the 'problems of women', the 'problem that has no name' in the symbolic language of the literary imagination, without the benefit of the feminist discourses which were to multiply within a few years of her suicide. Her profound, imaginative comprehension of these problems has touched chords for many women and often produced stark polarizations along the gender divide. Her writing reflects the experience of American women in the 1950s, the terror, the anger, the despair, and depicts an individual woman's attempts to overcome the sense of debilitation through wit, irony and the manipulation of symbolic discourses.

3   PIERCY: THE ART OF NAMING THINGS

Friedan's work came as an inspiration and salvation for a lot of isolated women, struggling as Plath had struggled with the seemingly irresolvable conflicts in female identity. For Plath, who committed suicide in early February 1963, it came too late. But it came at the right moment for the young working-class aspiring writer, Marge Piercy. Note how her tribute to Beauvoir, rehearses Friedan's central concept; that the lack of a name for the condition is part of the malaise:

> I read *The Second Sex* then [Chicago, August 1959]. She [Beauvoir] provided in *The Second Sex* an analysis for experiences that were familiar to me, but because you cannot, if you do not have a vocabulary, you cannot handle your own experience.

> One of the things that feminism does for women is name things. So that once you name something it exists for you, you can handle it in your mind, you can turn it around, you can decide what to do about

it. But if things have no names all you can do is feel this sense of uneasiness. It's a personal thing then, instead of being an issue it's your own problem: why do *I* feel weird, why do *I* feel strange, what did *I* do?

(Piercy, BBC 2, *Bookmark*, 1989)

Marge Piercy was born in 1936 in Detroit. She is one of the few American women novelists to describe herself as working class. Her writing is informed by the second wave of feminism, and by the activism of the new left in the 1960s, and this gives her a resource and a context in which to explore more analytically the issues which Plath wrestled with in isolation with uncanny prescience.

In a *City Limits* interview, Piercy describes the sense of marginality and insecurity she experiences, despite her success as a popular novelist; simply because she is a working-class woman novelist, writing political (i.e. leftist) and feminist texts, for a readership that is also predominantly female, working class:

> In America, if you write anything which has class politics or is feminist or of the left or has any sensibility that isn't the predominant media sensibility, you have difficulty getting published. ... I encountered that when I began writing and it's no less true today. In fact, it's getting worse all the time ...
>
> A lot of my work is writing about the lives of working class women. And as the situation gets worse, more and more people can't afford

(Left) Sylvia Plath (1932–1963). (Right) Marge Piercy (b. 1936)

to buy my books, which the publishing industry make more and more expensive. Even paperbacks are getting more expensive, and that's what most of the women who buy me buy.

If you have less money, books are the first thing you won't buy. So the economic climate affects all women in the arts, because most people who read us are so marginal economically.

(Piercy, 1984, p.18)

It is interesting the extent to which Piercy's sense of herself as a working-class woman author, constantly threatened by the 'masculine' world of capitalist economics, cost accountancy, etc. because of her 'failure' to conform to the 'predominant media sensibility', is actually worked out as a theme within the text of *Braided Lives*. Piercy denies that any of her books are strictly autobiographical, but concedes that 'the nearest is her novel of growing up in the fifties, *Braided Lives*' (ibid., p.19).

Braided Lives is a *Bildungsroman*, i.e. a novel of education — quite literally since it is about the protagonist's, Jill Stuart's, experience of university college education in the 1950s. It is specifically a female *Bildungsroman*. A *Bildungsroman* is about growing up and about intellectual growth; one could say that it has an aim, which is individual autonomy, the formation of the integrated, stable, mature adult personality. This is achieved through a characteristic movement between possible alternatives, until the protagonist's individual reality is established, both by identification with aspects of the alternative influences on offer; but even more by defining oneself clearly against the alternatives. In this respect *Braided Lives* could usefully be compared with Lisa Alther's *Kinflicks* (1977), which is also a novel of quest for female identity, and it also has to work out the protagonist's troubled relationship with her own mother, before she can move forward into her own future.

One of the major alternatives Jill has to negotiate is lesbian longing versus heterosexual experience. In fact adolescent lesbian experimentation and the distinct possibility of a conventional heterosexual marriage are both rejected, or grown through and beyond, in order to maintain her autonomy as a writer, as a feminist and as a political activist. So the major theme of this *Bildungsroman*, the development of Jill Stuart, by learning from her experiences at university, also makes this a *Kunstler-roman* — or the portrait of the artist as a young woman. This aspect is highlighted by the framing device.

The narrative of the 1950s is framed by the contemporary voice of the fictitious first person narrator, Jill Stuart who, having made it as a successful novelist and poet, is in 1982 reviewing her past, or as the opening chapter puts it, she 'Forces Herself on Herself'. *Braided Lives* is about a specific political issue, the politics of reproduction and of women's right to choose. Piercy uses the vehicle of popular fiction to dramatize the issues and attaches them to individual characters for immediacy and impact.

To begin with the novel seems to be more about the older Jill who, having succeeded, is reviewing the history of her development, presumably in order to come to terms with it, to understand it, and to be able to move forwards.

One needs history in order to comprehend the interaction between past experience and the present action. Women in particular need their history, or 'herstory'; because their experience tends not to be perceived as part of official histories, so *Braided Lives* is a process of 'telling it like it was', of foregrounding those elements which were important to young women at the time, even if they appear trivial and trivializing. It documents the ways in which growing up for a woman in the US in the 1950s was culturally specific, that the female 'rites of passage' were very different from the male, and that in the quest to construct her adult identity, a young woman was subject to a number of strong cultural, social and ideological pressures. So although this is a novel about the formation of an individual character, it is also quite consciously a novel about the social construction of gender roles, and of 'feminine' identity.

The issue of sexual/textual politics is treated both in the 'framing narrative', or 'narrative frame', and in the body of the text. The first boyfriend, Mike, is implicitly criticized for his phallogocentricity, his phallic power-play both in the field of aesthetics and in the back seat of his mother's car. One snatch of conversation will serve to demonstrate the distinction the author makes between the character of the aspiring male poet and the female, first person narrator:

> 'If you really love me, if you loved me as much as I love you, other people wouldn't matter. You wouldn't carry on about her.'

> 'She's in trouble! If you love somebody, why should it make you despise other people? I don't believe that!'

> 'Because you don't love me as much as I love you. You're scattered. All I need in this life are you, that letter Pound wrote me and a handful of truly great poems.'

> I would say food, water, a little sleep. Talk. Writing. Do I *need* him? What does it mean to be needed? 'You won't help us, so let's just forget it.'

> (Piercy, 1982, p.135)

Mike is referring here to arguably the most influential male literary modernist, Ezra Pound, famous for his energetic and somewhat idiosyncratic correspondence with aspiring young poets and intellectuals. Piercy is making a point about masculine art as phallogocentric, since Pound developed pseudo-scientific theories about the connection between the male orgasm and creative genius.

Within the framing narrative, we find this spoof, parody review of the masculinist literary establishment's aggressive criticism of feminist poetics:

Spring 1982, Bloodstone Review

Miss Stuart's seventh volume of poetry is crammed with reductionist simplistic snippets of women's lib cant. In describing a series of male/female encounters in which women are injured, raped, maimed, Stuart is unsympathetic to male needs. Individual poems stress only the woman's role and anguish, instead of taking a balanced view. Only the poems about good sex

*transcend this morbid polemical bias. When we men denigrate women, com-
pare them to mud, death, meat, sows, sloughs, sewers, traps, toilets, when we
equate them with mortality, contingency, nature, when we put down women
who put out and women who don't, we are merely being universal. Miss
Stuart is guilty of special pleading. In art there can be no special pleading for
women. Her poetry is uterine and devoid of thrust. Her volume is wet, men-
struates and carries a purse in which it can't find anything.*

Sydney Craw

(Piercy, 1982, p.404)

In the words of this masculinist critic, to be phallic, like Pound, is fine, to
write from the womb is definitely non-kosher. Yet this parody review
encodes Piercy's acknowledgement that Piercy herself, just as much as her
fictive narrator, risks being dismissed as marginal and guilty of special
pleading, because she writes from and about woman's experience of her
body and how that affects the way she can inhabit the social order: she also
risks being criticized for writing in the genre of the popular novel.

The notion that masculinist art is universal, whereas feminist literary production is non-universal, i.e. female, i.e. of lesser value, is critiqued by radical feminists such as Adrienne Rich. In her highly influential essay, 'When
We Dead Awaken: Writing as Re-vision', Rich describes the problems facing
a woman poet in the late 1950s: 'I had been taught that poetry should be
"universal", which meant, of course, nonfemale' (Rich, 1980, p.44).

Piercy is aware of the debate around women's writing. Radical feminists
such as Rich and Mary Daly were arguing for powerful gynocentric texts,
which foregrounded women's experience. One major influence on both of
them was Virginia Woolf, especially her prose such as *A Room of One's Own*
(1929), where she advocated a new type of fiction which accommodated
itself to the special rhythms of the female body. Anglo-American critics like
Susan Gubar had also argued for a woman's literature that took its formal
inspiration from the specifics of female biology and produced a cultural
artefact which reflected the complex experience of female sexuality (Gubar,
1986, first published in 1981). Piercy, both in her poetry and in *Braided Lives*,
which focuses on the single issue of contraception and abortion, embraces
many radical feminist ideas. However, she never suggests that the mythic
imagination can change society single-handed. In many respects she also
espouses socialist feminism. Indeed her consistent use of the genre of popular, realist fiction indicates this. She offers through the popular novel analyses of the social order, and the various ways it continues to marginalize
and oppress women. If her novels can be accused of trivializing women's
issues, by making it a matter of romance, lipstick, obtaining diaphragms,
and self-administered abortions, her message is that this is what women's
lives are socially determined to be about.

So *Braided Lives* takes from Friedan the awareness that women's lives are
trivialized by the feminine mystique, the awareness that young women are
not striving sufficiently to achieve autonomous identity but are in a state of
psychological dependency, or infantilism, expecting their future husband to

endow them with identity. *Braided Lives* could also be seen to conform to the conservatism of Friedan's analysis, which does not question the underlying structure of the family as a means of capitalist oppression. Piercy also needs the popular novel's solution of happy wedding bells ringing.

But Piercy's own political involvement and education was more radical than this. And I think this also emerges from a reading of the novel: Jill Stuart, the protagonist is involved in leftist politics at a time when it is dangerous, and oblique references are made to McCarthyism and to characters who are members of the Communist Party. In another novel by Piercy, *Vida* (1980), the predicament of an outlawed political revolutionary is foregrounded, and the drama there revolves around the conflict between revolutionary, terrorist politics and sexual politics. The women's movement arose in part from the failure of the left to take women seriously, both as an individual and as an issue. In the 1960s they were still fetching the six-packs and being told that everything would be OK — come the revolution sister. So Piercy's novel *Vida* reflects on the experience of a woman member of an extreme leftist, urban terrorist group, and about the frustrations and marginalizations which she experiences in the context of left-wing political activism.

Piercy inhabits a position somewhere between socialist feminist and radical feminist. In *Braided Lives* she seems to be moving towards a radical feminist tradition by foregrounding not the politics of the Cold War and McCarthyism but the politics of the battle for control over women's bodies. Her novel represents the ways in which women's bodies are their parents' and then their husbands' property; and how this situation is colluded in by the doctor who refuses contraception without proof of marriage, and by Mike, who refuses to contribute to the abortion fund, and by a husband who puts a pinprick in his wife's diaphragm, which eventually leads to her death after an illegal abortion.

SUMMARY

Piercy's writing arose from a reaction to the conservatism of the 1950s and to the inability of the 1960s' new left to recognize that it was perpetuating the oppression of women while fighting other types of political oppression. *Braided Lives* is an accurate reflection of how it was for women growing up in the 1950s. Moreover, it is only possible to see this clearly in the 1980s, after two decades of the most recent wave of the women's movement. The 1980s framing device is necessary because what we have is a novel which could not have been written at the time, which required the intervening years of consciousness raising groups, of feminist political activism, and the publication of a number of crucial (not seminal) feminist texts, in order to be able to *name* what was happening to women in the 1950s.

4 IN SEARCH OF THEIR MOTHERS' GARDENS?

Toni Morrison and Alice Walker are two African-American writers whose roots and inspiration are not only in the women's movement but also in the Black Power movement. Their writing reflects a different conflict of allegiances and a different position in US history, which complicates their cultural inheritance and their literary discourses.

In an article about Morrison's second novel, *Sula* (1975), Vashti Crutcher Lewis states:

> Research indicates that the cosmology and world-view of African-Americans is distinctly African, albeit we are not always consciously aware of this. It is to Toni Morrison's credit that she recognizes African tradition in African-American culture and chooses deliberately to write from an African point of view. In doing so, she removes much of the mystery of Black life and answers, to some degree, the ubiquitous question: What makes Black folk act that way?
>
> (Crutcher Lewis, 1990, p.323)

In the article Crutcher Lewis charts in detail the ways in which the two main protagonists of *Sula*, who are pariahs in their black American community, can be understood to be priest and oracle of the River-God and priestess or water spirit vowed to the same River-God. The plot and events which occur in the novel make perfect sense when perceived from an African point of view, but when viewed from an Anglo-American perspective they appear bizarre and inexplicable. For example, the title *Sula* is the name of the main female protagonist, and it is an African name. In both the Babangi and Kongo languages it has a range of meanings that indicate and reinforce the African cosmology that underlies the narrative; for example, 'to alter from a proper condition to a worse one', 'to be blighted', 'to fail in spirit', 'to be overcome', 'to be paralysed with fear', etc. Put this together with the fact that: 'Among the Ewe speaking people of West Africa, priests and priestesses are sacred, and they must not be insulted or in some cases even touched, and one must be careful not to jostle a sacred person by accident in the street' (Crutcher Lewis, 1990, p.323), and it begins to make sense when everyone in the community who comes into contact with this unrecognized, modern-day priestess, comes to a very nasty end!

However, although I am convinced by Crutcher Lewis's argument about the importance of Morrison's recognition of the way African culture and cosmology survive in modern American consciousness, I think it is important to realize that although Morrison writes with an awareness of an African sensibility and cultural formation, she also writes with an awareness of the modern American perspective, including its cultural blind spots. Hence she creates a dramatic tension in her writing, by playing with that clash between two different, indeed opposite, yet coexistent points of view and cultural outlooks. As a writer, some of the things she does must seem very obvious to her, but must also be written in the knowledge that they will initially at least be incomprehensible to a Western or Westernized mentality.

The major tradition of African-American writing which she has to draw upon is that of the slave narrative; these were authentic, first person accounts of the slave's experience of slavery, and of escape from slavery. The best example might by Harriet Jacobs, *Incidents in the Life of a Slave Girl* (1861). But this is a narrative in which the narrator feels unable to reveal all the details, 'because of [feminine/slave] modesty'. Toni Morrison has emphasized that this is a common characteristic of female slave narratives, and this relates to the reiterated phrase at the end of her book *Beloved*: 'It was not a story to pass on. ... It was not a story to pass on. ... This is not a story to pass on.' (Morrison, 1987, pp.274–5.) Morrison is aware that, while the nineteenth-century slave narrative did representatively tell the tale of the tribe, it also actively suppressed much of the story, from 'modesty'; from the fear of giving offence, from shame, perhaps even because of the lack of a written language with which to describe and inscribe certain aspects of African-American culture. The model of sentimental fiction provided a language in which certain things literally could not be spoken.

However, the nineteenth-century slave narrative did function as an historical document, unlike, Morrison would argue, twentieth-century autobiography, which she sees as having lost its representative status. In 'Rootedness: the Ancestor as Foundation', Morrison says:

> The autobiographical form is classic in Black American or Afro-American literature because it provided an instance in which a writer could be representative, could say, 'My single solitary and individual life is like the lives of the tribe; it differs in these specific ways, but it is a balanced life because it is both solitary and representative'. The contemporary autobiography tends to be 'how I got over — look at me — alone let me show you how I did it'. It is inimical, I think, to some of the characteristics of Black artistic expression and influence.

(Morrison, 1985, pp.339–40)

So in the slave narrative, and in Morrison's own fiction, the individual consciousness and experience is always representative, I would argue, of a tribal consciousness and of a cultural and political formation. Thus, *Beloved* draws upon the historical past, but has to do it in a different form from either the slave narrative, or the post Stowian[1] sentimental black novel. And it is a form which incorporates a 'tribal' African cosmology, and which restores to the past the incidents or occurrences which were left unsaid, unspoken and unrecorded or unwritten at the time.

In an article entitled, '"Somebody Forgot to Tell Somebody Something": African-American Women's Historical Novels', Barbara Christian reminds her reader that although African-American writers had written historical novels, they had tended to be about recent pasts, about the 1920s, 1930s and 1940s, about their mother's lives; but they had not been about the time when their

---

[1]Harriet Beecher Stowe's *Uncle Tom's Cabin* (1852) was arguably influential on the first African-American women novelists who followed Stowe in using the genre of sentimental fiction to describe African-American slavery and post-Abolition experiences.

foremothers were slaves. And she describes a phenomenon recalled by Alice Walker, Margaret Walker, the writer of *Jubilee*, and by Morrison: the way in which their families were ashamed of that past, and silenced the grandmother's reminiscences of slave times, or spoke in hushed whispers about those taboo aspects of their past. There was a concerted family and tribal effort to blank out, to forget the slave history, an effort which was concomitant with upward mobility and an espousal of 'all American' values and aspiration. Hence the importance of 'rememory' in the text of *Beloved*.

So from an initial childhood fascination with the bits of the past that the family spoke about 'in whispers' (Alice Walker, BBC documentary on *The Color Purple*) a new type of African-American historical novel has emerged in the past decade or so. Examples might include: Octavia E. Butler's *Kindred* (1979), Alice Walker's *The Color Purple* (1982), and Sherley Anne William's *Dessa Rose* (1986). Butler's *Kindred* is interesting because it uses the genre of science fiction in order to depict the contrast between the life of a female slave in Maryland around 1815–30, and that of a contemporary woman living in Los Angeles in 1976. The female protagonist, Dana, finds herself pulled back into her female ancestor's past to protect her ancestor's owner each time his life is endangered. Eventually she discovers that her foremother's owner, is also her ancestor, and that without her protecting him, he would not have survived to sire the line which became her own family. But in protecting him she is also witness to his cruelty perpetrated on her slave ancestors. So in science fiction form the novel investigates the complexity of emotions and passions felt between an American Negro slave and her white master, and felt by the modern product of this union. It faces the fact that the contemporary African-American can, and must, both hate and feel protective towards the perpetrators of the institution of slavery; so that, when delved into, family histories/'herstories' reveal many reasons for their having been a taboo subject.

In *Kindred* Dana is literally pulled back into the past each time her forefather/master is in danger, and can only get back to her present, when she is in even greater danger. The novel is framed by the fact that she eventually loses an arm in the passage between the past and present, because her master (Rufus) has attempted to rape her, and she resisted. It is a violent image of what it is like to remember the female slave past, and of the ways her past are inscribed in the bodies of the living present:

> I was back at home — in my own house, in my own time. But I was still caught somehow, joined to the wall as though my arm were growing out of it — or growing into it. From the elbow to the ends of the fingers, my left arm had become a part of the wall. I looked at the spot where flesh joined with plaster, stared at it uncomprehending. It was the exact spot Rufus's fingers had grasped.

> I pulled my arm toward me, pulled hard. And suddenly there was an avalanche of pain, red impossible agony! And I screamed and screamed.

> (Butler, 1988, p.261)

This sensational ending is immediately preceded by an image of the female slave, overlaid with a twentieth-century emancipated consciousness being faced with an almost impossible choice: submit to rape, or kill in 'self defence' your forefather, whom you have protected at incredible personal cost all his life. The trapped lost arm is an image of the violence to one's self and one's ancestor which that choice inevitably implies.

Morrison's *Beloved*, like *Kindred*, investigates an horrific image of the effect of slavery on a woman, and like *Dessa Rose*, it is based on a historical incident, but does not adhere to it. *Beloved*'s source is an actual incident which occurred in 1856, and which became something of a *cause célèbre* at the time. This was the case of Margaret Garner, a fugitive slave, who was pursued and recaptured along with her husband, and who in desperation tried to kill herself and her children as they were being recaptured. Significantly, Morrison has stated that 'she did not inquire further into Garner's life other than to note the event for which this slave woman became famous' (Christian, 1990, p.336).

The transformations which take place between the historical record and Morrison's text all tend to make this a woman's novel as well as a 'slave narrative'. The historical men are marginalized or suppressed or replaced by female figures (and a completely fictitious poor white girl is introduced), to make this novel highly matrifocal and gynocentric, or woman-centred. In 'Rootedness: the Ancestor as Foundation', Morrison says:

> That is the disability we must be on guard against for the future — the female who reproduces the female who reproduces the female. You know there are a lot of people who talk about the position that men hold as of primary importance, but actually it is if we don't keep in touch with the ancestor that we are, in fact, lost. The point of the books is that it is *our* job.
>
> (Morrison, 1985, p.344)

These remarks help explain what is happening in Butler's *Kindred*, where Dana does kill the ancestor (white) and in so doing loses not her entire self, but symbolically has an arm taken off to represent that self-inflicted trauma of trying to ignore an unspeakable past. The essay 'Rootedness: the Ancestor as Foundation' was written by Morrison before *Beloved*, but her comment about the attenuation which takes place when the female nurtures the female nurtures the female, should make the reader question any easy assumptions about *Beloved*. Is it a celebration of a matriarchal strength, or does it register regret at the way historical circumstances forced a woman like Sethe, the mother figure, in on herself?

As I have already said, the changes introduced between history and 'herstory' include the disappearing of various male characters, and also allow the circumstances of Sethe's escape from slavery. Her escape takes place while she is breast feeding the baby, later known in the text as Beloved, who has already been taken to safety by a train of fugitive slaves, and when she is nine months pregnant. She gives birth to her youngest child, Denver, while making her escape, with only the help of the fictitious poor white girl whom Morrison introduces into the novel. Prior to her escape she is tortured as part of a 'scientific' experiment, by being suckled by the two nephews of a character called Schoolmaster. This is a powerful, gynocentric passage, based entirely on maternal emotion and experience. The 'milking' of Sethe for Schoolmaster's experiment, the details of the separation of the lactating mother from the unweaned baby, and the birth in the bottom of a leaky boat assisted by a simple poor white girl are all potent expressions of specifically female, maternal experience.

And the crux of *Beloved*, is not Margaret Garner's sense that it is better to be dead than enslaved; but a far more subtle, maternal desire to protect and 'save' the beloved child, by sending her on before. That belief in crossing over hinges more on African cosmology than on Christian faith. Take away the African-American belief system and Sethe is crazy, mad as she seems to a minor character, Janey, when Denver eventually goes to ask for help for her mother:

> Janey seemed more interested in Sethe's condition, and from what Denver told her it seemed the woman had lost her mind. That wasn't the Sethe she remembered. This Sethe had lost her wits, finally, as Janey knew she would — trying to do it all alone with her nose in the air. Denver squirmed under the criticism of her mother ...
>
> (Morrison, 1987, p.254)

Much as the priest of the River-God, Shadrack, in her earlier novel, *Sula*, is actually perceived in the text by the folks of the Bottom as crazy and shell-shocked out of his wits, so here another character interprets Denver's

(Left) Alice Walker (b. 1944). (Right) Toni Morrison (b. 1931)

account of her mother's condition without the dimension of African-American insight and sensibility.

Morrison's sense that woman-identified women are denying life's fullness is substantiated, by the fact, that although the men are mainly written out of the text, Paul D., who was a former slave on the same plantation as Sethe, is allowed to come back and make a future with Sethe, once the ghost/demon has been finally — well almost finally — laid by the women: 'Only this woman Sethe could have left him his manhood like that. He wants to put his story next to hers. "Sethe" he says, "me and you, we got more yesterday than anybody. We need some kind of tomorrow"' (ibid., p.273). Rememory is important for both the individual and the community, but in the end the dead have to be buried.

Another theme of African-American writing has to do with the notion of author as shaman. Baby Suggs is a type of wise woman/priestess/shaman within *Beloved*, just as Shug Avery is a blues singer/founder of a church in Walker's *The Color Purple* and *The Temple of My Familiar*. But this role of female priest, shaman, healer and medium in touch with the spirit world is not confined to characters in their novels. It is also, I believe, the way in which both Alice Walker and Toni Morrison envisage their own role as novelist. Consider the end note to *The Color Purple*, which states succinctly: 'I thank everybody in this book for coming. A.W., author and medium.' Or consider what Morrison has to say on the subject:

> There are things that I try to incorporate into my fiction that are directly and deliberately related to what I regard as the major characteristics of Black art, wherever it is. One of which is the ability to be both print and oral literature: to combine those two aspects so that the stories can be read in silence, of course, but one should be able to hear them as well. It should try deliberately to make you stand up and make you feel something profoundly in the same way that a Black preacher requires his congregation to speak, to join him in the sermon, to behave in a certain way, to stand up and to weep and to cry and to accede or to change and to modify — to expand on the sermon that is being delivered. In the same way that a musician's music is enhanced when there is a response from the audience. Now in a book, which closes, after all — it's of some importance to me to try to make that connection — to try to make that happen also. And having at my disposal only the letters of the alphabet and some punctuation, I have to provide the places and spaces so that the reader can participate. Because it is the affective and participatory relationship between the artist or the speaker and the audience that is of primary importance, as it is in these other art forms that I have described.

(Morrison, 1985, p.341)

African-American writers, like Morrison and Walker, need to recover women's 'herstories' as much as Anglo-American writers. However, the history of slavery and the coming to terms with the cultural memories sometimes involves different priorities than Anglo-Americans'. Walker, in *In Search of Our Mothers' Gardens* (1983) embraces a sense of the past, and of the cultural and artistic achievement of the foremothers that coincides with the values of some radical feminists, but which other feminists would see as a type of collusion with patriarchally ascribed gender roles for women. In particular she argues that art is based on spirituality, and that the grandmothers and great-grandmothers of her generation displayed much spirituality and creativity, not in book production, since this medium was not available to them, but in other art forms, such as quilt making, colourful gardening and the blues. In an act of creative generosity she quotes Woolf's *A Room of One's Own* as an important text for women writers and interweaves references to African-American authors to illustrate its relevance as well as the differences felt by a woman writing in an African-American tradition (Walker, 1984, pp.231–43).

Walker's three most recent novels, *The Color Purple, The Temple of My Familiar* and *Possessing the Secret of Joy* form a trilogy which investigates different yet related aspects of the African-American cultural inheritance, including the transition from sharecropping to an urban, capitalist economy, the shamanic belief system which links African-American to both Latin American and African culture and politics, and most recently the effects of the widespread practice of female genital mutilation which has remained a taboo topic for even longer than the history of slavery. In all of these areas Walker's womanist consciousness facilitates a critique and revisioning of African-American traditions and beliefs that is perhaps only possible from a cultural position of double marginalization.

SUMMARY

African-American women writers could be said to suffer a double oppression or marginalization, in which white, middle-class feminists fail to perceive their African inheritance, and African-American men continue to oppress them because of their gender. However, there has been a renaissance in African-American writing in the last decade, to which a number of powerful women artists, including Alice Walker and Toni Morrison have contributed.

Their work has drawn on a specific African-American cultural inheritance, combined with versions of feminism which range from a generous spirituality to an incisive political commentary. One particular genre which writers such as Walker and Morrison have developed is the historical novel which revisits formerly taboo areas of African-American history, including the history of slavery and sharecropping.

5 MASCULINITY: JUMPING ON THE BAND-WAGON?

Beauvoir famously described woman as the 'Other' of the masculine subject. Her feminist study, translated in America in 1953, described the relation of the sexes as a lop-sided equation:

> The term *masculine* and *feminine* are used symmetrically only as a matter of form, as on legal papers. In actuality the relation of the two sexes is not quite like that of two electrical poles, for man represents both the positive and the neutral, as is indicated by the common use of *man* to designate human beings in general; whereas woman represents only the negative, defined by limiting criteria, without reciprocity.
>
> (Beauvoir, 1972, p.15)

The problem for woman was to become a speaking subject herself; to move from immanence to transcendence. It could be argued that the radical feminist philosopher, Mary Daly, has done just this in works such as *Gyn/Ecology* (1979), *Pure Lust* (1984), and *Intergalactic Wickedary* (1988). Rather than define woman as the 'Other' of the masculine subject and as the object of the masculine gaze and of masculinist cultural definitions, Daly transforms the concept of woman as other into the concept of Otherness. This is a transcendent state, moving beyond actual historical conditions and social conditioning into a realm of gynocentric meta-ethics. She draws on what Alicia Suskin Ostriker has referred to as 'a subterranean tradition of female self-projection and self-exploration', although it must be acknowledged that she is also influenced by the nineteenth-century American Transcendentalist tradition. However, if one adopts a rather pragmatic American attitude it is patently obvious that in the world of literary and cultural production, 'Women are doing it for themselves' (Eurythmics, with Aretha Franklin, 1985, on Eurythmics *Be Yourself Tonight*, RCA). So much so, that the recent move away from women's studies towards gender studies (Showalter, 1989), or in popular culture from the women's movement to the men's movement, appears to be using the strategies and the rhetoric of second-wave (radical) feminists to problematize not only femininity, but also masculinity and indeed all genders.

John Stoltenberg, for example, prefaces his powerful and moving text, *Refusing to Be a Man*, with the acknowledgement that it is feminism which has influenced his thinking about masculinity and patriarchal politics and culture:

> When the ideas of feminism first reached me about fifteen years ago, almost every detail of my life began to change, in ways I still don't fully comprehend. Since then I've been asked, probably hundreds of times, 'What got you so interested in feminism anyway?' The question, or a version of it, is usually asked with bewilderment, though sometimes with frank suspicion — as if growing up a man and becoming a feminist (a radical one, at that) were off the map of human possibility.
>
> I try to explain, as best I can, that beginning in 1974 I happened to be really challenged by some close women friends and some mind-

blowing feminist books and hours and hours of intense discussion — all of which is true as far as it goes. But like so many men I've met across the country through profeminist activism over the past decade and a half, I count myself part of the struggle for women's equality for reasons that are intensely personal — so personal, sometimes, they can't be glibly declared ...

What would happen if we each told the deepest truth about why we are men who mean to be part of the feminist revolution — why we can't *not* be part of it — why its vision of full humanity for everyone so moves us? What would happen if we dared? As the poet Muriel Rukeyser once asked, I wonder sometimes: would the world split open?

(Stoltenberg, 1990, pp.11–12)

As well as referring to the work of specific radical feminists and specific campaigns, such as Andrea Dworkin and Catherine A. MacKinnon's work and campaign against pornography, I think you can see from this extract that Stoltenberg has also been influenced by the powerful rhetoric of American radical feminists. Reading the radical feminist prose of Adrienne Rich, or the womanist prose of Alice Walker, one is struck by a particular kind of rhetoric which American feminists have developed since the 1970s. It is not always philosophically sophisticated, but it does combine intellectual concerns, allusions to poetry, to fiction and to myth, discussion of personal and family experience, of immediate social and political issues in a web of powerful and often highly emotive prose. It is beyond the scope of this chapter to trace the sources of this type of radical rhetoric but I would suggest that its roots come from a variety of sources: the essays of Virginia Woolf, the nineteenth-century American Transcendentalist and Abolitionist movements, and the powerful radical speeches of the 1960s Civil Rights leaders are all synthesized together with other literary and academic sources.

Even a book such as Robert Bly's *Iron John*, which attempts to empower and validate traditional types of manhood (not machismo) employs a discourse which is familiar to the readers of radical feminism. The emphasis on myth, ritual, sensitivity to individual feelings and experience, the male equivalent to the feminist consciousness raising groups of the 1960s and 1970s, strikes me as a woman reader as harnessing an available discourse about myth, which radical feminists have been drawing on since the 1950s when Neumann's *The Great Mother* (1955) first appeared in translation. Bly takes a different line on combat from Rich for example, but he does attempt to respect the women's movement, for example:

In general, I think each gender drops its own pain when it tries to carry the pain of the other gender. I don't mean that men shouldn't listen. But hearing a woman's pain and carrying it are two different things. Women have tried for centuries to carry men's pain, and it hasn't worked well.

(Bly, 1992, p.64)

At times he is guilty of the same essentialist thinking as radical feminists, at others he seems aware of more recent arguments about genders. Although his text begins with characterizations, not of 'masculinity', but of different types of American masculinities which are determined by the different social, political, economic and cultural determinants of each decade; his thinking does have a tendency to function through polarities. For example:

> Our obligation — and I include in 'our' all the women and men writing about gender — is to describe *masculine* in such a way that it does not exclude the *masculine* in women, and yet hits a resonant string in the man's heart. No one says there aren't resonating strings in a woman's heart too — but in the man's heart there is a low string that makes his whole chest tremble when the qualities of the masculine are spoken of in the right way.

> Our obligation is to describe the *feminine* in a way that does not exclude the feminine in men but makes a large string resonate in the woman's heart. Some string in the man's heart will resonate as well, but I suspect that in the woman's heart there is a low string that makes her whole chest tremble when the qualities of the feminine are spoken of in the right way.

> (Bly, 1992, pp.235–6)

This reflects, in my view, an underlying desire to redress the imbalance caused by the dynamic energy of the women's movement. He particularly rejects the 'femininity' of 'new men' and feels that this was not a healthy response to the challenge of the women's movement. Yet, if I continue the quotation into Bly's next paragraph, and in all fairness I should, we will find an acknowledgement of constructionist thinking: 'At the same time, we all know that there are in reality besides these two states, "feminine" and "masculine" all sorts of degrees, intermediate states, unions, combinations, special cases, genius exceptions, and so on' (ibid., p.236).

In recent years constructionists have offered meticulous philosophical analyses of how gender is arbitrarily constructed by cultural forces; and have revealed the extent to which gynocentric authors still collude with socially determined gender roles for women. The work of Madonna, very much a postmodernist artist, could be said to demonstrate their analysis (see Plate 3.1).

Bly's stated aim is to revive pagan ritual celebration of manhood; and again paradoxically this leads him back to a theme familiar to feminist thinkers:

> Powerful sociological and religious forces have acted in the West to favour the trimmed, the sleek, the cerebral, the noninstinctive, and the bald. ...

> Women's sexuality has suffered tremendously and still suffers from the tyranny of the bald, ascetic, and cerebral. The goddess Aphrodite, alive inside the female body, is insulted day after day.

> The same forces have doomed male sexuality to the banal and the profane and the hideously practical.

> (Bly, 1992, pp.247–8)

Although the text attempts to give back male rituals of initiation into manhood to contemporary men, what strikes me finally is that it speaks to both men and women, precisely because the concept 'man' still occupies two positions in our language and culture: that of the masculine gender and that of the neutral voice or utterance. The claim to universality which the language always makes for men and masculinity, which was seen as a disadvantage by Beauvoir, and by most feminists since her, now becomes a disadvantage for men who wish to speak of themselves among themselves. Showalter (1986a, pp.261–3) once suggested that in contemporary society men occupy a larger sphere, women a smaller and there is quite a considerable degree of overlap in the twentieth century unlike the separate spheres of the nineteenth century. But even in the twentieth century there remains a small area of female cultural space, existing outside of the dominant sphere; Showalter termed this 'the wild zone' from which feminists should speak. Now it seems to me, women have access to the language of 'universal' discourse, since they were always given that (even if not on equal terms), but women have also developed their own gendered discourses and men are finding it hard to find the inverse reflection of radical feminist enunciation for their own gender-specific utterances.

SUMMARY

According to radical feminism, men have constituted the dominant cultural group, masculinity has been equated with the norm, and language has encoded patriarchal values throughout history. It is only recently that cultural critics have isolated white masculinity as itself constituting a peculiar ethnic and cultural group, and that men have become more self-conscious about their gender formation.

Stoltenberg describes himself as a radical feminist and analyses many of the cultural formations of masculinity, especially in relation to sexuality, in a manner which complements the campaigns of American feminists during the past two decades. Bly, on the other hand, while trying to be sympathetic to women and to feminist concerns, seeks to redress an imbalance which he believes second-wave feminism has been partly responsible for. Ironically, he uses many of the resources familiar to radical feminists in his revisionist reconstruction of empowered manhood.

6 CONCLUSION

American radical feminists posit that sexual oppression is the primary oppression upon which all other oppressions are based. They emphasize the importance of the female body, and envision and celebrate female power in mythological, neological and visionary modes. Their voice has been very important in American culture during the 1970s and 1980s and has informed the work of a number of women writers. Their influence is traceable even in the work of African-American writers such as Morrison and Walker, where we find the mythological and visionary notion of the woman author as shaman.

Socialist feminists are a necessary counter-balance to the inspirational texts of gynocentric authors, since they acknowledge the importance of social factors in determining gender role models. But their impact has not been so prominent, especially in popular culture, party because of the failure of the new left in the 1960s to take sufficient account of women's problems and oppression. However, their thinking pervades the work of some women writers, especially those who, like Piercy, identify themselves as working class.

Since the 1950s American women have spoken in a variety of voices about female experience in their culture. Some have been feminists, some not; but most have been touched by the power of radical feminism which itself was energized by the widespread radicalism of the 1960s. American radical feminists have intervened in many aspects of literary and cultural production as well as in many popular protest movements. I have concentrated on a few, representative novels by women authors, and referred to the prose of liberal and radical feminist writers in order to illustrate one aspect of an extraordinarily diverse and energized renaissance in women's cultural production which has occurred in the US over the last three decades.

REFERENCES

Alther, L. (1977) *Kinflicks*, Harmondsworth, Penguin.

Beauvoir, S. de (1972) *The Second Sex*, Parshley, H.H. (trans.), Harmondsworth, Penguin (first published in 1953).

Bly, R. (1992) *Iron John*, London, Element.

Braxton, J.M. and McLaughlin, A.N. (eds) (1990) *Wild Women in the Whirlwind: Afra-American Culture and the Contemporary Literary Renaissance*, London, Serpent's Tail.

Butler, J. (1987) 'Variations on sex and gender: Beauvoir, Wittig, Foucault' in Benhabib, S. and Cornell, D. (eds) *Feminism as Critique*, Cambridge, Polity Press, pp.129–42.

Butler, O.E. (1988) *Kindred*, London, Women's Press (first published in 1979).

Christian, B. (1990) '"Somebody forgot to tell somebody something": African-American women's historical novels' in Braxton, J.M. and McLaughlin, A.N. (eds), pp.327–41.

Crutcher Lewis, V. (1990) 'African tradition in Toni Morrison's *Sula*' in Braxton, J.M. and McLaughlin, A.N. (eds), pp.316–25.

Daly, M. (1979) *Gyn/Ecology*, London, Women's Press.

Daly, M. (1984) *Pure Lust*, London, Women's Press.

Daly, M. and Caputi, J. (1988) *Websters' First New Intergalactic Wickedary of the English Language*, London, Women's Press.

Firestone, S. (1979) *The Dialectic of Sex: the Case for Feminist Revolution*, London, Women's Press (first published in 1970).

Friedan, B. (1963) *The Feminine Mystique*, London, Penguin.

Gubar, S. (1986) '"The Blank Page" and the issues of female creativity' in Showalter, E. (ed.) (1986b).

Morrison, T. (1975) *Sula*, New York, Bantam.

Morrison, T. (1977) *The Song of Solomon*, London, Chatto & Windus.

Morrison, T. (1985) 'Rootedness: the ancestor as foundation' in Evans, M. (ed.) *Black Women Writers*, London, Pluto Press.

Morrison, T. (1987) *Beloved*, London, Picador.

Piercy, M. (1979) *Woman on the Edge of Time*, London, Women's Press.

Piercy, M. (1980) *Vida*, London, Women's Press.

Piercy, M. (1982) *Braided Lives*, London, Penguin.

Piercy, M. (1984) Interview in *City Limits*, 15/21 June, pp.18–20.

Plath, S. (1982a) *The Bell Jar*, London, Faber & Faber (first published in 1963).

Plath, S. (1982b) *The Journals of Sylvia Plath*, New York, Dial Press.

Rich, A. (1980) *On Lies, Secrets and Silences: Selected Prose 1966–1978*, London, Virago.

Showalter, E. (1986a) 'Feminist criticism in the wilderness' in Showalter, E. (ed.) (1986b), pp.243–70.

Showalter, E. (ed.) (1986b) *The New Feminist Criticism*, London, Virago.

Showalter, E. (ed.) (1989) *Speaking of Gender*, London, Routledge.

Stoltenberg, J. (1990) *Refusing to Be a Man*, Glasgow, Fontana/Collins.

Walker, A. (1983) *The Color Purple*, London, Women's Press.

Walker, A. (1984) *In Search of Our Mothers' Gardens*, London, Women's Press.

Walker, A. (1989) *The Temple of My Familiar*, London, Women's Press.

Walker, A. (1992) *Possessing the Secret of Joy*, London, Jonathan Cape.

Woolf, V. (1981) *A Room of One's Own*, London, Granada (first published in 1929).

FURTHER READING

Dinnerstein, D. (1987) *The Rocking of the Cradle and the Ruling of the World*, London, Women's Press (first published in 1976).

Fuss, D. (1989) *Essentially Speaking: Feminism, Nature and Difference*, London, Routledge.

Griffin, S. (1984) *Woman and Nature: the Roaring Inside of Her*, London, Women's Press (first published in 1978).

O'Neill, W. (1989) *Feminism in America: a History*, Oxford, Transaction (2nd rev. edn).

Ostriker, A.S. (1987) *Stealing the Language: the Emergence of Women's Poetry in America*, London, Women's Press.

Plath, S. (1977) *Johnny Panic and the Bible of Dreams: and Other Prose Writings*, London, Faber & Faber.

Rossi, A. (1988) *The Feminist Papers: From Adams to de Beauvoir*, Boston, Northeastern University Press.

HOLLYWOOD: THE ECONOMICS OF UTOPIA

Richard Maltby and Kate Bowles ★

1 WHAT IS HOLLYWOOD?

Hollywood is one of the United States' most popular export successes. It joins Levis and Coke in having become so much a part of everyday life in even distant and scarcely Westernized areas as to seem, paradoxically, less an *American* product, and more a part of an international mass culture in which we all share. Visitors to California, the scenic backdrop to tens of thousands of movies and television productions, find themselves recognizing pieces of the Hollywood picture: Bel Air homes, the Santa Monica freeway, or the Pacific coastline. But the imaginary Hollywood into which the local cinema is transformed by the screening of a movie cannot be found, and of all the tourist sites around the Los Angeles suburb which is called, quite misleadingly, 'Hollywood', it is perhaps the famous Hollywood sign which is the most poignantly disappointing. Seen from vantage points around the city, the cultural icon of the souvenir shops is in fact unexpectedly remote, undersized and often in disrepair. Originally erected by a property developer in 1923, it is not so much a signpost to the stars as a small, bald statement, standing for something which is impossible to locate precisely because it is everywhere.

Our familiarity with Hollywood's America is similarly deceptive: the movies operate like postcards to furnish us with a selective and distorted sense of having seen the view for ourselves. In order to widen our perspective, it is first important to define what we mean by Hollywood. Hollywood is not simply, or wholly, a synonym for 'The American film industry'. There are movies made by independent producers working outside the Hollywood system which offer a challenge to the recognizable Hollywood style while continuing to speak to us in an American accent; the products of other national film industries have often copied the formats and techniques of Hollywood movies. Far from being natives born into a particular economy and mode of production, the citizens of Hollywood can be both foreign and transient: directors, technicians and stars on temporary contracts for the duration of one production. Hollywood's product range includes movies made for television as well as for the movie theatre, together with an array of associated merchandising, and its investment holdings reflect the interests of corporate business culture as much as those of the movie industry itself. Its earnings come not only from American theatres, but substantially from the foreign market and international video sales. These conditions have not always applied, and certainly do not prohibit the exploration of American themes in Hollywood movies, but they should complicate our interpretation of Hollywood as a purely American product, designed with only American consumption in mind.

Of course, Hollywood's institutional history is bound up with the political, economic and social development of the United States. None the less, the extent of these connections cannot be deduced from the movies alone. Even when Hollywood seems to deal straightforwardly with historical themes, 'based on a true story', there are many factors working to increase the inevitable casualties and distortions of story-telling. This is as true of movies telling the story of Hollywood as of those whose project is the history of the US; the facts are routinely rearranged in the services of entertainment and, ultimately, of box-office success. In *Singin' in the Rain* (1952), for instance, Cosmo (Donald O'Connor) discovers the principles of sound dubbing by standing in front of Kathy (Debbie Reynolds) and miming while she sings behind him. This is much livelier, and funnier, than a literal account of the rather mundane process whereby multiple channel recording and post-synchronization were developed. It does not describe Hollywood's industrial processes, but it is true to the principle that underlies Hollywood's presentation of itself in star biographies and studio histories alike: that the history of entertainment must itself be entertaining.

In order to appreciate Hollywood's role in interpreting America to itself and to the world, it is therefore crucial that we understand the nature and function of entertainment. Although entertainment is pervasive and economically powerful, it evades definition: it is much easier to agree upon what it is *not* (work, or science, or politics, for example) than what it is. Our problems in defining entertainment are symptomatic of the place it occupies in our lives. Precisely because entertainment represents a pleasurable and therapeutic distraction from our more important concerns — the things we are obliged to do — little attention has been paid to examining what entertainment is, or what it does. For most of the twentieth century, Hollywood has been synonymous with entertainment, the name for the principal form of commercially produced non-work. In 1925 an advertisement for Paramount pictures promised its readers that 'All the adventure, all the romance, all the excitement you lack in your daily life are in — Pictures'. It urged them to 'Go to a motion picture ... and let yourself go. ... Out of the cage of everyday existence! If only for an afternoon or an evening — escape!' (Lynd and Lynd, 1929, p.265). The 'wonderful new world' they could escape to was Hollywood, the 'Metropolis of Make-Believe', as it was called in *A Star is Born* (1937).

Richard Dyer describes the place to which we escape for our entertainment as a revised, 'utopian' version of our own world (Dyer, 1977). Like most utopias, the world it displays is one which is based on the real world, but which is able to behave differently. When Superman leaps over tall buildings in a single bound, the tall building is part of a landscape we know and understand, and Superman looks superficially like us, but he is able to do something we recognize as being extraordinary and, in some sense, 'unreal'. However, within the context and logic of utopia, his behaviour is appropriate and justified. Even in less fantastic circumstances, the principle continues to apply: the hero is raked with gunfire and survives (*Lethal Weapon*, 1987); the enemy can be brutally murdered without fear of consequence (*Fatal Attraction*, 1987); the lovers meet again when they might easily have missed each other (*Casablanca*, 1942). In entertainment's utopia, rare events and unusual coincidences become commonplace experiences; issues and conflicts are clear, rather than being cluttered and confused with irrelevant information; solutions and consequences are correspondingly less complicated and less ambivalent.

What is the effect of this combination of close resemblance and acute strangeness? In 1937, successful screenwriter Frances Marion argued that, above all, Hollywood's audience

> wants to be 'sent home happy'. It looks to the photoplay to provide it with a substitute for actual life experience, and to function in such fashion the screen story must contain elements that are emotionally satisfying. Something approaching the ideal life is what this audience prefers to see, rather than life as it actually knows it. It wants to see interesting things which, within the limits of possibility, might happen to it; preferably things to which its own day dreams turn.
>
> (quoted in Ricketson, 1938, p.13)

In claiming to provide something 'approaching the ideal life' which at the same time falls in with the audience's own 'day dreams', Hollywood represents itself as benevolently fulfilling its purpose of entertaining as many of the people as it can, for as much of the time (see Plate 4.1).

But if Hollywood is an American version of Utopia, or vice versa, it is also the synonym for what Umberto Eco has called 'the heavy industry of dreams in a capitalist economy'. Hollywood's status as dream *factory*, show *business* has always been a paradoxical part of its appeal and one of the reasons for denying its products the status of art. In her examination of Hollywood in 1950, anthropologist Hortense Powdermaker saw in Hollywood 'a caricature and overelaboration of the business motives and goals of our society' (Powdermaker, 1950, p.314). 'In Hollywood, the concept of a business civilization has been carried to an extreme. Property is far more important than man and human values have to struggle hard to exist at all.' But Hollywood's glamorization of its capital strength was entirely selective, concerned primarily with spectacle and display. Running parallel to this was an equally strong tendency towards denial of the profit motive: the business side of the show. As Powdermaker noted, 'while the heroes in Hollywood are those with the most money, in the movies we find the opposite extreme' (ibid., p.313). Thus the entertaining version of Hollywood, invented by press and publicity agents and reproduced in Hollywood's movies about itself, diverted public attention away from the routine, mechanical, standardized aspects of the industry's central operations (distribution and exhibition) towards its more attractive, glamorous periphery (production).

Mindful of Hollywood's enduring use of self-dramatization as disguise, the account that follows is organized precisely to emphasize the continuities of Hollywood's development as an industry. We shall concentrate on discussing, in a chronological framework, some of Hollywood's industrial practices, such as self-regulation, rather than describing the aesthetic virtues or sociological significance of a few particularly celebrated movies. This stress on Hollywood's industrial nature is at odds with critical approaches that emphasize individual authorship (auteurism), or generic similarity among Hollywood movies. It is, however, not entirely incompatible with these approaches, and we will conclude by looking at the problems and the rewards associated with the study of genre, using the example of the Western. It is often argued that the historical persistence of a genre such as the Western implies that it has a significance beyond the practicalities of industrial production, a status approaching that of folklore or mythology. The persistence of this argument, as much as of the genre itself, requires that we address the operation of genre in Hollywood. But Hollywood's reflection of, and influence on, American culture cannot be accounted for solely by the conventions of genre. To appreciate Hollywood's complex relationship to American culture, we need to look beyond genre to the way that such everyday phenomena as the family, romance, heroism, femininity and childhood have been represented in different genres and at different times, in the context of changing industrial and technological circumstances.

SUMMARY

'Entertainment' offers us an escape into a world which resembles our own, but which is able to behave differently: Utopia.

As one of the principal forms of commercialized entertainment, or non-work, Hollywood is both an American product and a primary component of international popular culture.

In order to appreciate Hollywood's place in American culture, we need to examine the movies in the context of the industrial and social circumstances which produced them.

2 PATENTING CINEMA BEFORE HOLLYWOOD

The development of the necessary technology for cinema entertainment was not predetermined by any social or cultural demand, but resulted from an opportunistic assembling of mechanical and chemical inventions whose origins lay in nineteenth-century scientific investigations. Celluloid, the material which was found to be sufficiently thin and flexible to be coated with light-sensitive chemicals and passed through a projector at a constant speed, was originally used as a substitute for ivory in the manufacture of false teeth; likewise, the basic electro-mechanical components of the movie projector — its light and motor — were hardly invented with that application in mind. Moving picture pioneers such as Eadweard Muybridge and E.J. Marey were chiefly interested in scientific or educational applications, in recording the physiological details of movement, for example. Neither thought of using their discoveries for anything as frivolous as telling stories for public entertainment, although Muybridge envisaged the rather morbid private application of the moving picture as an extension of the photographic record, preserving images of loved ones to be viewed after their deaths.

It was quickly realized that this technological discovery could be deployed in more diverting ways, to profit from the significant conceptual shifts in definitions of work and leisure at the turn of the century. The earliest machines for presenting moving pictures, such as Edison's and Dickson's Kinetoscope of 1891, aimed to use them for home entertainment, more in anticipation of the video player than the cinema. However, what came to distinguish the movies from the other new media of the turn of the century was that, unlike photography, the gramophone, or later radio and television, the cinema was the only entertainment medium *not* targeted at the domestic market. Not until the 1980s was the theatrical identity of the cinema challenged by video. By 1895, on the other hand, the Cinématographe constructed by the Lumière brothers in Paris had made possible the projection of the moving image for public viewing, and America entered the twentieth century with moving pictures forming part of the vaudeville theatre line-up. Each of the short topical films, scenic views, and comic or dramatic sketches lasted up to two minutes.

At this stage, the producer companies sold their films direct to exhibitors, who played them until they wore out. This unsophisticated system of distribution made it difficult for any projectionist to provide much in the way of variety. In 1903, film exchanges were established, allowing exhibitors to rent and return prints to an intermediary third party. This greatly expanded their repertoires, lowered their costs and increased their profits, to a level that made possible the opening of special theatres dedicated to the exhibition of moving pictures. The 'nickelodeons' began to appear in America in 1905, initially charging five cents admission (hence the name). In just over a decade the moving picture show became part of a cheap night out for the mass American public, who had by now seen such comparatively lengthy productions as Edwin Porter's *The Great Train Robbery* of 1903, running at twelve minutes, and a fifteen-minute version of *Uncle Tom's Cabin*, also produced by Porter for the Edison company. Until 1910, most films were of about that length, while a typical programme in one of the 10,000 theatres in the US might last for an hour.

As with the formation of any new industry, the priority for the individual pioneers was to establish their own domination of the new market, chiefly by taking out patents on their inventions that would inhibit the development of rival technologies, and then suing each other. Out of the ensuing tangle of lawsuits there emerged a patent stand-off, with Edison holding the patent for production equipment, and the Biograph company holding the patent for essential projection technology. Although other smaller companies were in operation, Edison and Biograph dominated, and their subsequent mutual co-operation indicated the industry's inclination towards a monopolistic structure. The Motion Picture Patents Company (MPPC), formed in

In 1903 The Great Train Robbery *was one of the first pictures to demonstrate that the cinema could tell a gripping story. Critics have often since described it as the first important Western, but at the time it was publicized as a faithful re-enactment of actual events*

1908, was designed to reinforce the combined supremacy of the few bigger companies by charging licence fees to the many smaller ones who, in retaliation, formed associations of their own. In 1910, the MPPC created its own distribution organization, the General Film Company, and this provoked the first of many anti-trust manœuvres against the new industry. The conflict of interests between the small number of large producer–distributor companies and the large number of small exhibitors was evident in these legal arguments, and has remained the industry's central structuring tension throughout its history. The larger companies were, however, powerful enough to impose their terms of trade on smaller producers and exhibitors alike, and stabilize the market. This was a key factor in protecting the American industry against other developing national movie industries which might target America as a possible export outlet.

The decade after 1908 also saw the industry's relocation from the East to the West Coast. The advantages were clear: California was cheaper, the weather was reliable, there was a friendly civic administration in Los Angeles, and a range of impressive and varied scenery within easy reach of the city. At the same time the motion picture producers were consolidating their financial position by streamlining their production processes as far as possible. Initial production of topicals and scenics had largely given way to the making of short fiction films. These were much easier and cheaper to produce on a regular basis. They also had the added advantage of supplying (and encouraging) popular demand for fictions as a form of entertainment, an appetite whetted by the press and theatre since the turn of the century. As the story films could be produced most cheaply and regularly in specially built studios, the industry therefore began to organize itself around a studio system of production. By 1911, when the first studio was built in Hollywood itself, Los Angeles had already become the second largest production centre after New York, with companies building studios in several of its suburbs. Three years later, when Carl Laemmle opened his Universal City production plant, Los Angeles boasted that 80 per cent of the country's motion pictures were produced there. By 1917, therefore, the invention of 'Hollywood' had secured its own metaphorical patent.

SUMMARY

Cinema technology was assembled from existing nineteenth-century scientific inventions: electro-mechanical components and celluloid.

Producers initially made short non-fiction films, often on location, and then moved into story-film production, which adapted well to industrial conditions of studio production.

There has been tension since this early stage between the few large producer–distributor companies and the many smaller exhibitor companies. However, as the larger companies were quickly able to establish their domination of the process, stabilizing the industry as a whole, American movie-making secured a competitive position in the international market from the outset.

When the industry moved its base from the East (New York) to the West Coast (Los Angeles), 'Hollywood' became synonymous with American movie-making.

3   SILENT HOLLYWOOD: DEVELOPING THE CLASSICAL STYLE

From this early stage Hollywood production processes resembled a factory system, but its products were more diverse, and more complex, than those of the other new industries. The complexity lay partly in the way in which some of the workers became components in the package which the industry sold to consumers. In the early 1910s individual performers began to be identified as 'picture personalities'. The designation 'star' had its origins in the theatre, but the star system rapidly developed into a crucial element in the Hollywood production system, constructing the fan as a consumer, and the star as commodity, around whom a galaxy of other commodities revolved. To each movie appearance, the stars brought a fixed and reliable set of characteristics, which the fan magazines, in circulation from 1912, could reveal as extending into their personal lives. These magazines inspected the lives of Hollywood's glamorous, exemplary Americans in intimate detail, charting their romantic ups-and-downs and their brand-name preferences with equal concern (Plate 4.2). In addition, they contributed substantially to the status of those stars who, like Mary Pickford and Douglas Fairbanks, were an important American export. When Pickford and Fairbanks married in 1920, for example, a crowd of 300,000 turned out to see them pass through Moscow on their tour of the European continent.

Given the industry's spectacular expansion during these early years, it is not surprising that there were many legislative attempts to supervise its progress, and to control the potential for moral degradation which the nickelodeons in particular seemed to represent. Aware of the need for self-regulation in the face of threatened state intervention, the industry assembled its own National Board of Censorship in 1909, but was none the less subjected to external censorship legislation in a number of cities, beginning with Chicago in 1907. In 1915, these moves were given constitutional validation by the Supreme Court, which declared motion pictures were 'mere representations of events, of ideas and sentiments, published and known'; the motion picture industry was 'a business, pure and simple ... not to be regarded ... as part of the press of the country, or as organs of public opinion' (quoted in Mast, 1982, p.142). This judgement established the legality of state censorship of the movies, and its consequences obliged the industry to make sure that their product was acceptable not only to their customers but also to the guardians of American public culture. It was not overturned until 1952.

The decision came within days of the opening of *The Birth of a Nation*, D.W. Griffith's virulently racist epic of the Civil War and Reconstruction. *The Birth of a Nation* was hailed by some for its innovations in screen narrative, and denounced by others for its damaging social effects. Leading Progressive reformer Jane Addams called it 'a pernicious caricature of the Negro race', and advocated its censorship on the grounds that it was 'unjust and untrue' (quoted in Schickel, 1984, p.283). The National Association for the Advancement of Colored People accused it of gambling 'on the public ignorance of our own history' and 'permanently lodging a radically false conception in the public mind' (quoted in Geduld, 1971, p.101), far from the last time that such a charge was brought against Hollywood's products. Despite the huge commercial success of *The Birth of a Nation*, the threats of local legislation to censor or control movies in the name of public order discouraged Hollywood from making socially or politically provocative films.

Virtual monopoly control over the domestic market gave Hollywood the necessary economic support for aggressive expansion into the foreign market from a very early stage, and it achieved a dominant position world-wide during the First World War. Provided a movie could recoup its costs in the North American market, overseas takings represented a clear profit, and this made it possible to sell to overseas distributors at lower prices, undercutting the local competition. By the late 1920s, Hollywood received approximately 35 per cent of its total income from the foreign market. Deprived of revenue even in their own countries, Hollywood's foreign competitors were unable to compete, resorting instead to the defensive strategy of petitioning their governments to impose limits on the number of American movies their exhibitors could import. It has remained a commonly held view, on both sides of this unequal trade relationship, that Hollywood is selling more than movies to the world's audiences, and it is this sense in which Hollywood is believed by its supporters and detractors alike to be the conduit of American values and American consumer goods to the world. This belief underpins the industry's relationship to American politics. 'Trade', declared the State Department during the 1920s, 'now follows the films', to the tune of one dollar's worth of export goods for every foot of film shipped abroad. Hollywood was thus able to offset against its early encounters with state censorship the strategic, selective political support which any new revenue-generating industry could expect, particularly in the interpretation of anti-trust laws.

Looking at the full range of Hollywood's holdings, therefore, from real estate and equipment via the movies themselves to the less tangible assets of in-house celebrities and lifestyle messages, the similarities between the movie business and other parts of the new urban industrial culture were partly obscured. Nevertheless, some important production principles were shared among them, chiefly the drive to maximize production efficiency and regularize market demand. The public should be able to rely on a motion picture to provide a certain kind of entertainment, in the same way that a Ford car would provide a certain kind of transport; to this end, the Hollywood product should be recognizably standardized. However, sufficient variety should be included in order to encourage the public to buy the product again; standardization should therefore be modified by means of differentiation. The product on offer was not so much the movie itself as a way of spending time: surveys in the 1920s suggested that 68 per cent of the audience went to the movies for the 'event', while only 10 per cent went specifically to see the feature.

The movie theatre itself offered one highly standardized part of the entertainment package, but the principal mechanism whereby standardization was modified by differentiation lay in Hollywood's narrative style. As silent films grew into full-length features, a reliable yet widely variable formula needed to be found in order to prevent them from becoming either unmanageably disorganized and incapable of being taken in at a sitting, or unbearably routine, discouraging the audience from returning to the theatre. What emerged has become known as the Classical Hollywood style, marked out by a strongly linear progression of events, in which all information was potentially relevant, and nothing was redundant, random, or unresolved. Characters behaved with consistency, and yet provided the range and depth of dramatic focus that prevented the stories from becoming dull; plots unfolded according to the imperatives established at the outset, yet with sufficient pace to keep the audience interested and anxious (but not too anxious). Because this causally motivated and tightly edited narrative style naturalized itself in the expectations of its audiences, it is now difficult to appreciate the extent of its artificiality, or to imagine that there might be alternatives to its story-telling conventions.

Stylistic conventions were similarly negotiated for camera placement, shot construction, editing and continuity, in order to ensure that maximum success was achieved by the motion pictures as visual narratives. Although it often advertised the 'realism' of its spectacles, Hollywood did not deploy the available technology to minimize the difference between art and life. Instead, its practice was to celebrate its craft, drawing attention to its skill in manufacturing illusions, and to the opulence of its fabrications. Advances in moving picture technology therefore offered the audience the maximum degree of pleasure available from watching cinema *as* cinema, enjoying each new technical accomplishment and thereby appreciating the ways in which the medium differentiated itself from other forms of public entertainment. As is still the case, it was in the interests of movie-makers that the audience be aware of the budget: the lavish sets for the epics of Cecil B. deMille reminded the audience that the cinematic *mise-en-scène* was far grander than that which theatre could produce; likewise, the car chases of the Keystone comedies operated as much to display to the audience the current state of camera technology as to advance the story. But because the conventions remained consistent and, when necessary, unobtrusive, they acted to naturalize the aesthetic of the narrative movie. By knowing when and how to keep their technical presence discreet, movie-makers ensured that the audience felt at home in what continued to be extremely artificial surroundings.

As the Classical Hollywood style developed, so did the organization of the motion picture industry. The manufacturing companies that had first dominated the industry in the MPPC declined in importance. The new powers had their origins in exhibition or distribution, and by 1918 the future structure of the industry had become clear. Industrial power, and the great majority of production, was concentrated in a few vertically-integrated companies. A vertically-integrated company is involved in all three branches of its business: manufacture, wholesale and retail. A vertically-integrated food company, for instance, might own the plantations where its crops are grown, the canning factories where they are processed, the trucks that deliver the cans and the grocery stores in which they are sold. A small number of vertically-integrated companies, all pursuing the same business strategies, can between them dominate an industry. Within the motion picture industry, the architect of vertical integration was Adolph Zukor, the founder of the Famous Players production–distribution company, who added a chain of theatres to his operations in the years immediately after the First World War. In response, the largest exhibition consortium, First National Pictures, began producing its own movies, competing for the services of Zukor's stars. During the 1920s a series of mergers produced three, then four, vertically-integrated companies which dominated the industry: Paramount, which included Famous Players; Warner Bros., which expanded greatly in the late 1920s and took over First National; Loew's, Inc., the parent company of MGM; and Fox, which became Twentieth Century-Fox in 1935. In 1919, the industry's three biggest stars, Mary Pickford, Douglas Fairbanks and Charlie Chaplin, together with D.W. Griffith, attempted to exercise their market power by forming United Artists to distribute their own productions, but they simply never made enough movies to rival the major vertically-integrated companies.

The grandiose interiors of picture palaces impressed patrons with their elaborate architecture. Seating as many as 4,000, they offered their audiences an experience of luxury and grandeur they were unlikely to experience anywhere else except at the movies

These firms used the power that vertical integration gave them in three ways. First, they concentrated their theatre ownership in the most profitable sector: the first-run theatres in the major metropolitan centres. Built between the mid-1910s and the late 1920s and decorated in elaborate styles borrowed from Europe, the Orient and ancient history, these picture palaces complemented the often exotic nature of the motion pictures themselves. Audiences might, for instance, see Rudolph Valentino in *The Sheik* (1921) or Douglas Fairbanks in *The Black Pirate* (1926) in a theatre decorated like a moonlit Italian Renaissance garden or a palace in Baghdad. The nickelodeons had made their name — literally — by being cheap entertainment, but Hollywood's rapidly evolving economic logic argued that the evidence of big spending made better business sense. For the clerks and shopgirls of American cities, as much as for Hollywood's expanding middle-class audience, a night at the picture palace might now last two-and-a-half hours, and include a musical overture, a live 'presentation' stage show, a newsreel and several other shorts as well as the main feature, all accompanied by a live orchestra of as many as 50 players. Despite their extravagances, the picture palaces were highly profitable operations, and as democratic as they were vulgar: their inventive grandeur was available to anyone with the price of admission — except for black viewers who, if they were admitted, were seated in a segregated section, usually the balcony.

Extravagance in production was the second element in the major companies' consolidation of their dominance of the industry. During the 1910s and 1920s the costs of movie production, and particularly the salaries paid to stars, rose rapidly, creating a huge barrier to entry into film production for any new company. Thirdly, in their role as distributors, the major companies used their market power to dictate terms to the majority of the country's 20,000 exhibitors. The main element of this control was block booking, in which the distributor insisted on selling movies in groups of up to 50, guaranteeing the exhibition of the full line of product. Distributors also dictated the order in which theatres could show movies, ensuring that the most expensive theatres in each location played the movie first. So while movies such as *Why Change Your Wife* (1920), *Flaming Youth* (1923) and *Gentlemen Prefer Blondes* (1927) appeared to celebrate the adventurous and carefree nature of modern life, their images of extravagance were part of a general industry strategy by which the majors both demonstrated and consolidated their oligopoly power (an oligopoly is created when a small number of competitive firms control a market). Meanwhile hard-headed business negotiations were being conducted on Wall Street in order to continue Hollywood's programme of expansion of both studio facilities and, economically much more important, theatrical real estate.

Hollywood style was similarly aligned to an ethic of private consumption. The stars continued to represent all the pleasures of the new hedonism, based on material prosperity; as idols of consumption they taught their audience some of the skills needed to enjoy what advertising counsellor Christine Frederick called the new doctrine of 'consumptionism … the greatest idea that America has to give to the world; the idea that workmen and masses be looked upon not simply as workers and producers, but as consumers' (quoted in Maltby, 1989, p.10). But with the pleasures came dangers, at least as the guardians of traditional morality saw it. Mary Pickford's divorce from Owen Moore and marriage to Douglas Fairbanks in 1920 gave ammunition to newspaper writers and moral reformers. The death of star Wallace Reid from drug addiction, the unsolved murder of director William Desmond Taylor in a cloud of circumstances hinting at sexual deviance, a studio cover-up, and the involvement of several stars, and most notoriously of all, the trial of comedian Roscoe 'Fatty' Arbuckle for the manslaughter of 'starlet' Virginia Rappe provided the evidence to support accusations that behind the images constructed by Hollywood's publicists lay a 'real' world of moral turpitude.

The public obsession with the sexual lives of celebrities, which has been a feature of Hollywood and stardom ever since, comes in part from the movies' own preoccupation with heterosexual romance as a major element in nine out of ten plots. But it also results from a more general cultural inclination to prioritize sex as being the central indication of private, 'real' identity. Hollywood participated enthusiastically in the revision of codes of sexual behaviour in the 1920s, providing images that provoked considerable anxiety in culturally conservative quarters about the influence of the stars on young consumers. Rudolph Valentino displayed a disturbingly exotic brand of male sexuality in movies such as *The Four Horsemen of the Apocalypse* (1921) and *Monsieur Beaucaire* (1924), raising concerns about the effects of movie-going upon impressionable young women, and provoking racially-inspired anxieties about Hollywood's representation of an idealized American manhood. Meanwhile, the antics of Hollywood heroines created even more anxiety. Clara Bow, the screen embodiment of the flapper, became known as the 'It' girl after English novelist Elinor Glyn identified her as possessing 'It', a 'strange magnetism which attracts both sexes', composed of self-confidence and poise (quoted in Walker, 1968, p.38) (Plate 4.2). Less sophisticated or more puritanical minds than Glyn's, however, understood 'It' as little more than sexual provocation, and feared for its effect on their children.

In 1922, the major companies established a trade association for the industry, the Motion Picture Producers and Distributors of America, Inc. (MPPDA), with a leading Republican politician, Will H. Hays, as its President. Its main purpose was to safeguard the political interests of the emerging oligopoly, and to turn aside threats of legislation or court action that might impose a strict application of the anti-trust laws to the industry. It also standardized intra-industry relations and trade practices, and stabilized relationships between distributors and small exhibitors. Its most visible activity, however, was the management of the industry's public relations, less with those people who actually went to the movies than with 'the classes that write, talk and legislate' (Hays, 1932). The MPPDA had as one of its founding objectives the maintenance of 'the highest possible moral and artistic standards of motion picture production', and in pursuing this objective the industry, through the Association, implicitly accepted the idea common among Progressive reformers that 'pure' entertainment — amusement that was not harmful to its consumer — was a commodity comparable to the pure meat guaranteed by the Food and Drug Administration (Moley, 1946, p.227). On the whole, despite the anxieties provoked by Arbuckle, Valentino and Bow, the industry's strategy of defensive self-regulation was successful throughout the 1920s. The coming of sound, however, complicated this picture as well as several others.

SUMMARY

Hollywood 'stars' quickly became part of the package which the industry sold to its consumers; fan magazines documented and encouraged this trend.

The intensity of the cinematic spectacle, together with its popularity, attracted the attention of moral reformers to its potential for harm, and the principle was established that cinema should be subject to internal self-regulation and external censorship.

Hollywood developed a 'classical' narrative pattern designed to make movies comprehensible to the audience, and capable of being reproduced to order on an increasingly industrialized scale. Like many other new products, movies were to be both *standardized* and *differentiated* in order to build a loyal consumer following.

The industry consolidated into four major *vertically-integrated* companies controlling production, distribution and exhibition, and established a trade association, the Motion Picture Producers and Distributors of America, Inc. in order to protect their interests and to oversee self-regulation.

4 SOUND, THE DEPRESSION, AND THE PRODUCTION CODE

The introduction of sound to popular cinema during the late 1920s was less a technical innovation than a business venture, spearheaded by Warner Bros. and Fox as part of their programmes of expansion, aimed at improving their share of the exhibition market. The driving forces behind the development of sound, however, were the two corporate giants behind the other entertainment innovation of the 1920s, radio: Western Electric, the manufacturing subsidiary of AT&T, and the Radio Corporation of America (RCA), part-owned by General Electric. Initially, neither movie company looked to sound as a way of adding dialogue to feature movies: Fox produced Movietone newsreels, and Warners made Vitaphone shorts, starring some of Broadway's most famous vaudeville performers such as George Jessel and Irving Berlin. The first full-length movie with a soundtrack, *Don Juan* (1926), had no dialogue, simply a recorded musical accompaniment that replaced the live orchestra in the theatre. Within a year, Warners were experimenting with making sound a component of features: in *The Jazz Singer* (1927), Al Jolson sang four songs, and the movie proved enormously popular with audiences. Jolson's next movie, *The Singing Fool* (1928), broke box-office records everywhere it played and convinced any remaining sceptics of the greatly increased profits to be made with sound. The other major companies agreed terms with Western Electric in 1928, and began producing 'all-talking' pictures in 1929, the year in which sound technology spread out from the major cities to most of the 15,000 theatres in the US. By September 1929, the industry's remarkably smooth and well-planned conversion to sound was complete. Sound also brought into being the last of the industry's major companies when RKO was created out of the amalgamation of a number of smaller distribution and exhibition organizations in order to exploit RCA's rival sound system.

As with many of Hollywood's technological shifts, sound created some drawbacks, many of which have been mythologized by Hollywood's own accounts of the transition. The mechanical recording of sound had been available since the 1870s, but the synchronization of sound and image for cinema entertainment took longer to perfect. Introducing microphones to the studio resulted in some difficulties with the noise levels of the camera motors, and attempts at soundproofing initially restricted camera movement, although not to the extent that mythology suggests. Other optical effects were temporarily restricted, and in front of the camera, performance styles were gradually adjusted to take account of the growing significance of dialogue rather than expression. The precipitate decline of some silent stars' careers — John Gilbert is the most famous — had less to do with the alleged inadequacies of their voices than with the shift in acting style and movie content that came with sound, making the histrionics of the romantic melodramas in which they starred seem comic rather than grandly passionate.

More important than these essentially cosmetic reorientations was the impact of dialogue in determining the interpretation of otherwise ambiguous scenes within the movies. In a cinema of gesture and expression, it had been possible for movie-makers to attribute salacious content to the mind of the beholder; with spoken dialogue rendering the content of each scene much more explicit, it became harder to sustain the denials. This shift had particular consequences within the foreign market, not simply because the movies were audibly Americanized by the transition to sound, but because the extent to which an individual movie could be tailored to suit local sensitivities by changing its intertitles was greatly reduced. The process of translating language, let alone political or social niceties, became far less flexible. The increasingly critical role of self-regulation, under the MPPDA's supervision, was due not so much to the fact that, as MGM's head of production Irving Thalberg put it, characters could now 'delicately' discuss subjects 'the silent picture was forced to shun', as to this loss of flexibility brought by sound technology.

At MGM in the early 1930s, Louis B. Mayer (centre) ran the studio, but Irving Thalberg (second from left) supervised production. F. Scott Fitzgerald based the character of Monroe Stahr, The Last Tycoon *of his last novel, on Thalberg, who died in 1936 at the age of 37*

Thalberg argued that motion pictures did not present their audiences with new attitudes, but simply reflected those they already had. 'The motion picture', he insisted, 'is literally bound to the mental and moral level of its vast audience' (Thalberg, 1930). Other voices, however, were less tolerant, and because of the industry's vulnerability to legislation, it was forced to attend to the anxieties of an increasingly insecure Protestant provincial middle class. Even though movie advertising was all many of Hollywood's critics saw, this was enough to suggest that permissive representations of sex and violence were designed to cater to the baser instincts of 'morons', a term widely used to refer indirectly to the immigrant working class. Along with the road house and the dance hall, therefore, the movie theatre was denounced as a site where provincial values (and children) were endangered by the incursions of a modernist, metropolitan culture widely regarded as alien — a word which was often, but not always, a synonym for Jewish.

The industry responded to these pressures by introducing the Production Code in 1930. The Code was a corporate statement of policy about the appropriate content of entertainment cinema that acknowledged the possible influence of movies on the morals and conduct of those who saw them. It represented the industry's acceptance of its difference from the book, magazine or theatre business, because of the difficulty in confining movies to 'only certain classes of people. The exhibitor's theatres are built for the masses, for the cultivated and the rude, the mature and the immature, the self-respecting and the criminal' (Moley, 1946, p.224). The Code was designed to ensure that the movies only provided their customers with what it called 'correct entertainment'. 'No picture shall be produced', it announced sternly, 'which will lower the moral standards of those who see it'. Movies were thus endowed with an affirmative cultural function that was dramatically at odds with a view of art as a vehicle of social criticism or negation. In this aspect, much more important than its famously trivial requirements that, for instance, one of the four participating feet remain on the floor during a love scene (to avoid what was delicately known as the 'horizontal embrace'), the Code had a determining effect on movie content throughout the Classical period of studio production, and contributed significantly to Hollywood's avoidance of contentious subject matter.

Perhaps surprisingly, however, the effect of the Code was not so much to rule out the *double entendre* as to create precisely the environment in which it could flourish. As one of the Code's first administrators explained, in order to entertain their undifferentiated audience, the movies needed a system of representational conventions 'from which conclusions might be drawn by the sophisticated mind, but which would mean nothing to the unsophisticated and inexperienced' (Joy, 1931). Far from narrowing the available readings of a movie, the industry was endeavouring to restore some of the ambiguity that it had lost in the transition to spoken dialogue. This was perhaps most obvious in dealing with representations of sexuality, but it applied equally to Hollywood's representation of other subjects.

These renegotiations over content took place against a backdrop of considerable economic instability in Hollywood, as elsewhere. The transition to

sound had encouraged all the major companies to embark on ambitious programmes of expansion, particularly in their real estate holdings, and these
had cushioned the industry against the initial impact of the Crash in 1929.
The Depression, however, exposed the excessive ambition of this expansion
on borrowed money. By 1933 the majors found themselves in the hands of
their Wall Street creditors. Nevertheless, with the consumers' real spending
power being squeezed, the diversionary appeal (and the low cost) of the
movies survived a temporary and partial decline in the industry's box-office.
Stock in Hollywood's intangible assets — stardom, glamour, the capacity to
keep up appearances — remained high. Moreover, the actual changes in
ownership, as the companies passed in and out of Wall Street control, did
not manifest themselves in explicit changes in the product; it was in the
interests of the industry's creditors that output remained efficient, reliable
and in line with demonstrated public demand. When the financial situation
stabilized, the industry was dominated by the 'Big Five': Paramount,
Loew's, Inc. (MGM), Warner Bros., RKO, and Twentieth Century-Fox; with
three smaller companies (appropriately, the 'Little Three'): Universal, Columbia, and United Artists. What had appeared to be a period of upheaval had
in fact been one of further consolidation.

Much the same was true regarding movie content. Although a growing chorus
of voices denounced the moral evils of the movies, it would be wrong to conclude that movies themselves became more salacious or vicious between 1930
and 1934. The early 1930s was a period of increasing moral conservatism in
American culture, and the film industry was not alone in failing to pedal back-
wards fast enough to satisfy 'the growing demand for a return to decency in
all of our leisure pursuits'. The brief cycle of gangster films inspired by press
coverage of Al Capone in 1930 and 1931 provoked much criticism, as did
Hollywood's more sustained interest in the careers of 'fallen women', such as
Joan Crawford in *Possessed* (1931) or Marlene Dietrich in *Blonde Venus* (1932).
Although the Production Code saw to it that crime was never seen to pay, it
was none the less the case that with stars such as James Cagney playing the
gangster, and Jean Harlow playing the fallen woman, a certain inevitable
glamour attached to their characters. There was a danger that the precarious
balance of ambiguity might tip towards support for the wrongdoers, to the
extent 'that the double standard shall be seriously affected'. This was precisely
what the industry was accused of in 1933, with the publication of the Payne
Fund Studies into the effects of motion pictures upon American youth, and in
particular by the sensationalist popularization of their findings, Henry James
Forman's book *Our Movie Made Children*.

In 1934, the industry responded to this growing external pressure with what
appeared as a great public *mea culpa*, in which it confessed to previous
moral laxity and promised to implement the Production Code fully in
future. It appeared, too, that the missionary responsible for its conversion
was the Catholic church, which had organized its laity into the Legion of
Decency and threatened a boycott of 'unclean' movies. In reality, this was a
stage-managed Hollywood melodrama, concealing delicate negotiations
between the MPPDA and the Catholic hierarchy over a mutually beneficial
public performance that would result in the effective enforcement of the

Production Code by the existing machinery, without inflicting major economic damage on the industry. In its own economic and political self-interest, the industry was obliged to accept a culturally conservative definition of the function of movie entertainment. As the editor of an industry trade journal explained in 1936, the motion picture business was 'vulnerable to, and on occasion menaced by, all the governments there are, abroad and at home, including national, state and city legislators' (*Motion Picture Herald*, 1936).

Within the broad categories of what historian Tino Balio has called 'production trends', Hollywood's selection of material was organized mainly around relatively brief cycles. A movie's commercial success led the studio that had produced it to try to replicate the formula, while other studios tried to imitate it, and the cycle lasted for as long as it proved popular. In due course, any commercial formula was likely to be repeated, but this procedure meant that Hollywood's production needed to be attuned to relatively short-lived changes in public mood, as well as to the more stable elements of audience demand. The 'fallen woman' cycle and the gangster movies, for example, can be seen as part of the industry's attempt to investigate the previous decade and to join the coalition of social forces attributing America's present problems to the vices of the past. Beyond these specificities, however, these movies were as liable as any Hollywood product to recycle the principal, standardizing story-line of heterosexual romance which was such a helpful organizing device in Classical Hollywood narratives.

The success of these romantic story-lines and in particular the persistence of the vigorously attractive male star (in the person, for instance, of Clark Gable), concealed a crisis around masculinity in a decade of high unemployment, when the male breadwinner could no longer count on being a hero even in his own home. Hollywood's biggest star in the mid-1930s, Shirley Temple, almost invariably played an orphan child in search of a father around whom she could construct a family (Plate 4.3). As Hollywood emerged from what Robert Sklar has called its 'Golden Age of Turbulence', the second half of the decade saw the studio system of production operating with a sense of certainty that it understood and could satisfy the demands of its predominantly middle-class audience (Sklar, 1975, p.175). 'Screwball' comedies represented women as irresponsible, in need of male authority. The hero-figures of the late 1930s — James Stewart, Mickey Rooney or Henry Fonda, for instance — were representatives of small-town, middle-class virtue, and a cycle of successful historical biographies also emphasized that American virtues were rooted in its rural past, whether that was the log cabin of *Young Mr. Lincoln* or the *ante-bellum* plantation of *Gone With the Wind* (both 1939).

Economically, the industry's most successful period was during the Second World War when audiences had fewer durable goods on which to spend their money. Movie theatres themselves were no longer the ornate palaces of the 1920s; now a neighbourhood theatre would probably offer a double bill, including a low-budget B-feature (often made by one of Hollywood's 'Poverty Row' studios such as Republic or Monogram which specialized in such productions), as well as the newsreel, comedy or cartoon shorts, and the main attraction. Shows would run for three hours or more. Theatres also now sold candy and popcorn, and most theatres installed air-conditioning in the late 1930s, providing a quite separate reason for going to the movies in the hot summer months, previously the time of the year with the lowest movie attendances. Granted the status of an 'essential industry', Hollywood enlisted in the war effort 'to arouse the emotions of the apathetic and direct the energies of the frustrated' (quoted in Maltby, 1989, p.114). In *Casablanca* (1942), Humphrey Bogart's Rick Blaine embodies the spirit of pre-war American isolation ('I stick my neck out for nobody', he declares), until he is reminded of his idealism by the revival of his romance with Ilsa Lund (Ingrid Bergman). Bogart's character was an American heroic archetype put to propagandist purpose: the man reluctantly drawn into a violent conflict he cannot avoid without compromising his principles. On the whole, Hollywood's war was played out by stereotypes of one kind or another, frequently in familiar crime movie plots converted into espionage stories.

Meanwhile, the major companies were encountering a familiar obstacle. Always vulnerable to the criticism that their industrial structure was monopolistic, the Big Five were finally forced by the Supreme Court in 1948 to separate the exhibition side of their business from their production and distribution operations. This verdict, which was known as the Paramount decision, undermined the economies of scale that had provided the rationale for the studio system of production, and signalled the beginning of the end of the Classical Hollywood cinema, although it took more than ten years for the decision to be implemented fully. The studios had, however, been preparing themselves to scale down production since their practice of distributing movies in blocks had been drastically curtailed in the early 1940s. A shift towards the production of fewer but more expensive movies occurred, and was accompanied by an increase in the number of independent production companies centred on an individual producer or star. Independently produced movies were still distributed by the major companies, but their rise represented a shift away from the studio system and its volume production. By 1955, when RKO ceased operations, many of the small neighbourhood theatres had closed their doors.

SUMMARY

The introduction of sound made movie content significantly less ambiguous, and it therefore became harder for producers to adapt movies to sensitive market areas, particularly overseas.

Criticism of the industry's moral standards grew, and in 1930 the industry responded by establishing its own Production Code, admitting responsibility for affirming cultural values, rather than offering social criticism, while at the same time exploiting the workings of the Code in order to allow *double entendre* and innuendo to continue in the mind of the 'sophisticated' viewer. Increasing conservatism in America, rather than increasingly salacious content, brought about a stated recommitment to the Code in 1934.

The coming of sound cushioned the industry from the immediate impact of the Depression, but also encouraged over-expansion, and the major companies came under Wall Street control during the 1930s, eventually consolidating as five major and three smaller companies.

After a financially successful period during the Second World War, the industry was investigated as a monopoly, and was compelled by the Supreme Court in 1948 to separate the exhibition side of its business from the production–distribution axis.

Classical Hollywood, whose stylistic features had firm industrial origins, thus approached the end of its cycle for industrial reasons.

5 PARANOIA AND DOMESTICITY: THE POST-WAR DISSOLUTION OF CLASSICAL HOLLYWOOD

Hollywood's uncertainties in the post-Second World War period were most visible in a disparate group of movies that became known as *films noir*, a term first used by French critics to describe the visual and thematic hallmarks they identified in movies they saw when their cinemas were opened to American pictures after the war. Part of what united these movies was their unsettling visual style, which used dramatic contrasts in lighting, distortions in camera angles and uncomfortable shot compositions (see Plate 4.4). An important source for this style had been Orson Welles' first movie, *Citizen Kane*, a thinly disguised biography of newspaper magnate William Randolph Hearst. Received with much criticism for its content on its release in 1941, its style and appearance (expressionist lighting, deep-focus photography and disrupted narrative relying heavily on flashbacks) became increasingly influential as the decade wore on. *Films noir* were noticeably more cynical than Hollywood conventionally allowed; the happy ending was far from guaranteed, and lovers were almost as likely to kill each other as to marry. Whether he was a war-veteran thriller hero or a comic suburban patriarch, the post-war male hero found himself struggling to make sense of his unevenly lit surroundings and his own psychological maladjustment. Women were increasingly represented as malevolent figures, masculinized by their wartime experience. Marriage no longer provided a safe haven, and if the outside world was full of beautiful women, movies such as *Gilda* (1946) and *Out of the Past* (1947) made it clear, even in the gloomiest lighting, that they were up to no good.

As the paranoid hero of *film noir* wrestled with his own deficiencies in a hostile world, paranoia as a political motif began to appear across a broad range of American institutions. If America had been slow to enter imaginatively into the Second World War, no such prompting was required with the first perceived threat to national stability in the post-war period: communism. The demonstrated potential of the new atomic technology raised the stakes almost beyond comprehension, and yet the real threat of communism was popularly believed to be approaching mainland America by much more insidious routes — infiltration, subversion and mind-control. Once again, Hollywood's mass appeal made it a large and obvious target for those seeking to anticipate communism's point of entry into American life, and in October 1947 the House Committee on Un-American Activities (HUAC) opened its investigation into 'Communist Infiltration of the Motion Picture Industry'. Members of the industry were called upon to testify against their colleagues, and refusal to do so was taken as hostility to the objectives of the Committee. The first group of 'unfriendly witnesses', known as the Hollywood Ten, served one-year prison sentences for contempt of Congress for refusing to answer what became known as the $64,000 question: 'Are-you-now-or-have-you-ever-been-a-member-of-the-Communist-Party?' Many more, however, found themselves blacklisted on the basis of the most innocent political gestures and past associations. Careers were destroyed by little more than rumours, with many blacklisted personnel forced to leave Hollywood or work under assumed names.

Hollywood's conformity undoubtedly reflected the industry's timidity as well as its consistent desire to avoid political controversy, but it was also in keeping with national sentiment. Movie producers behaved no worse (if also no better) than university administrators, business executives or union leaders; it was merely that some of the Hollywood victims of McCarthyism and the anti-communist witch hunts were more prominent public figures. The climate of the time was perhaps most exactly caught in *On the Waterfront* (1954), a crime melodrama set and shot in the New York dockyards, in which Marlon Brando's rebel hero is eventually persuaded to testify to the Crime Commission investigating waterfront corruption. The movie, scripted and directed by 'friendly witnesses' who had 'named names' before HUAC to save their careers, received the industry's accolade by winning eight Oscars in 1955.

On the Waterfront established the Method acting style as a new Hollywood orthodoxy. It was also a political parable for the 1950s, providing a complex quasi-religious vindication of the decision to inform

What made *On the Waterfront* such an embodiment of its period was not only its characterization of the informer as hero, but also its inversion of the utopian relationship between Hollywood and the United States. *On the Waterfront* explains that the waterfront 'ain't America'; in the paranoid climate of the early 1950s, Hollywood's version of America was often dystopian. In keeping with a growing public belief in the existence of 'organized criminal conspiracies' more or less interchangeable with communist operations, crime movies treated 'the mob' as a business; some interpretations reversed the metaphor to see business being represented as criminal. And if Hollywood's America was not being infiltrated by communist conspirators or Mafia criminals, it was subject to the *Invasion of the Body Snatchers* (1956), or *Them!* (1954), giant mutant ants created by nuclear accidents or misguided experiments.

There was now a second imperative to improve production quality rather than increase quantity. The post-war audience had more money to spend on consumer goods, including entertainment, and movie audiences had risen to an all-time high in 1946. But there was a significant newcomer competing for the leisure dollar: television. This had been a technical possibility as early as 1927, but one which it did not prove convenient to distribute on a mass scale until the post-war suburban building boom had established the nuclear family in its bunker as the nation's strongest defence against communism. Between 1947 and 1954, the number of television sets in the US grew from 14,000 to 32 million. Movie audiences, on the other hand, declined: by 1953, only half the number of people in the US were going to the movies as had attended in 1946.

Kevin McCarthy and Dana Wynter discover the 'pods' that will replace them in Invasion of the Body Snatchers. *After a lengthy examination of the merits and trials of living in a community 'without passion', referring as much to suburban conformism as to communism, the movie altered its original, pessimistic ending to allow the FBI to step in and save the world. In* Them!, *nuclear experiments produced a race of giant ants that threatened to destroy civilization as Americans of the 1950s knew it*

With its audience threatening to desert the movie theatres for the privacy of their own new homes, Hollywood struggled at first with a series of innovations largely designed to convince the public that the silver screen still held the monopoly on technical wizardry. Most of these efforts either required expensive theatre modifications or, like 3-D, turned out to be short-lived gimmicks. Only the CinemaScope version of widescreen achieved the degree of success necessary to justify widespread conversion. Meanwhile, just as movies had done previously, television (bolstered by advertising) came to be part of modern culture to an extent that its absence quickly became unthinkable, and the movie industry, which had always acknowledged the business advantages of tactical co-operation, put away its 3-D glasses and set about accommodating the new arrival.

The centre of television production followed the movie industry's shift from East to West and by 1956 television Western series such as *Gunsmoke* and *Cheyenne* were being produced in Hollywood. With relatively low production costs and a guaranteed local and overseas market, these series took the place of B-movies in the industry's economic rationale. A second source of revenue came from the sale of film libraries to television programmers. In addition, as the threat of consumer boycotts continued against advertisers sponsoring programmes with any taint of radicalism, television was obliged to steer a narrowly conservative course, and Hollywood was able briefly to assume the mantle of social commentary in movies such as *The Defiant Ones* (1958), at least where there was a box-office advantage to be gained by doing so.

Nineteen-fifties suburbanization was not so much America's retreat into middle-class isolationism as the rediscovery of the domestic frontier. After the Depression and the restricted availability of consumer goods during wartime, the opportunity to participate in a consumer-led economic boom was a golden one. Although the paranoid hero took some convincing, once the movie and television industries were working together to sell the American way of life and to denounce its opponents, the pitch was attractive. Fortunately for the movie industry, however, the suburban fortress sheltered a powerful unit of disaffection: the teenager. Just as the nuclear family was settling down at home, this new dissident consumer was showing ever greater inclination to go out. With increased spending power and unprecedented mobility, the car-crazy teen gave Hollywood yet another new market in which to expand. As the neighbourhood theatres closed, the drive-in theatres opened, and by 1956, the 'passion pits' accounted for a quarter of Hollywood's box-office.

The potential this new audience represented was twofold. In the first place, with their attention only intermittently on the screen, teenagers did not demand high production values or social comment so much as spectacle, horror, and above all, duration. Accordingly, exhibitors assembled double- and triple-bills of specially-produced low-budget 'teenpics'; Paramount's *The Blob* and *I Married a Monster from Outer Space* was a successful combination in 1958. Even while staving off criticism that Hollywood was, as usual, catering to any vulnerable audience who could afford to pay, movie producers saw a second way to make money out of the new subculture, in making movies *about* teenagers. Just as many of the movies of the 1930s had purported to criticize the vices of the 1920s while giving them generous screen-time, so many of the teenpics could be defended as investigations into the new phenomenon, or even critiques of the threat to American values it represented. Hollywood was playing its neatest sleight of hand, making movies full of thrills for its teen customers, with a message no responsible parent could afford to ignore. *The Blackboard Jungle* (1955) defended its representation of juvenile delinquency in schools by claiming in its opening titles that 'public awareness is a first step toward a remedy for any problem' — language that echoed the self-justifications of friendly witnesses before HUAC. This did not prevent the movie from being denounced by moral conservatives, among them the American Ambassador to Italy, who insisted that it be withdrawn from the Venice film festival. The publicity from that denunciation, in turn, did the movie no damage at the box-office.

The sympathetic attention given to the moral conflicts faced by America's sons and daughters in movies such as *The Wild One* (1954) and *Rebel Without a Cause* (1955) boosted the careers of Marlon Brando and James Dean, among others; the paranoid hero had fathered the troubled, mumbling teen. In its treatment of women, Hollywood demonstrated something of a breast fixation, with the blossoming careers of Jayne Mansfield, Jane Russell, and Marilyn Monroe. But despite their amplitude, these women were scarcely destined for motherhood, and with so many absences at its heart, Hollywood's nuclear family hollowed out into the unhappy shell displayed in the 'family melodramas' such as *All That Heaven Allows* (1955) and *Bigger than Life* (1956). Ambivalence surrounding women's changing social position found articulation in the work of Alfred Hitchcock. Many Hitchcock heroes were neurotic or mother-fixated, and yet with sufficient residual paranoia to suspect the manipulations and betrayals of the beautiful women around them, whose obsession appeared to be with their bachelor eligibility.

Hitchcock's movies, particularly those of the late 1950s and early 1960s, have provided fertile soil for subsequent critical interpretation, whether that criticism has sought to elevate the director to the status of artist or to psychoanalyse the movies as texts or cultural symptoms. Through his television series, *Alfred Hitchcock Presents*, Hitchcock became the first director-as-star since Chaplin, and the only director then working in Hollywood whose name on a movie was likely to boost it at the box-office. Movies such as *Rear Window* (1954), *Vertigo* (1958) and *North by Northwest* (1959) guaranteed their audiences suspense by propelling them, along with their characters, into a malevolently chaotic world. They appeared to take a sadistic pleasure in manipulating audience emotion, and uncovering the guilt, madness and sexual obsession lurking beneath the placid surface of American normality.

Although it is an exaggeration to suggest that any one movie could represent the end of Classical Hollywood, Hitchcock's *Psycho* (1960) would come as close as any. Taking to new extremes many tendencies of the previous decade *Psycho* systematically violated the certainties upon which the

Alfred Hitchcock described Psycho *as 'a fun picture ... it's rather like taking [the audience] through the haunted house at the fairground.' Film critics have not necessarily concurred with the director's view, but most have agreed that it is 'clearly a seminal work ... Since* Psycho, *the Hollywood cinema has implicitly recognized horror as both American and familial.' (Robin Wood)*

Classical Hollywood audience had been encouraged to base its confidence. In a move that would prove enormously influential, it brought horror home to small-town America, to the family and to the bathroom. For its heroine (Janet Leigh) there was to be no ending, happy or otherwise — the great secret which the publicity campaign surrounding the movie's release was at pains to protect was that the leading character in whom the audience would have innocently invested the greater part of its sympathy and attention was to be murdered in Hollywood's most famous shower scene, less than half-way into the movie. This was not merely a violation of the conventions concerning screen violence, but of the narrative codes whereby the standardized Hollywood product had made movie-going a reliable, comprehensible and, above all, repeatable experience since the 1920s. With the climax coming too violently and too soon, the audience was offered no clear moral direction concerning the remaining characters, save a growing suspicion that the villain might be the victim, and that the director did not have their welfare at heart. In an important sense, therefore, it became *un*safe to go to the movies, as Hollywood emerged into its 'post-Classical' phase.

SUMMARY

The post-Second World War period saw the production of the Hollywood *film noir*, with distinctive visual motifs and a more noticeably cynical or threatening content, in which the paranoid hero featured prominently.

Hollywood's popularity and capacity for influence brought it to the attention of the House Committee on Un-American Activities and many personnel were blacklisted as former communists or sympathizers. This, together with extreme developments in science, further encouraged an aesthetic of paranoia even as Hollywood attempted to champion the values of home and the suburbs.

The introduction of television required Hollywood to redefine itself in order to keep its market share of the leisure dollar. After experimenting with various gimmicks, the industry addressed itself to the most rapidly expanding consumer group, who were socially inclined to find entertainment outside the home: teenagers.

As popular concern grew, Hollywood began to confirm its own suspicions about the nuclear family while further distancing itself from the restrictions experienced by television; the post-Classical box-office appeal of 'unpleasure' was heralded by movies such as *Psycho*.

6 HOLLYWOOD SINCE 1960

By the 1960s, the imperatives and the aesthetics of Classical Hollywood had largely shifted into television, the mass entertainment medium to which America had now become habituated. With the destabilizing of the old studio production system, following the Paramount decision, the Hollywood majors concentrated on differentiating their product with increasingly spectacular budgets, leaving routine production to the television serials. Despite the equally spectacular failure of the most expensive film yet made, *Cleopatra* (1963), the studios persisted in the strategy of high-budget epic production, preferring to base their confidence on the extraordinary success of *The Sound of Music* (1965), which proved difficult to repeat. As the industry struggled through the decade to rediscover a formula that would win back the domestic audience, it became increasingly reliant on the foreign market, responsible for 50 per cent of its earnings and now also a market for American television.

With the situation more stable abroad than at home, Hollywood turned to making movies overseas — 'runaway productions' — and in some cases internationalized its casts. After 1960 it became progressively more difficult to sustain definitions of media production in nationalist terms, or to argue that American movies represented a distinctively American set of ideas or political doctrine. But if the idea of Hollywood, and the imaginary America it represented, became irreversibly internationalized, the profits from the international film industry still found their way back to the American economy. American dominance of distribution companies, and widespread investment in foreign film-making, ensured that profits continued to accrue even when foreign product was being distributed. It is worth remembering that billion dollar industries generate as much support for their governments in terms of tax revenue as they may in terms of political or social ideas.

As the remaining studios were assimilated into larger American conglomerates (Paramount being bought up by Gulf & Western, with interests primarily in steel, mining and plastics, for example), some of the industry's internal structures came under pressure. In 1967, with audience figures improving for the first time since 1946, *The Graduate* and *Bonnie and Clyde* enjoyed the kind of success for which the industry had been hoping. Both addressed the changing tolerances of a domestic audience whose family entertainment needs were already safely taken care of by television. In 1968 the Production Code was replaced by a ratings system, and this made possible the more explicit representation of sex and violence, within the new restricted categories, under the guise of 'realism'. Movies with this draw card were also able to return to a lower budgetary scale and, as it became clear that the family audience had transmuted into the youth audience, with a significant increase in attendance among 18–25 year olds, movies such as *Easy*

Advertisements for Bonnie and Clyde *appealed to the youth audience of the late 1960s with this description of the protagonists: 'They're young. They're in love. And they kill people.'*

Rider (1969) catered to the new post-teen consumer by extending and adapting the low-budget 'schlock' aesthetics of the drive-in teenpics.

The rise of independent production of this kind alerted the market to the possible profitability of new directors and new modes of movie-making. The early 1970s saw a short-lived 'Renaissance' in Hollywood production when the hope was briefly entertained that increasingly explicit sex and violence might lead, within the logic of an anti-establishment aesthetic, to a new political or 'art' status for the Hollywood movie, without consequent loss of commercial viability. During this period American universities also began to offer film courses, which appeared to validate the movies' claim to institutional respectability. At the same time as these claims to political radicalism or high cultural significance were being made, however, the mushrooming pornography industry was taking advantage of the new ratings system which had defined a market niche for the explicit sex movie, and for a few years in the early 1970s some of this industry's products, such as *Deep Throat* (1972), found their way into the nation's movie theatres.

Although the Renaissance failed to live up to expectations, Hollywood initially preserved the capacity for limited self-criticism and commentary upon other American institutions. With individual stars becoming increasingly influential, or 'bankable', to the extent that their presence gave some financial security to movies with otherwise difficult content, Hollywood began to examine its own institutional and cultural significance in 'revisionist' movies. *The Wild Bunch* (1969), *McCabe and Mrs Miller* (1971) and *Ulzana's Raid* (1972) questioned the assumptions of earlier Westerns, for instance. The revelations of the Watergate scandals and the failed war in Vietnam damaged public confidence in democratic structures, and although Hollywood did not discuss Vietnam openly until the end of the 1970s, the institutional crisis in both domestic and foreign policy was projected across a range of 'disaster' movies in various forms. Any radical critique, however, was dissipated in the narration of highly individualized tales of neurosis and disillusionment.

This depoliticization is hardly surprising: popular movies may well function as frameworks within which specific anxieties can be expressed, but they can seldom be satisfactorily treated as fixed, transparent metaphors, each with a single, correct interpretation. Commercial factors require that even a movie as overtly political as *All the President's Men* (1976) should also appeal as a star vehicle for Robert Redford and Dustin Hoffman. And while it is possible, and useful, to read the blockbuster movie of the decade as an attack on incompetence, denial and corruption among elected officials, with particular reference to Watergate (which came to a head in 1974), *Jaws* (1975) is none the less very much a movie about a shark.

Obscured by the Renaissance and post-Renaissance mirage of a return to low-budget independent production, individual creativity and 'art', the industry's investment stakes rose with the production of each blockbuster speculation, continuing the pattern of conglomeration and diversification of holdings. While most Hollywood movies are now produced by independent production companies they continue to be financed and distributed by the major companies, which are themselves components of multinational media conglomerates such as Time-Warner Inc. or Rupert Murdoch's News Corporation, which owns Twentieth Century-Fox. The Japanese electronics corporation Sony's purchase of Columbia Pictures in 1989 signalled a likely trend in the merging of 'hardware' and 'software' concerns, a development at least as significant as the implications the purchase had for the further internationalization of American culture (Schatz, 1993, pp.8–36).

The concentration of media ownership has not been significantly alleviated by the changes in technology which the industry has experienced since 1980. Although the video-cassette appears to increase consumer choice at least about the circumstances of consumption, and thus to challenge the very nature of cinema as public entertainment, the economic reality is that the conglomerates have found ways of repeat-selling the same products by redistributing them in video form throughout both the domestic and foreign markets. In some cases, movies may actually 'première' on video, bypassing the cinema altogether. Television presales have also become increasingly significant in the guarantee of financial backing for a project, with the result that Hollywood movies in one format or another are now really quite difficult to miss. Extending this saturation logic, the movie itself is now accompanied by a package of associated merchandising: the novelization (or the reprint, with movie stills, of an original novel), the book-of-the-filming, the soundtrack, clothing, confectionery, toys, stationery and so on.

The content of Hollywood's recent movies, however, provides scant evidence of these changes to its corporate structure and product range. Perhaps the closest any movie has come to analysing contemporary Hollywood is *Wall Street* (1987) (Plate 4.5), not concerned with the movie industry as such, but with the transnational and largely abstract management of capital, which made infamous the corporate ethic: 'Greed is good'. *Wall Street* explains the apparent paradox of the 'art market', which is more about 'market' than 'art', in terms that have some consequence for our understanding of Hollywood as an essential unit in a mature capitalist economy: 'The illusion has become real, and the more real it becomes, the more desperately they want it. Capitalism at its finest'. This is not to suggest that the illusion has been mistaken for the object it represents, but that the illusion (the painting, the movie) has acquired enormous material significance in its own right.

This returns us to one aspect of Hollywood's 'realism': to what extent can we read Hollywood's movies for signs of contemporary America, when the essence of movie-making is not to inform but to entertain? As Hortense Powdermaker noted, 'minority groups, insecure and fearful in general, pass over the usual Hollywood stereotyping of all peoples, noting only when one of their own group appears untruthfully portrayed' (Powdermaker, 1950, p.72). Hollywood in the 1980s dispatched America's ethnic and political conflicts into deep space or projected them into the future, constructing elaborate technological dystopias in which the fruits of human endeavour became thrillingly excessive, while the consequences of aggression were effectively depoliticized. The question of fair or equal representation is clearly redundant when the minority concerned are chest-busting aliens, for example. But Hollywood's representational practice is only fractionally more significant when the minority group is identifiable or 'real', even though particular movies continue to act as catalysts for protest groups. As one critic argues, the descendants of Thalberg's 'sophisticated' audience 'know that life isn't like the movies, that Hollywood distorts and simplifies in order to dramatize. There's a big difference between suspending disbelief and believing everything you see' (Young, 1992).

SUMMARY

After exploring the market potential of the spectacular, big-budget production, Hollywood turned its attention elsewhere, both to the foreign market, and to the possibility of greater investment in overseas production. Nationally, the remaining studios were absorbed into larger industrial conglomerates with diverse business interests such as Gulf & Western (Paramount).

At the same time, there was a brief rise in independent production, and, with the introduction of a ratings system to replace the Production Code in 1968, the possibility arose that increasingly explicit movies might allow Hollywood to be both commercially successful and politically anti-establishment.

Business imperatives determined the outcome of this negotiation, as new technologies, particularly video, came on to the market, and as media ownership became further concentrated under multi-media conglomerates such as Time-Warner Inc.

We therefore need to find a way of understanding Hollywood's products which takes into account the full complexity of economic and social interests which actually enable movie-making to take place.

7 STUDYING HOLLYWOOD: THE APPEAL OF GENRE CRITICISM

Generic categories appeal to film scholars principally because they appear to provide a consistency within Hollywood cinema that withstands the interventions or intentions of individual film-makers. A generic framework makes it possible to discuss the inscription of collective social and historical meanings within particular movies. The search for America in Hollywood's utopian reconstruction of the known world is made much easier by the identification of these recurrent preoccupations and, at a sophisticated level of analysis, by observing the ways in which they change over time. For audiences, the appeal of the genre movie is the opportunity it presents to add to an accumulating store of knowledge, and to confirm or revise existing expectations. In this sense, its reward to the attentive, knowledgeable viewer is similar to that offered by the star vehicle to the fan. Over time, the frame of reference grows ever more dense and extensive, although we should bear in mind that viewers forget as well as remember, and that the whole field of generic knowledge is unlikely to be available to any given audience, even to *aficionados*.

Of all Hollywood's output, Westerns have been the easiest to identify generically. There is widespread agreement that this category, characterized by exceptionally clear visual markers (costumes, setting) and gestural codes, formulaic plots and ritualized performances, is the place where America negotiates with itself over the nature of its occupation of the continent, its priorities in terms of individual, family and community values, and its relationship to progress, civilization and government (see Plate 4.6). In its discussion of men taming a wilderness and transforming it into a garden, for example, the Western mythologizes the notion of American individualism as a civilizing force, and yet at various times, the values represented by nature and by culture are changed according to contemporary preoccupations. In *Broken Arrow* (1950) and *Dances with Wolves* (1990), for instance, civilization's malaise is registered through a celebration of the 'natural' nobility of its savage opposite, the Indian.

The persistence of the Western, which made up 25 per cent of Hollywood's output between 1926 and 1967, has led some critics to look on it as a transhistorical phenomenon. Writing in 1953, French critic André Bazin argued that the genre addressed basic human realities through the mythologization of a particular phase of American history: 'we find at the source of the Western the ethics of the epic and even of tragedy ... because of the superhuman level of its heroes, and the legendary magnitude of their feats of valor' (Bazin, 1967, p.147). As an epic it works determinedly towards its final chapter: the shoot-out, the last stand, the rescue of the captives. According to Robert Warshow, the morality play character of these dramatic resolutions gave 'the figure of the Westerner an apparent moral clarity which corresponds to the clarity of his physical image against his bare landscape; initially at any rate, the Western movie presents itself as being without mystery, its whole universe comprehended in what we see on the screen' (Warshow, 1985, p.438). In its key structuring opposition between values associated with individualism (the outlaw) and those representing the community (the lawman), the Western is seen to address a specifically American cultural anxiety about the need to preserve both sets of ideals by dramatizing the conflict between the individual and society at the historical moment when America was formed as a modern nation. These dramatizations have changed as the political or cultural concerns of American society have shifted, so that the history of the Western is often also understood as an allegorical history of twentieth-century America: a history in which generic evolution is seen to trace a line of thematic development from 'straightforward storytelling to self-conscious formalism' (Schatz, 1981, p.38).

Many Westerns themselves deal with the inevitability of historical change, and with the exclusion of the frontier hero from the society his actions have brought into existence. At the end of *Stagecoach* (1939), the Sheriff acquiesces in the outlaw's escape from 'the blessings of civilization', while *My Darling Clementine*'s (1946) outlaw hero Doc Holliday is redeemed by his death. In such Classical Westerns the official hero and the outlaw hero overcome their differences in a larger battle to protect civilization from a greater savagery (Ray, 1985, pp.59–66). In *The Man Who Shot Liberty Valance* (1962, and directed, like the two Classical films, by John Ford) the death of the individualist hero is greeted with melancholy regret and a strongly nostalgic awareness of the price paid for the democratic populism (perfectly embodied by James Stewart) that replaces him. But by the 1970s, as America experienced turmoil at home and overseas, 'revisionist' Westerns such as *Pat Garrett and Billy the Kid* (1973) argued that the threat to the values of the West no longer lay in the savagery of nature, but in the corruption and corporate self-interest of civilization. The heroic frontier community has been replaced by something more meagre: the Santa Fe 'Ring' who hire Garrett to track down Billy, and then themselves kill Garrett when the job is done.

Although production declined throughout the 1980s, critical and academic interest in the Western eventually endowed the genre with sufficient cultural respectability for Clint Eastwood's *Unforgiven* to win the Oscar for Best Picture in 1992, only the second Western to do so since *Cimarron* in 1931. Widely acclaimed as a masterly revision of the genre which has already been extensively revised, *Unforgiven* pays repeated homage to previous Westerns and their creators. Eastwood, its ageing and compromised protagonist, is a focus for the movie's self-consciously elegiac investigations into the nature of heroism and history-making, until he literally fades into the sunset of legend in the final shot. More emphatically, however, the movie asserts a contemporary relevance in its discussion of the moral pitfalls of gunfighting, thus offering the concerned liberal audience a politically correct position from which to enjoy the hero's triumph in the shootout. Of course, since much of the Western's appeal is to nostalgia, it is hardly surprising that the genre has been declared dead many times in its history. But it has never, until now, died of respectability.

This form of generic history is, however, very selective in the thematically resonant movies from which it chooses to generalize. Most analysis of the genre has been concentrated around a relatively small group of A-budget movies made between 1945 and 1965, and has largely ignored the great majority of Westerns made on low budgets for the bottom half of double bills. This suggests the extent to which criticism has understood genre in Hollywood quite differently from the industry itself, which categorizes its product by budget size and by the audience sector to whom it is primarily appealing, organizing its production schedules around cycles and sequels rather than genres as such. Not surprisingly, the two sets of categories frequently fail to correspond, and in some cases directly contradict one another. In complete contrast to the identity which movie *criticism* assigns to the maligned category of 'melodrama', for example, the movie *industry* defined action movies, crime stories and thrillers as 'melodramas'. 'Women's films' such as *Stella Dallas* (1937) were usually called 'dramas'; far from being disparaged, as subsequent criticism has assumed, the 'woman's film' was a relatively high-status and high-budget category of production, with only musicals and 'prestige' pictures seen as being more important.

In the case of the Western, production declined precipitously after 1970, with barely a handful being made during the 1980s. Hollywood's apparent abandonment of what had been its most common genre raised questions about the critical arguments that claimed that the Western was central to the expression of an American mythology. Had the mythology changed, so that the Western was no longer relevant? Had the mythology migrated elsewhere, to other genres, and if so, had it changed in the process? Or had Hollywood somehow stopped articulating American mythology? It is possible to detect Western-style elements in any movie where civilization is threatened, as undeniably it is in *Aliens* (1986), for example. We can even extend our investigation retrospectively, and argue that the self-sacrificial exit of the 'uncivilizable' hero in order to preserve the sanctity of the hearth is as much as a feature of *A Star is Born* (1937), in which the dissolute ex-star Frederic March drowns himself to prevent his wife destroying her successful career, as it is of *The Searchers* (1956), in which John Wayne, his quest for his niece completed, returns to the desert out of which he came. At some stage in our pursuit of generic features, however, we have to concede that we risk

John Wayne, icon of American masculinity, as the complex racist Ethan Edwards in The Searchers, *contemplating the evidence of a war party attack on his brother's family. At the end of his quest to rescue his niece from the degradation of miscegenation, Edwards himself cannot re-enter civilization, but is doomed to 'wander forever between the winds', like the Indian whose corpse he has earlier mutilated*

classifying most of Hollywood's movies as thinly or thickly disguised Westerns, when perhaps it would be more accurate to define all of them, including the Westerns, simply as Hollywood's means of reproducing its most popular motifs in order to continue to entertain its international audience.

Throughout its history Hollywood has noted our wishes and fulfilled them. It is in this sense that the behaviour of the Western is neither distinctive nor definitive, but rather is consistent with Hollywood entertainment as a whole. We have not been required to believe in Hollywood's description of America or its version of history for longer than the duration of the movie. No matter how vividly we have experienced its imaginary landscapes and utopian possibilities, we leave the cinema reminding ourselves that what we have seen was 'only a movie'. Our relationship to these fictions is, however, complicated by our dismissal of them as mere entertainment. Hollywood's most profound significance lies in its ability to turn pleasure into a product we can buy in the entertainment supermarket: capitalism at its finest. We therefore need to attend closely to the industrial and economic processes involved in the manufacture and marketing of these transient images, as well as to their content, if we are to appreciate the full complexity of our relationship to Hollywood, and Hollywood's relationship to American culture.

SUMMARY

One way in which scholars have approached Hollywood is to classify its products according to a generic system which bears some resemblance to the industry's own sense of production cycles and trends, but which elsewhere departs from industrial concepts over genres such as 'melodrama', for which entirely conflicting definitions exist.

The Western has a particular appeal for genre criticism as it is unusually easy to define and identify. It has therefore been possible to claim that the Western is the location of Hollywood's most consistent articulation of American mythologies and anxieties. Recurrent themes include tensions between individual and community, nature and civilization, heroism and domesticity.

This interpretation of the Western's significance is problematized by the actual decline in production of Westerns in the post-Classical period. Has Hollywood stopped articulating the founding myths of American culture? Are these now being articulated in a neighbouring genre? Or are all Hollywood movies merely variations on the Western in different settings?

Returning to the industrial account of Hollywood as an institution, we argue that the resolution to this paradox lies in Hollywood's history of turning the pleasure of entertainment into a product which we will repeatedly consume. The Western in its heyday was a particularly successful example of this, and it is therefore not so much the definitive Hollywood movie type, but is consistent with Hollywood entertainment as a whole.

REFERENCES

Bazin, A. (1967) 'The evolution of the Western' in Gray, H. (trans.) *What is Cinema? vol.2*, Berkeley, University of California Press.

Dyer, R. (1977) 'Entertainment and Utopia', *Movie*, no.24, pp.2–13.

Geduld, H.M. (ed.) (1971) *Focus on D.W. Griffith*, Englewood Cliffs, Prentice-Hall.

Hays, W. (1932) Draft of '1932 Annual Report of the MPPDA', Will H. Hays Archive, Department of Special Collections, Indiana State Library, Indianapolis (unpublished).

Joy, J. (1931) Jason Joy to James Wingate, 5 February. Production Code Administration Case file, *Little Caesar*, Department of Special Collections, Margaret Herrick Library of the Academy of Motion Picture Arts and Sciences, Los Angeles (unpublished).

Lynd, R.S. and Lynd, H.M. (1929) *Middletown: a Study in Modern American Culture*, New York, Harcourt, Brace & World.

Maltby, R. (ed.) (1989) *Dreams for Sale: Popular Culture in the 20th Century*, London, Harrap.

Mast, G. (ed.) (1982) *The Movies in Our Midst: Documents in the Cultural History of Film in America*, Chicago, University of Chicago Press.

Moley, R. (1946) *The Hays Office*, Indianapolis, Bobbs-Merrill.

Motion Picture Herald (1936) 'Whose business is the motion picture?', 11 February, pp.15–16.

Powdermaker, H. (1950) *Hollywood the Dream Factory: an Anthropologist Looks at the Movie-Makers*, Boston, Little, Brown.

Ray, R.B. (1985) *A Certain Tendency of the Hollywood Cinema (1930–1980)*, Princeton, Princeton University Press.

Ricketson, F.H. (1938) *The Management of Motion Pictures*, New York, McGraw-Hill.

Schatz, T. (1981) *Hollywood Genres: Formulas, Filmmaking, and the Studio System*, New York, Random House.

Schatz, T. (1993) 'The new Hollywood' in Collins, J., Radner, H. and Collins, A.P. (eds) *Film Theory Goes to the Movies*, London, Routledge.

Schickel, R. (1984) *D.W. Griffith and the Birth of Film*, London, Pavillion.

Sklar, R. (1975) *Movie-Made America: a Cultural History of American Movies*, New York, Random House.

Thalberg, I. (1930) 'General principles to govern the preparation of a revised Code of Ethics for talking pictures', Production Code file, Motion Picture Association of America Archive, New York (unpublished draft).

Walker, A. (1968) *Sex in the Movies*, Harmondsworth, Penguin.

Warshow, R. (1985) 'The Westerner' in Mast, G. and Cohen, M. (eds) *Film Theory and Criticism: Introductory Readings*, New York, Oxford University Press.

Young, T. (1992) 'The lust picture show', *Guardian*, 17 May, p.28.

FURTHER READING

See Sklar (1975) in the references.

Balio, T. (ed.) (1990) *Hollywood in the Age of Television*, Cambridge, Mass., Unwin Hyman.

Bordwell, D., Staiger, J. and Thompson, K. (1985) *The Classical Hollywood Cinema: Film Style and Mode of Production to 1960*, London, Routledge & Kegan Paul.

Gledhill, C. (ed.) (1992) *Stardom: Industry of Desire*, London, Routledge.

Schatz, T. (1988) *The Genius of the System: Hollywood Filmmaking in the Studio Era*, New York, Pantheon.

IDEOLOGY AND DIVERSITY IN AMERICAN TELEVISION

Andrew Goodwin ★

One can begin to understand a peculiarity of the American way of producing and consuming television by looking at an issue of the weekly *TV Guide* which many households use to pick their way through the schedule. *TV Guide* has been published by Murdoch Magazines since 1988 when Rupert Murdoch's News Corporation bought Triangle Publications. It has approximately 230 pages of which 170 are devoted to daily programme listings and a further fifteen or so detail each movie shown on television during the week. There is so much listed in *TV Guide*, and so little space, even with the typeface shrunk almost beyond the scope of human vision, that many of the descriptions are extremely brief, often amounting to no more than the title of the show. In any given time slot, say 6 p.m. to 6.30 p.m., there can be 25 listings, and these do not include many of the cable stations available, or any reference to satellite TV services. To help viewers find their way round the schedule the guide offers a two page grid for each evening (see Figure 5.1). Typically there could be 50 or more services included here, although this does not include all the television coming into the home if cable TV is available.

On a given evening a typical viewer of American television might have about 500 programme options. It is worth remembering that in these circumstances, which, as we will see, are likely to appear absurdly straightforward when compared to the technological choices facing viewers in the next century, there is an important sense in which television in America seems not only abundant beyond belief, but also beyond anyone's control, including that of the putative viewer. Increasingly, TV technologies are focusing on ways of making the choices more accessible: the remote control unit, gadgets which allow easier programming of video-cassette recorders, and TV screens with additional windows which permit the viewer to preview one channel while watching another. Indeed, there is now a cable TV channel, the Prevue Channel, devoted exclusively to telling the viewer what is on the other channels. But the truthful answer to the question, what's on television?, is often: who knows? The bewilderment tells us something important about America's increasingly noisy and overcrowded televisual market-place.

This chapter will offer a guide to the historical development of television in the US, in order to explain how its institutions operate. In doing so we will confront the issue of the relationship between free market economics and cultural diversity. Does a television system run for profit and funded by

Monday Evening

	6:00	6:30	7:00	7:30	8:00	8:30
2	Married...	Murphy Brown	Cheers	Love Connection	Movie: *Romancing the Stone*	
3	NBC News	News	Fresh Prince	Blossom	Movie: *Bloodlines, Pt. 1*	
4	News	Entmt. Tonight	Fresh Prince	Blossom	Movie: *Bloodlines, Pt. 1*	
5	News	Current Affair	Evening Shade	Hearts Afire	Murphy Brown	Love & War
6	Business Report	MacNeil, Lehrer	California's Gold		Travels	
7	News	Jeopardy!	Wheel of Fortune		FBI: The Untold	Amer. Detective
8	News	Jeopardy!	Wheel of Fortune		Fresh Prince	Blossom
9	MacNeil, Lehrer		Business Report	Being Served?	Travels	
10	News	Wheel of Fortune	Jeopardy!	Cops	Evening Shade	Hearts Afire
11	News	Entmt. Tonight	Inside Edition	Current Affair	FBI: The Untold	Amer. Detective
13	News	Hard Copy	Current Affair	Entmt. Tonight	FBI: The Untold	Amer. Detective
14	Noticias	Noticiero	Mágico Juventud		Capricho	
20	Mission: Impossible		In the Heat of the Night		Nat'l Geographic: On Assignment	
22	Shining Time	Long Ago...	Ghostwriter	Club Connect	In the Mix	
26	Grecian Spotlight	ABS/CBN News	News		News	News
31	Golden Girls	Designing Women	Roseanne	Dear John	Movie: *Babylon 5*	
35	Love Connection	Studs	Roseanne	Designing Women	Movie: *Loose Cannons*	
36	Hunter				Movie: *Babylon 5*	
38	Phillippine Newswatch	Vien Thao	Today's Japan	News	Chinese Mini-Series	Chinese Sitcom
42	Cheers	Cosby Show	Roseanne	Cheers	Movie: *Romancing the Stone*	
44	Roseanne	Roseanne	Star Trek: The Next Generation		Movie: *The Outlaw Josey Wales*	
46	News	Rush Limbaugh	Crimewatch		Evening Shade	Hearts Afire
48	Noticias	Noticiero	Guadalupe		Kassandra	
50	Star Trek: The Next Generation		News	Golden Girls	M*A*S*H	
60	Mystery!		Being Served?	EastEnders (7:35)	American Experience (8:15)	
60	Today's Japan	John McLaughlin	Destinos		Gardens of the World	Mystery!
67	Noticias	Noticiero	Mágico Juventud		Capricho	

CABLE-TV CHANNELS

	6:00	6:30	7:00	7:30	8:00	8:30
A&E	Sherlock Holmes Mysteries		Lovejoy		Evening at the Improv	
AMC	Movie: *The Big Lift*				Movie: *The Buccaneer*	
BRV	Movie: *David and Lisa* (5:00)		John Neumeier		Movie: *May Fools*	
CNN	Larry King Live		News		Sports	Moneyline
CMT	Stand-Up	Almost Live!	Short Attention Span Theater		Big Laff Off	Comics Only
DSC	Europe: This Great Notion		Kayapo		Natural World	
ESN	College Basketball (4:30)	College Basketball: Oklahoma State at Oklahoma				SportsCenter
FAM	Life Goes On		Waltons		Young Riders	
LIF	Supermarket	Shop/Drop	Unsolved Mysteries		L.A. Law	
	Joms		Liquid TV	Half Hour Comedy	Classic MTV	Prime Time
MTV	...Would You Do?	Wild & Crazy Kids	Looney Tunes	Bullwinkle	Get Smart	Superman
NIK	College Basketball (5:00)		Warriors Pregame	NBA Basketball: 76ers at Warriors		
TNN	Movie: *Coma* (5:05)				Movie: *Rape and Marriage: The Rideout Case* (7:20)	
	Nashville Now		Ralph Emery		Club Dance	
	NBA: Celtics at Pistons (5:00)		Movie: *The Spikes Gang* (7:20)		Murder, She Wrote	
USA	Gladiators		Quantum Leap		Movie: *The Spirit of 76*	

PREMIUM CHANNELS

	6:00	6:30	7:00	7:30	8:00	8:30
DIS	Movie: *Care Bears Movie II: A New Generation*			W'derland	Avonlea	Making Their Mark (8:50)
HBO	Movie: *The Empire Strikes Back*					Movie →
	Movie: *Just One of the Guys* (6:15)				Movie: *All-American Murder*	Movie →
MAX	Movie: *Hang 'Em High*				Movie: *Sudden Impact*	
SHO	Movie: *The Search for Signs of Intelligent Life in the Universe*				Movie: *Once upon a Crime*	
TMC	Movie: *The Adventures of Robin Hood* (5:30)				Movie: *The Spirit of '76*	

PAY-PER-VIEW CHANNELS

	6:00	6:30	7:00	7:30	8:00	8:30
VC1	Movie: *Single White Female*				Movie: *Raising Cain*	
VC2	Movie: *Single White Female* (5:00)				Movie: *Single White Female*	
VC3	Movie: *Single White Female* (5:00)				Movie: *Single White Female*	

San Francisco Metropolitan Edition

March 1, 1993

	9:00	9:30	10:00	10:30	11:00	11:30
2	Movie (Cont.)		News		Cheers	Murphy Brown
3	Movie (Cont.)		News		News	Tonight
4	Movie (Cont.)		News	Hard Copy	News	Tonight
5	Movie (Cont.)		News		News	Sweating Bullets
6	Northern Exposure		Renaissance		Charlie Rose	
6	American Experience				Charlie Rose	
7	Movie: *They've Taken Our Children, Part 1*				News	Nightline
8	Movie: *Bloodlines: Murder in the Family, Part 1*				News	Tonight (11:35)
9	Lucy Jarvis Classics		Viewpoints		Charlie Rose	
10	Murphy Brown	Love & War	Northern Exposure		News	Arsenio Hall
11	Movie: *They've Taken Our Children*				News	Nightline
13	Movie: *They've Taken Our Children*				News	Nightline
14	Cara sucia		Cristina		Noticiero	Los Gómez
20	Twilight Zone		WKRP	Bob Newhart	Untouchables	Off the air
22	Nova		MacNeil, Lehrer		NHK News	RAI News
26	Cantonese Drama		Mandarin Drama		Golden Girls	Designing Women
31	News		News	Night Court	Arsenio Hall	Comm. Progs.
35	Movie (Cont.)		News		News	
36	Religious Prog.		Wonder Years	All in the Family	News	Comm. Progs.
38						
42	Movie (Cont.)		News		Married...	Star Trek...
44	Movie (Cont.)		News	Arsenio Hall		Montel Williams
46	Murphy Brown	Love & War	Northern Exposure		News	Sweating Bullets
48	Película: *Será anunciada*				Película: *Será anunciada*	
50	M*A*S*H (Cont.)		Headline News		Commercial Programs	
60	American Experience (Cont.)		American Experience (10:15)		We Do the Work	
60	Discovering Mexico		Washington Week	To the Contrary		
67	Cara sucia		Cristina		Noticiero	Los Gómez

CABLE-TV CHANNELS

	9:00	9:30	10:00	10:30	11:00	11:30
A&E	David L. Wolper Presents		Sherlock Holmes Mysteries		Lovejoy	
AMC	Movie: *The Snake Pit*					
BRV	Movie (Cont.)		Movie: *David and Lisa*			
CNN	News	Crossfire	Larry King Live		News	Sports
CMT	A-List	Kids in the Hall	Saturday Night		Stand-Up	Whose Line?
DSC	Europe: This Great Notion		Kayapo		In Wildness	
ESN	College Basketball: UNLV at New Mexico State				Sports Reporters	SportsCenter
FAM	Father Dowling Mysteries		700 Club		Screecrow and Mrs. King	
LIF	Movie: *Shattered Innocence*				Thirtysomething	
	Prime Time (Cont.)		Sex in the '90s		Half Hour Comedy	Grind
MTV	Mary Tyler Moore	Dick Van Dyke	Dragnet	Alfred Hitchcock	Lucy Show	F Troop
NIK	NBA Basketball (Cont.)		Hockey Week	Inside Skiing	NBA Basketball: 76ers at Warriors	
TNN	National Geographic Explorer (9:20)				Movie: *Ironclads* (11:20)	
	Nashville Now		Nashville Now		Ralph Emery	
	Miller & Company					
	Movie: *The Courtship of Eddie's Father* (9:20)				Screecrow and Mrs. King	
USA	WWF Wrestling		Matlix		MacGyver	

PREMIUM CHANNELS

	9:00	9:30	10:00	10:30	11:00	11:30
DIS	Movie: *Casablanca*				Main Event: Frank Sinatra in Concert	
HBO	Movie: *The Wild One* (Cont.)		Movie: *Conquest of the Planet of the Apes*		Movie	
	Movie (Cont.)		Movie: *Dance with Death*		Iceman Tapes	Movie (11:50)
MAX	Movie (Cont.)		Clint Eastwood		Movie: *Pale Rider*	Movie (11:45)
SHO	Movie (Cont.)	Jim Carrey (9:35)	Movie: *Ultimate Desires* (10:05)		Movie: *Irreclads* (11:20)	
TMC	Movie: *The Rapture*				Movie: *The Long Good Friday*	Movie (11:50)

PAY-PER-VIEW CHANNELS

	9:00	9:30	10:00	10:30	11:00	11:30
VC1	Movie (Cont.)		Movie: *Stay Tuned*			
VC2	Movie: *Single White Female*				Movie: *Single White Female*	
VC3	Movie: *Single White Female*				Movie: *Single White Female*	

San Francisco Metropolitan Edition

Figure 5.1 An evening's programmes from TV Guide

advertising revenue somehow guarantee or enable social pluralism? And are there questions other than diversity at stake? The chapter will also explore the problem of national stability in the US and the role of television as an agent for social legitimation. These issues will be considered in part through an encounter with some historical trends in programming, a short case study of MTV: Music Television, and some comments on the future of American television.

1 DEVELOPMENT OF THE AMERICAN MODEL: ANARCHY IN THE USA

Today, because of the nation's size and diversity, the mass media are central to any understanding of American culture and society. It could be argued that the media are fundamental in any advanced, industrialized, or post-industrial, society. But the United States is unique in being a technologically sophisticated nation spanning several time zones, in which questions of national identity remain fluid. American television reflects this temporal fragmentation: it should be noted that TV programmes are not necessarily broadcast simultaneously. But television also reflects a deep need to construct unity, both around a national identity and around the practices of consumerism. These issues of politics and culture can be addressed when we have understood something about the structures and economic organization of American television.

The history of television in the US is a story of the emergence and consolidation of centralized centres of cultural power, followed by the erosion and diffusion of that power. In this respect, its development is surprisingly similar to the chronology of TV in the UK, where the authority of the BBC–ITV duopoly has been diminished in recent years by challenges from Channel 4, home video, satellite and cable television. The specifics of the US case are, however, quite different and considerably more complex.

1.1 THE BIG THREE

The centralized power brokers in US television were, until recently, the so-called 'Big Three' networks which broadcast terrestrially: the National Broadcasting Corporation (NBC), Columbia Broadcasting System (CBS), and the American Broadcasting Corporation (ABC).

- NBC was created in 1926, following RCA's pioneering work in the development of television technology (prompted in large part by the ambitious vision of David Sarnoff). NBC was co-owned by RCA, General Electric and Westinghouse. It began broadcasting from the Empire State Building in 1933 and introduced commercial television at the 1939 World's Fair in New York. In 1959 it broadcast the first regular colour programming, beginning with the series *Bonanza*. NBC's heyday was the 1980s when it screened ambitious and popular TV series such as *Hill*

Street Blues, Saturday Night Live and *Late Night with David Letterman.* NBC is now solely owned by General Electric.

- CBS was created in 1928, when William S. Paley bought the Columbia Phonograph Company and immediately changed its name. CBS has been the home of many classic TV shows and personalities, such as the Edward Murrow–Fred Friendly current affairs programme *See It Now,* which ran from 1951 to 1958, the show *Face the Nation* in which leading politicians spoke with journalists, Walter Cronkite's evening news broadcasts, and classic situation comedies such as *I Love Lucy,* the 'rural' or 'idiot' sitcoms such as *The Beverly Hillbillies* and the more sophisticated programming that followed this, like *The Mary Tyler Moore Show* and *Maude.* In recent years CBS has been saddled with the image of being the stuffiest of the Big Three, although it should be noted that it has been associated with many extremely controversial shows, such as *The Smothers Brothers Comedy Hour,* and *All in the Family,* the American equivalent of *Till Death Us Do Part.* CBS is now part-owned by Laurence Tisch, who has a controlling interest in the company.

- ABC was created in 1943 when NBC sold off its Blue network, one of its two radio networks (the other being the Red network), on the orders of the government-run Federal Communications Commission. Traditionally the least successful of the Big Three, ABC scored successes in the 1970s with its popular show *Happy Days* and its screening of the *Roots* mini series; in the 1980s ABC's *Roseanne* was consistently one of the highest rated shows. It is now owned by Capital Cities/ABC, a newspaper group.

Until the 1980s the Big Three dominated American television, holding onto a combined share of 90 per cent of the total TV audience as late as 1978 (Turow, 1992, p.2). They are each run for profit and funded exclusively via advertising. Advertising rates are negotiated on the basis of the size and sometimes composition of the audience. This information comes through the ratings systems, whereby each individual show is assigned ratings points and audience share. Ratings points are the number of households which tune into a given programme and audience share is the percentage of TV sets turned on which were tuned to a particular show.

Like many aspects of American culture, television is centred on localized, as opposed to national, institutions. The Federal Communications Act of 1934 established the local TV station as the entity legally responsible for all its output, regardless of the origin of programming. In practice, much of this programming is produced by the networks, because most of the local stations are 'affiliates'— they are attached to one of the Big Three who provide the bulk of the programmes, including such flagship shows as the evening news and most prime-time programming (everything screened from 8 p.m. to 11 p.m.; although some West Coast stations are experimenting with prime-time from 7 p.m. to 10 p.m.). On network affiliates, about 5–10 per cent of programming is locally produced, while 25–30 per cent comes from syndicators and 65 per cent from the networks (Becker and Roberts, 1992, p.317). Syndicators are independent producers who make programming such as game shows or one-off 'movies of the week' and sell them to local stations. Increasingly syndicators also produce situation comedies, talk shows, and 'infotainment' news shows like *Hard Copy* and *A Current Affair*. Most shows are syndicated nationally, so that while the local station is the focus of the American TV system, most of the shows that most people watch are the same across the country. Since only 5–10 per cent of programming is locally produced, the CBS affiliate in San Francisco, KPIX, for example, is likely to be screening programming that is very similar to WROC, the CBS affiliate in Rochester, NY.

A Public Broadcasting System (PBS) was established in 1967, through the Public Broadcasting Act. In ratings terms PBS is insignificant: a wag once observed that the audience for public TV is so tiny that you need a search warrant to find it. Like the *New York Times* or *Washington Post*, however, public TV forms an important element in élite culture, often screening prestigious British 'quality' drama and documentary programming. Among its more successful shows have been comedies such as *Fawlty Towers*, drama productions such as *Upstairs, Downstairs* (screened under the rubric of *Masterpiece Theater*) and its own children's programme *Sesame Street* (1968 début). PBS is a non-profit system funded by a grant from the government, by public institutions such as schools and universities, by private donations (some from individual viewers), and by corporate sponsorship. Like commercial TV, public television is federalized, with local stations showing a combination of locally produced, nationally produced and imported programming. Although public TV is non-commercial and does not carry advertising, the 'enhanced underwriting' giving credit to corporate sponsors increasingly resembles the format of the TV commercial.

1.2   CHALLENGES TO THE BIG THREE

Since the 1980s the power of the Big Three networks has been eroded on many fronts. One challenge came from the independents. Initially these were over-the-air stations which were unaffiliated with a network, and which almost exclusively screened syndicated programming, almost all of it comprising re-runs of series originally shown on the networks. Syndicated re-runs are another peculiarity of the American system. Following a successful first run in prime-time on a network, a popular situation comedy or game show may then go 'into syndication'. Here the rights to the repeats are sold to a syndicator and packages of the programme are then purchased by local stations across the nation. Consequently a popular programme like the sit-com *Murphy Brown* can be simultaneously available on a weekly basis as a first run show on the network and its affiliates, and then also seen as repeats, often on a daily basis, on local independent stations. Many independent stations schedule blocks of old sitcoms, back to back, for two or three hours at a time in late afternoon and early evening. The independent stations eventually built larger audiences by expanding from a purely over-the-air service with the arrival of cable television, a second key element in the decline of the networks.

Community Antenna Television Systems, which was originally the name given to cable television, used to pipe television into those communities who could not receive over-the-air broadcasts, perhaps because of geography. Eventually cable expanded into other markets, until it now covers 56 per cent of American households with over 50 million subscribers. Cable TV is provided by local cable operators who transmit both 'dedicated' cable networks and other network, affiliated, independent, and public TV services. 'Dedicated' cable systems are based on 'narrowcasting' — selecting a carefully targeted audience whose demographic profile is desirable for advertisers — unlike the Big Three, who have traditionally sought to maximize audiences. Dedicated types of programming include news (Headline News and Cable News Network: CNN), sports (ESPN and Sports Channel America), music (MTV), and movies (Home Box Office, Showtime and Cinemax). Exceptions are those services dedicated to one type of audience, such as Black Entertainment Television, which targets African-Americans with a mixture of news and light entertainment programming. The cable operators provide a 'basic' package which usually includes CNN, ESPN, the Arts and Entertainment network and other services. A small number of independents have been able to build national audiences via cable distribution. The most well-known of these 'superstations' is Ted Turner's WTBS in Atlanta.

The structure of the cable television industry, like broadcast TV, involves a separation between producers and distributors. While the cable networks compete to a certain extent — Home Box Office (HBO) and Showtime are rivals in the movie market-place; Bravo and the Arts and Entertainment network compete for 'quality' television audiences — the cable distributors are almost exclusively local monopolies. These local cable operators charge a fee to subscribers for the cable service. Local cable operators are financed through these revenues and also through local advertising. Viewers may opt to pay additional sums for 'subscription only' channels like HBO, the Disney Channel, and the adult Playboy channel, and consumers may also choose to pay an extra fee for special 'pay-per-view' live broadcasts of major sports events and rock concerts. The cable networks themselves are financed via a share of these additional payments, or through national advertising.

Other threats to the dominance of the Big Three are home video, satellite television, and the emergence of a fourth network, the Fox Broadcasting Corporation, owned by Murdoch's News Corporation. Fox TV began broadcasting in 1986, building its schedule in a shrewd and original manner, by initially programming for only two nights of the week. This enabled the new network to keep its costs down in its early and most financially vulnerable years. Fox increased its programming by small increments each year, adding additional nights as its revenues increased. Deals were struck with independent television stations across the US, each of which carries a common core of Fox programming in prime-time and on Saturday mornings. Hit shows like *The Simpsons* and *Married … With Children* often generated significant ratings shares to take Fox into a position to challenge the dominance of the Big Three, leading industry commentators to speculate on whether it may eventually replace one of the majors. In 1993 Fox began air-ing programmes seven nights a week.

Home video and satellite TV are also important additions to the TV menu. As in the UK, direct broadcast by satellite services are expanding in America. While domestic use of video-cassette recorders took off more slowly than in the UK, by 1992 there was a VCR in 70 per cent of American homes (Becker and Roberts, 1992, p.364).

The shift in power from the networks and their affiliates to the indepen-dents and cable has been dramatic. Some commentators have gone so far as to predict the end of the networks, beginning with the collapse of one of the Big Three. From 1978 to 1990, the total share of the audience obtained by the Big Three has declined approximately from 90 per cent to 65 per cent (Figure 5.2).

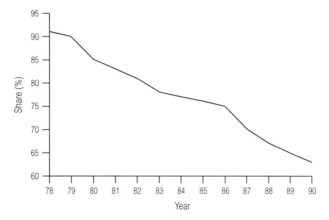

Figure 5.2 *Combined prime-time share of ABC, CBS and NBC, 1978–90*

(Source: Turow, 1992, chart 1.1)

It is a paradox that the relatively unrestricted nature of market relations in the TV industry takes place in a constitutional environment that provides for a seemingly more formalized relationship between government and the mass media than is the case in the UK, where television is, even in the 1990s, more tightly regulated. The key difference is the presence in the United States of a written Constitution. No understanding of the US media is possible without an account of the role of free speech in the American Constitution. The Bill of Rights appended to the US Constitution states that 'Congress shall make no law ... abridging the freedom of speech, or of the press', a statement that has been taken by extension to refer to the mass media and which is also embodied in the First Amendment to the Consti-tution. However, as Joseph Turow points out, this founding principle of American culture and society does not consider the relationship between freedom and the market-place:

> The amendment does not insist that speech and the press ought to be free in some broad, abstract sense. Rather, it specifically refers to freedom from congressional control ... The issue of private control over the avenues of knowledge — by advertisers, media conglomerates, or other means — is not a concern of the First Amendment.
>
> (Turow, 1992, p.56)

Turow's point is important because it shows us that there is no inherent contradiction between American ideals and the fact that censorship, self-censorship and control in US television occur through economic mechanisms mediated through advertising power. Indeed, this power is precisely *facilitated* by weak and relatively passive forms of government regulation which result from these constitutional concerns.

SUMMARY

Until the 1980s the Big Three networks (ABC, CBS, and NBC) dominated US television. They are run for profit and funded by advertising negotiated on the basis of information from the ratings system. Non-profit making Public Service Broadcasting is insignificant in terms of ratings.

Since the 1980s the power of the Big Three has been challenged by cable TV and the independents (especially by those who have been able to build national audiences via cable distribution). Other challenges have come from home video, satellite TV and Fox TV.

2 'MANY ALTERNATIVES BUT NO MORE CHOICE'

Many critics of the structure of US television suggest that it is not only anarchic to the point of being unable to systematically address issues of quality, since there is no central authority with sufficient power to even ask this question, let alone regulate in favour of quality programming, but that it is progressively widening the gap between the 'information rich' and the 'information poor'. Furthermore, it is argued by Bagdikian (1987) and others that the appearance of diversity is misleading, for two reasons. First, the appearance of multiple points of ownership hides a consolidation of power. Like the boxes of cereal or soap powder at the supermarket which hide the small number of producers through a proliferation of brand names, competitors in the TV market may turn out to be nothing of the sort. VH-1 and MTV are apparently competing all-music video channels on cable, for instance. In fact, they serve different markets — VH-1 is aimed at 25–54 year olds and MTV at 12–34 year olds — and the same corporate master, since both are owned by Viacom International. The multiple system operators in the cable industry are so powerful that in 1986 four companies provided programming to about 27 per cent of the cable television audience (Becker and Roberts, 1992, p.324). Secondly, the market-place itself produces a uniformity of programming, regardless of who owns and controls the production process. This is because ownership of the programming or of distribution channels is less significant than the power of advertisers in shaping programme content. The drive to create a 'media environment' conducive to selling goods and services, and the need to construct the appropriate audiences may be more significant than questions of corporate ownership. W. Russell Neuman makes the argument forcefully when he writes:

> Despite the proud independence of the fourth estate, and the entertainment industry more generally in the United States, the net result is that what most people hear and see in the mass media is remarkably uniform in content and worldview. That uniformity is not the result of a nefarious ring of scheming conspirators; it is structural. It derives from the critical-mass mathematics of the marketplace.
>
> (Neuman, 1991, p.130)

In response to this critique the defenders of the current system argue that it has produced diversity in programming and that private investment in TV has produced new technologies which enhance choice in other ways; for instance, the VCR gives us more flexibility about what we watch, when we watch and how we watch; the remote control unit enables us to mute out commercials, or zap from station to station to avoid them. Benjamin Compaine suggests that new technologies expand consumer freedom, arguing that:

> The empirical evidence indicates that the media structure in the United States is by far more open, diverse, and responsible to the public need and wants than at any time in history, notwithstanding the contrary sense that is suggested by the headlines created when media companies merge. There are no headlines proclaiming [the] arrival of a new journal or the growth of phenomena such as Cable News Network. Independent *ad hoc* television networks are another subtle but substantial change in the balance of media competitiveness.
>
> (Compaine, 1993, p.278)

If we look, for instance, at the debate about cultural imperialism and the 'one-way flow' that exists in the television industry (see Schiller, 1969; Tunstall, 1977; Fejes, 1981) then the new technologies, while they have not significantly undermined global inequities, have contributed to a lessening of centralized Western cultural power. In the US today it is possible to encounter non-American international perspectives on politics and current affairs on cable. The independents also carry entertainment programming from different parts of the world and the home video market sustains a thriving polyglot culture of imported Vietnamese, Taiwanese and Japanese videos.

It might also be noted that by the mid-1980s the declining ratings of the major networks brought about some level of innovation and experimentation. TV executives concluded that viewers needed to feel that there was something special about the fare offered in prime-time. Searching for a way of marking out differences for aesthetic strategies that would create an exciting identity for network television, the Big Three, especially ABC which was targeting a younger audience, encouraged a certain amount of risk taking. For instance, both Steve Bochco (*Cop Rock*) and David Lynch (*Twin Peaks*) were given free rein to create bizarre and sometimes puzzling television dramas. Critics of the system insist, however, that not only did these more adventurous experiments not last — *Cop Rock*, a musical about cops, was cancelled after only a handful of shows, and *Twin Peaks* lasted only two seasons — but that the most significant area of innovation proved to be 'trash TV' or 'tabloid TV', reality based programming like *Hard Copy, A Current Affair, Inside Edition, Rescue 911, America's Funniest Home Videos* and *I Witness Video*, which often sensationalized sex, violence and crime. However, even this last development is quite complex and contradictory, for it can be argued that 'infotainment' shows help to undermine the credibility of conventional journalistic practices that have for years been criticized by academics, thus achieving something that scholarly criticism alone could never have done (see Goodwin, 1993).

These debates will be pursued further later in this chapter. First we must consider one or two fundamental concepts in the study of television and how they may apply to the patterns of programming on American television and to the central controlling mechanism of advertising revenue.

SUMMARY

Despite the proliferation of channels, American television does not offer the viewers 'real' choice. Viewers are confronted by essentially similar programming. Innovation is not fostered and is not given the opportunity to develop an audience.

3   IDEOLOGY AND CONSUMERISM

The concept of 'ideology' is central to any understanding of contemporary culture. The term has numerous meanings, some of them conflicting, and is the subject of some extremely complex and acrimonious debates (see Brunt, 1990; O'Shaughnessy, 1990; Thompson, 1990; Lewis, 1991). For our purposes ideology can be understood in a broad sense as it relates to the notion of social legitimation, which is to say: how is it that societies manage to reproduce themselves? We often take for granted that our social world will continue to be there each morning when we awake. As we expect the sun to come up, so we expect existing social structures to be maintained. In revolution or during periods of social crisis, however, while the sun may still come up, the continuation of the social structure is less reliable. Sociologists have observed that the continuation of social structures depends at least in part on the maintenance of common ideas and beliefs.

A broad definition of ideology seeks out those ideas which are part of a wider system of beliefs, which are historically contingent, and which help to maintain the status quo. Leaving aside for the moment the question of whether or not ideology is seen to originate with a ruling class or whether it is generated from below, we might still investigate television in the US as an ideological force which helps to keep the family of Americans together, but together in particular ways. Despite its reliance upon ideas of freedom and liberty, in what ways can American television be seen as an ideological agent? How does TV in the United States help to sustain the status quo? Let us consider a mechanism in American television which is central to this issue: advertising.

One way in which the question of ideology has been answered is through an analysis of the role of advertising and consumerism. Americans know that advertising is everywhere, and most Americans know that the 'almighty dollar' rules. The point here is that Americans are not taken in by the role of the sales pitch in their culture, although they do accept it.

A look at the ratings system will show that there are some peculiarities in the relationship between viewers and programmes that might not be apparent at first sight. It was Dallas Smythe (1977) who first noted that the American television system positions the viewer as a commodity. Communications theory models of the media which base themselves on sender–message–receiver paradigms encourage us to think of the TV programme as the message and the audience as the receiver. However, as Smythe pointed out, since US television is not based upon commodity production, but is almost entirely advertising funded, it is necessary to ask: who is the customer and what is the product?

What then are the implications of advertising funding for programming policy? Defenders of the current system argue that it provides autonomy from the state, as there is little or no government funding, in line with the spirit of the First Amendment, and because the market-place services audience demand. Smythe argues that American television is concerned with the production of audiences, who are then sold to advertisers. Thus, it is the advertiser who is the receiver in this communication chain, while the viewer is the 'product'. This has important implications for arguments about market-place democracy. In defence of commercial television it is often suggested that this system 'gives the public what it wants'. In this model of consumer sovereignty the viewer is all powerful, because TV producers seek to maximize audiences; hence, what we want to watch will be served by the market. Smythe's analysis of the relations between audiences, TV producers and advertisers breaks the logic of implied consumer sovereignty, because it is clear that with the exception of the Public Broadcasting System, television institutions in the US are not serving 'the public'; they are serving those consumers whom advertisers wish to reach.

A-8 *Nielsen* NATIONAL TV AUDIENCE ESTIMATES — EVE.THU. APR.29, 1993

TIME	7:00	7:15	7:30	7:45	8:00	8:15	8:30	8:45	9:00	9:15	9:30	9:45	10:00	10:15	10:30	10:45
HUT	47.6	48.9	50.0	52.3	56.1	58.9	60.2	62.1	64.3	65.8	66.0	65.9	61.6	59.9	58.0	55.6

ABC TV — MATLOCK THE FINAL AFFAIR (PAE) / PRIMETIME LIVE

	8:00	8:15	8:30	8:45	9:00	9:15	9:30	9:45	10:00	10:15	10:30	10:45
HHLD AUDIENCE% & (000)	13.1	12,200							14.0	13,030		
TA%, AVG. AUD. 1/2 HR %	19.9	11.6*	13.0*		13.7*		14.2*		20.5	14.8*		13.3*
SHARE AUDIENCE %	21	20*	21*		21*		21*		24	24*		24*
AVG. AUD. BY 1/4 HR %	11.3	12.0	12.9	13.0	13.6	13.9	14.4	14.0	14.9	14.7	14.1	12.5

CBS TV — TOP COPS / STREET STORIES / PICKET FENCES

	8:00	8:15	8:30	8:45	9:00	9:15	9:30	9:45	10:00	10:15	10:30	10:45
HHLD AUDIENCE% & (000)	7.5	6,980			7.8	7,260			8.9	8,290		
TA%, AVG. AUD. 1/2 HR %	11.9	7.2*	7.7*		11.2	7.7*	7.9*		12.3	8.3*		9.5*
SHARE AUDIENCE %	13	13*	13*		12	12*	12*		15	14*		17*
AVG. AUD. BY 1/4 HR %	7.5	6.9	7.3	8.1	7.7	7.7	8.3	7.5	8.1	8.6	9.5	9.6

NBC TV — CHEERS-THU (R) / WINGS / CHEERS / SEINFELD (R) / L.A. LAW

	8:00	8:15	8:30	8:45	9:00	9:15	9:30	9:45	10:00	10:15	10:30	10:45
HHLD AUDIENCE% & (000)	11.6	10,800	13.1	12,200	20.8	19,360	20.1	18,710	12.4	11,540		
TA%, AVG. AUD. 1/2 HR %	14.3		15.3		23.5		22.3		16.6	12.8*		12.0*
SHARE AUDIENCE %	20		21		32		30		21	21*		21*
AVG. AUD. BY 1/4 HR %	10.7	12.4	12.7	13.6	19.9	21.7	20.0	20.2	13.4	12.1	11.9	12.1

FOX TV — SIMPSONS / MARTIN / ILC:GREATEST BITS 4 / ILC FIRST SEASON (R)

	8:00	8:15	8:30	8:45	9:00	9:15	9:30	9:45
HHLD AUDIENCE% & (000)	12.1	11,270	11.2	10,430	8.2	7,630	6.9	6,420
TA%, AVG. AUD. 1/2 HR %	14.1		12.9		9.7		8.1	
SHARE AUDIENCE %	21		18		13		10	
AVG. AUD. BY 1/4 HR %	11.2	13.0	11.2	11.2	8.6	7.8	7.0	6.9

INDEPENDENTS (INCLUDING SUPERSTATIONS EXCEPT TBS)

	7:00	7:30	8:00	8:30	9:00	9:30	10:00	10:30
AVERAGE AUDIENCE	12.3 (+F)	13.2 (+F)	5.9	6.1	6.0	6.3	12.9 (+F)	11.3 (+F)
SHARE AUDIENCE %	25	26	10	10	9	10	21	20

PBS

	7:00	7:30	8:00	8:30	9:00	9:30	10:00	10:30
AVERAGE AUDIENCE	1.5	1.5	1.9	2.2	2.0	2.2	1.7	1.5
SHARE AUDIENCE %	3	3	3	4	3	3	3	3

CABLE ORIG. (INCLUDING TBS)

	7:00	7:30	8:00	8:30	9:00	9:30	10:00	10:30
AVERAGE AUDIENCE	8.6 (+F)	10.3 (+F)	10.9	12.0	11.9	13.0	13.9 (+F)	12.1 (+F)
SHARE AUDIENCE %	18	20	19	20	18	20	23	21

PAY SERVICES

	7:00	7:30	8:00	8:30	9:00	9:30	10:00	10:30
AVERAGE AUDIENCE	1.6	1.4	1.8	1.9	2.3	2.5	3.2	3.4
SHARE AUDIENCE %	3	3	3	3	4	4	5	6

Figure 5.3 Nielsen ratings chart: on this particular evening NBC's Cheers obtained the highest rating of 20.8, reaching over 19 million homes

Eileen Meehan (1990) and Ien Ang (1992) have both shown how an analysis of the ratings system is quite revealing in demonstrating the constructed nature of these figures. Statistics produced by the A.C. Nielsen company and the Arbitron Ratings company are not only vulnerable statistically (because of their use of small samples: 4,000 households represent the entire nation in the Nielsen ratings, for instance) but are also concerned with the creation of a product through the packaging of an audience, to be sold to advertisers, rather than measuring consumer satisfaction. Meehan and Ang show how the measurement of audience figures is determined by what advertisers want to know. Given the dubious basis of the figures, it would be quite accurate to say that the ratings are in a sense a fiction which advertisers have agreed upon; as long as everyone consents to play the game by the same rules then the business of selling audiences can proceed, regardless of whether or not the system actually reflects any meaningful 'reality'. One example of the skewing of ratings is the widespread practice of screening often highly sensational programming which is expected to draw larger than usual audiences during 'sweeps' months. The 'sweeps' are the months when ratings figures for local stations are computed, which will subsequently form the basis for negotiations between those stations and their advertisers. 'Sweeps' months are, then, a game; their ratings neither reflects the true popularity of programmes, nor the popularity of the regular schedule. 'Ratings are tools designed by firms to achieve economic success — control over ratings production. Forms of measurement are selected on the basis of economic goals, not according to the rules of social science.' (Meehan, 1990, p.127.) Yet these figures are the very basis of programming policy in American television (see Figure 5.3).

SUMMARY

It has been argued that American TV is concerned with the production of audiences for advertisers. Programming is based on the ratings system which is a measure of audience statistics determined by what advertisers want to know.

4　DIVERSITY, STANDARDIZATION AND SOCIAL POWER

These issues can be further developed through a questioning of the impact of advertising funding upon programming policy. It is frequently suggested that new programmes are rarely given a chance to survive on American television, because network nervousness over falling ratings and, therefore, falling advertising revenue leads shows to be cancelled prematurely, often after only a handful of airings. In a typical television 'season', September to May, the majority of new programmes will not survive the first few months; many pilots for new series will be scrapped before they reach the screen at all, falling victim to early 'pre-tests' in which marketing techniques are used to test a show on a small audience. These strategies do not serve to nurture new talent or encourage innovation and risk taking, since pre-testing of cultural products is notorious for underscoring conservatism. The consequence of this has been described as a system which works by rewarding 'least objectionable programming'; in other words, those shows which offend the smallest numbers of people, regardless of the numbers who are actually *satisfied* by the programming.

Another criticism of America's advertising-funded system arises from the theory that there is a time lag in the relation between social trends and TV programming, which is caused by advertiser anxiety. Susan Horowitz (1987) put forward this idea in her work on situation comedies, arguing that sitcoms *do* reflect social trends, and *do* engage with serious topics and social conflict; however, this kind of subject matter is ready for prime-time only after it has been sufficiently sanitized through repeated exposure elsewhere in the culture. Once a 'controversy' becomes acceptable to mainstream audiences, then sitcoms adopt it as a theme of social relevance. An example is the topic of divorce, which was already a well-established trend in American society in the 1960s, but which could not be acknowledged *even as a possibility* in 1970, when producers came to CBS with the idea of *The Mary Tyler Moore Show*. The actress Mary Tyler Moore had previously portrayed Rob Petrie's wife Laura on *The Dick Van Dyke Show*; CBS was nervous not only that divorce would alienate viewers but that it would be thought that Mary Tyler Moore had somehow been divorced from Rob Petrie/Dick Van Dyke (see Gitlin, 1983, p.214). And so her character was presented as a single career woman. Not until 1988 was Moore able to play a divorcee — in the short-lived *Annie McGuire*.

As late as 1992, Republicans could label *Murphy Brown* socially disruptive for its portrayal of single motherhood, when the then Vice-President Dan Quayle used it to provoke an argument about 'family values'. However, this example also reminds us that while the time lag theory may explain something about social conservatism in prime-time, the Republican Party's desire to pick a fight with the television industry was also built on the proposition that television does not share its values. Throughout prime-time, and especially in situation comedies, television had lambasted the ideals of the Reagan–Bush administrations; from the parodistic depiction of the Reaganite son of ex-hippie parents Alex P. Keaton in *Family Ties*, through a sympathetic engagement with the tragedy of AIDS in *Designing Women*, and the relentless liberalism of *Murphy Brown* with its continuing critique of the battle between news-as-truth and TV-as-business, to the savage anti-fundamentalist satires of *The Simpsons*.

However, the fact that television in America may sometimes support a liberal agenda does not render it non-ideological. Some analyses of American TV have suggested even deeper-seated flaws in the system, resulting in part from advertising funding, which brings about standardization and political bias. Certainly the need to create a positive, upbeat environment for the promotion of consumerism in the commercial breaks suggests that tragedy, intractable problems and situations which do not lend themselves to easy solutions are likely to find television a hostile place. Todd Gitlin (1987) argues that prime-time offers 'happy solutions' to 'unhappy situations' and that through this mechanism, for instance in situation comedies, television is able to address social issues while maintaining a positive glow in the living room. In an analysis of *Miami Vice*, Gitlin (1986a) looks at the impact of car commercials on TV aesthetics, arguing that the appeal of this show is to surface affect, to momentary emotion, the celebration of colour and movement, at the expense of character, depth or narrative: just like a commercial, in fact. Mark Miller (1986) goes further still and argues that prime-time is in fact a riot of consumerism, in which the 'correct' values are inculcated into viewers through programming itself; he gives the example of the centrality of consumer goods in *The Cosby Show* and links this point with a critical discussion of the 'neo-feminism' of television, which is, he claims, a disguised effort to tell us that we are what we buy, not what we do.

It can also be argued that while entertainment programming, which is seen as less serious than news, may sometimes explore a liberal social agenda, documentary and news programming is more tightly policed for 'objectivity' and is also more likely to buttress traditional American values of patriotism, individualism and free-market economic relations (see, for example, Hallin, 1989). The New York based group Fairness and Accuracy in Media (FAIR) has undertaken extensive content analyses of TV news to reveal biases which work in favour of established power, of big business and government, and towards white, upper middle-class men. Significantly, two FAIR researchers found public television's nightly news show *The MacNeil-Lehrer News Hour* to be every bit as biased politically as commercial television news, such as the notoriously conservative ABC programme *Nightline* (Lee and Soloman, 1990).

More recent research suggests that this lack of objectivity in news and current affairs programming combines with a systematic 'bias against understanding' in which the extremely condensed and visually-driven agenda of TV reporting fails to educate or inform. Studies of TV coverage of the Gulf War of 1991 and the US Presidential election of 1992 undertaken at the University of Massachusetts showed that the more viewers watched television the *less* they knew about current events (Lewis *et al.*, 1991, 1992). This research parallels the 'cultivation analysis' of the audience pursued over the last 20 years by George Gerbner and his colleagues at the Annenberg School in Philadelphia. This work has attempted to demonstrate that heavy viewers of television tend to adopt the world-view of TV's agenda, whereas light viewers are less inclined to see their lives in the terms set out by television (see, for example, Gerbner *et al.*, 1986).

However, the impact of television is very complex as Lewis (1991) and Morley (1992) have shown. What we do know is that different audiences will react differently to the same message. An excellent example of this idea is laid out in a study of the American audience for *The Cosby Show*, where it is shown that white and black Americans find quite different messages in the programme (Jhally and Lewis, 1992). For many African-Americans, *Cosby* represents a bold effort to break down stereotypes and provide white and black viewers alike with an improved role model of the black American. But for many white viewers *Cosby* was used to show that racial discrimination was a thing of the past and that social equality had now been achieved. Since it can be empirically demonstrated that this is *not* the case, *Cosby* was allowing its white audiences to believe that which was wrong but nevertheless comforting, whilst at the same time, the very same episodes sent a positive message to many African-Americans. This research is an important example of the multiple interpretations that are possible, especially when a mass medium is central to such a diverse and multi-cultural society. If television is polysemic — containing many meanings — anywhere in the world, then it will certainly be polysemic in the United States.

Research on the political and social effects of American television has undergone a major re-think in recent years, in part because of the new influence in American academic life of British cultural studies, often drawing on the work of the Birmingham University Centre for Contemporary Cultural Studies (see Clarke, 1992; Grossberg, 1992). Cultural studies research has been extremely critical of the American sociology of mass communications, and of what is often seen as overly-simplified Marxist criticism of the media. In place of these approaches cultural studies offers an account of the television text which is often based on semiotic, structuralist and psychoanalytic methods (see Brunt, 1990) and an account of the audience which emphasizes consumer autonomy, popular pleasures and audience activity (see Morley, 1986, 1992). This work tends to stress the polysemy of the TV text, as in John Fiske's (1990, pp.1–20) account of a segment of the comedy-drama *Hart to Hart*. Similarly, Ang's (1985) research on *Dallas* focused on how the audience, in this case, Dutch viewers, used the programme and made sense of it in relation to their own lives. Another example of cultural studies research which lays stress on audience empowerment and textual pleasure is Constance Penley's (1992) research on 'Trekkies' who re-frame the show *Star Trek* through fan clubs, and in some instances via the production of pornographic fanzines featuring Spock and Captain James T. Kirk.

The cultural studies approach to understanding audiences adds an important and useful perspective to the study of American television. It is especially significant for its effort to validate popular and apparently 'trivial' cultural forms; and this is important when we consider the long legacy of European condescension towards American culture, and a long-standing tendency, still apparent today, to assume a totally unwarranted dismissive and superior attitude when looking at the US from across the Atlantic.

The cultural studies approach does not, however, succeed in replacing earlier paradigms. There are a number of limits that must be acknowledged here. First, as Lewis (1991) points out, to demonstrate that television's messages are polysemic and may be decoded in a variety of ways by different audiences does not mean that television has no effect, or that audiences are free to choose any possible meanings; rather, we should conclude that television's effects are complex, and that audience meanings will be determined by a process of negotiation that occurs when a TV text meets a set of pre-existing discourses stored in the heads of its viewers. Neither does the fact of discovering audience activity and textual polysemy mean that television is not ideological. Ang (1985) is careful to point out that her research reveals *Dallas* to be *potentially* 'feminist' but rarely so in *actual* audience interpretations.

Secondly, as Lull (1990, pp.16–17) has argued, cultural studies research runs the risk of being too shoddy in its engagement with the empirical moment, especially when it dabbles in psychoanalytic theory. Many of the efforts to hypothesize psychological and psychoanalytic processes working within the TV audience are thought-provoking and suggestive for future empirical research (e.g. Mellencamp, 1990a); what they are not, yet, is *convincing*. The task of studying the empirical meanings of emotion and affect in television is a job that remains to be done, and may best be tackled by social psychologists, rather than cultural studies theorists.

Thirdly, it can be argued that the emphasis on the text–audience relation can sometimes lead to a neglect of the real power which exists in media institutions. If TV consumption is a process of negotiation between readers and texts, then it needs to be said that the bargaining process at the table of meaning-production is not necessarily fair. The word 'negotiation' hides as much as it reveals, since it tends to downplay the inequities inherent in the dominant ways of organizing mass communication in industrial societies. Which is to state an obvious point: the power to control the content of television programmes, and the form of their transmission (the schedule) does not lie with the American pubic. While there is feedback of a rudimentary kind between the television institutions and their audiences, it is flawed and inadequate. Audience 'freedom' to re-read the *CBS Evening News* or *Matlock* or *As the World Turns* is only ever a resistive freedom to re-contextualize; it rarely crosses over into the power to re-frame how others will interpret a show, or (more radically) into the ability to mass produce new meanings. A major factor here is the absence of a strong public service tradition, which means that the kinds of 'access' programming made available to non-professionals on UK television is virtually unheard of in American TV.

SUMMARY

Marketing techniques are used to pre-test shows and the system rewards 'least objectionable programming'.

There is a time lag between social trends and their portrayal in programmes. TV tends to reaffirm mainstream values and positive solutions, with news and current affairs programmes biased in favour of dominant interests.

Programmes are polysemic, they can mean different things to different groups. This is stressed in recent cultural studies research, which is an interesting, although limited, approach to understanding TV audiences.

5   A CASE STUDY: MTV

Many of these issues regarding audience readings, text analysis and institutional power can be seen at work in the developing history of the world's first all-music television service, Music Television. MTV is part of MTV Networks, originally owned by Warner-Amex (a consortium which brought together the music industry interests of Warner Bros., with the banking corporation American Express). It was sold to Viacom International in 1986. MTV began transmission in August, 1981 and is targeted at 12–34 year olds. It is available to 57.3 million cable subscribers in the US, but its actual audience is considerably smaller than this: often MTV has attracted a less than 1.0 share, meaning that less than 1 per cent of potential viewers — in most markets, basic cable subscribers — tuned in. Many people believe that MTV operates like a radio station with the VJs (video jocks) playing videos live, in real time. In fact most MTV transmissions consist of pre-recorded VJ-segments which are slotted-in between videos and commercials by an engineer.

Goodwin (1992, pp.131–55) argues that MTV's programming history can be understood in terms of a shift from a commitment to particular musical genres (British New Wave and American 'album-oriented rock'), which built on the 'narrowcasting' strategies of both radio and cable TV, to a more ambitious desire to emulate print media pop culture outlets such as *Rolling Stone* and *Q* magazines. This has led MTV to develop non-music programming (political coverage, game shows, movie reviews, and *Real World* — a 'real life' tele-vérité soap opera), to screen a broader range of music than in its early years, and to announce its intention to split into three discrete services sometime in 1993 or 1994.

In 1985 MTV Networks launched VH-1, a similar service aimed at 25–54 year olds, which was built on the foundation of a failed rival service, Ted Turner's Cable Music Channel (see Denisoff, 1988). VH-1 has been less successful at attracting audiences than MTV and is not as widely available on cable systems in the US. In August 1987, in another effort to expand, MTV Europe began broadcasting. It was initially funded by MTV Networks in conjunction with British Telecom and Robert Maxwell's Mirror Group Newspapers. The latter partner has since dropped out. MTV's global reach now extends to over 75 countries, including MTV Japan, MTV Australia and MTV Latin America. The programming on these localized MTVs, including MTV Europe, is often quite different than on MTV in the US, although many non-music programmes are shared. The *potential* world audience for MTV is 231 million households.

MTV is not only influential; more importantly, it is also typical. Much popular commentary has credited the station with an impact on television (CNN, *Miami Vice*, 'trash TV'), cinema (*Flashdance*, *Wayne's World*), advertising (McDonald's, Coke and Pepsi ads which look like mini-music videos), the music industry itself (the *Unplugged* programme has encouraged artists to release all-acoustic albums), and even politics (Bill Clinton credited MTV with helping him to win the 1992 Presidential election). However, MTV is better understood as a new form which is symptomatic of trends within the culture industries. Foremost among these are the fusion of advertising and programming and increasing use of avant-garde aesthetic techniques in mainstream TV.

As we have seen, American television is not produced as a commodity to be bought and sold in the market-place. Instead, advertising funding is primary. New cable services such as MTV have as their foundations the identification of a target audience with sufficient disposable income to attract advertisers. Given that advertisers have not always found it easy to 'narrowcast' to the young audience, the fusion of pop music and television is the perfect vehicle for reaching that group. MTV has been described as the most researched service in the history of television, and it is interesting to note that the methodology utilized was 'psychographics' — an approach to the consumer taking into account leisure spending and cultural attitudes, alongside more familiar parameters such as income, gender and ethnicity (Denisoff, 1988). The consumerist underpinning of MTV is also revealed in the programming itself, which is mostly a form of advertising: the video clips shown on MTV are advertisements, financed by record companies, and they are primarily designed to sell records, cassettes and compact discs (see Figure 5.4). With the exception of the monies spent by MTV to secure 'exclusivity' deals with six major record companies (deals which give MTV a 30 to 60-day window in which no rival service may screen a video), the promotional video clips are thus free of charge. This method of financing a television service parallels other developments in American television, such as the 30 minute 'infomercial' (a paid programme which often looks like a talk show or documentary, but which is actually a commercial) and the routine use of children's TV shows to plug products aimed at children: such as *Teenage Mutant Ninja Turtles* or *X-Men* (see Engelhardt, 1986).

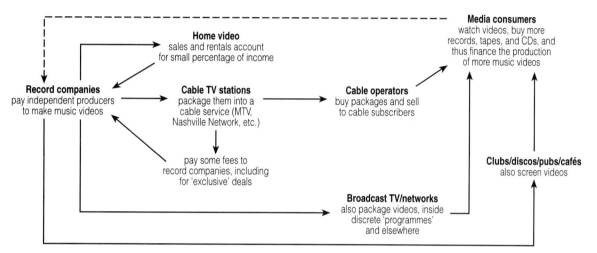

Figure 5.4   *The music video cycle*

Here we might consider the work of Nick Browne, who has studied the made-for-TV movie through the concept of a televisual 'super-text'. Browne suggests that a vital link between political economy and text analysis can be made if we consider all the material transmitted during a television broadcast as one text: that is to say, the advertisements, trailers, continuity and station identification materials constitute, alongside the programme itself, a televisual super-text. Browne then identifies coherence in the super-text, at two levels of linkage between programming and commercials. First, he suggests that television's fragmentary and segmented form creates temporary disequilibriums which are resolved through the restoration of the 'lost object', the commodities advertised in commercial breaks: 'Though interruptive, the ad, in its role as agent of symbolic restitution for a lack in the narrative proper, constructs a kind of narrative pleasure that assures formal resolution and confers on the represented object the status of good object.' (Browne, 1987, p.596.) Secondly, Browne argues that the tacit contract between viewers and advertisers — that we agree to be exposed to a sales pitch in exchange for the experience of 'free' television — constitutes a naturalizing discourse that imports the alienated relations of production into our 'leisure' time: a position which is very close to the arguments made by the Frankfurt School concerning the commodification of our so-called 'free' time (Adorno, 1991, pp.162–70).

> In 'free' television, the general possibility of 'entertainment' is exchanged for the willingness of the audience to be subjected to a view of something specific — the objects displayed in ads … The literal circuit of exchange is closed when the viewer, through the relay of the represented object, purchases the actual object in whose price the invisible cost of the motivating ad is hidden. The actual commodity, then, is the ultimate referent of the television discourse … Television presents and sustains consumption as an answer to the problems of everyday life. It articulates and, at the same time, dissolves the difference between the 'supertext' and 'supermarket'.
>
> (Browne, 1987, p.596)

Applied to MTV, these arguments are extremely pertinent. The notion of the commodity as a 'lost object' which restores order to an imperfect world has dual application in relation to music television; for while Browne's argument can be applied to, say, the advertisements on MTV, it is also highly suggestive of the relation between the clip and the commodity it promotes. Logos, album designs, and star-imagery are central elements of the video clip, and may thus function as the clue to the object-to-be-restored within each segment.

Sometimes this device is actually narrativized. For instance, the clip of Nelson's song *Love and Affection* opens with a male teenager crying in his room while in the next room his father argues with his mother. The teenager then escapes into a fictional Nelson world, via a huge poster on his wall where he finds, to borrow Dyer's (1977) terms, energy, abundance and community in Nelson's performance of *Love and Affection*. As is often the case in music videos, this 'fantasy' turns out to be 'real': a feather obtained in the 'fantasy' is then present in his room when the teenager returns to the 'real' world. Similarly, in Poison's *Nothing But a Good Time*, a male teenager is washing dishes in a restaurant while listening to rock music on the radio when his boss enters, to berate him for working too slowly. Disgruntled and upset, he escapes through a door and into an alternative reality, where Poison are performing their song. On his return to the kitchen, the dishes have magically been cleaned during his absence. ZZ Top's videos have often used this same technique, through the magical agent of the key, which contains the 'ZZ' of the group's name, to their car, The Eliminator. In both *Gimme All Your Lovin'* and *Legs* this key/car provides a young male with access to sex, romance and escape from his small-town life: Browne's argument could hardly be made more explicitly relevant than it is in these clips. This link takes on even greater significance when current songs (and perhaps their video imagery) are used in television commercials: for instance, in the Genesis Michelob spot that used *Tonight, Tonight, Tonight*, or in Robert Plant's Coca Cola ad, which used *Tall Cool One*. Sometimes it is just the visual imagery that is used: a commercial for Chic perfume utilized the imagery for Chris Isaak's *Wicked Game* clip, so that the product seemed to be the 'solution' to the romantic angst of that song.

Music video clips enhance television's ability to forge this ideological nexus between texts and commodities, since their narratives can stage dramas which offer the star/musical object as 'solution' to a much greater degree than did televised performances of a song prior to MTV. Furthermore, the development of dedicated music television services opens up possibilities for programming that highlight consumption, through VJ/host presentational material, complementary star profiles and interviews, news and reviews of new tours, movies, videos and albums, and celebratory documentaries such as MTV's *Rockumentary*.

MTV is thus a hybrid form, like so many 1980s cultural objects, mixing programming and promotion, and simultaneously serving both the music and television industries. It is also a hybrid in another sense which is typical of contemporary American television, for MTV offers a visual style which sometimes appears experimental, avant-garde and perhaps modernist. While many areas of MTV are quite traditional in aesthetic terms, many of the videos, for instance, look like mini-documentaries which have been cut to a very fast rhythm, others are visually disturbing and may look strange to viewers of more mainstream television programming. The same can be said of MTV's attitude, which is well summed-up by its old slogan: MTV — BETTER SORRY THAN SAFE. In this respect MTV echoes those areas of network TV output mentioned earlier, like *Twin Peaks*, which have broken with the mainstream aesthetics of prime-time. Like *Twin Peaks*, and perhaps *Northern Exposure*, MTV often seems to be suffering from a case of terminal irony, never able to take itself seriously, and always ready to pull the rug from under itself. It was MTV, after all, which in 1989 awarded Neil Young 'Best Video of the Year' for his *This Note's For You*, after effectively banning the clip from its schedule! Where *The Simpsons* mixes a conventional cartoon format with radical and anti-conservative politics, so MTV often hides a trenchantly liberal political agenda under its cloak of consumerism. Its news programming has been consistently anti-Republican, pro-environment, anti-racist and sometimes pro-feminist. In its visuals MTV is known for being both frenetic and oblique — two features which it shares with rock and pop music, and which arise out of the musical and lyrical content of those forms (see Goodwin, 1992). But this style is also seen elsewhere on American television; it has leaked into news and current affairs shows, and into some drama.

What does all this mean? At first sight, this account of MTV may suggest that this new service is nothing less than an Orwellian plot designed to further the dark ends of multi-national capitalism. As is so often the case with popular culture, the reality is a good deal more complex.

Because of its need to recruit young, counter-cultural viewers, there is a necessity for liberal discourses on MTV. To the extent that MTV marks itself out from 'normal' television and attempts to promote a rock 'attitude' it has been far more resistant to censorship than has, say, the BBC. Where the BBC engaged in massive censorship during the Gulf War (banning dozens of records because they might allude to the conflict, for instance), MTV screened the anti-war video made by Julian Lennon and friends, *Give Peace a Chance*.

Because MTV is a dedicated service, committed to the promotion of an 'alternative' culture (however cynically or self-servingly), it has an investment in risk-taking that public service and commercial networks alike do not share. One result of this is that MTV has opened up the political agenda on television, by using programming criteria which reflect the values of rock 'n' roll rather than the values of paternalist broadcasting institutions. Secondly, professional ideologies in broadcast journalism — while they are by no means pervasive in music television — do surface and thus open up a liberal space in which critical distance can sometimes occur between the music television texts and the commodities it promotes.

The relationship between advertising revenue and political attitudes can be a complex issue, too. While the need to promote sets clear aesthetic limits on what can be said in a music video (see Laing, 1985; Goodwin, 1992), the search for advertising revenue can also take television in unexpected directions. In the 1970s, as Gitlin (1983) has shown, the 'turn toward relevance' in situation comedy was underwritten by a desire, especially on the part of CBS, to reach new, younger, more affluent consumers. Thus the network dropped highly successful, but rather conservative, programmes like *The Beverly Hillbillies* and *Petticoat Junction* because they attracted the wrong demographic groups; replacing them with innovative shows like *All in the Family* and *M*A*S*H*. Similarly NBC, in the early 1980s, promoted 'quality television' and in particular the drama *Hill Street Blues*, which was supported despite very low initial ratings, in the hope that quality TV would deliver quality audiences (see Feuer *et al.*, 1984; Feuer, 1987).

At MTV there is evidence that the network's move toward socially responsible news coverage was motivated in part by advertising concerns. A recent report on MTV provides us with this information: 'There is more than civic virtue at work here: MTV thinks that a weightier image will attract sponsors that have shunned it in the past. Indeed, the network recently signed up Ford Motor Co. and American Telephone and Telegraph Co. as new advertisers.' (Landler, 1992, p.62.) Aaron Cohen, head of AT&T's advertising agency supports this account: 'When MTV is out there trying to get young people involved in the political process, it's a perfect environment for a blue chip client.' (Quoted in Robins, 1992, p.1.) This argument demonstrates a contradiction between the anti-democratic nature of advertising-funded television (not everyone's 'vote', as a viewer, is equal) and its overt political content: desirable, better-educated, upscale viewers may demand liberal programming, and — in the case of MTV — 'quality' programming may attract advertisers because of what it says about the network.

SUMMARY

MTV has had a significant impact on American cultural and aesthetic values. Other art forms have been influenced by the MTV style. It is clearly directed at a young audience with disposable income — an attractive audience for advertising.

> MTV takes an overt liberal position on social issues such as the environment, but aligns it with a heavy emphasis on consumerism.

6 CONCLUSION: IMPLICATIONS FOR TUBE FUTURES

Intellectuals in the US tend to be even more dismissive of television than their European counterparts. In part this is no doubt explained by the prevalence of advertising, which is found to be distasteful or simply distracting, and by the perceived aesthetic poverty of the programmes themselves. However, one factor is more fundamental: there is no central national cultural institution, like the BBC, with which intellectuals can identify, or feel obliged at least to keep up with and perhaps participate in. Hence a continuing and apparently endless trend in American literary culture centres on the production of books which mostly seem to reiterate the same essential point: TV is bad (Mander, 1978; Postman, 1985; McKibben, 1992). Contrary to common belief, it is not at all unusual to encounter scholars, writers and even students who do not possess a television set. Clearly such people are in a small minority, but this is none the less significant because it speaks to the marginalized position of the medium, in élite terms, in comparison with Western Europe. A commonly seen bumper sticker in liberal-intellectual neighbourhoods reads simply: KILL YOUR TELEVISION. The role of television in attempting to unite citizens of all classes in the UK simply does not apply in the same way to American television. And yet it remains the case that network television has been, until recently, a unique institution in its ability to reach most of the population simultaneously — an important function in such a huge and diverse nation.

One problem in understanding American television lies in the tendency for print-based intellectuals to dismiss the medium on the wrong grounds. First and foremost, it is necessary to reject the 'technological determinism' implied both by negative dismissals of television and by celebratory projections into the future which stress the power of new inventions, such as interactive TV and virtual reality. Raymond Williams (1974) and others have identified technological determinism as an approach which sees cultural history as driven by new media technologies. In that account social trends in mass culture are assumed to stem from new inventions and technologies. In contrast to this view Williams shows how the technology of television is shaped by social, economic and political decisions.

The most significant technological development on the horizon for American television is the shift from analogue to compressed-digital transmission of TV cable services. This development will enable cable TV operators to offer perhaps as many as 500 channels. Tele-Communications Inc., of Colorado, has announced its plan to begin such services as early as 1994 (Kolbert, 1993; Dibbell, 1992). What this suggests is the strong possibility of increasing fragmentation or 'de-massification' of the audience, along the lines considered by Neuman (1991) in his account of the decline of the mass audience.

This fragmentation and fracturing of markets and of taste leaves open the question of the relationship between television and national identity. If American television is, as this chapter has suggested, a complex phenomenon which contains deeply ideological appeals to consumerism and a relatively (and carefully contained) oppositional liberalism, how will this well-established ideological mixture fare if technological and social forces combine to break up the mass audience? The citizens of the US are wrestling with the relationship between ethnic and national diversity on the one hand and the social consequences of the free market on the other: will the possibility of 500 channels catering for every conceivable market niche be so disruptive that America itself will fracture? This issue is complex, and nobody yet has all the answers. But it may be the case that national identity in the United States is so invested in consumerism that American television can both multiply *and* unify.

REFERENCES

Adorno, A. (1991) 'Free time' in Bernstein, J.M. (ed.) *The Culture Industry: Selected Essays on Mass Culture*, London, Routledge.

Ang, I. (1985) *Watching Dallas*, London, Methuen.

Ang, I. (1992) *Desperately Seeking the Audience*, London, Routledge.

Bagdikian, B. (1987) *The Media Monopoly*, Boston, Beacon Press (2nd edn).

Becker, S. and Roberts, C. (1992) *Discovering Mass Communication*, New York, Harper-Collins (3rd edn).

Browne, N. (1987) 'The political economy of the TV (super) text' in Newcomb, H. (ed.).

Brunt, R. (1990) 'Points of view' in Goodwin, A. and Whannel, G. (eds).

Clarke, J. (1992) *New Times and Old Enemies: Essays on Cultural Studies and America*, London, HarperCollins.

Compaine, B. (1993) 'The expanding base of media competition' in Alexander, A. and Hanson, J. (eds) *Taking Sides: Clashing Views on Controversial Issues in Mass Media and Society*, Guilford, Conn., Dushkin.

Denisoff, S. (1988) *Inside MTV*, New Brunswick, Transaction.

Dibbell, J. (1992) 'It's the end of TV as we know it', *Village Voice*, 22 December.

Dyer, R. (1977) 'Entertainment and Utopia', *Movie*, no.24.

Engelhardt, T. (1986) 'Children's television: the shortcake strategy' in Gitlin, T. (ed.) (1986b).

Fejes, F. (1981) 'Media imperialism: an assessment', *Media, Culture and Society*, vol.3, no.3.

Feuer, J. (1987) 'MTM: quality television' in Newcomb, H. (ed.).

Feuer, J., Kerr, P. and Vahimagi, T. (1984) *MTM: 'Quality Television'*, London, British Film Institute.

Fiske, J. (1990) *Television Culture*, London, Routledge.

Gerbner, G. *et al.* (1986) 'Living with television: the dynamics of the cultivation process' in Bryant, J. and Zillman, D. (eds) *Perspectives on Media Effects*, Hillsdale, NJ, Lawrence Erlbaum.

Gitlin, T. (1983) *Inside Prime Time*, New York, Pantheon.

Gitlin, T. (1986a) 'Car commercials and *Miami Vice*' in Gitlin, T. (ed.) (1986b).

Gitlin, T. (ed.) (1986b) *Watching Television*, New York, Pantheon.

Gitlin, T. (1987) 'Prime time ideology: the hegemonic process in television entertainment' in Newcomb, H. (ed.).

Goodwin, A. (1992) *Dancing in the Distraction Factory: Music Television and Popular Culture*, Minneapolis, University of Minnesota Press.

Goodwin, A. (1993) 'Riding with ambulances: television and its uses', *Sight and Sound*, vol.3, no.1.

Goodwin, A. and Whannel, G. (eds) (1990) *Understanding Television*, London, Routledge.

Grossberg, L. (1992) *We Gotta Get Out of This Place: Popular Conservatism and Postmodern Culture*, New York, Routledge.

Hallin, D. (1989) *The 'Uncensored War': the Media and Vietnam*, Berkeley, University of California Press.

Horowitz, S. (1987) 'Sitcom domesticus' in Newcomb, H. (ed.).

Jhally, S. and Lewis, J. (1992) *Enlightened Racism:* The Cosby Show, *Audiences and the Myth of the American Dream*, Oxford, Westview Press.

Kolbert, E. (1993) 'Deciding what to watch when 500 channels await', *New York Times*, 4 January.

Laing, D. (1985) 'Music video: industrial product, cultural form', *Screen*, vol.26, no.1.

Landler, M. (1992) 'The MTV tycoon', *Business Week*, 21 September.

Lee, M. and Soloman, N. (1990) *Unreliable Sources: a Guide to Detecting Bias in News Media*, New York, Lyle Stuart.

Lewis, J. (1991) *The Ideological Octopus: an Exploration of Television and its Audiences*, London, Routledge.

Lewis, J. *et al.* (1991) *The Media and the Gulf War*, Center for the Study of Communication, University of Massachusetts at Amherst.

Lewis, J. *et al.* (1992) *Images/Issues/Impact: the Media and Campaign 92*, Center for the Study of Communication, University of Massachusetts at Amherst.

Lull, J. (1990) *Inside Family Viewing*, London, Routledge.

McKibben, B. (1992) *The Age of Missing Information*, New York, Random House.

Mander, J. (1978) *Four Arguments for the Elimination of Television*, New York, Quill.

Meehan, E. (1990) 'Why we don't count: the commodity audience' in Mellencamp, P. (ed.) (1990b).

Mellencamp, P. (1990a) 'TV time and catastrophe, or beyond the pleasure principle of television' in Mellencamp, P. (ed.) (1990b).

Mellencamp, P. (ed.) (1990b) *Logics of Television: Essays in Cultural Criticism*, London, British Film Institute.

Miller, M. (1986) 'Prime time: deride and conquer' in Gitlin, T. (ed.) (1986b).

Morley, D. (1986) *Family Television*, London, Routledge.

Morley, D. (1992) *Television, Audiences and Cultural Studies*, London, Routledge.

Neuman, W.R. (1991) *The Future of the Mass Audience*, Cambridge, Cambridge University Press.

Newcomb, H. (ed.) (1987) *Television: the Critical View*, Oxford, Oxford University Press (4th edn).

O'Shaughnessy, M. (1990) 'Box pop: popular television and hegemony' in Goodwin, A. and Whannel, G. (eds).

Penley, C. (1992) 'Feminism, psychoanalysis and the study of popular culture' in Grossberg, L., Nelson, C. and Treicher, P. (eds) *Cultural Studies*, London, Routledge.

Postman, N. (1985) *Amusing Ourselves to Death: Public Discourse in the Age of Showbusiness*, London, Penguin.

Robins, M. (1992) 'Blue chip ad buyers want their MTV', *Variety*, 29 June, pp.1/86.

Schiller, H. (1969) *Mass Communication and American Empire*, Boston, Beacon Press.

Smythe, D. (1977) 'Communications: blindspot of Western Marxism', *Canadian Journal of Social and Political Theory*, vol.1, no.3.

Thompson, J. (1990) *Ideology and Modern Culture: Critical Social Theory in the Era of Mass Communication*, Cambridge, Polity Press.

Tunstall, J. (1977) *The Media Are American*, London, Macmillan.

Turow, J. (1992) *Media Systems in Society: Understanding Industries, Strategies and Power*, New York, Longman.

Williams, R. (1974) *Television: Technology and Cultural Form*, London, Fontana.

FURTHER READING

See Gitlin (1983, 1986b) and Mellencamp (1990b) in the references.

Barnouw, E. (1982) *Tube of Plenty: the Evolution of American Television*, Oxford, Oxford University Press (rev. edn).

Berg, L.V. and Wenner, L. (eds) (1991) *Television Criticism*, London, Longman.

O'Connor, J.E. (ed.) (1983) *American History/American Television: Interpreting the Video Past*, New York, Frederick Ungar.

DRAMA

Matthew Roudané ★

1 THE THEATRICAL LANDSCAPE

Twentieth-century American drama appears as divided as the culture dramatized by its playwrights. The poets and painters of the twentieth century respond to the same outer landscape, but the dramatists capture a fragmented outer world, perhaps with a greater sense of immediacy, but surely with a greater sense of communal spectacle. If the theatre is the most public of the arts, then 'it offers the opportunity of acting out anxieties and fears which are born in the conflict between private needs and public values' (Bigsby, 1984, p.1). Indeed, the relationship between the public issues of a nation and the private anxieties of its citizens informs all serious American drama. This public/private confluence gives the genre its particular ambivalence and intensity, and American drama replicates the sweep and play of American culture. Put another way, American drama stages a nation thinking (or not thinking) in front of itself. American drama charts a culture that thrives on theatrics, performance, spectacle: from elections to executions, from World Series to world summit meetings, America is a culture that loves to watch the watchers watching the watchers watch. In American drama, life imitates art as much as art imitates life.

This chapter surveys selected playwrights who have shaped twentieth-century American drama. This discussion of major and minor dramatists provides a representative sampling of the American dramatic imagination. The major figures — O'Neill, Williams, Miller, Hansberry, Albee, Shepard and Mamet — best capture the emotional intensity of the genre. But many lesser known playwrights — from Glaspell to Norman — exert an important influence on the American stage. This chapter, then, considers dramatists whose plays are essential to understanding American drama as well as those whose works are often ignored, though they contribute significantly to our critical understanding of the field. This chapter also alludes to some of the major themes of American drama. Bigsby identifies some of these major themes as objectifying a sense of *loss*: a loss of physical, mental, and moral space. So the major thematic and cultural features of American drama — the role of truth and illusion; of ritualized forms of expiation; of authentic communication; of the primal family unit; of the myth of the American Dream; of racial identity; of consciousness; and of death itself — all connect with this multilayered sense of loss. American dramatists are at their best when juxtaposing a deeply personal feeling of loss with an outer public world that, more often than not, only intensifies a condition of alienation.

Despite the modernity of twentieth-century American drama, there remains an ancient quality about the asymmetries and psychological dislocations, the confrontations and rebellions, that animate the plays. American dramatists have learned from their past — from Sophocles, Shakespeare, and Shaw — about the civic function of the theatre. From Eugene O'Neill to David Mamet, American dramatists believe that the theatre is a valid forum for charting the spiritual triumph, or failure, of the body politic. Arthur Miller spotlights the civilizing influence of drama, a quality that he contends shapes American drama:

> See how the plays that we call great have made us somehow more civilized. The great Greek plays taught the western mind law. They taught the western mind how to settle tribal conflicts without murdering each other. The great Shakespearean plays set up structures of order which became part of our mental equipment. In the immense love stories, the wonderful comedies, there's all sorts of color. But back of these plays is a civic function. The author was really a poet-philosopher.

(Roudané, 1987, p.374)

American dramatists, despite differences of race, class, or gender, address the civic and personal dimensions of the theatre to which Miller alludes. American plays emerge as paradigms of public interests and private desires, paradigms that transcend geographical place and historical fact, and through such transcendence attain the universality that Aristotle thought essential for all great art. Behind the modernity of the dramas considered here lies some of the primal furies shaping ancient Greek tragedies, Elizabethan histories, and modern British comedies. And the overall influence, forged out of the crucible of the performing arts, seems militantly civilizing.

2   BEGINNINGS: EUGENE O'NEILL AND SUSAN GLASPELL

Eugene O'Neill (1888–1953) is generally regarded as America's greatest dramatist. Born in New York, his father, James O'Neill, was a noted actor who packed the family from city to town while touring on the American theatre circuit — the only thing Eugene could predict was his father's nightly performance, a dreaded experience that would continue for three decades. His mother, Ella Quinlan, became seriously ill while pregnant with her second child, who later died. Treated with morphine, she became a life-long addict. Eugene used these familial experiences, revealing his family as hiding behind lies, 'pipe dreams' that masked inner betrayals and moral weaknesses. O'Neill endured alcoholism, drugs, and survived what he called the 'tyrannies' of his Irish Catholicism, and these private concerns manifest themselves in his plays.

Moved from one school to another, O'Neill entered Princeton University in 1906, only to be expelled a year later. Although married in 1909, O'Neill drifted around much of the globe as a gold prospector in Honduras, and as a sailor on ships destined for Europe and South America. O'Neill lived the life as a derelict in New York waterfront bars and seedy flophouses, and knew pimps and whores while continually drinking. In 1912 he contracted tuberculosis, and during a year-long hospital stay he read European philosophy and drama. He was particularly impressed with August Strindberg. It was during this time that he committed himself to serious writing and in 1914 published *Thirst and Other One-Act Plays*. He enrolled in George Piece Baker's English 47 playwriting course at Harvard University, and in 1916 became involved with the Provincetown Players, who produced *Bound East for Cardiff*, which drew on O'Neill's sea adventures. Suddenly O'Neill's contrived earlier melodramas evolved into authentic plays.

O'Neill represents the birth of modern American drama. While most theatre groups in the US imported plays from abroad, the Provincetown Players focused on American works. The Players were a group of actors and playwrights committed to staging works that were fresh, new, sometimes awkwardly innovative. Free from broad commercial pressures the Players were a perfect group for the idealist O'Neill, whose intense plays about truth and illusion, the decline of Christianity, and the ascendancy of materialism were too shocking for most Americans whose native theatre had been British classics or superficial melodramas. Working with Susan Glaspell, George Cook, and others, O'Neill's early works were nurtured by the Provincetown Players. He thrived on what Era Pound would soon proclaim: to make art new. Theatrically inspired by Strindberg, philosophically fuelled by Nietzsche, and psychologically intrigued by Freud and Jung, O'Neill experimented in his early career with a variety of dramatic forms.

In the 1920s, O'Neill moved to Broadway. During this decade he seemed as comfortable with a more realistic work like *Desire Under the Elms* (1924), which is a reworking of the Phaedra–Hippolytus–Theseus tragic myth, as he did with his more experimental plays, such as *The Emperor Jones* (1920) or *Strange Interlude* (1928), an eight-hour long play which uses revealing 'asides' that exteriorize suppressed desires. *The Emperor Jones*, whose daring set drained the Players of their entire budget, was archetypal in texture, expressionistic in technique, it featured drums and lighting to spotlight such inner emotions as fear, confusion, and celebration, emotions that dominate the play. This work was also one of the first American plays with a black hero and a mixed-ethnic cast.

Just as theatre-goers were intrigued by the gloomy and painful world of *Anna Christie* (1921), so were they provoked by the class conflicts in *The Hairy Ape* (1922), where Yank struggles to 'belong' within a society that has no place for this lower-class stoker. When *The Hairy Ape* opened on 9 March 1923, the Mayor of New York tried to close the show, while the public flocked to see the first successful expressionistic play written by an American.

Preoccupied with dramatic forms that would accommodate his tragic vision, O'Neill, in the 1920s and 1930s, produced *Marco Millions* (1923), a satirized view of a salesman; *The Great God Brown* (1926), complete with Greek masks to better stage an Apollonian–Dionysian conflict; and *Lazarus Laughed* (1928), which calls into question the pursuit of materialism by interfolding in the action Greek choruses, references to the Bible, the use of masks, large crowds of people, and stylized laughter. *Mourning Becomes Electra* (1931), which in its original took three days to perform, reinvents Aeschylus's *Oresteia* in the context of the American Civil War. Many felt that such plays as *Lazarus Laughed, Marco Millions, Dynamo* (1929), and *Days Without End* (1934) marked the decline of his mimetic powers. When, in 1936, O'Neill won the Nobel Prize, most thought his best work was behind him.

However, in 1932 O'Neill planned a cycle of plays charting the fortunes of several generations of an American family: *A Tale of Possessors Self-Dispossessed*. Suffering from Parkinson's disease he completed only *A Touch of the Poet* (1935–42) and *More Stately Mansions* (1935–40). Interestingly, though, in the late 1930s and early 1940s he would write his greatest plays. Returning to the power of realism and autobiography, O'Neill produced *The Iceman Cometh* (written 1939, published 1946), *Long Day's Journey into Night* (written 1940, published 1956), and *Hughie* (1941).

For O'Neill, illusions and booze are the only forces that enable his characters to endure this world, a world in which the individual is reduced to an insignificant speck in the universe over which he or she has little or no control. Caught in an increasingly mechanized America, caught in the aftershocks of their own hubris, caught by their inability to accept the 'Real Thing', O'Neill's heroes revert to a reliance on illusions as the only way to cope with life's absurdities and personal betrayals. Larry in *The Iceman Cometh* tells Rocky, 'the lie of a pipe dream is what gives life to the whole misbegotten mad lot of us, drunk or sober', to which Rocky replies, 'De old Foolosopher' (O'Neill, 1957, p.10). Most of O'Neill's figures appear as 'Foolosophers' who seem emotionally paralysed by their 'pipe dreams'. Despite their romantic impulses and earnest desires to reach a higher consciousness, O'Neill's heroes emerge as tragic figures, in the specifics of whose fall the playwright sets forth the tragedy of existence itself. As Mary Tyrone says in *Long Day's Journey*, 'I really love the fog … It hides you from the world and the world from you' (O'Neill, 1956, p.98). This retreat into a metaphorical fog characterizes O'Neill's characters and anticipates their ultimate doom.

Of the many other playwrights during the first half of the twentieth century, Susan Glaspell (1876–1948) emerged as an important voice. Working closely with her husband, George Cram Cook, Glaspell helped establish the Provincetown Players. Their summer home on Cape Cod became part of a Bohemian group of writers and artists whose radical views of art, politics, and human relationships provided a fertile ground for new theatre. Glaspell's *Suppressed Desires* (1915) was the first play staged by the Provincetown Players. A two-act satire on Freudian psychoanalysis, the play spoofs both Freud and those who blindly subscribe to Freudian thought, even if they, like the play's heroine, do not know the first thing about psychology. *The Verge* (1921) is a markedly complex and experimental piece, a psychodrama whose stylized language calls attention to Claire Archer's state of mind as she experiences a mental collapse. As Claire says, 'it's hard to ... get past what we've done. Our own dead things ... block the way' (Bigsby, 1987, p.77). The metaphor underpinning the play stems from its title: at the start we see a Claire who is on the *verge* of mental collapse; at the final curtain we see a Claire who has passed the precipice and is about to enter a world of madness.

Many regard *Trifles* (1916) as Glaspell's best short play. A highly gripping realistic drama in one act, *Trifles* embodies questions about truth, power, and gender. A murder mystery, the play revolves around Minnie Wright, who is suspected of killing her husband John. The investigators called in tell the women, who they assume to be trivial, to stay in the kitchen so that the men can uncover the truth. The truth, of course, lies concealed in the kitchen, and only the women are able to discover it. The 'trifles' of a woman's world are ignored by men, though it is the intelligence of the females that calls into question the ability of the men in this play and, by extension, in US culture, to find the truth. With these plays, and *The Outside* (1917), *The Inheritors* (1921), and others, Glaspell is being rediscovered as the important playwright she always was.

SUMMARY

American drama appears as divided as the culture dramatized by its leading theatricians.

O'Neill, who represents the birth of modern American drama, was the first to establish serious drama in the US and is considered America's most important dramatist.

Glaspell, a contemporary of O'Neill, also made major contributions. In her psychological dramas, concern with female identity, and work with the Provincetown Players, Glaspell has recently been recognized for her significant work.

3   SATIRISTS, REALISTS, AND EXPERIMENTERS

O'Neill dominated the first half of twentieth-century American drama. But other playwrights emerged from O'Neill's long shadow, especially between the wars. Ruby Cohn (1988) breaks the writers of this period into three major groups: the social satirists, the social realists, and the occasional experimenters.

After the First World War and the Depression, many American writers produced ironic critiques of the myth of the American Dream, a myth promising a pot of gold at the end of the rainbow for any individual who works hard and achieves religious fulfilment through economic salvation. Americans are not the only ones who dream of monetary as well as spiritual fulfilment, but most Americans perceive their country as a mythicized place where dreams very well may come true. Individuals enjoyed religious freedom in this Brave New World, and poverty-stricken and homeless immigrants established successful businesses. At the same time, many felt betrayed by the Dream. Dramatists felt a moral imperative to take measure of an increasingly bewildering America. Thus such social satirists as Maxwell Anderson, Philip Barry, S.N. Behrman, Rachel Crothers, George Kelly, and Robert Sherwood became theatrical voices to be reckoned with. Similarly, Lillian Hellman, Sidney Howard, Sidney Kingsley, and Clifford Odets may be thought of as social realists. Hellman (1905–1984) sparked debate with *The Children's Hour* (1934), in which a child spreads a tale concerning lesbianism that leads one of her schoolteachers to commit suicide, while her *The Little Foxes* (1939) depicts corruption in a Southern family. Odets (1906–1963) used the Depression and the failure of the American Dream myth as the ideological backdrop for *Waiting for Lefty, Awake and Sing,* and *Paradise Lost* (all 1935).

The occasional experimenters include Elmer Rice, William Saroyan, and Thornton Wilder. Rice was an innovator; his *Street Scene* (1929), set in a lower middle-class apartment in New York on a hot summer day, was a stunning portrait of violence. The play that best reflects Rice's sense of the absurd is *The Adding Machine.* Produced by the Theatre Guild in 1922, *The Adding Machine* was unlike any play ever viewed on the American stage, shaped as it was by a series of highly surrealistic scenes involving Mr Zero, the protagonist. Saroyan (1908–1981), too, felt that art and politics could coexist in the theatre. In his uneven fables of American dreams, such as *My Heart's in the Highlands* and the more popular *The Time of Your Life* (both 1939), he juxtaposes important social concerns with optimistic, all-American characters. His characters reflect a kind of naïve cheeriness that, as the Depression yielded to the Second World War, never quite squared with the moral seriousness of the era. Still, *The Time of Your Life* appealed to a central part of the American psyche: the work ethic and a Walt Whitman-like celebration of democracy.

The work of Thornton Wilder (1897–1975) remains important. The *Matchmaker* (1954) was transformed into *Hello, Dolly!*, one of the most successful musical comedies. In 1938 he staged his most famous play, *Our Town*, which is discussed in Chapter 10, then in 1942, as the war escalated, he captured the anxieties of a world on the brink of destruction with *The Skin of Our Teeth.* Wilder had been greatly influenced by his friends Sigmund Freud, James Joyce, and Gertrude Stein, whose ideas manifest themselves in the form and structure of *The Skin of Our Teeth.* After the Second World War, Wilder saw the play produced in a bomb-devastated building in Germany. He was profoundly touched by the final scene when Hester's words took on an added poignancy: 'How will a man choose the ruler that shall rule over him? Will he not choose a man who has first established order in himself?' (Wilder, 1970, p.136.) Wilder's faith in humanity is a central theme of his work.

SUMMARY

Many playwrights of the 1920s and 1930s saw drama as a model for a critique of American society. Often experimental in form and social in theme, the plays of the period replicate the tension between public virtue and private desire, between a mythicized vision of what America could or should be versus what America, in fact, was.

4   THEATRICAL RENAISSANCE

The 'character' of American drama changed on or about December 1944, when Tennessee Williams staged *The Glass Menagerie*. Within the next five years the American stage would be forever altered: while Williams would follow *The Glass Menagerie* with *A Streetcar Named Desire* in 1947, Arthur Miller wrote *All My Sons* (1947) and *Death of a Salesman* (1949). O'Neill dominated the early twentieth century; Williams and Miller unquestionably influenced the later half.

Tennessee Williams (1911–1983) was born in Mississippi and lived there until his travelling salesman father moved the family to St. Louis in 1918. Williams called the move a 'tragic' one. Years later he mentioned that his childhood experiences in Missouri marked 'the beginning of the social consciousness which I think has marked most of my writing'. Dealing with an over-protective mother, a maniacal father, and a mentally troubled sister, Williams's familial experience heightened his psychological perception, a perception that informs his work. Thematically and culturally, Williams's plays are marked by his life-long preoccupation with the role of the artist and dreamer, the lover and lunatic. They chart cosmic waifs who drift through private anxieties and public exposures with few prospects of redemption.

If O'Neill is the tragic dramatist, and Miller the social playwright, Williams is a poet of the heart. Like O'Neill, Williams draws upon his own familial disappointments, reworking painful encounters into lyrical stage moments. Such experiences are evident in *The Glass Menagerie* which Williams calls 'a memory play'. He portrays the psychohistory of the Wingfield family through the reminiscences of the protagonist and narrator, Tom, who clearly resembles the playwright himself, as Laura and Amanda mirror his sister and mother. Tom addresses the audience: 'Yes, I have tricks in my pocket. I have things up my sleeve. But I am the opposite of a stage magician. He gives you illusion that has the appearance of truth. I give you truth in the pleasant disguise of illusion.' (Williams, 1970a, p.22.) In the play, Amanda seems fixed on finding a 'gentleman caller' for her fragile and withdrawn daughter, Laura. But Amanda lives mostly in an illusory world, dwells on the past, and pushes her children. The attractive and shy Laura plunges deeper into her imaginary world of glass animals, and Tom labours by day in a factory — dreaming of becoming a writer. When Jim, an old high school acquaintance, calls on Laura, he reveals that he is set to marry, thus dashing Amanda's plans for some emotional rescue for her daughter, and herself. With Amanda bereft and Laura alone, Tom, like his never-seen father, abandons the family. An authentically moving, dream-like play, *The Glass Menagerie* was financially successful and enabled its author to devote the rest of his life to writing.

A Streetcar Named Desire is Williams's masterpiece. Starring Marlon Brando, the play ran for 855 Broadway performances. A smouldering tale of sex, the South, and the collapse of self-reliance, it centres on Blanche Dubois, who, after losing the family home in Belle Reve, travels to New Orleans to live with her sister Stella. However, Stella's husband, Stanley Kowalski, feels threatened by Blanche, and the two remain on a fatal collision course, which climaxes when Stanley rapes Blanche. The play ends with Blanche, about to be taken to a mental hospital, uttering one of the most famous lines in all American dramatic literature: 'I have always depended on the kindness of strangers' (Williams, 1970b, p.142).

Although Williams is best known for *Menagerie* and *Streetcar*, he wrote over 30 plays, and composed verse, fiction, and a shrill autobiography. His other notable plays include *Summer and Smoke, Camino Real* (both 1953), *Cat on a Hot Tin Roof* (1955), *Suddenly Last Summer* (1958), and *Night of the Iguana* (1961).

If Williams can be viewed as the lyrical romantic, Arthur Miller may be seen as a theatrician of the ethical. A dedicated social dramatist, his social realism stems from growing up during the Depression of the 1930s. Born in Manhattan in 1915, his mother was a schoolteacher and his father a coat manufacturer. The family business, doomed by a failing economy in 1929, had to move to Brooklyn. After high school Miller took a job in a car parts warehouse for two years because he had no money to attend college — saving his pay cheques for tuition, he enrolled at the University of Michigan and there discovered a talent for writing.

Miller's first Broadway play, *The Man Who Had All the Luck* (1944), closed after only four performances. His next work, however, garnered favourable reviews, and *All My Sons* (1947) generated popular interest. On 10 February 1949, with the première of *Death of a Salesman*, Miller became one of America's most influential dramatists. Abandoning a conventional stage, Miller collaborated with Jo Mielziner to provide a non-realistic set for *Death of a Salesman*. Willy Loman's house has invisible walls and the play relied on special lighting effects and the sound of a flute to bend time: the past, present, and even future are seamlessly melded into a dramatic whole so successfully that theatre-goers forgot they were watching certain key events that happened a lifetime ago, but whose consequences infiltrate the present condition of the Loman family. *Death of a Salesman* was originally entitled *The Inside of His Head*, and this first working title suggests something about the essence of the play: within Willy Loman's consciousness are the values and dreams that drive him. The play is about the last day in the life of a travelling salesman whose distorted acceptance of an American work ethic — the American Dream — prefigures his tragic fall.

The Glass Menagerie in its first year on Broadway: Amanda (Laurette Taylor) stands over her daughter Laura (Julie Haydon)

A Streetcar Named Desire with Marlon Brando, Kim Hunter, and Jessica Tandy (1947)

Director Elia Kazan (right) discusses the set for Death of a Salesman with Lee J. Cobb (who plays Willy Loman), Mildred Dunnock (Linda Loman), and Arthur Kennedy (Biff) (1949)

Willy's is a language of cliché and platitude. He tells Biff and Happy, his boys:

> Bernard [a friend] can get the best marks in school, y'understand, but when he gets out in the business world, y'understand, you are going to be five times ahead of him. That's why I thank Almighty God you're both built like Adonises. Because the man who makes an appearance in the business world, the man who creates personal interest, is the man who gets ahead. Be liked and you will never want …

> (Miller, 1949, p.33)

Willy's discourse is also a language of denial and evasion. And yet Miller somehow elevates a rhetoric of the banal to true poetry: 'I put thirty-four years into this firm … and now I can't pay my insurance! You can't eat the orange and throw the peel away — a man is not a piece of fruit!' (Ibid., p.82.) When Willy screams these lines, most theatre-goers respond on a gut level. For this is a play about loss, not merely the loss of one's job in a competitive America, but also about the loss of one's self. Willy feels burdened by a world weariness, a sense of unfulfilment, yet, as Charley (a neighbour) says, 'Nobody dast blame this man. You don't understand: Willy was a salesman … He's a man way out there in the blue, riding on a smile and a shoeshine. And when they start not smiling back — that's an earthquake.' (Ibid., p.138.) So much of the cultural power of the play resides not in the melodramatic surface events but in its subtext: in the deeper, existentialist realm of what it means to be fulfilled in one's life. Metaphorically as well as psychologically, there are two Willy's in the play — the travelling salesman who will forever remain the Lo-Man in business, and the Willy of consciousness, the real Willy who is most content when using his hands, planting seeds in his garden.

Willy emerges as a modern day tragic anti-hero in that his hubris, or overweening pride, certifies his fall. One fateful night in Boston years earlier, Willy had an affair with The Woman, only to be discovered by Biff, who was struggling to graduate from high school. Biff feels a Hamlet-like sense of betrayal; that he caught his father with someone other than Linda shatters Biff. He drifts for a decade from job to jail, and returns to 'find himself', as his mother Linda says. As in much of Miller's work, the pastness of the past reinvents itself in the world of the present action. Feelings of guilt, shame, betrayal, loss, pity, and fear commingle in *Salesman*, for Willy commits suicide, hoping the insurance will provide for his family in ways he never could. The play ran for 742 performances, and with this work Miller 'successfully touched a nerve of national consciousness' (Bigsby, 1984, p.248).

He retouches that nerve, with varying degrees of success, throughout his work. In 1950 he adapted Ibsen's *An Enemy to the People*, and followed this with *The Crucible* (1953), which seems to be about the 1692 Salem witchcraft trials but also may be viewed as a work concerned with anti-communist hysteria during the McCarthy era. Following his divorce from Marilyn Monroe, Miller returned to serious dramaturgy with *After the Fall* (1964). A play of consciousness, it remains one of Miller's most personal works as it explores — by implication only — his past life and marriage in a poignant quest of self-disclosure and self-understanding.

Miller's plays transcend local history while exploring those very historical factors — and the value systems underpinning them — that are wedded to American culture. The private experience of the common person defines, for Miller, the public issues of a nation and, finally, of human existence itself. 'His real achievement … is as a writer whose plays have proved so responsive to the shifting pressure of the social world and whose characters embody that desperate desire for dignity and meaning which is the source of their wayward energy, their affecting irony and their baffled humanity.' (Bigsby, 1992, p.125.)

SUMMARY

Williams and Miller launched an American theatrical renaissance after the Second World War, extending the moral seriousness and technical virtuosity that O'Neill, Glaspell, and others had first established in the first half of the twentieth century. Williams is a lyrical poet of the heart while Miller is more of the social realist.

5   REJUVENATION IN THE 1960s: EDWARD ALBEE

The traditional narrative history of American drama usually sees Edward Albee (b. 1928) as the next major force in the American theatre. In fact, he was largely responsible for rejuvenating American theatre in the 1960s. First staged in Germany on 28 September 1959, his *The Zoo Story* is a classic which embodies many of the qualities that have since come to characterize vintage Albee. The necessity of ritualized confrontation, the primacy of communication, the paradoxical mixture of love and hate, the cleverly abrasive dialogues, the religious and political textures, the tragic force of abandonment and death, and the penalty of consciousness all coalesce in *The Zoo Story*.

Albee generates much tragic tension by yoking opposites together. Peter, the passive listener, lives on the East Side of New York, and his world seems well-ordered. He represents the businessman, the upper middle-class family man. Jerry, on the other hand, lives on the West Side, and his is a sordid world. He appears as the battle-fatigued loner, searching for meaning in an increasingly bewildering America. Jerry reflects that 'sometimes a person has to go a very long distance out of his way to come back a short distance correctly' (Albee, 1973, p.21), and such a reflection culminates in a fatal chance meeting in New York's Central Park, a meeting that turns into a life-

and-death struggle. For Jerry has decided to make 'contact' with Peter by shattering his comfortable world. Hence the verbal jest turns to the physical assault, which ends with the ritualized suicide/murder of Jerry.

When he impales himself on the knife held by a terrified Peter, Jerry not only gains a kind of purpose and expiation for which he has been searching, but also shatters Peter's predictable world. Whether seeing Jerry as a psychopath living in a 'zoo' (New York), Christ-figure, or shaman, critics generally acknowledge Albee's chief cultural point: to present a Peter who, through 'the cleansing consciousness of death' (to use Albee's words), progresses from ignorance to awareness through Jerry's self-sacrifice. By mixing pity, fear, and recognition in the play's closure, Albee transfers the tragic insight Peter gains to the audience. For Albee, communication shatters isolation.

The American Dream (1960) only enhanced Albee's reputation. Regarded as America's first significant contribution to the Theatre of the Absurd, it is a satiric attack on a culture that places its faith in a consumerist, materialist world. Post-Eisenhower America, with its unfettered enthusiasm for wealth and security as an anodyne for the horrors of two world wars and a depression, prompted Albee to ironize 'the myth of the American Dream'. Satiric in tone, absurdist in technique, American in cadence, *The American Dream* was Albee's attack on what he saw as American complacency. The play offended many. With its domineering Mommy, weak Daddy, rejected Grandma, and banal Young Man (the embodiment of the Dream), the play was, as Albee wrote in a preface to the work, 'an attack on the substitution of artificial for real values in our society, a condemnation of complacency, cruelty, emasculation and vacuity; it is a stand against the fiction that everything in this slipping land of ours is peachy-keen'. The play reflects, many felt, the hypocrisy of much of American life: relationships are subordinated to social categories, and often these categories function as psychological screens behind which the characters lose all sense of original thought. But above all, the play outlines a universal theme: 'a personal, private yowl' that charts 'the anguish of us all' (Albee, 1973, pp.53–4).

His best known play, *Who's Afraid of Virginia Woolf?* (1962), earned him the reputation of being a nihilist, moralist, allegorist, existentialist, charlatan, or absurdist. However one regards the play, his first full-length Broadway effort ranks with the very best of the American theatre. Realism and theatricalism crystallize in *Who's Afraid of Virginia Woolf?* Its verbal duelling, sexual tension, and unexpected exorcism within a claustrophobic set generate mystery and excitement. The play goes like this: after a Saturday night party at the home of the president of a small New England college, George, a history professor and Martha, his wife, have a young couple over for a night-cap. Nick, a newly hired biology professor and Honey, his wife, suddenly find themselves in the middle of a marital duel. Through a night of booze and games, George and Martha gradually draw the unsuspecting couple deeper into their own bizarre reality by telling mysterious, often witty, stories about their past, which may or may not be true. After nearly four hours of fighting, George and Martha finally come to terms with the fact

George (Arthur Hill) and Martha (Uta Hagen) in
Who's Afraid of Virginia Woolf? *(1962)*

that their lives have been largely wedded to illusions, and that they have lost sight of objective reality. As it turns out, George and Martha have nurtured a fictional son for years, and this illusory boy has become a reality for them. The audience, however, is aware of this only at the climax of the play — until then, we think that, indeed, they have a son. The play reaches its climax with the exorcism of the son-myth. With their illusion banished, George and Martha, and probably Nick and Honey, begin the arduous task of facing life without illusions.

Who's Afraid of Virginia Woolf? is Albee's most affirmative work. Beneath the playfully devastating gamesmanship lies the animating principle of love which unites its players. Near the end George explains to Honey: 'When you get down to bone, you haven't got all the way, yet. There's something inside the bone ... the marrow ... and that's what you gotta get at. [*A strange smile at Martha.*]' (Albee, 1962, p.213.) The 'marrow' allusion provides a key dramatic moment, for George realizes what needs to be done to save, not his marriage, but his and Martha's very existence: the son-myth crippling their world must be confronted and purged from their psyche. The 'marrow' allusion signifies George's awareness that stripping away the illusion governing their lives is necessary for survival.

The play's ending stages the revisioning process Albee insists is necessary for his characters' spiritual aliveness. The hatred between George and Martha gives way to rapprochement, rapprochement to relationship, and relationship to love. These connoisseurs of verbal duelling now communicate directly. Once so ennobled by their verbal inventiveness, conferring upon an illusion the status of objective reality, George and Martha are brought to earth, not merely by sacrificing their son, but also by sacrificing the very language which defined their moral imagination. The game-playing, for now, is all over. The ending of *Virginia Woolf* heralds the first step in living authentically. For O'Neill illusions help; for Albee they destroy.

In 1964 Albee staged the baffling *Tiny Alice*, a play concerned with the role of truth and illusion and the way in which the truth/illusion duality influences one's religious convictions. *A Delicate Balance* (1966) explores those who have shifted their stance toward living in tragic ways. The play does not chart cataclysmic changes but rather subtle shifts in human relationships: from engagement to habit, from commitment to estrangement, from love to indifference. All of the characters have let vital lies, or illusions, slowly take over their lives. Although some come to an awakening, Albee suggests that the others, on the brink of living honestly, succumb to the illusions that so distort their existences.

If self-reliance juxtaposed with the collapse of moral nerve forms a pattern in Albee's work of the 1960s — *Tiny Alice*, *A Delicate Balance*, and his most experimental work, *Box* and *Quotations from Chairman Mao* (1968) — then self-betrayal and death inform his work during the 1970s. *All Over* (1971), originally entitled *Death*, concerns the pressures death exerts on those still living. Culturally, the play extends the author's absorption with individual and social response toward death and dying. A companion to *All Over* appeared as *Seascape* (1975), a play first called *Life*. Two sea lizards, Sarah and Leslie, emerge from the sea only to stumble on a very human couple, Nancy and Charlie. The play dramatizes an evolutionary learning process, combining fantasy, myth, and everyday experience. The plot melds animal instinct with human reason, asking its audience to consider what happens to the individual if the human spirit withers because pure reason has usurped intuition. After *Seascape*, Albee continued to produce and direct, but without the power of the earlier work. Still, his clever use of language and moral seriousness make Albee a major figure.

SUMMARY

Albee rejuvenated the American theatre in the 1960s. His witty dialogues of cruelty and social commitment extended the legacies of O'Neill, Williams, and Miller. He was one of the first alternative dramatists to make a successful move to Broadway.

6   BROADWAY AND THE MUSICAL

Since Albee was one of the first 'Off Broadway' artists to bring European absurdism to Broadway audiences, perhaps it is sensible here to consider the status of Broadway and the musical at the time he staged *Who's Afraid of Virginia Woolf?* Broadway and the musical have long, complex, and interesting histories. Some feel that the musical may be America's 'major' contribution to the stage. Certainly Oscar Hammerstein II (1895–1960) and Richard Rodgers (1902–1979) combined dance, song, and fiction in a very original manner in *Oklahoma!* (1943). They also produced *Carousel* (1945), *South Pacific* (1949), and *The King and I* (1951), which most Americans consider classics. Similarly, Alan Jay Lerner (1914–1986) and Frederick Loewe (1904–1988) delighted the American public with *My Fair Lady* (1956), their musical adaptation of Shaw's *Pygmalion*. And Leonard Bernstein (1918–1990) and Arthur Laurents (b. 1918) produced *West Side Story* (1957) — a modern musical reinvention of Shakespeare's *Romeo and Juliet* which pits rival street gangs in New York against each other.

While most 'serious' dramatists laboured in relative obscurity, Broadway staged some extremely popular plays during the 1962–3 season, the year of *Virginia Woolf*. Richard Sheridan's eighteenth-century comedy *The School for Scandal* and a musical adaptation of Charles Dickens' *Oliver Twist* attracted supportive crowds. The Actors' Studio Theater staged two well-received revivals: O'Neill's *Strange Interlude* and George Bernard Shaw's *Too Good to be True*. Moreover, several holdovers from previous seasons were crowd pleasers. *The Sound of Music* was still attracting audiences after 1,424 performances. Other successful shows included *How to Succeed in Business Without Really Trying* (679 performances); *A Man for All Seasons* (638); *No Strings* (506); and *A Funny Thing Happened On the Way to the Forum* (447). Several other major productions that finally closed during the season of *Virginia Woolf* were *My Fair Lady*, after six years and 2,715 performances; *Camelot*, after 873 performances; and *Carnival*, after 719. Clearly on one level Broadway exhibited a degree of vitality.

But as much of this sampling of the early 1960s Broadway fare suggests, mainstream American theatre in New York seemed woefully inadequate in qualitative terms. While European theatres were typically staging plays imbued with ethical import and political textures, many Broadway theatres tended to produce superficial works. The politicized revolts of contemporary European dramatists were not to be found in a commercially-based Broadway aesthetic. If a play was 'safe' — if it would not offend too many and would sell at the box-office — it might see a healthy stage life. Experiments in performance theory and practice, politically extreme works, plays that challenged the conservative tastes of Broadway were found beyond the Great White Way (as Broadway is called) — in university and regional theatres, and 'Off Broadway'. A Broadway play's vitality often seemed measured in commercial value.

So when Albee emerged in the 1960s, superficial plays or guaranteed classics saturated the market. Today, Broadway remains in a precarious state. Arthur Miller wrote in January 1993 that

> the demise of the Broadway theatre [is part] of a whole cultural shift. In New York, of course, it's a question of real estate and the costs of production. In a few weeks there will be only a couple of straight commercial plays on Broadway, and 19 dark Broadway theaters. The theater culture in this city has been dispersed. It's been going on for about 25 years now, and I think it has almost completed its devolution.
>
> (Miller, 1993)

Miller is right — the most vibrant and original theatre takes place in 'Off Broadway' and off-'Off Broadway' theatres — small non-commercial houses spread throughout New York. Albee was also right when, in 1962, he called Broadway the true theatre of the absurd, mainly because of its crass commercialism. The dispersal goes much further, for it is in the regional theatres in Omaha, St. Paul, Seattle, Chicago, Atlanta, and Charleston, as well as in the hundreds of university theatres across the country, that one discovers 'real' theatre. But most regional directors confess that, unless they balance Caryl Churchill or Tom Stoppard with Shakespeare or a popular comedy, they risk losing season ticket subscribers — and money. So Broadway and the musical have their legitimate place in the American theatre, if only because they draw large crowds with escapist fare that prompts laughter.

One of the most prolific Broadway dramatists is Neil Simon: his nearly 50 comedies, musicals and screenplays 'define' Broadway. He is famous for writing funny plays that celebrate family and marriage through their treatments of parenting, divorce, sibling rivalry, sexual awakening, and adultery. *Barefoot in the Park* (1962), *The Odd Couple* (1965), *California Suite* (1977) and *Biloxi Blues* (1985) have become household titles for most Americans — even if they have not actually seen Simon on TV or the stage. Despite an overreliance on gag one-liners and problems with plot structure, Simon's work is exceedingly popular with traditional audiences whose morality may be better reflected in *The Star-Spangled Girl* (1966) than in Beckett's *Waiting for Godot*.

SUMMARY

Broadway, ever on the verge of financial collapse, has a long and vital history in the narrative of American drama — with an unabashed emphasis on spectacle, glitz, and one-liners. The musical in particular appeals to traditional audiences who enjoy a good laugh. Although most 'serious' dramatists and theatre-goers scoff at the banality of Broadway, it occupies a central, if superficial, role in American drama.

7   SAM SHEPARD

In 1963 Sam Shepard, a nineteen year old engaged in a youthful quest from California, wound up in New York where he was, in his own words, 'cleaning up dishes and bringing Nina Simone ice'. Today, with some 50 plays, many call Shepard the dominant dramatist of his generation. By 1965, at least six Shepard plays were staged in various small theatres in New York. In 1970, he staged *Operation Sidewinder* at New York's Vivian Beaumont Theater, a public theatre in Lincoln Center. A full-length play with an extremely complicated set that precluded an off-'Off Broadway' début, *Operation Sidewinder* takes place in the West, features a huge mechanical snake designed to make contact with outer-space travellers, and includes Hopi (Native American) snake dances and military scenes. A financial failure that drew mixed reviews, *Operation Sidewinder* reminded Shepard that he should never let a production be taken out of his artistic control again.

By the mid-1970s, Shepard became involved with the Magic Theater in San Francisco. He directed *Action* and *Killer's Head* (both 1975) at the Magic, after both plays had ended their run in New York. As his reputation grew, Shepard continued to stage many of his plays first at the Magic Theater and then at 'Off Broadway' houses throughout New York. 1976 signalled the start of Shepard's most productive decade, with plays which secured his reputation as one of America's best theatricians. Several of them not only won Shepard various prestigious awards, but spoke to a whole new generation of theatre-goers in a language, style, and theme that exuded a fresh — and authentic — resonance.

Shepard seems at his best when exploring his unique interpretation of 'the myth of the American Dream'. *Seduced* (1978) serves as a useful illustration: the protagonist, Henry Hackamore, is really Howard Hughes, one of America's more celebrated and enigmatic cultural icons, the ultimate embodiment of wealth, power, and perversity. If the opening scene established Henry's eccentricities — Henry meticulously covers his body with Kleenex — Shepard confirms Henry's paranoia moments later. Luna, one of Henry's former lovers summoned to his Mexican compound, must surrender her purse, lest Henry be attacked by assassins. So Henry instructs Raul, his bodyguard, to 'Put the contents in a plastic bag. Take the bag to the parking lot. Drive the Chevrolet back and forth over the bag sixteen times. Collect the smashed remains and put them in another bag. Take that bag to the beach. Rent a small boat. Row out to the twenty-mile limit. Dump the bag. Abandon the boat and swim to shore.' (Shepard, 1984, p.246.) This is one of the many humorous scenes, but such comedy quickly darkens. For in his misanthropy, Henry plays out the fractured inner reality of a deranged consciousness, a consciousness not so much aligned with a human being as with an object, some part belonging to the wreckage of a cultural landscape. This is why Henry exclaims: 'Look at it growing! Hotels! Movies! Airplanes! Oil! Las Vegas! ... I'm the demon they invented! Everything they ever aspired to. The nightmare of the nation! It's me, Raul! Only me!' Shepard presents a Hackamore who loves Las Vegas, Shepard's symbol of an American wasteland. This American Dream seduces, betrays, rapes Henry: 'I was taken by the dream and all the time I thought I was taking it. It was a sudden seduction, Abrupt. Almost like rape. You could call it rape. I gave myself up. Sold it all down the river.' The play ends with Raul's betrayal of Henry. Forcing the eccentric to sign over all assets, he blasts Henry with a pistol, Shepard's last rape symbol. But Henry does not die. Instead, he ends the drama with a haunting monody: 'I'm dead to the world but I never been born' a testimony to the illusory resilience of the myth of the American Dream — destructive as it may be (ibid., pp.274–6).

Curse of the Starving Class (1976), *Buried Child* (1978), and *True West* (1980) form a 'family trilogy'. In *Curse of the Starving Class* we see that beneath the bland surface of a 'typical' family lies a multilayered 'curse' whose various sources reveal themselves through each character. Shepard develops the play's central metaphor: hunger. These family members hunger for fulfilment; yet it is clear that the family remains psychologically starved, forever cursed. The curse also extends with the Oedipal dimensions of the play: the father and son antagonism, and the notion that the curse Ella, the mother, depicts is hereditary, figure prominently in the action.

Buried Child explores father–son relationships by charting three generations in a single family. Like the other two plays in the trilogy, *Buried Child* reveals an American family that jars with sentimentalized versions of the ideal family that saturated American television and popular magazines in the 1950s. It seems to be about an ordinary family. However, violence and sterility hover beneath the veneer of familial unity and the family seems doomed by some fatal genetic flaw. Shepard never specifies who is biologically or even psychologically responsible for this family's fate — until we see just how strangely the major characters interact with each other.

True West raises questions about individual, familial, and cultural identity. The play concerns two brothers: Austin, a Hollywood screen-writer, an educated young urban professional, and Lee, an uneducated derelict, a robber who spends much of his time drifting in the desert. Austin has come to 'Mom's house' so that he can be alone and write. Lee intrudes unexpectedly — just as he intrudes into nearby houses to steal televisions. In this play, though, he ends up stealing something else. When he discovers Austin, he steals his brother's writing career and very identity. Austin, too, metamorphoses into a Lee-like figure. They are almost like two halves of the same person, one representing a violent part, the other an intellectual part. The play ends with a dazed mother returning to find her two sons locked in mortal combat, her kitchen trashed, suggesting that the merging of identities will not be complete, or whole. *True West* becomes a parody of a Western movie. While Austin and Lee duel, Shepard implies that they are fighting for some mythic terrain, for there has never been nor will there ever be a 'true West'. Like the desert world of their invisible father, Lee and Austin's world is a fabrication, a lie of the mind, the 'true West' of some misspent collective imagination. There is no resolution at the end of *True West*, just a portrait of a family incapable of listening, understanding, loving.

Love and hate, expulsion and inclusion intermingle in Shepard's *Fool for Love* (1983), a play filled with a violent love, a primal sexual connection between man and woman. In *A Lie of the Mind* (1985) he continues to explore the destabilized family and illusions that emotionally paralyse. The play hints at unspeakable secrets — incest, murder, and other crimes of the heart. Shepard's heroes are fuelled by unseen presences, felt absences. In his preface to *The Unseen Hand* (1969), Shepard describes the pressure his main characters experience: 'What's happening to them [individuals trapped in an alienating world] is unfathomable but they have a suspicion. Something unseen is working on them. Using them. They have no power and all the time they believe they're controlling the situation.' (Shepard, 1972.) This is precisely the paradox that the Shepard hero too often feels.

SUMMARY

Shepard may be the most important contemporary American dramatist. With his motifs from myth and popular culture, his sense of buried truths, and an unyielding critique of the American Dream myth, Shepard has qualitatively enhanced the genre. He defines something of the spiritual profile of the US through intense examination of the primal family unit, the mythic American West, and the violence that commingles in each of his characters.

8 FEMINIST CONCERNS

In many important respects, women dramatists in the US would probably agree with Shepard's idea that 'something' is 'using them', though the sources of such pressure are many, and the plays reflecting women's concerns are equally diverse. While many women dramatists produced important work before 1960, their work tended to map out a patriarchal world from fairly traditional perspectives and dramatic modes. However, since the 1960s, women dramatists have produced works that are more radicalized. While invoking a term like 'feminist' may not always accurately reflect all of the following dramatists' beliefs, most of them seem to agree that women have been marginalized and trivialized. So their work makes women central participants in the action. The claim of the poet Adrienne Rich — that for many women writing is nothing less than an act of cultural survival — seems confirmed in the performance theories and practices of many women dramatists.

One critic has called Megan Terry (b. 1932) 'The mother of American feminist drama'. Hers is a political theatre that has been obvious since she joined Jo Ann Schmidman to become playwright in residence at the Omaha Magic Theater in 1974. Hers is a women's centred stage which critiques stereotyped gendered representations while offering affirmative images of women who are recovering their feminine strength and dignity. Terry was a founding member of two influential groups: the Women's Theater Council and, with Joseph Chaikin, the Open Theater. In nearly 30 years of playwriting, Terry is largely responsible for injecting 'transformational' acting and sets into the American stage. Her work stands as a model of alternative creative structures that subvert traditional realism, a realism that Terry contends perpetuates patriarchal attitudes. Hence her feminist stance dramatizes the importance of breaking with the status quo, of transforming the present into a Brave New World, based on women's perspectives.

She energized the American stage with *Viet Rock* (1966), an antiwar play and rock musical that opened at the La Mama Experimental Theater Club in New York. The play is more like a movie with its transformational cuts after each scene. Actors take on at least a dozen differing roles throughout a play that, by clear implication, traces US involvement in Vietnam. Theatre-goers watch as characters are drafted into the war and as they participate in fighting; the play closes with a circle of corpses on the stage.

While working with the Open Theater, Terry produced several plays and collaborated with Jean-Claude van Itallie and Sam Shepard on *Nightwalk* (1975), the Open Theater's last production. Terry's other notable plays (of some 60) include *Approaching Simone* (1970), which is based on Simone Weil, the French philosopher and mystic. Many critics feel that *Approaching Simone* may be her best work. An earlier play, though, illustrates her feminist vision as well. *Keep Tightly Closed in a Cool Dry Place* (1965) presents three jailed men who have been convicted of killing one of their wives. In keeping with Terry's 'transformational' dramaturgy, the men suddenly change into soldiers, led by General Custer, who dismember an Indian; then they metamorphose into Captain John Smith, who saves two members in his expedition team. Other scenes revolve around the wife's murder. Terry also interfolds in the action aspects of popular culture — gangsters, drag queens, machines, media types, entertainers — whilst gathering circumstantial evidence about the woman's murder.

Her first full-length work after joining the Omaha Magic Theater was *Babes in the Bighouse* (1974). This play, which uses comedic transformations, takes place in a women's prison, and Terry deftly exposes the relationship between dehumanization, incarceration and sexual stereotyping. After *Babes in the Bighouse*, her work intensifies in its feminist textures. In *American King's English for Queens* (1978), Terry stages the ways in which a male-generated language enables people in power to manipulate and subjugate others, especially women. Concerned with an inherent sexism in our discourse, this play reveals a family who has adopted a feral child, Morgan. The family's oldest daughter announces that 'We'll have to think of a way we can teach her to talk without making her feel that being a girl is not as good as being a boy' (quoted in Cohn, 1991, p.76). Other social and feminist concerns are evident in such plays as *Goona Goona* (1979), which addresses domestic violence, and *Hothouse* (1974), a surprisingly realistic play for Terry which charts feminine strength as seen through three generations of hard-loving and hard-drinking women. From *Attempted Rescue on Avenue B* (1979) to *Walking Through Walls* (1987), Terry presents a theatre dedicated to the exploration of serious social issues from a female perspective.

Maria Irene Fornés has produced compelling plays concerned with female community. Born in Cuba in 1930, Fornés moved to the US in 1945. During the mid-1950s she toured Europe, hoping to become a painter. In Paris, she saw Roger Blin's production of Beckett's *Waiting for Godot* and, upon returning to the US in 1957, committed herself to the theatre. Working within the creative environs of the avant-garde, she produced *There! You Died* (1963; revised and retitled *Tango Palace*, 1964) and *Dr. Kheal* (1968), two plays written in the absurdist tradition. A technically versatile dramatist of at least 20 plays, she also wrote a successful musical, *Promenade* (1965) and a powerful ritual-participatory drama, *A Vietnamese Wedding* (1967). Her work since the 1970s becomes increasingly intense, serious, experimental, and she is perhaps best known for *Fefu and Her Friends* (1977), which explored the issue of women's identity.

In *Fefu and Her Friends*, we watch Stephany Beckman (Fefu) and her seven women friends as they circulate through a house set in New England on a spring day in 1935. The friends gather to plan a fund-raiser for their local school. The characters are colourful, different: the demonstrative Emma, the former lovers Cecilia and Paula, the couple Cindy and Christina, the supportive Sue, and Julia, who is in a wheelchair. But just when we think this might be a celebration of sisterhood, Fefu turns on Julia, telling her that she can walk and that she can fight against her hallucinations. Christina intervenes, and Fefu takes out her gun. We hear a shot. Fefu comes back — with a dead rabbit. Her play-closing lines are 'I killed it … I just shot … and killed it … Julia.' (Quoted in Cohn, 1991, p.80.) The other women comfort Julia, who is bleeding, as the lights go down. Although we are not sure if she is dead or just wounded, Julia, Fornés implies, may emerge triumphant over Fefu.

In *The Danube* (1982) Fornés considers the connections between love, language, politics, and dramatic characterization itself, while her *The Conduct of Life* (1985) examines military and sexual pressures in Latin America. *Mud* (1983) depicts the domestic life of Lloyd, Henry, and Mae, raising disturbing questions about gender and power. This ill-fated lovers' triangle presents a Mae who tries to lift herself out of the metaphorical mud entrapping her, but her impulse to escape Lloyd, who says to her, 'I'll kick your ass', and Henry, who struggles to be 'decent', is cut short by death. The play's fragmentary construction perfectly captures the breakdown of relationship. Mae says at the end, 'I'm going to find myself a job, and a room to live in. Far away from you. Where I don't have my blood sucked.' (Fornés, 1993, pp.936, 943.) But Lloyd kills her with a rifle as they 'freeze' at the final curtain. Fornés's non-realistic and visual dramas make her one of the more important alternative dramatists in the US.

Most female playwrights have had a difficult time infiltrating into 'mainstream' theatre. Indeed, many lesbian and feminist dramatists choose to avoid Broadway. Marsha Norman (b. 1947), however, has chosen and succeeded in staging important work on Broadway. Norman addresses such issues as female identity, mother–daughter relationships, connections between food and women's sense of self, though less from the perspective of a feminist and, she claims, more from the view of examining the human condition through female characterizations. Norman has contributed to a new realism in recent theatre because she replicates the everyday, commonplace, unidealized lives of women who dwell within working-class homes. She exploits a regional dialect that is filled with dry humour and authentic self-disclosure.

Getting Out (1977) presents one woman who has just been released from prison. Norman dissolves realism, however, when Arlene appears as two women: Arlie and Arelene. The two women on the stage at the same time enable Norman to chart the transformation of Arlie into Arlene — the protagonist before and after her imprisonment — and allow her to show Arlie, the jailed adolescent, and Arelene, the adult trying to start a new life for herself as they interact with their-selves. The play stages the problem of how Arlene must learn to integrate the vastly differing parts of her personality into a new whole.

As a playwright in residence at the Actors Theater in Louisville, Norman wrote *Third and Oak* (1978) and *Circus Valentine* (1979). She also composed *Holdup* (1983), a play about fables of the American West told by her grandfather. She produced *'night, Mother* in 1983 at the American Repertory Theater in Cambridge, Mass. and, later, the play moved to Broadway for an important ten month engagement. *Traveller in the Dark* (1984) reveals her interest in philosophy as the protagonist, a cancer surgeon, struggles with a guilty conscience.

To date her reputation stems mainly from *'night, Mother*. This play moves quickly to its climax when Jessie, the divorced daughter now living at home with her widowed mother, calmly announces, 'I'm going to kill myself, Mama', and we watch as she fulfils her promise. This is not the standard fare for Broadway: it is a play about suicide, about Jessie's heroic struggle to come to terms with her life and there is an oddly consoling, reasonable side of Jessie that emerges. She attempts to take control of her life, a life that has been filled with disappointment: 'What if you are all I have and you're not enough? What if the only way I can get away from you for good is to kill myself? What if it is? I can *still* do it!' (Norman, 1983, p.72.) Jessie hungers for a reckoning, for spiritual nourishment that has forever eluded her. Norman describes the door of the set as a door which 'opens onto absolute nothingness' (ibid., p.3), and it is behind the door that Jessie kills herself.

SUMMARY

Women's theatre, seeking to make visible uniquely female perspectives, validates the triumphs, desires, and pressures women face in a sexist America. Although Terry, Fornés, and Norman often present problematic and death-saturated plots and characters, their contributions define the importance of locating a recoverable female self.

9   AFRICAN-AMERICAN DRAMA

Of the many African-Americans who have braved a mainstream American theatrical heritage that placed political, racial, and financial barriers before them, several have emerged to contribute significantly to American drama. Although a number of black people wrote for the stage prior to the Second World War, Lorraine Hansberry (1930–1965) was the first black woman to have a play produced on Broadway. *A Raisin in the Sun* (1959) helped open doors on Broadway that hitherto had remained closed to black playwrights. Her professed artistic goal was to make visible her world and her people to all Americans. *A Raisin in the Sun* opened at the Ethel Barrymore Theater on 11 March 1959 and ran for 530 performances. Directed by Lloyd Richards and starring the then unknown Sidney Poitier, the 29 year old Hansberry was hailed as the most dynamic woman playwright in the US.

The play chronicles the Younger family, who disagree on how to spend their dead father's insurance money. Mama wants to purchase a new home, thus getting her family out of a Chicago South Side ghetto, but Walter, her son, wants to invest the money in a liquor store business. While Mama makes a down payment, she gives the remaining money to Walter, who loses it all in a business deal. Adding to familial tensions is Mama's daughter, who rejects God, turns down a wealthy suitor, and is attracted to a Nigerian student who says he will take her to Africa. The play ends when Mama leads her family to their new home, located in a white suburb. Despite all the tensions, the pride of the Younger family emerges. A play showing authentic concerns of black people, *A Raisin in the Sun* remains a classic of the American stage.

Hansberry died young, and on the day her second play, *The Sign in Sidney Brustein's Window* (1965), appeared. A play about a Jewish intellectual in the 1950s who laments that the socialism of the 1930s has been lost and who advocates societal change, it foreshadowed the 1960s social upheavals in the US. Hansberry had also finished another play, *Les Blancs*, which her playwright husband, Howard Nemiroff, staged on Broadway in 1970. It features Tshembe, a black African intellectual who reflects on his personal attitudes toward Europe and Africa. Uncomfortable with his place in both cultures, he realizes that he must accept and live within his own history. Pan-African in spirit, *Les Blancs* reflects Hansberry's deep interest in personal heritage. Her last play, an assembly of letters, early writings, and notes arranged by her husband and entitled *To Be Young, Gifted, and Black* (1971) added to her reputation. In her realistic portraits of black family life, she tackled such issues as racism, abortion, manhood and womanhood, and she broke down racial stereotypes.

Adrienne Kennedy (b. 1931) creates disjointed images, a collage of inner thoughts and reflections that make for sparkling theatre. Her best play remains *Funnyhouse of a Negro* (1964). In this highly symbolic play, Queen Victoria, Jesus Christ, the Duchess of Hapsburg, and Patrice Lumumba (the Zaïrean political figure, assassinated in 1961) enact the dreams and worries of Sarah, the mulatto heroine who struggles with her persona, her family's ideas, and her sense of ethnicity. The historical and symbolic figures in the play are people, Kennedy tells us, who were part of her day-dreams as a child. These historical figures became aspects of Sarah's own self, though they increasingly grow more disturbing. Feeling the pressure of divided loyalties, Sarah ends the play, rope around her neck, by committing suicide. Expressionistic and revealing of a black woman's consciousness, Kennedy's plays deepen as they explore the unconscious. If her plays in the 1970s seem more realistic, she returns to a surrealistic mode in *A Movie Star Has to Star in Black and White* (1976).

Ntozake Shange (b. 1948) combines jazz, dance, poetry, and visual images within her work. A major contributor to the emerging black feminist movement, Shange explores the plight of urban black women through experimental plays that are closer to staged poetic reflections. Her work, for some, remains controversial because of her less than flattering portraits of black males. *for colored girls who have considered suicide/when the rainbow is enuf*, first performed in bookstores and women's bars in San Francisco in 1974, is a choreopoem — a combination of dance and chanting/dialogue which seems closer to poetry than drama — spotlighting women's oppression and spirit. With many successful runs throughout the country in the mid-1970s, it established her reputation. From *Negress* and *Where the Mississippi Meets the Amazon* (both 1977) to *Spell #7* (1981), Shange celebrates what Alice Walker calls a 'womanist' vision, a vision outlining the transcendent power of women. During an interview with Marilyn Stasio in 1977 at the Blackstone Theater in Chicago, Shange said: 'Men consider the theatre their space, their *male* space', and went on to note that was why she liked staging her work in non-traditional theatre spaces: bars, street corners, and the like. She added, 'I'm not interested in converting a bunch of men to what I believe. My job is to get these men to give me some of their tools, a piece of their space, so I can do what I have to do. Once I get in, you see, then I can set all the terms myself.' (Stasio, 1977, pp.29–30.) Such terms are imagistically staged when the women in *for colored girls*, simply known as Lady in Orange, Lady in Pink, and so on, enact Shange's theatre of resistance.

While Shange and other black women articulated a female response to experience, several black males staged decidedly masculinist responses. Amiri Baraka, born in Newark, New Jersey in 1934 (as Everett LeRoi Jones), remains the most influential revolutionary playwright in the black theatre. After serving in the air force, he settled in Greenwich Village in 1958, where he enrolled at Columbia University and married a white woman (the issue of interracial marriage may be seen in *The Slave*, 1964). In all his writings, Baraka defines an emerging black militant aesthetic. Such militancy emerged not only from living in a racist society, but also from a visit to Cuba in 1960. Baraka, part of a delegation of black people invited to celebrate Castro's revolution, felt inspired to develop a uniquely black artistry and culture, based on a new revolution that would try to eliminate social injustice in a white-dominated America. His plays, the best of which were written during the height of the Civil Rights movement in the 1960s, are imbued with the full force of a new black power, and these plays typically address how white liberal attitudes, while seemingly a good thing for black people, ultimately turn into yet another block toward the larger and more compelling revolution that privileges black culture, power, and identity. In 1964, Baraka's *The Eighth Ditch*, *The Baptism*, and *Dutchman* were staged in New York.

Dutchman indicts a racist world by dramatizing an intense confrontation between Lula and Clay. The action unfolds in a subway car where Lula, a young white woman, is attracted to the middle-class Clay, a young black man. 'Come on, Clay. Let's rub bellies on the train' (Baraka, 1964, p.31), she says in an increasingly tantalizing and inflammatory language. Lula realizes that if she is to seduce Clay, she has to change him, alter his essential blackness, by making him a fantasy of a white imagination. Clay refuses, and delivers a cogent statement concerning the importance of his black identity. With indifferent white subway riders all around, Lula murders Clay for rebuffing her entreaties. After plunging the knife twice into his chest, Lula screams, 'Get this man off me! Open the door and throw his body out' (ibid., p.37), which the white riders do. The play's title rekindles images of the *Flying Dutchman*, the ship of the dead said to haunt the ocean. Baraka's subway becomes an ironized version of such a ship, a ghost ship, with all its ghostly versions of a racist America that will murder the Clays of the world.

Baraka also composed *The Toilet* (1964), *Experimental Death Unit #1* (1965), and *J-e-l-l-o* (1965), plays about black activism in America. When Malcolm X was assassinated and when the Watts Riots in Los Angeles occurred, Baraka became even more militant, as seen in his later plays such as *The Death of Malcolm X* (1969). In 1968 Baraka, in his ongoing efforts to validate African-American values, changed his name from LeRoi Jones after becoming a Kawaidi Muslim.

Ed Bullins also made an important contribution to black theatre. Born in 1935 and raised in a south Philadelphia slum, Bullins' work, like his own life, is rough and uncompromising. He served as Cultural Minister for the Black Panthers in San Francisco, but resigned in 1967 because of clashes over art and political ideology. Inspired by Baraka, Bullins stages what he calls a 'theater of black experience'. Of the nearly 40 plays he has written, the following are regarded as his best: *Clara's Ole Man* (1965), *Goin'a Buffalo* (1968), *In the Wine Time* (1968), *The Duplex* (1970), and *In New England Winter* (1971). In these plays Bullins presents those in the ghetto with rage and dignity.

Charles Fuller (b. 1939) brings a different voice to the black theatre. Whereas Baraka and, to a lesser extent, Bullins have been criticized for a didacticism that subverts artistic integrity, Fuller has received praise for balancing racial identity and black concerns within a more organic dramatic form. His three most significant plays to date, *The Brownsville Raid* (1976), *Zooman and the Sign* (1980), and *A Soldier's Play* (1981) suggest that, unlike Baraka, Fuller outlines a black experience that is integrated with white American life. While Fuller spells out two communities in his work — one black, one white — he also presents a theatre in which the two worlds integrate.

A Soldier's Play, a murder mystery which concerns black racism, is set in Fort Neal, Louisiana in 1944. A black officer, Waters, has been murdered, and

Davenport, a black Washington lawyer, investigates. During his questioning of the all-black army outfit, Davenport learns the men's assumptions — that the Ku-Klux-Klan murdered Waters. Davenport thinks that there probably was some white conspiracy, but he discovers the murderer to be Peterson, one of the black soldiers. Each character in the play represents some aspect of the African-American personality, Fuller suggests. Waters is the tyrant, one who voices black on black racism: 'Them Nazis ain't all crazy — a whole lot of people just can't fit into where things seem to be goin' — like you, C.J. The black race can't afford you no more.' (Fuller, 1982, p.72.) Waters terrorizes the country bumpkin C.J. to the point where he commits suicide. Peterson hates Waters because Waters is a racist, a Nazi figure himself. Thus the military 'boot camp' becomes a symbol of entrapment. When Davenport, the play's hero, solves the mystery, Fuller breaks stereotypical impressions of blacks. Davenport's honesty defines his heroism, and Fuller reveals the humanity of a black man in ways that Baraka has elected not to do.

August Wilson, born in Pittsburgh in 1945, exemplifies the most important work in the black theatre during the past decade. The son of a white man and a black woman, Wilson claims that 'the black Americans have the most dramatic story of all mankind to tell', an observation that remains detectable in his plays. His father never lived with the family, and his mother, a native North Carolinian, moved to a Pittsburgh slum to work, struggling to keep her family together.

While he became involved in the Civil Rights movement, Wilson composed plays in Pittsburgh and soon moved to St. Paul to take a job writing play skits for the Science Museum of Minnesota. He founded the Playwrights Center in Minneapolis where his play about a gypsy cab station, *Jitney* (1982), was produced. His first success, *Ma Rainey's Black Bottom* (1984), the first of a planned ten-play sequence about African-American experience, is about Ma Rainey, the famous black blues singer. The play dramatizes how white managers and executives exploited Ma Rainey. Further, Levee, one of several black musicians in the play, has a dream of leading his own band in the hope of establishing himself as an important jazz musician. However, memories of seeing his mother raped by a gang of white men haunt him. Levee wants to 'improve' the musical session he is involved in by harmonizing the old jazz tune *Black Bottom* in a new jazz style, but Ma Rainey demands that they play the tune in the old way. He succumbs to the pressure, and the play ends on a painful note.

Fences (1985) captures the life of Troy Maxon, a garbage collector living in a black tenement in Pittsburgh in the 1950s. Troy, ever struggling to keep his family together, rebels: he searches for his rights, though he knows that, at the age of 53, he has been fenced in by the myth of the American Dream. The father/son tensions are also felt throughout this play, and Rose, Troy's wife, appears as the strongest character, for she is able to deal with her husband's fear of death and her son's youthful anger.

Wilson's *The Piano Lesson* (1987), *Joe Turner's Come and Gone* (1986), and *Two Trains Running* (1990) reflect his life-long project of highlighting African-

American heritage. Lloyd Richards, former Dean of the Yale School of Drama, has directed all of Wilson's major work and in his introduction to *Fences* calls him 'one of the most compelling story tellers to begin writing for the theatre in many years' (Wilson, 1986, p.vii).

SUMMARY

African-American dramatists have emerged since the 1960s to produce plays that capture the spirit and conditions of what it means to live in a racist America. From Hansberry to Wilson, they validate the necessity of a spiritual Civil Rights movement, one based on coming to terms with their heritage and black identity.

10   OTHER VOICES

In a country as heterogeneous as the United States, many playwrights may be loosely aligned with their respective national, sexual, or ideological groups. For example, there are over 100 Chicano theatre companies, with Luis Valdez being the most prominent dramatist for his culture.

Born in 1940 to farm-working parents in Delano, California, Valdez studied drama at San Diego State University. Initially associated with the San Francisco Mime Troupe, he founded El Teatro Campesino (The Farmworkers' Theater) in 1965 as a response to a farmworkers' strike at the Delano grape plantation. Featuring brief political plays, often on issues about farm labour, Valdez created two dramatic forms: *actos*, which are brief satires about the exploitation of fieldworkers; and *mitos*, which are lyrical, poetic plays about Chicano life. Valdez draws on American and European dramatic heritages, but he also interfolds in the dramas Mexican theatrical traditions that originated in the seventeenth century. In the 1960s and early 1970s, El Teatro Campesino gained international recognition with its tours in Europe and America, and Valdez also wrote and directed the popular Hollywood film *La Bamba* in 1987. His *Los Vendidos*, or 'the sellouts', is his most popular and best work. Set in Honest Sancho's Used Mexican Lot, the play reveals stereotypes that an Anglicized America imposes on Chicano people.

As Valdez explored Chicano life, so David Henry Hwang presents plays about the cultural and political lives of Asian-Americans. His first play, *F.O.B.* (1980) — 'fresh off the boat' — stages the anxieties arising between Chinese immigrants new to the US and their assimilated, acculturated relatives and friends. He explores similar themes in *The Dance of the Railroad* (1981) and in *Rich Relations* (1986). Born in Los Angeles in 1957, Hwang's most remarkable achievement so far is *M. Butterfly* (1988). This is a dazzling play in which Hwang offers a social critique of Western attitudes toward Asians. He explores sexist and racist conceptions, particularly regarding how many Western men fantasize about, and exploit sexually and socially,

Asian women. The play's main character, Gallimard, a French diplomat, falls in love with Song Liling, an opera singer who he spots while she performs the death aria for Puccini's opera, *Madame Butterfly*. Hwang subverts audience expectation when we see that Song is really a man who goes along with the love affair with Gallimard so *he* can spy for the Chinese government.

SUMMARY

Valdez and Hwang produce plays that reflect their respective cultural heritages. More importantly, they call into question Anglicized attitudes toward immigrants through their social critiques of American culture.

11 DAVID MAMET: THEATRICIAN OF THE ETHICAL?

David Mamet (b. 1947), one of America's most influential newer voices, is an ethicist. He animates his stage through language that explores the relationship between public issues and private desires, and the effects of this relationship on the individual's spirit. Mamet replicates human commitments and desires in demythicized forms: commodity fetishism, sexual exploitations, botched crimes, assaults, business transactions enacted by petty thieves masquerading as business associates, and human relationships whose only shared feature is the absence of love. Mamet seems at his best in criticizing what he feels is a business-as-sacrament mentality that has led to corruption of the social contract and his heroes' ethics.

His first plays outline issues to which he often returned. In *Duck Variations* (1974) two men in their 60s sit on a park bench, and their duologue reveals their insignificance. The two men come too close to talking about their own finiteness, and so both replace honest conversation with banal talk, their way of avoiding their fear of death. *Sexual Perversity in Chicago* (1975) presents 34 scenes dealing with sex. The play opens in a singles bar, where Bernard tells his friend Danny in graphic detail about a recent sexual encounter he has had with a woman. Bernard and Danny's conversations are carnivalesque dialogues filled with obscenities. Deb and Joan, the central females in the drama, seem little better off, as Bernard's sexist remarks are matched by Joan's hostile responses to Danny. This is a world in which Eros has been defleshed and where loneliness dominates.

These earlier plays stand as examples of Mamet's interest in portraying people whose lives have been reduced to nothingness, a motif refined in later works. *American Buffalo* (1975) concerns small-time thieves. They find a rare buffalo nickel in Don's junkshop, where the play unwinds, a nickel that motivates them to rob the man from whom Don supposedly purchased the coin. Don orchestrates the robbery plans, which the younger Bob will try to pull off. Teach, a nervous man with a swagger, insists that he, a man, do the job. A long honour-among-thieves conversation ensues in which Teach's lines brilliantly reflect Mamet's vision. Free enterprise, Teach lectures Don, gives one the freedom 'To embark on Any Fucking Course that he sees fit … In order to secure his honest chance to make a profit.' (Mamet, 1977, p.73.) He quickly adds that this does not make him 'a Commie' and that our 'country's *founded* on this, Don. You know this.' The robbery never takes place, but near midnight Bob returns with another buffalo nickel. Don seems embarrassed and Teach becomes agitated, hitting the boy several times. Bob reveals that he bought the coveted nickel, made up the story about a rich coin collector, and suggested the burglary. Although the play ends when Teach attacks Bob and trashes the entire junk shop, we sense a precarious friendship remains. If the characters do not realize how much they have buffaloed themselves, the audience does.

Mamet's preoccupation with a business-as-sacrament mentality is extended in *Glengarry Glen Ross* (1984). The play dramatizes the real estate sales profession as seen through the plight of small-time salesmen: greed lies at the centre of the play. The title refers to the Florida swamps, not the Scottish Highlands, which indicates just how much the playwright wishes to ironize experience in this drama. Roma emerges as the star of the sales team, and he also appears as the most complex. Whereas the others talk, Roma produces. He almost succeeds in swindling the unsuspecting customer, who nearly gets locked into buying suspect real estate. Roma and his colleagues distort language and action to justify their work, thus charting ethical perversity in America.

Speed-the-Plow (1988), which featured Madonna as Karen, extends Mamet's business plays. Set in Hollywood, the play centres on Bobby Gould, the recently promoted Head of Production for a Hollywood film company, and Charlie Fox, a friend who shows him a 'buddy prison' film script. They sense a hit because of a macho star who will fill the lead role. The plot thickens when they have to read a serious novel for cinematic possibilities, and when a temporary secretary, Karen, enters and Charlie bets $500 to see if Bobby can seduce her. Karen, however, preaches the 'truth' to Bobby, who decides to replace the 'buddy prison' script with a film based on the novel (on radiation). An outraged Charlie assaults Bobby when he hears this, and rages at Karen, '[You're] A Tight Pussy wrapped around Ambition' (Mamet, 1988, p.78). Charlie throws Karen out, and he and Bobby are friends again, and will produce the banal 'buddy' film. A lack of trust animates this play in which men appear as spiritual kin of those in Mamet's earlier plays.

Oleanna (1992) is a play about sexual harassment. A male college professor, John, and a female student, Carol, are in his office; she is there because of difficulties in his class. John, who is under tenure review, offers help. The professor listens as she confesses, 'I don't understand what anything means … and I walk around … with this one thought in my head. I'm *stupid*.' (Mamet, 1993, p.36.) He offers Carol some advice and a consoling hand. However, later, Carol accuses the professor of sexism and sexual harassment. He calls her back to the office in a failed attempt to clear up misunderstandings. By the end, the college suspends John and he may be facing charges of rape. Reduced to a grovelling figure, John appears in stark contrast to the suddenly articulate Carol. John explodes, slugging and tackling Carol, and sealing his fate — though he in fact never raped Carol.

In *Oleanna*, Mamet returns to a world in which the gaps between words and deeds remain. He invites us to respond to questions of censorship, political correctness, representations of women, and so on. The title of the play, taken from a folk song, alludes to a nineteenth-century escapist vision of Utopia. *Oleanna* suggests the impossibility of such a vision.

SUMMARY

Mamet's work returns to broader social questions about communication and community. He is most comfortable, and at the height of his aesthetic power, when he replicates anger and betrayal, mystery and assault in the American business world, and when he deepens social satire into private loss.

12 CONCLUSION

Although there is no single unifying theory that encapsulates what is most distinctive about American drama, several important patterns are noticeable. Many American plays focus on the family and are often set in a middle-class home 'that proves to be a jail for the sensitive protagonist' (Cohn, 1988, p.1117). The pressures of a consumerist world typically conspire with the protagonist's own moral weakness, resulting in plays that often end up as modern tragedies. Feelings of physical, mental, and moral loss dominate much of American drama too. Playwrights interfold the public issues of a nation with the private tensions of the individual, and the confluence of the public and the private are often acted out through ritualized forms of confrontation and expiation. Many American dramatists present characters who confer upon an illusion the status of objective reality — as if some 'pipe dream' is somehow the 'Real Thing'. So when the dramatist concentrates on the family, communication, consciousness, myths of the American Dream, female bonding, race, ritualized forms of expiation, and so on, it is because of a moral impulse to distance oneself from a pervasive sense of loss. That many of the heroes in the plays fail to transcend such loss does not negate the importance, American dramatists suggest, of relocating one's essential self. American theatre is, perhaps, best thought of as a drama of the Disunited States of America. It seems fair to say that the American stage, after years of growing pains, has finally achieved an authenticity that validates its place in American literary culture and history.

REFERENCES

Albee, E. (1962) *Who's Afraid of Virginia Woolf?*, New York, Atheneum.

Albee, E. (1973) *The Zoo Story (and) The American Dream*, New York, Signet.

Baraka, A./LeRoi, J. (1964) *Dutchman (and) The Slave*, New York, Morrow.

Bigsby, C.W.E. (1982, 1984, 1985) *A Critical Introduction to Twentieth-Century American Drama, vols 1, 2, 3*, Cambridge, Cambridge University Press.

Bigsby, C.W.E. (ed.) (1987) *Plays by Susan Glaspell*, Cambridge, Cambridge University Press.

Bigsby, C.W.E. (1992) *Modern American Drama 1945–1990*, Cambridge, Cambridge University Press.

Cohn, R. (1988) 'Twentieth-century drama' in Elliott, E. *et al.* (eds) *The Columbia Literary History of the United States*, New York, Columbia University Press, pp.1101–25.

Cohn, R. (1991) *New American Dramatists 1960–1990*, New York, St. Martin's.

Fornés, I.M. (1993) 'Mud' in Worthen, W.B. (ed.) *The HBJ Anthology of Drama*, New York, Harcourt Brace Jovanovich, pp.934–43.

Fuller, C. (1982) *A Soldier's Play*, New York, Hill & Wang.

Mamet, D. (1977) *American Buffalo*, New York, Grove.

Mamet, D. (1988) *Speed-the-Plow*, New York, Grove.

Mamet, D. (1993) *Oleanna*, New York, Vintage.

Miller, A. (1949) *Death of a Salesman*, New York, Viking.

Miller, A. (1993) 'We're probably in an art that is — not dying', *New York Times*, 17 January, section H, p.5.

Norman, M. (1983) *'night Mother*, New York, Hill & Wang.

O'Neill, E. (1956) *Long Day's Journey into Night*, New Haven, Yale University Press.

O'Neill, E. (1957) *The Iceman Cometh*, New York, Vintage.

Roudané, M. (ed.) (1987) *Conversations with Arthur Miller*, Jackson, University Press of Mississippi.

Shepard, S. (1972) *The Unseen Hand and Other Plays*, New York, Urizen Books.

Shepard, S. (1984) *Fool for Love and Other Plays*, New York, Bantam.

Stasio, M. (1977) '"For colored girls who … ": an interview with playwright Ntozake Shange', *Stagebill*, December, pp.28–30.

Wilder, T. (1970) *Three Plays by Thornton Wilder*, New York, Bantam.

Williams, T. (1970a) *The Glass Menagerie*, New York, New Directions.

Williams, T. (1970b) *A Streetcar Named Desire*, New York, Signet.

Wilson, A. (1986) *Fences*, New York, New American Library.

FURTHER READING

See Bigsby (1982, 1984, 1985, 1992) and Cohn (1991) in the references.

Adler, T.P. (1987) *Mirror on the Stage: the Pulitzer Prize as an Approach to American Drama*, West Lafayette, Purdue University Press.

King, B. (ed.) (1991) *Contemporary American Theater*, New York, St. Martin's.

Krutch, J.W. (1957) *The American Drama Since 1918*, New York, Braziller (rev. edn).

Meserve, W.J. (1969) *An Outline History of American Drama*, Totowa, Littlefield Adams.

Miller, J.Y. and Frazer, W.L. (1991) *American Drama Between the Wars*, Boston, Twayne.

Roudané, M.C. (ed.) (1993) *Public Issues, Private Tensions: Contemporary American Drama*, New York, AMS Press.

POPULAR MUSIC

Jeremy Mitchell and John Pearson ★

1 INTRODUCTION

Music is a social activity and music, culture and society are related in a complex manner. Indeed one author has suggested that 'Societies and the individuals who constitute them have been as inalienably and essentially shaped by music as they have by language' (Shepherd, 1992, pp.152–3). Certainly in the United States today music is everywhere, on television and radio, in films and as background 'muzak' in buildings and shopping malls. But music also plays the same functions in America as it does in other cultures. It is played as ceremonial music, the national anthem, to reinforce national identity, or is associated with particular roles as in the playing of *Hail to the Chief* for the President. Music also functions in a similar way as art or entertainment — serious music developing from the European classical tradition — and there is music connected with particular groups within the wider society.

However, America differs from most other cultures in that it is, as Ian Bell suggests in his overview, a constructed culture, one concerned 'about newness, about continual self-creation … [it] is always to be viewed as heterogeneous rather than homogeneous … [with] tensions between unity and diversity.' All of this is reflected in American music within which different traditions coexist and interact to produce distinctively American musical forms. For example, there are areas in which the polka, imported from middle Europe, is still played and enjoyed for entertainment, but at the same time new music is continually produced for mass popular consumption.

There is an American tradition of classical, 'serious', music associated with composers such as Ives, Copland, Barber and Glass but such music is usually played for relatively small concert audiences. Popular music, produced as entertainment for a mass audience is largely an American creation. It is linked in its modern form to technological innovation and associated with the development of recording which recreates and disseminates music. This was done initially through the phonograph but later it took place through radio, film, television and video as well. Music became a commodity produced and marketed by the music industry on a mass scale. As Jeremy Mitchell notes *Livery*

Stable Blues, a record made by the Original Dixieland Jazz Band in 1917, was the first record to sell a million copies; it must have been *heard* by many times that number. Recording disassociates music from the performer and increases the potential audience. At the same time popular music became something that could cut across the diversity of American culture, and create a sense of commonality. Because America was becoming a mass society in the early years of the twentieth century it was inevitable that popular music should become a mass music too. (The technological influence is sometimes more direct than this; the 78 r.p.m. record lasted about three minutes, so this became the initial 'standard' length of a popular song!)

This chapter examines two strands of twentieth-century American music, jazz and rock 'n' roll. The treatment is approximately chronological and together covers a period from about 1920 to 1965. The two musics have a great deal in common: both originally developed in the South, within the black community, and both had roots in the blues. Both are urban musics, and both encountered hostility and resistance within the dominant white culture. Finally both were affected by the dynamics of the popular music industry and were, to some extent, absorbed and appropriated by those outside of the communities within which they originated. But here too both reflect the wider currents of economic and social change in twentieth-century America.

There are differences between them too. During the swing era, from perhaps 1935 to 1942, jazz was closely associated with popular music but after the latter date this is no longer the case. After 1942 jazz develops as an international art and entertainment music for a more restricted audience. The jazz musician is perceived more as a creative artist and jazz itself is increasingly considered a 'serious' cultural product.

At first rock 'n' roll followed a similar course. Its growing popularity also depended upon records, radio and the music industry. John Pearson draws a direct parallel between rock 'n' roll in the 1950s and swing in the late 1930s. But rock 'n' roll, unlike jazz, did not become a 'serious' minority music, it became 'a profitable and permanent part of American popular culture'. So both musics illustrate aspects of American culture, the music business in general and its reflection of broader economic and social change.

If rock 'n' roll lives on in contemporary American popular music then this is true of other American musics too. Jazz and rock 'n' roll are not the only American musics. Some of the analysis applies equally to country and western, cajun and zydeco, bluegrass music or the blues itself. There are still other identifiable strands of American music which reflect the diverse nature of American culture. In America new forms of popular musics emerge, stage musicals such as *Oklahoma!* and *West Side Story* which combine popular song with dance and drama. But a popular music concerned with the continual creation of the new, and with selling a product to a mass audience, is a peculiarly American creation and both jazz and rock 'n' roll have at times contributed to the underlying process of continual self-creation which characterizes pop music from the early 78 r.p.m. records to the latest music video.

JAZZ: 1920–45

> Louis Armstrong's trumpet speaks to the possibilities available to the individual in a democracy.
>
> (Wynton Marsalis)

Jazz is one of the most distinctive American cultural creations, and one in which African-Americans play a distinctive and major role. But why did jazz develop in the United States? What is the relationship between jazz and American culture or between jazz and popular music? At one level jazz resulted from a conjunction of specific musical, social, and economic circumstances; African-Americans and their social conditions have a major influence on its evolution. At a deeper level the cultural connection is summarized by the comment of Wynton Marsalis (quoted in Peretti, 1992, p.1), a contemporary trumpet player who performs both jazz and classical music.

The origins both of the word and the music are the subject of debate — we do not know where 'jazz' came from, although in the late nineteenth century the word had an association with speed and excitement. Similarly while we know that jazz as a music existed from the early years of the twentieth century it is difficult to date its origin more precisely.

There is a further complication. Jazz originated as a social music, played for social events and for entertainment. Some of the most successful jazz musicians, like Louis Armstrong, have been entertainers in a wider sense. But today jazz, like classical music, is a minority art form and it is played more as a music to listen to than as pure entertainment. This means that the story of jazz is also partly an account of its changing relationship with popular music and the music industry.

This part of the chapter examines the links between jazz and American society in the period when the music spread widely, between 1920 and 1945, and encountered hostility too. Rapid change in jazz occurred simultaneously with developments in the popular music industry, the spread of records and growth of radio broadcasting. For a short period big band jazz *was* popular music but after 1945 the two diverged and the relationship between them is now less direct. However, the roots of contemporary jazz in terms of performance, repertoire and relationship to the music industry, lie in this earlier period, and still reflect some of the important contributions made by individual musicians at this time.

2 ORIGINS

In 1919 the Swiss conductor Ernest Ansermet went to hear several performances by the Southern Syncopated Orchestra (SSO) at the Philharmonic Hall in London. The SSO was a group of black American musicians and the concerts consisted of a mixture of music — spirituals and rags, classical music as well as light pieces by Stephen Foster — together with an instrumental blues by the clarinettist Sidney Bechet. It was the last item which most excited Ansermet's attention:

> There is in the Southern Syncopated Orchestra an extraordinary clarinet virtuoso who is, so it seems, the first of his race to have composed perfectly formed blues on the clarinet. I've heard two of them which he had elaborated at great length, then played to his companions so that they could make up an accompaniment. Extremely difficult, they are equally admirable for their richness of invention, force of accent, and daring in novelty and the unexpected. Already they gave the idea of a style and their form was gripping, abrupt, harsh, with a brusque and pitiless ending like that of Bach's second Brandenburg Concerto. I wish to set down the name of this artist of genius; as for myself, I shall never forget it, it is Sidney Bechet ... What a moving thing it is to meet this very black, fat boy with white teeth and that narrow forehead, who is very glad one likes what he does, but who can say nothing of his art, save that he follows 'his own way', and then one thinks that this 'own way' is perhaps the highway the whole world will swing along tomorrow.
>
> (quoted in Chilton, 1987, p.40)

If jazz is defined as 'a music created mainly by black Americans in the early 20th century through an amalgamation of elements drawn from European, American and tribal African musics. A unique type it cannot safely be categorized as folk, popular or art music, though it shares aspects of all three' (*The New Grove Dictionary of Jazz*, 1988, p.580), or as 'an instrumental blues, featuring individual and collective improvisation and a unique "swinging" of the beat' (Peretti, 1992, p.21), then it is clear that the SSO did not play jazz. But the music they played, and Ansermet's comments, give an idea of some of the musical sources from which jazz developed, and there is great prescience in his remarks on its future growth.

The context and timing of the concert were important. The US had entered the First World War on the side of the Allies and the troops sent to Europe were accompanied by bands. Some bands toured with great success and after the war others followed. So Ansermet was able to hear the SSO in London. But in addition to their historical interest his comments hint at some of the constraints and tensions that influenced the emergence and development of jazz. The first is its problematic relationship with popular music. Jazz may have 'developed from a functional music (fulfilling the needs of its audience) to a modernist art (which by definition rejects the conventions and expectations of its audience)' (Giddins, 1990, p.36) but in its early years it was a music of, and for, entertainment and is closely linked to the wider entertainment industry.

Again, Ansermet clearly recognized the individuality of Bechet's music. His review has been used as evidence of the early European appreciation of the status of jazz as art — and the jazz musician as an artist. He notes Bechet's blues playing, although with the SSO this took place in a non-jazz context.

However, his comments touch on two important musical points. One is the range of influences that contributed to jazz as a music, the other is the relationship between the individual and the group within the process of making music. Early jazz is usually seen as a collective music; individual musicians, of whom Bechet is an important example, transformed it into a music which is predominantly a vehicle for individual, solo expression, a music in which improvisation plays a central role. Bechet's blues were probably a mixture of improvised and non-improvised elements. In jazz the balance between these two, as well as the relationship of leadership, composition and group music making to improvisation, and the role of the individual, is one which shifts and changes as jazz develops.

The date of the SSO performance is significant; after 1919 jazz can be clearly identified as a distinct musical form and was increasingly disseminated to a wider audience through records. It marks the end of the war and the beginning of a period of rapid social change in the US. The two are related for 'social change is the engine driving jazz' (Peretti, 1992). At the same time there was a growth in the entertainment industry to cater for a larger, more mobile population which now had different expectations. This is reflected too in the popular music of the time, in the recording industry and in the growth of the cinema, theatre and dance hall as places of urban entertainment.

But importantly the SSO was a black orchestra. Jazz is inextricably linked to the black experience in America and draws on earlier black music as a major source. The relationship between jazz, which was initially produced in a black urban subculture, and the wider white society is a complex one. In the 1920s public performance was segregated, black performers could play for a white audience but mixed groups did not perform in public. The entertainment industry is a product of the wider social context, and popular taste usually reflected the interests of the white majority, who dominated and controlled the entertainment industry too. So for black musicians the context of music making often reflected the racial discrimination found in the wider society.

The reaction to jazz amongst the white majority was initially hostile. For white society, jazz, like ragtime before it, and rock 'n' roll later, was perceived by some as a threat to fundamental values. Jazz was the 'devil's music'. A headline in the *Ladies Journal* in 1921 asked 'Does Jazz put the Sin in Syncopation?' (quoted in Harvey, 1991, p.134). This association was partially reinforced by the introduction of Prohibition in 1920. Music — including jazz — formed part of the underground entertainment culture which arose in response to Prohibition, a world which also included night-clubs and illegal drinking places. The association between these and organized crime is well known and some of this association rubbed off on jazz which became linked to 'low life', and jazz musicians came to be perceived as outsiders. This was one of the attractions of the new music, particularly to the young, and it became part of a revolt against established values. Jazz was associated with modernity, with youth and change, and the jazz musician became a symbolic figure of revolt.

SUMMARY

Jazz draws on several musical traditions but is closely linked to the black experience of America.

While we cannot date its origin precisely we can say that jazz existed by the end of the First World War.

The production of jazz reflected the pattern of discrimination found in the wider society, and jazz and jazz musicians were initially viewed with some hostility.

3   GROWTH

Jazz first entered the popular music mainstream with a record of *Livery Stable Blues* made by the Original Dixieland Jazz Band in 1917, the first gramophone record to sell a million copies. But theirs was an imitation of black jazz played by a white band, and their popular success was short, 'by 1924 the group had passed into history' (Schuller, 1968, p.182). However, their 'hot' music was an inspiration to a generation of young white musicians, and their initial success meant that record companies tried to record other similar music. So it is from the early 1920s that we have aural evidence of the development of jazz as a music.

While we cannot date the origin of jazz we do know the importance of New Orleans in its early development. The city, and Louisiana generally, had a rich and varied musical culture with an extensive tradition of social music making. Before 1920 much of the South was still a rural society but while it drew from rural music such as the blues, and from earlier African-American music, jazz is essentially an urban music. It was made possible by the coexistence of several musical traditions in an urban milieu and it developed within the wider economic context of urban life. In New Orleans there was a coming together of rural and urban folk music, of black American and European traditions, and it was here that jazz seems to have originated. Oral evidence suggests that it was being played by the early years of the twentieth century and identifies important early bandleaders such as the trumpeter Buddy Bolden. By the date of the Original Dixieland Jazz Band recording, and certainly by the end of the war, there were many marching bands playing jazz at a range of social functions in New Orleans. After the First World War there was extensive black migration from the rural South to the urban north, particularly to Chicago and New York. Musicians, and music, formed part of that migration, with the result that jazz travelled north too: 'Everyone who has even the slightest contact with the music called jazz has heard the proposition that the music was born in New Orleans, came up the Mississippi to Chicago, and from there spread out to points East (notably New York)' (Morganstern, 1977, p.133).

This may be an over-simplification both of the pattern of migration and the spread of jazz but there is some basis to it; John Chilton's *Who's Who of Jazz* gives biographical details of 427 important jazz musicians who were born in the South before 1915. Between 1917 and 1941 over 80 per cent of them had migrated to the north. The trek north was made for economic as well as social reasons — musicians earned more in northern urban centres — and migration helped the spread of jazz both directly and through its imitation by others. With growing economic prosperity the market for jazz grew, in live performance and through record sales. The record industry had started early in the century and by 1921 over 100 million records were sold annually. Sales of phonographs also grew spreading music more widely in both geographic and social terms. Sales of records and phonographs continued at a high level throughout the 1920s only falling after 1929. Following the success of the Original Dixieland Jazz Band companies looked for other musical novelties to sell records, and this in turn meant that other jazz bands were recorded.

Records did more than just link jazz to the entertainment industry. Live jazz was played in dance halls and night-clubs but listening to a record cuts out the extra-musical context and provided opportunities for musical imitation. Duke Ellington recalled that he learnt to imitate the stride pianist James P. Johnson by slowing down a piano roll and putting his fingers on the depressed keys of a piano. Records served a similar role in inspiring and teaching other musicians and once it was recorded the spread of jazz was rapid. (A fact that was appreciated by musicians; the New Orleans trumpeter Freddie Keppard turned down the opportunity to make the first jazz records as he 'didn't want people stealing my stuff off records'.) Many of the memoirs of musicians from the 1920s stress the importance of records in influencing their musical development. Record companies recognized the existence of different markets and by the early 1920s there were separate records for the black market, the so-called race records, which feature jazz and blues singers. These were sold in black neighbourhoods in northern cities and available through mail-order in the South.

The Creole Jazz Band led by the trumpet player Joe 'King' Oliver (1885–1938) was amongst the earliest black bands to make records. Oliver himself first achieved local fame and pre-eminence in New Orleans and had made the journey north to Chicago in 1918. By the time he recorded in 1923 his band was amongst the most popular of the bands playing for dances on Chicago's South Side.

The resulting records are amongst the early classics of recorded jazz, but listening to them now through the fog of the early acoustical recording technique, and with a gap of 70 years, it is difficult to assess the importance and contemporary influence of the band and its music. One commentator suggests that: 'Oliver's Creole Jazz Band represents one of jazz's great achievements … It proved, for example, that planning, organisation, and discipline are not incompatible with jazz expression; but at the same time, they must not become autocratic and rigid procedures incapable of assimilating new ideas.' (Schuller, 1968, p.77.) Oliver's band had a major impact on other musicians; some of the young white Chicago musicians who heard the band in person were overwhelmed by the force and inventiveness of the music, and for many its music defines the classic collective New Orleans style.

(Left) King Oliver (centre with trumpet) and members of his band supporting the Chicago White Sox during the 1919 World Series. (Right) Louis Armstrong, 1932: a studio portrait taken in London during his first visit to Europe. Note the Le Corbusier chair

But the band had a further link to the subsequent development of jazz. It included the young Louis Armstrong (1900–1971) who more than any one individual shaped and influenced the future course of the music. The outlines of his life and career are relatively well known. He was born poor in New Orleans and was sent to reform school where he learnt to play the cornet. He showed natural talent as a musician and leader, fronting marching bands and working on the Mississippi riverboats and elsewhere. In 1923 Oliver sent for him to come and play second cornet in the Creole Jazz Band. At first his playing complemented that of Oliver but after a few months he was encouraged to strike out on his own and he left to join the Fletcher Henderson band in New York. There he rapidly established himself as a major musical influence on the emerging jazz community.

Over the next few years Armstrong recorded intensively both with his own small groups — the Hot Fives and the Hot Seven — as well as with other leaders and as an accompanist for many blues singers. His records were a success within the black community and he became popular for his singing as well as his trumpet playing. Both on record and in performance he demonstrated the musical possibilities of jazz and the expressive potential of the jazz solo. By the end of the decade he was leading a large band which became a vehicle for his talent and showmanship, and he was on his way to becoming a commercial success in the wider world of popular music. Throughout the 1930s he consolidated this success by recording popular songs, appearing in films and becoming a touring entertainer.

His career continued until his death in 1971; his life was one of non-stop performance of music, and through records, films and tours he emerged as a world star. In later life he toured for the US State Department, a recognition of the status of jazz as a cultural export. But his influence on the development of jazz was most profound in the few years immediately after he left the Oliver band. It was Armstrong who more than any other individual transformed jazz into a music dominated by the improvising soloist. His example touched and influenced all musicians at the time, not only trumpeters but other instrumentalists and singers too. After the 1920s his popular success was based both on singing, and on trumpet playing — as well as his mugging and performing for a predominantly white audience.

To listen to the records Armstrong made with the Henderson band in 1925 gives some indication of his influence. Such records are frequently only listenable for Armstrong's contribution; the other instrumentalists sound stilted and from another era, playing a form of dance band music rather than jazz. Other musicians 'caught up' with Armstrong fairly quickly but 'what is it that distinguishes Louis from the rest? Why does an Armstrong solo stand out like a mountain peak over its neighbouring foothills?' (Schuller, 1968, p.91). There are probably four essential reasons:

> (1) his superior choice of notes and the resultant shape of his lines; (2) his incomparable basic quality of tone; (3) his equally incomparable sense of swing, that is, the sureness with which notes are placed in the time continuum and the remarkable varied attack and release qualities of his phrasing; (4) and, perhaps his most individual contribution, the subtly varied repertory of vibratos and shakes with which Armstrong colours and embellishes individual notes.
>
> (Schuller, 1968, p.91)

These four elements can be heard in his solos from the beginning of his recording career. The daring and authority of his playing developed rapidly in the five years after leaving Oliver, culminating in *West End Blues* (recorded in June 1928) which is a dazzling display of the possibilities of jazz as a vehicle for the individual soloist. But subsequently his career reflects the wider tensions affecting all jazz. From 1929 to 1947 he played mostly with big bands of relatively inferior musicians who acted as a foil to his musical and technical accomplishments. His recorded repertoire was composed largely of the popular songs of the day, or new versions of tunes he had recorded earlier. Armstrong came to see himself as an entertainer, giving the public what it wants, rather than as a continually creative artist. He adapted to the commercial demands of a largely white audience which made him unpopular with younger musicians. But he was well aware of external events and the continuing racial injustices of the wider society. In 1957 he criticized President Eisenhower for not taking action against the anti-school integration campaign in Arkansas, and in 1965 he made further comments about civil rights. But in general he accepted a separation of his role as an entertainer from events in the wider society. His importance in the development of jazz is difficult to minimize; musically it was 'through Louis

Armstrong and his influence [that] jazz became a truly twentieth century language. And it no longer belonged to New Orleans but to the world' (Schuller, 1968, p.88).

While Armstrong was influencing jazz as a solo art other musicians were expanding the role of the composer. In some of the recordings by his Red Hot Peppers (1926), Jelly Roll Morton (1890–1941) was perhaps the first to achieve a new balance between improvised solos and a more formal preconceived musical structure. However, in the longer term the music and example of Duke Ellington (1899–1974) were more influential. Ellington did not come from New Orleans, he was born in Washington DC to a relatively affluent middle-class family. He started a band there but by the mid-1920s he had moved to New York, the centre of the music industry. Like Morton he was a piano player and, like Morton too, he found a way of combining the strengths of individual players within a more structured musical setting. By 1927, 'after long experience playing Tin Pan Alley pop songs, hot jazz numbers, and the blues, Ellington has evolved a style that drew upon all these genres, as well as African-American folk music ... ' (Tucker, 1991, p.258). This can be heard on records of his early compositions such as *Creole Love Call* or *Black and Tan Fantasy*, both recorded in 1927.

A publicity photograph of the Duke Ellington Orchestra during its residence at the Cotton Club

In the same year Ellington and his band started a five-year residency at the Cotton Club in Harlem. Here they played for a white audience, and made live radio broadcasts. Ellington gradually expanded his band and shaped his music to draw on the abilities of his instrumentalists, a practice summarized in the phrase that 'his real instrument was his band'. His music evolved in sophistication and complexity. As he experimented with musical form he came up against the limitations of the recording possibilities of the time, in particular the three minute format of records. From the early 1930s he wrote longer pieces, culminating in *Black, Brown and Beige*, an attempt to illustrate the history of the American Negro in music. This was premièred in 1943; it ran for about 40 minutes and was judged a critical failure.

Ellington was both composer and performer, and wrote many pieces which have entered the jazz repertoire. Like Armstrong his career was long but the band he had between 1940 and 1941 is usually held to have been his most creatively successful. Like Armstrong too, he travelled to Europe in the 1930s where he found a reception that was less tinged with the racial prejudice that still existed in America. In Europe jazz was treated with greater seriousness and the jazz musician was viewed more as an artist rather than an entertainer. Although he was popular and successful in the 1930s Ellington never achieved the financial rewards that were gained by some of the white bands in this period, he was perhaps less central to the popular music of the swing era.

SUMMARY

Jazz is essentially an urban music and its spread is associated with the wider pattern of black migration after the First World War.

The growth of jazz is closely paralleled by that of the music industry: the growth of the record industry in the 1920s and commercial radio in the 1930s.

Improvisation plays a major role in the evolution of jazz and the history of the music is closely linked to the contributions of key individual musicians.

4 TRANSFORMATION

'The Jazz Age is over ... it extended from the suppression of the riots of May Day 1919 to the crash of the stock market in 1929 — almost exactly a decade' (F. Scott Fitzgerald, quoted in Shaw, 1987, p.14). In economic terms this may have been so but in cultural terms it was not. As Ogren has noted:

> Jazz was indeed a powerful new music ... It arose to popularity amidst strident criticism and extravagant praise. Detractors criticised jazz's musical characteristics — unless they dismissed it as noise —

and its origins in lower-class black culture. Jazz lovers hailed the same sounds as everything from exciting entertainment to an antidote for repressive industrial society.

(Ogren, 1989, p.7)

In the early 1920s jazz was blamed for many perceived social ills from the breakdown of the moral order, to the increase of illegitimacy and the downfall of young women (Leonard, 1987, p.13). By the end of the decade this criticism was less strident, in part perhaps because of the general economic difficulties, and the end of the 'jazz age' that Fitzgerald notes. The economic consequences of the Crash for the entertainment industry included a decline in record sales from over 100 million a year in 1927 to about 6 million in 1932. Sales of phonographs fell too from around a million a year to less than 40,000.

This decline affected jazz and jazz musicians. In the 1920s blues singers had enjoyed widespread popularity too, through records and within the black community, but this decreased by the end of the decade. Bessie Smith (1895–1937) had been a major singer and performer, recording frequently up to 1929. Yet in 1930 she made only eight records, in 1931 six and in 1932 none. She recorded only four more sides, in 1933, before her death in 1937. The decline was due both to economic circumstances and to changing popular tastes. Race record sales decreased and the popularity of blues decreased too. The blues remain a central element in jazz but blues singers never recovered the wider popularity they enjoyed in the 1920s. (Blues singing was an

Bessie Smith: the 'Empress of the Blues'

area in which women were prominent; in instrumental jazz there were women performers — and all women bands as Placksin (1985) has documented — but like much of popular music, and the entertainment industry in general, jazz was male dominated.)

Records sales may have declined but radio grew more important and it was radio that brought jazz and jazz-influenced music to a wider, national audience in the 1930s. In 1934 the white clarinettist Benny Goodman (1909–1986) formed a big band. Goodman was born in Chicago the eighth of the eleven children of a poor Russo-Jewish immigrant family. He was a member of the generation of young white musicians influenced by early black jazz and other 'hot' music. He had been making records since he was seventeen, and earning a living as a professional musician even before that. He survived the worst years of the Depression by working in radio orchestras, the pit bands of Broadway musicals and night-club bands. On forming a big band he had been persuaded to hire the black Fletcher Henderson, himself a former leader of a big band, to write arrangements for him. But the key factor in Goodman's swift rise to fame and fortune in the mid-1930s was his appearance on the National Biscuit Company's *Lets Dance* programme on Saturday night. This lasted for three hours and was broadcast coast to coast. Because of the continental time difference the show went out on the air late in the east but at prime-time on the West Coast.

Jitterbugging to the Benny Goodman Orchestra: Paramount Theater, 1937

After forming his band Goodman took it on a coast to coast tour in 1935. The story of the band's tour is well known. At first their appearances across the country were disastrous and it was only when they reached California that their popularity with the young became apparent. Towards the end of their appearance at the Palomar Ballroom Goodman thought that their engagement there was to be terminated too and so the band played the more jazz oriented and exciting numbers which had featured in their radio broadcasts. The crowd of young people went wild. The swing era had begun: 'that remarkable period in American musical history when jazz was synonymous with America's popular music, its social dances and popular entertainment.' (Schuller, 1989, p.4.) For a brief period, possibly until America entered the Second World War or the advent of the recording ban imposed by the American Federation of Musicians in 1942, jazz and popular music were more closely linked than before or since. Goodman is remembered as the 'King of Swing'. The years after the success at the Palomar brought him remarkable success in popular terms — both financial and social with appearances in film, hit records and so on. Big band jazz was *the* popular music and his example was imitated by other jazz bands playing similar music for dancing and entertainment.

Radio began to replace records as a key medium for commercial success. Appearances on radio were live and it was only later that stations came to rely on records. The spread of radio, and the syndication of programmes, created a more national market for music and brought new bands to national attention. John Hammond first heard the Count Basie band — perhaps the most important new jazz big band of the second half of the 1930s — on his short-wave car radio in Chicago. They were playing at the Reno Club in Kansas City. Hammond was so excited by the music that he drove down to hear the band in person, and then helped arrange their passage to New York, a record contract and a wider audience. (Except that Basie was persuaded to sign for a record company under a contract which paid him a low flat fee for a set number of records; few recording artists were then paid on a royalty basis.)

Such music was everywhere, not just on the radio but on juke-boxes, in films, clubs, and ballrooms. The white bands often featured an instrumentalist leader such as Artie Shaw, or the Dorsey brothers or Glenn Miller. Black bands were successful too, for example those led by Chick Webb, Jimmie Lunceford, Earl Hines and the vocalist/entertainer Cab Calloway, but they did not enjoy the same degree of financial success as white bands. In the music industry both music making and audiences were still largely segregated although there were some tentative moves towards racial integration towards the end of the 1930s (black and white musicians had recorded together from the 1920s).

But if financial and popular success favoured the white bands, some leaders used their popularity to introduce tentative steps towards racial integration. Goodman influenced other bands too in playing with a small group as well as his big band. The first of these more jazz oriented combos was a trio featuring black pianist Teddy Wilson (1912–1986) but this was later expanded to a quartet, and eventually, between 1939 and 1941, a sextet featuring the pioneering electric guitarist Charlie Christian (1916–1942) and other black instrumentalists. Other bandleaders also featured one or more black musicians: the singer Billie Holiday appeared with Artie Shaw, the trumpeter Roy Eldridge with the Gene Krupa band and so on. But such crossings of racial boundaries, and tentative steps towards integration, were usually taken at great personal cost, as the memoirs of musicians from the period show.

The big band was the dominant instrumental group but not all records were made by big bands. Some successful singers were accompanied by small groups. Between 1935 and 1942 Billie Holiday recorded many of the popular songs of the day accompanied by small groups of musicians, and the singer/entertainer Fats Waller, who perhaps tapped the popular market in the same way as Armstrong, was always backed by a small band.

But control of the entertainment industry remained in white bands. Younger black musicians saw themselves as being 'ripped-off' by white musicians who 'stole their music' and enjoyed the economic benefits which were rightly theirs. These economic and social complaints were two factors which fed the discontent of younger musicians some of whom, by 1940–1, were also becoming dissatisfied with swing as music — it was increasingly rigid and formulaic, geared to the needs of a mass music market rather than exploring musical possibilities and the potentialities of personal expression.

These tensions and changes within jazz were obscured by wider problems, in particular the US participation in the Second World War, which changed the whole economic and social environment of the music industry. Perhaps pure entertainment music was no longer appropriate for a nation at war, but the economics of the industry changed too. Many musicians were drafted into the forces. Restrictions were placed directly on entertainment through a tax, and briefly a curfew. Radio made increasing use of records rather than live performances. Amplification meant that a small group could be heard as well as a big band, so technological change helped to accelerate the demise of the big band. None of these changes by themselves explains the end of swing and the big band era but, by the mid-1940s, mass taste had changed, popular music and jazz diverged. Popular music came to be centred more on singers and eventually most large bands went out of business, the only one that survived to the end of the decade was that led by Duke Ellington.

This transformation in music and music making is linked to a change in the audience for jazz and the milieu in which it is created. Swing bands played for participatory entertainment — for dancing in ballrooms or clubs. After the mid-1940s jazz becomes primarily a music to listen to and is played either in small clubs or at concerts. This shift reinforced the changing self-perception amongst jazz musicians who came to see themselves more as artists than as entertainers, playing for themselves and their fellow musicians as much as for the public. This was certainly the case with the style of jazz called bebop which had evolved by 1945. The younger musicians associated with bebop, which was harmonically and rhythmically more sophisticated than swing, at first cultivated a deliberate aggressive exclusivity towards other musicians — especially white musicians — and their audience.

Bebop seemed to present a marked break with previous styles of jazz. This was partly because of the conditions in which it emerged and the hostility that existed between young players and older musicians who frequently could not master the new music, and in part because a recording ban makes it difficult to appreciate how bop was related to, or evolved from, earlier jazz styles.

However, bebop was not the only post-swing development in jazz; around 1940 the jazz world had been changing in other ways. While younger musicians expressed their dissatisfaction with swing by seeking new modes of musical expression in bebop, others, who were equally dissatisfied with the effect of commercial pressures on jazz, sought to re-create a pure jazz from the past. Their efforts brought the rediscovery of older musicians such as Bunk Johnson (1889–1949), and the revival of a New Orleans style music. So from the mid-1940s jazz includes a plurality of differing modes of musical expression — a 'modern' and a 'traditional' jazz. In time a degree of musical and critical tolerance evolved but in the early years of modern jazz after 1945 some acrimony existed between proponents of the differing styles of music.

These changes were accompanied by a widening of the audience for jazz. In the Second World War, as in the First, American troops travelling overseas took their culture with them. This included music as well as dance and dress. The appeal of jazz spread geographically. This was not new, jazz musicians had travelled widely before 1939, but it was from the late 1940s that it became more common. Jazz ceased to be a solely American music and became international in performance as well as appeal. The first important non-American jazz musician was probably the gypsy guitarist Django Reinhardt and he has been succeeded by others. The pattern of diffusion and imitation that occurred in the US was repeated in a larger setting. Jazz is now a world music although still predominantly an African-American one. It is characterized by improvisation and self-expression, and has continued to change and develop. The bebop of 1945 was only the beginning of this process; in turn it has been succeeded as 'modern jazz' by a succession of other styles — cool jazz, hard bop, modal jazz, free jazz, and fusion. Jazz has also assimilated influences from other musical traditions and become a world music.

Jazz has made the transition from a social music existing in a specific subcultural setting to an international art form; it has been described as 'America's classical music' and, like classical music, it is now performed by professionalized, trained musicians, and is discussed and appreciated as a cultural phenomenon. Like classical music too its audience is a minority one and if it has retained any link with popular music this is now a much more tenuous one than was the case earlier in its history.

SUMMARY

In the decade after 1935 jazz and popular music were closely linked through the success of figures such as Benny Goodman.

From the 1930s radio began to replace records as the most important means for achieving popular success and played a key role in nationalizing popular music.

Control and benefits within the music industry still reflected the pattern of racial inequality within the wider society.

The changes in jazz at the end of the swing era reflected wider social and cultural changes as well as purely musical considerations.

After the Second World War jazz became an international music in terms both of audience and participants; it ceased to be solely an American art form.

5 CONCLUSION

I started with a quotation from Wynton Marsalis which directly linked the development of jazz to broader aspects of American culture. A related point was made by the pianist Thelonious Monk who suggested that 'jazz and freedom go hand in hand' (quoted in Morganstern, 1977, p.134). The account given here suggests that the linkage between jazz and the wider culture is less direct than Monk and Marsalis imply and that its history is also influenced by economic, social and technological factors. But the connection may be more fundamental: ' … jazz, in essence, is a music that pits the individual against the collective in a symbiotic relationship — a kind of democracy in microcosm — and without the slightest doubt an art that could have been created only in an atmosphere of freedom, actual or potential.' (Morganstern, 1977, p.134.) To which one can only say: perhaps, although negative evidence partially supports this suggestion. Authoritarian regimes tend to try and control non-conformist behaviour, and jazz musicians have often been viewed as subversive individualists. But the social and political freedom in which jazz originated was less than complete which makes the achievement of early musicians such as Armstrong or Ellington even more impressive, a triumph of art over social and economic circumstances.

Dizzy Gillespie (1917–1993), one of the architects of bebop — and a candidate for President in 1964 — remarked that 'Jazz is too good for Americans'. He was reacting to the lack of critical and cultural appreciation of jazz in America, and the social disadvantages still facing many black Americans. Both of these are changing, but the evolution of jazz will probably continue to reflect musical influences as well as wider cultural and economic pressures.

ROCK 'N' ROLL: 1945–65

In February 1993 the music magazine *Billboard* announced that for the first time its top ten most popular songs were all by artists of colour. That music from many ethnic communities within the US now has this opportunity is a significant accomplishment if looked at in the context of changes in popular music over the past 50 years. While popular music charts of some form have long existed, they have often been a reflection of a dominant white, middle-class culture, while at the same time being inclusive of various types of music. The history of popular music parallels other aspects of American culture during the twentieth century; the slow incorporation of opinions, ideas, values and peoples from outside mainstream white culture. It is a story not without struggle or independent of other changes in society. Carl Haverlin, who was President of Broadcast Music Inc. from 1947 to 1964, in speaking about the sort of music his organization promoted, said in the mid-1950s that rock 'n' roll was 'a vast democratization, a world democratization. It is the tempo of the Nigerian drum and it is worldwide'. Such an enthusiastic endorsement, and it was echoed by the musicologist Alan Lomax who saw rock 'n' roll as 'the healthiest manifestation yet in Native American Music', suggests that in the early history of rock 'n' roll music we can perhaps identify one of the focal periods of the desegregation of American popular music. It was not the first such episode, ragtime and jazz had already made their mark, but rock 'n' roll is important because it is the first music that is fully identified with the youth of the US.

Looking back it is sometimes difficult to comprehend the changes that have occurred in the music industry since 1940. Rock 'n' roll, and later rock, have become terms without limit, describing not just music, but attitudes, generations, artists, and eras. Yet it is the period from 1945 to 1965 that can best illustrate the significance of rock 'n' roll for it is in these years, loosely defined, that we can identify the forces that fostered the widespread use of the term 'rock and roll'. The origins of what we know as rock 'n' roll, and the development of this music into a profitable and permanent part of American popular culture can best be understood in parallel with discussions about the music business in general, as well as in the context of changing economic and social conditions. Shumway (1991) has argued that rock 'n' roll, as a cultural practice, and not just as music, developed because of the conjuncture of particular social conditions and technological developments.

6 A COLLECTION OF MUSICAL STYLES

The accepted story of rock 'n' roll is of a music formed in the late 1940s and early 1950s through a fusion of various musical styles, mostly with origins in the Southern states and including blues, hillbilly, cajun, gospel, boogie-woogie as well as strains of popular music. Of these styles blues (with its characteristics of vocal improvisations, use of non-diatonic scales, and verse and bar patterns) was the most important, especially in the post-Second World War urban blues styles. During the 1950s rock 'n' roll became increasingly accepted by the youth of the US (and subsequently by the youth of the world), first breaking into the popular music charts in the most noticeable way with records by Bill Haley. According to Stephen Tucker,

> rock and roll is the generic term used to describe the dominant strain of American popular music from 1955–65. In general, rock and roll was teenage oriented dance music that synthesized elements of black and white folk and popular musical styles, specifically and most conspicuously, rhythm and blues and country, or hillbilly, music.
>
> (Tucker, 1989, p.1028)

This popularity was conditioned by the limited appeal of the early 1950s pop music to the new phenomenon of the 'teenager'. Sociologist Phillip Ennis describes what happened:

> a new music arrived in the US around 1950 and by 1965 it had fully matured as the 7th stream of American popular music [surviving] among the six other streams that gave it life. These other streams are called pop, black pop, country pop, jazz, folk and gospel. Each of these musics, from their central cores and from their boundary zones with the others, successively touched and mixed, producing rock and roll. It was a boisterous and infectious music, directed to, and embraced almost exclusively by, young people. Rock and roll began with teenagers and was adopted later by college students and those of college age. Together they forged a musical ambience in which they could sing and dance and that would accompany them on a journey of confrontation with the adults who ruled their homes, their schools and their nation.
>
> (Ennis, 1992, p.17)

Whether we finally accept either of the two accounts there is still a consensus view. The early 'stars' of rock 'n' roll were often Southern but were soon followed, in the late 1950s, by artists whose regional origins were more difficult to place and who were, generally, younger than the earlier rock 'n' roll singers, almost to the point of being the same age as the listeners. George Melly has described the increasing popularity of rock 'n' roll in the UK as the 'revolt into style' and, in many ways, this is what happened in the US in the years 1955–65. There was soon opposition to the perceived excesses of rock 'n' roll and the music industry responded by toning down the lyrical content of songs in order to make the music more attractive to the growing teenage market, by increasingly sophisticated instrumentation, and by suggesting self-censorship by radio stations of the more crude examples of youth music. In the late 1950s and early 1960s 'record companies sought to produce bland, well crafted songs for the teenage market, to groom performers as teenage entertainers. The primary aim was to give singers the right image, to create teen idols who looked the part' (Frith, 1981, p.23). The excitement of rock 'n' roll had worn thin by the early 1960s, though many of the styles which went to make up rock 'n' roll continued to evolve and excite listeners outside of the popular music culture (much as they had done in the late 1940s and early 1950s); it was only the unexpected and unprecedented popularity of the Beatles, and other British groups, that both restored some originality and vitality to rock 'n' roll and ensured the commercial success of this style of music. By the late 1960s, 'rock and roll' had become 'rock' and had become, perhaps for the first time, an integral part of the popular musical scene, no longer dominated solely by dance oriented music or by musical styles whose origins were to be found in the South but rather aimed at a more varied listening and record-buying audience, with an increased emphasis on 'meaningful' lyrics and instrumental experimentation.

Like all encapsulated histories this story contains some elements of truth. While rock 'n' roll has often been told in terms of the 'great men' theory (and it was, for the most part, male dominated, a situation reflected in the lyrics, the stars, important disc jockeys, record producers, etc.), or in terms of 'hit records', some understanding of non-musical conditions that facilitated this new music offers a more comprehensive approach in showing a relationship between music and culture in general. Even suggesting that rock 'n' roll was 'new, bursting up on the world in 1955' obscures the fact that rock 'n' roll as a music merely emphasized trends that had been visible for some time, and as a term tells more about the state of US race relations and the music industry than it describes a musical style. In other words rock 'n' roll should be studied against a background of social, cultural, economic, technological and even political conditions. These forces had an impact on musical styles that were based on Southern rural styles, both black and white, reliant on Southern fundamental church music for expressiveness and emotion, and which became nationally recognized and popular in the 1950s. An understanding of these changing forces is a necessary adjunct to a chronological account of artists and songs.

In other words rock 'n' roll does not describe a musical style but an assortment or fusion of a variety of musical idioms. Elvis Presley, in this light, is not so much the first of the 'rock 'n' rollers' (as opposed to making the first rock 'n' roll records), as he is a continuation of the tradition of great Southern rural singers. Sam Phillips, who first recorded Elvis, is credited with saying that if he could find a white boy who could sing like a black singer he would make a million dollars. If, in fact, he did make this claim, the significance lies not in that he was the first to express such a sentiment but rather that he was part of the continuing tradition of American popular music that is always looking to find ways of having white musicians translate black musical styles into commercial success. In the late 1940s and early 1950s rhythm and blues singers and groups such as Wynonie Harris, Joe Turner, Roy Brown, Ruth Brown, Fats Domino, the Dominoes, the Orioles, and the Clovers were beginning to record music that appealed to both young white listeners and to hillbilly singers who continued their tradition of incorporating blues riffs and mannerisms into their music. In a sense it is the timing of the national and international appeal of these various styles that is of interest.

Elvis Presley performing on the Louisiana Hayride

Blues is 'perhaps the last great folk music that the western world may produce' (Oliver, 1982, p.168) and it is with blues that rock 'n' roll begins. It is without question that blues, in its commonly accepted musical form, is the most important element in twentieth-century American music. If it is vital to the origins of jazz it is equally vital to the origins of rock 'n' roll music. 'From being a music of a racial subculture in the US it became, from the late 1950s, the root and stem of modern popular music.' (Oliver, 1984, p.3.) As blues developed in the Southern states, interacting with and influencing Southern rural white music, so the changes in, and to, the South altered blues and fostered changes in Southern music that come to be more recognizable as rock 'n' roll. Indeed the interchange between black and white music and musicians is one that is still in need of much investigation, especially in the context of a politically conservative, racially segregated South. 'Negro music is always radical in the context of formal American culture' (Jones, 1963, p.235) and as the mainstream music industry ('tin-pan alley' for want of a better term) took over aspects of blues 'in the process the music was standardized, its more complex rhythms diluted and its lyrical content trivialized' (Barlow, 1989, p.114). It is this radical nature of black music that appeals to white musicians and listeners and which regularly breathes some freshness into American popular music. *Variety*, in the late 1930s, said of swing, and it is equally applicable to what became called rock 'n' roll, that 'what will be evolved will be a white man's style of swing retaining Negro bounce but coupling it to more respect for the melody'.

SUMMARY

Rock 'n' roll is a fusion of several musical styles; it has roots in rhythm and blues in particular, and beyond that other Southern black music. It became widely popular as a teenage dance music in the 1950s.

Although rock 'n' roll refers to a style of music social, cultural, and economic and technological factors were also important in its origins and success.

Starting out as a black music its commercial success and wider popularity followed its acceptance in the predominantly white popular music industry through performers such as Elvis Presley.

7 THE 1940s: WAR, MIGRATION AND URBANIZATION

The Second World War marks, in a number of ways, the coming of the new styles of music. Sosna (1987) has argued that the Second World War had more of an effect on the South than the Civil War — certainly by the end of the war changes in music and society had occurred that fostered what almost a decade later would be called rock 'n' roll. Among these we can mention: population migration out of the rural South and into Southern urban areas, the growing role of radio and the prominence of disc jockeys, the battles within the music industry over publishing and performing rights of musicians and recorded music, the technological developments associated with recording music, the popularity of juke-boxes (over 400,000 in the US by 1942) and their effect on the music industry and the first significant cross over into the best selling lists of hillbilly and urban blues. Certainly hillbilly music found its first national market during the war years; perhaps not surprising given the number of Southern whites who worked in northern cities, the rise of hillbilly radio programmes throughout the US and the fact that a third of all the US armed forces during the war spent some time in the South. Less easy to articulate is the sense that the war marked the divide between the era when the song was more important than the performer and the era when the performer's interpretation of the song was what mattered. In summary, the opportunities open to blues and hillbilly music after 1945 far exceeded the years prior to 1940 when these styles were popular regionally and records sold in almost insignificant numbers. Or as Tosches has so eloquently expressed it, 'rock and roll emerged in the middle of a war, when the world was mad' (Tosches, 1991, p.2).

The Second World War exacerbated the trend of Southern blacks and whites leaving the rural areas of the South for urban areas, both in the South and in the northeast, mid-central region and the West Coast. By 1960 9 million had left the South; although migration had not begun with the war, it reached its highest point in the 1940s when 1.5 million black people and nearly 900,000 white people left, including, as just one example, a quarter of the black population of Mississippi. The war assisted the industrial development of the South, allowing displaced Southern farmers, sharecroppers and tenant farmers to find jobs in Southern cities, providing an alternative to moving out of the South. From 1940 to 1945 the Southern farm population decreased by one fifth or 3,350,000. However, the South did not become urban, in the accepted sense of the word, until 1960; 40 years after the nation as a whole. This transition from a rural to an urban society or, perhaps more accurately, the movement of millions of rural, working-class Southerners to the cities, is perhaps the vital social factor in the development of rock 'n' roll music. If we accept the importance of Southern based musical styles to rock 'n' roll then we can explain rock 'n' roll as being 'found' at that period in US history when the South itself was becoming more urban and when Southern migrants still retained links to the South. The best of rock 'n' roll underlines this transition and expresses, musically, both older rural traditions and new urban ones. By the end of the 1960s rock music had moved further away both from its Southern roots and its roots in blues. It can perhaps be suggested that the high points of American rock 'n' roll music are to be found at the times when African-Americans were making adjustments to urban America; the period from the mid-1940s to the 1950s, the Civil Rights era, and, to carry this idea beyond the scope of this chapter, similarities can be seen with the recent economic deprivation found in urban areas and the parallel rise of rap music.

It is in the 1940s that we first see substantial evidence that Southern rural music was becoming more urbanized and nationally popular. Rural blues, while still significant and still appreciated by many older African-Americans, was slowly being replaced by blues music that had adopted certain traits from swing jazz, boogie-woogie and gospel quartets, and had developed in order to meet the demands of urban environments and audiences. While some rural blues artists (including those who had migrated to northern cities) such as Leadbelly, John Lee Hooker and Muddy Waters remained popular, it is the more urban artists such as Louis Jordan, Mahalia Jackson and Nat King Cole that found favour among black audiences. Shaw (1978) has summarized this change by suggesting that 'if blues was trouble music, and urban blues adjustment song, then rhythm and blues was good time dance music'. Among the characteristics of this new urban black music (sometimes called 'jump blues' or more usually rhythm and blues) are increased importance of saxophone and electric guitar, a patterned bass which holds the recording together (a change that was exaggerated once electric bass guitars became common in the 1950s), increasing use of riffs and drumming off the beat, and emphasis on loudness and dancing.

In the 1940s Muddy Waters (right) moved from Mississippi to Chicago and began to distinguish himself as the premier urban blues singer, electrifying his band yet maintaining very close musical links with pre-war Southern rural blues. Ella Mae Morse and Louis Jordan (top row) are examples of the types of music that, while sharing Southern origins, had developed to such an extent that their records became hits on the popular charts. Both Morse and Jordan appealed to younger white listeners who would not have been attracted by the music of Waters. It was the music of Morse and Jordan, among others, that pointed the way to rock 'n' roll

Hillbilly music also went through a period of popularity after the Second World War, and diverged along two separate paths. Bluegrass and old time country, or mountain music, remained true to the earlier forms of mountain music; while some hillbilly music, especially honky-tonk and hillbilly boogie, began to adapt to the changing environment, listening to and learning from black music and indeed white gospel music. Hillbilly artists as diverse as Ella Mae Morse, Hank Williams, Tennessee Ernie Ford, Merrill E. Moore and the Delmore Brothers introduced aspects of boogie-woogie and blues into their music, producing the more invigorating examples of hillbilly music. This had always been the case but now this music was appealing to record buyers outside of the South. (In the early 1950s both Tennessee Ernie Ford and Merrill E. Moore had enthusiastic followers in the UK.)

An important aspect of both hillbilly, especially western swing, and rhythm and blues was dance. However, while black music continually adapted to social changes, hillbilly music, even in the brief glory of rockabilly, remained determinedly rural and traditional. It is this aspect of hillbilly music that diminished its importance after the mid-1950s. While remaining a popular music it becomes less a catalytic music for young Americans.

The increased emphasis on the beat was partly a result of the influence of swing jazz and boogie-woogie, partly a result of the demands made by dance audiences (often in large, crowded urban dance halls) and partly because, in the early 1940s, it became possible to electrify instruments. And not only was it becoming increasingly easy to electrify musical instruments, it was also becoming easier to record and listen to the music. What we witness, in the decade after 1945, is music coming in from the margins of America, ably assisted by technology.

SUMMARY

The period immediately after the Second World War saw extensive social and technological change. There was extensive migration from the South to the north, both of blacks and whites; there was also migration from rural to urban areas in the South.

At the same time the environment for the dissemination of music changed. There was a growth of radio, which tended to play more records as opposed to live music, with a nationalizing effect upon popular music. Records also became more widely heard in public places through the spread of juke-boxes.

These changes brought a degree of cross-fertilization between different idioms, and this together with developments in technology helped to create a new music. The electrification of instruments, particularly the guitar, allowed the music to be amplified for urban dance halls.

8 TECHNOLOGICAL CHANGES IN THE MUSIC INDUSTRY

Technological changes, as well as migration, allowed Southern rural musical forms to be heard far beyond the borders of the old South and far beyond the settlement patterns of Southern migrants. Even within the South the increasing use of electricity and new technologies (especially radio and record players) had an effect on more traditional forms of music as well as on the predominantly rural nature of the South. As early as 1926 *Variety* commented that 'the talking machine to the hillbilly is more practical than his bible', emphasizing that creed and allegiance is to the 'Bible, the Chautauqua, and the phonograph' (quoted in Passman, 1971).

There are three important elements here, elements that continue to affect popular music: the ability of technology to change the sound of the music, the recording of the music and who listened to the music. Electrification of both instruments and the means of recording had a startling effect on music, beginning in the mid-1920s when records were first made through an electrical rather than mechanical process. Acoustic blues and hillbilly music, paralleling developments in jazz, became acquainted with electrical instruments in the mid-1930s. While the importance of musicians such as Charlie Christian and Eddie Durham in popularizing the electric guitar is openly acknowledged, the pioneering work of other electric guitarists like Bob Dunn and Eldon Shamblin in western swing and T-Bone Walker in blues (all guitarists that worked in the southwest, rather than the older South) showed that even rural styles of music were not stagnant. The noisier large urban dance halls necessitated not just an emphasis on the beat, provided by drums and a larger rhythm section, but also promoted the use of electrified instruments. The guitar is the most obvious of such instruments and Palmer (1991) has written evocatively of early 1950s electric blues guitarists and how they were the precursors of modern rock guitar. Pianos, saxophones and harmonicas were also audibly augmented by amplifiers and microphones. And the increasing loudness of the instruments allowed a totally different kind of vocalist to perform, a vocalist who used a microphone and yet still had to strain to be heard above the band. In many ways it was these forms of music, on the periphery of the popular music scene, that were the most adventuresome in their adaptation of technological changes. However, it is the guitar that became the instrument of rock 'n' roll. From its beginnings as a rural, acoustic instrument, it was, by the mid-1950s, the most purchased musical instrument in the US and by 1963 sales of guitars were greater than all other musical instruments combined.

The increasing use of technology by the music industry and society at large also fostered changes in how music was recorded and heard. The utilization, in the late 1940s, of tape recording of music not only allowed greater sophistication in recording but was also one of the reasons for the large increase in recording companies, especially small 'independent labels', because recording through the medium of tape was easier and cheaper than former methods. The quality of recordings also improved as master tape replaced shellac masters and ease of distribution increased when 45 r.p.m. records (as well as albums) began to rival 78s. Small independent record companies — lacking large capital backing and distribution networks — also flourished because they, unlike such 'major' companies as Victor, Decca and Columbia, satisfied a musical demand by displaced Southerners. For example, in the rhythm and blues field from 1949 to 1953 only 8 per cent of *Billboard*'s 50 best selling records were from major labels. However, independent labels should not be viewed as all that was good in rock 'n' roll, their importance lies in marketing a product that was, to a great extent, ignored by major labels and for which there was a demand. In doing so these labels provided opportunities to songwriters, producers and singers that existed nowhere else. Today major music conglomerates are the norm and it is sometimes difficult to understand and accept the visibility of smaller record companies and their contribution to the changes that occurred in the 1950s. Without such companies as Speciality, Imperial, Sun, Chess, Atlantic, Duke, Modern, Stax, Tamla Motown, Apollo, and the hundreds of others that appeared and disappeared, the opportunities offered to artists as diverse as Jerry Lee Lewis, the Miracles, Chuck Berry, Little Richard, James Brown, Otis Redding, Johnny Cash and Elvis Presley would have been greatly reduced and the future of American popular music would have been very different.

SUMMARY

Technological change was important in producing rock 'n' roll. The electrification of instruments, particularly the guitar, allowed the music to be amplified for urban dance halls.

The use of technology enabled more sophisticated recording and lowered production costs for record companies. This led to a growth in the number of small independent record companies, and it was these companies which were important for the success of rock 'n' roll as they provided opportunities for music, and musicians, ignored by the major record companies.

Changes in the format of records made distribution easier, and increased the potential market; in addition there was a new market for this music amongst the displaced Southerners who had moved to the north. The demand was not at first met by the major record companies.

9   DISC JOCKEYS, RADIO AND ROCK 'N' ROLL

The story of rock 'n' roll music is intimately connected with the development of TV, recording equipment, and especially radio. Radio, in its many forms, has become increasingly a musical medium, but this was not always the case, and indeed the fight to have recorded music played over the airways in place of live music is a story of its own. The early 1940s witnessed a partial resolution of three important conflicts within the music industry, all of which had dramatic, albeit unforeseen, affects on the popularity of Southern music. First, it was legally decided, against the wishes of record companies, that recorded music could be played by radio stations, which directly contributed to the rise of the disc jockey. Secondly, this right to play records over the air was maintained, even in the face of a three-year strike by the American Federation of Musicians (AFM) (during which very few recordings were made in the US). Thirdly, in response to a demand by the established, and tin-pan alley dominated, American Society of Composers, Authors, and Publishers (ASCAP) for an increase in royalties for music that was played on radio, the radio owners responded by organizing their own music licensing organization, Broadcast Music Inc. (BMI), banned ASCAP music from the airwaves and looked around for non-ASCAP musicians and song-writers. BMI found these artists in the very types of music that ASCAP had deliberately ignored: blues and hillbilly singers. If this was serendipitous for the musicians concerned it was catastrophic for ASCAP.

In the early 1930s it was estimated that 40 per cent of American families had radios. By 1938 this figure was 82 per cent. In that year 69 per cent of all rural families also had radios, listening, on average, five and a half hours a day. By 1940 about 90 per cent of US cities with a population of over 50,000 had at least one radio station. But it was the years after 1945 that marked the change in what was heard on these radios. From 1947 to 1951 performances of BMI material on radio increased almost 100 per cent, and that of ASCAP by 50 per cent. Country music shows had increased in number and reputation, led by the *Grand Ole Op'ry*, but also including the *Louisiana Hayride*, the *Chicago Barn Dance* and the *Wheeling Jamboree*; powerful radio stations set up in Mexico beamed country music all over the US; and, slowly but surely, radio stations, even white owned stations in the South, started to realize the importance of a black listening audience and began to cater for their tastes. It was 'the small independent stations, the type empowered [by agreement with the AFM to play records instead of use live musicians] … and encouraged to program phonograph records [that] became the fastest growing entity in radio' (Ennis, 1992, p.136).

By the early 1950s, when there were over 2,000 licensed AM radio stations in the US, the opportunity to hear music that was usually consigned only to records before the war had startling effects. Radio had achieved a near total saturation: 96 per cent of the population and 95 per cent of American households had at least one radio. The growth of radio stations aimed at black listeners (and working-class black listeners) provided the opportunity for the spread of black-based music beyond the areas where black people lived. Many Southern whites, growing up in a racist, segregated environment, both heard black singers in person and heard this exciting, invigorating music over the airwaves. While many important Southern white singers, such as Jimmie Rodgers, Hank Williams, Bob Wills, Bob Monroe and Carl Perkins give credit to blues singers who they personally knew, others, such as Elvis Presley and Buddy Holly found their inspiration by turning the dial. For example, Bob Monroe grew up in a much more rural area than Elvis and Buddy Holly who lived in urban areas where white and black people were more segregated. DJ Gene Nobles of WLAC radio in Nashville stated quite succinctly the role of radio for many young whites when he said: 'we played records that you thought you could only get on the wrong side of town and told you where to get them on the right side of town'.

Since the late 1940s radio has played an important part in the development of rock 'n' roll music, not least with the introduction of transistor radios in the 1950s. While the number of records sold increased dramatically from the early 1950s and while the sophistication of record players, and later cassette and compact disc players, has fostered this growth, the role of radio in the growth of rock 'n' roll should not be underestimated. In the early 1960s there were over 3,000 AM stations, some broadcasting over large areas of the US, some with very limited coverage, and nearly 700 FM stations. The amount of popular music, as well as rhythm and blues and hillbilly, which was played on these stations was immense, and most of it was recorded. Radio 'created national crazes, taught Americans new ways to talk and think and sold them products they never knew they needed' (Lewis, 1991, p.2). It also brought strange new music into homes all across the US through such stations as WDIA in Memphis (which claimed to broadcast to 10 per cent of black Americans), WLAC in Nashville, WERD in Atlanta, KXLW in St. Louis, KRKD in Los Angeles and WYLD in New Orleans. Integral to these and other radio stations was the work, and fame, of such disc jockeys, both black and white, as Zenas Sears, Alan Freed, Al Benson, Tommy Smalls, Bill Randle, John R., Hoss Allen, Jack Cooper, Dewey Phillips, Hunter Hancock and even B.B. King and Rufus Thomas. Many of these DJs became famous and influential, none more so than Alan Freed. By the early 1950s a music publisher was moved to comment that 'a hit is a hit only 50% on its merit: the other 50% is the treatment the DJs give'.

DJ Alan Freed (centre) was influential in promoting black rhythm and blues to a white audience on his Cleveland radio programme Moondog's Rock 'n' Roll Party

SUMMARY

From the early 1940s radio stations increasingly played records, and conflict within the recording industry produced opportunities for music recorded by the smaller labels. These developments made the role of the disc jockey important in influencing the commercial success of particular records.

The growth of radio played a major part in bringing rock 'n' roll to a wider audience; the change from live music to records, the growth in the number of radio stations, the spread of radio ownership as radios became smaller and cheaper all contributed to a growth in availability of 'strange new music' such as rock 'n' roll.

10 OPPOSITION TO ROCK 'N' ROLL

The music that was programmed by DJs was not always a welcome sound in the homes of America. The 1950s witnessed the first major concern about music that was liked by young, and especially young white, Americans. There had been concerns expressed before about some of the sexual connotations found in blues, and even hillbilly music, but as such music was only bought by black people and hillbillies this concern was limited. Indeed, from the 1920s, record companies had realized that there was a market in the rural South for such music; such records, however, were not easy to obtain elsewhere. Art Satherly, who recorded many of the early hillbilly singers of the 1920s and 1930s, said that 'the music then was all Broadway stuff. If a song hadn't been written by the coffee and cake boys in New York, then it wasn't supposed to be a song. They didn't figure anyone else was smart enough to know anything about music people would buy' (quoted in Hurst, 1989, p.67).

The sudden explosion of rhythm and blues onto the airwaves and into the charts in the 1950s brought a very different response. The 1950s mark the first, but not the last, appearance of opposition to rock music, an opposition based on the fact that the music did not conform to prevalent, conservative views of American society and furthermore that such music encouraged lewd dancing, fostered un-American attitudes towards sex, led to riots and showed entirely too much dependence on jungle rhythms and identification with black society. What made middle-class America even more uncomfortable was the importance of dance to rock 'n' roll. As Ennis (1992, p.48) has suggested, 'when dance rises in popularity, questions of the audiences' ethnicity, race, class, gender and age usually surface'. It is true that much of this opposition in the 1950s was based on the fact that the integral elements of the music were black (as indeed they were later, for example, with rap music) and were little understood, and less liked, by those who controlled the media and who were self-appointed guardians of decency (in the late 1960s the opposition to rock music was focused on its appeal to a youth movement that found little right with American culture). The 'shock was not musical but ideological; it was the overtly assertive social intermingling of black and white that was threatening' (Frith, 1981, p.24). Whether it was the apparent suddenness with which this new music appeared, or whether it was the prejudice against black music and its perceived influence on whites, the reaction against what was collectively called rock 'n' roll was intense and, to some degree, effective. In the mid-1950s changes occurred, both in response to the attack on rock 'n' roll and in response to the economic potential perceived in this music, by the music industry, that defined how rock 'n' roll would be packaged for the next decade.

Radio became increasingly formatted. Even though the utilization of FM radio in the 1960s allowed more musical experimentation, the origins of Top 40 radio, and the subsequent decline in the importance of disc jockeys who played what they wanted (or what they were paid to play), are to be found in the 1950s. The response of radio, to control what was played, was in reaction to an attack on two fronts: first, governmental inquiries into both Payola (illegal inducements to DJs by record companies to play certain records) and the ownership of radio, inquiries which took place towards the end of the 1950s and which all too often turned into attacks on rock 'n' roll by government officials; and, secondly, the hysterical reaction against the animalistic urges perceived in rock 'n' roll music, a reaction led by churches, educators and White Citizens Councils. Many antagonists were in fact members of the music establishment. As examples (quoted in Hill, 1991), in February 1955 *Variety* printed a 'Warning to the music business' against songs that 'attempted a total breakdown of all reticence about sex'. In 1958 Frank Sinatra declared that 'rock and roll smells phoney and false, it manages to be the martial music of every side-burned delinquent on the face of the earth'. Even the sociologist Vance Packard claimed, before a Congressional Committee, that 'our airways have been flooded in recent years with whining guitarists, [and] obscure lyrics about hugging, squeezing and rocking all night long'. The *New York Times* asked 'what is it that makes teenagers throw off their inhibitions as though at a revivalist meeting'. An apt comparison to anyone who understood Southern religion and the part it played in this new music.

Defending American youth against corruption was the theme that united all those who found fault in rock 'n' roll music, whether it relied too much on black influences, fostered political dissent, showed support for the devil or communism, contained obscenities, or degraded musical ability. The reaction in the 1950s was such that record companies, radio and TV fostered a less dangerous form of rock 'n' roll, whether through cover versions of black people's records by white artists (often with lyric changes), by self censorship on what records were played, by denying certain artists access to TV appearances, by curtailing the independence of disc jockeys, or by promoting teen idols who stressed more harmless lyrics, replacing obvious illusions to sex with rather more innocent suggestions. As early as March 1957 *Cashbox* commented: 'the type of Rock 'n' Roll that originally excited the kids … has quietly receded into the background and has been replaced with a softer version with emphasis on melody and lyric ... and listening to the story that goes with the song.' *Cashbox* concluded that 'it seems that the initial impact of the "big beat" has worn away' (quoted in Gillett, 1972, p.57).

SUMMARY

Rock 'n' roll, like jazz and ragtime before it, was viewed initially with hostility for its perceived emphasis on sex and 'social intermingling of black and white'. It was attacked by the musical establishment and older stars.

It was seen as a danger to the wider society. Attempts were made to curtail its expressiveness by producing a more toned down version of the music by white artists both on television and records.

11 REGIONAL MUSIC AND A NATIONAL INDUSTRY

Is the opposition to rock 'n' roll representative of what happens when a regional culture comes into conflict with a national one? Daniel (1990) has written that 'the South gave license to musical genius', but it was genius little understood by the music industry. Once urban blues and hillbilly became popular enough to be threatening to the mainstream pop music industry, this assertive culture responded. Cultural élitism in the music industry was nothing new in the 1950s. The early pioneers of both radio and recordings (including Thomas Edison, Emile Berliner and Lee De Forrest) viewed their products as allowing the spread of high culture and were often aghast at some of the entertainment that was on offer. The bitter battle between ASCAP and BMI, in the 1940s (and renewed in the 1950s), culminating in Congressional hearings into radio ownership supported by ASCAP, is another example of a prevailing view as to what was good music and what was not. Can it be confidently stated that what in fact happened to rock 'n' roll was the assimilation of marginalized musical styles into mainstream popular music, enriching the latter but returning many of the other styles back to the periphery? For instance, during 1955 a number of hillbilly and rhythm and blues songs reached the 'pop charts' (e.g. *Maybellene* by Chuck Berry, *Tweedle Dee* by Lavern Baker, *Ain't That a Shame* by Fats Domino, *Tutti Frutti* by Little Richard, and *Sixteen Tons* by Ernie Ford) but 1955's top selling records of the year shows very few of these songs, especially by the original artists: it was often cover versions by white artists (e.g. Pat Boone, Georgia Gibbs, and Perry Como) that were successful.

One of the myths about the 1950s, and of later decades, is of the musical dominance of rock 'n' roll music. There are many hit records in the 1950s and 1960s that are not rock 'n' roll at all. A look at the top ten best selling single records of the 1950s would show no rock 'n' roll record at all. In 1957 a poll of the musical tastes of high school pupils would indicate that the top five favourite male singers were Pat Boone, Elvis, Tommy Sands, Perry Como and Harry Belafonte! The clash between, on the one hand, a young, maverick music industry that was based on Southern musical styles and that took advantage of new means of recording and broadcasting and aimed its product at working class, older, black and white people (even if that product was increasingly bought by young whites) and, on the other, a popular music industry that was New York- and Hollywood-dominated was a clash in which the balance of power lay with the establishment. Ahmet Ertegun, the founder of one of the more long-lived independent record labels, Atlantic Records, suggested to his producers that

> the kind of record we have to make must work like this. There's a black cotton picker who lives in a cabin 27 miles out of Opooloosa. It's Friday night and the cat is all tapped out. It's 10 o'clock and he's lying back in his chair, dozing and listening to the radio. He listens, gets up, gets dressed, drives the 27 miles into town and buys the record.
>
> (quoted in Shaw, 1978, pp.370–1)

While such an attitude might have produced exciting music it was not the way the established music industry worked or profited. As far back as 1899 the *Musical Courier* had said of ragtime, that it was 'a wave of vulgar filthy and suggestive music [that] has inundated the land … it is artistically and morally depressing and should be suppressed by press and pulpit'. Astonishing words, because they could be used exactly to describe the music industry's determined resistance to jazz, blues, hillbilly, rock 'n' roll and British beat groups. Yet at the same time this industry showed a remarkable capacity for assimilating these musical styles and turning them to its own advantage. It is of some significance that although most of the major American rock 'n' roll stars of the 1950s and early 1960s recorded, initially, for independent labels it was the major companies, with some exceptions (such as Atlantic and Motown) that eventually prospered. Distribution concerns, payment problems for both royalties and records ordered, pressing delays, and the antagonism of large record companies were some issues that forced many small record labels out of existence. In the years 1946–52 it is estimated that 163 records sold over a million copies. Only five were recorded by companies other than Columbia, Victor, Decca, Capitol, MGM or Mercury. While the situation improved for independent labels later in the 1950s, by 1969 it is estimated that five major manufacturers, Columbia, Warner-Seven Arts, RCA Victor, Capitol-EMI, and MGM, controlled more than half the market. Of the remaining share approximately 35 per cent was divided between 100 smaller companies (Gillett, 1972; Sanjek and Sanjek, 1991). With this as a context it is perhaps no coincidence that Elvis became such a star only after he left a small label and signed with RCA Victor. The reason was perhaps less to do with his music, and more to do with the exposure that Victor could afford. Shumway (1991) has argued that Elvis became important not because of his records but because of his TV shows. The same could be said of the Beatles. There were almost 700 TV stations in 1960 and already they had begun to play their part in both introducing rock 'n' roll singers to the nation as well as supporting the rise of less dangerous artists and identifying, through shows such as *Bandstand* and *Shindig*, that the audience for rock 'n' roll was young teenagers. Compères such as Ed Sullivan, Perry Como, the Dorsey Brothers, and Steve Allen brought artists as disparate as Elvis, Bo Diddley, Jerry Lee Lewis, Buddy Holly and Carl Perkins to areas far from the South.

While a small record label could exist by selling a limited number of records to a selected audience a large record company could not afford to limit its scope in such a way. This was especially true with the changes that occurred in the US population after 1950. Record companies that recorded blues and hillbilly were content to sell their product to older black and white people and while this audience grew after the Second World War (to the extent that some blues and hillbilly records did sell a million copies), the turning point was the discovery of this music by the new phenomenon of the teenager and the discovery of the teenager by the music industry. By 1956 there were already 13 million teenagers spending $7 billion a year. Also in 1956 record sales increased by 45 per cent over the previous year. It is significant that in the same year it was estimated that disc jockeys commanded 68 per cent of the airtime on radio. The birth rate after the war rose dramatically and the discovery that there was a large, very young, and relatively well-off audience that liked rock 'n' roll had a fascinating effect on the larger record companies and the cultural watch-dogs. The music had to be suitable for these youngsters; increasingly the product of the record companies was aimed at a purchaser who was young, white, middle class and probably female. In a little over a decade there had been an incredible change in who bought records and to whom more and more records were directed. It was realized that working-class teenagers were starting to show some originality in musical taste; in the late 1950s and into the 1960s, firstly middle-class teenagers and later middle-class youth were accorded status as the focus of rock 'n' roll purchasing. And, in the main, the records that were being sold were 45 r.p.m. (interestingly, though perhaps not surprisingly, the 78 r.p.m. record remained popular longer among hillbilly and blues audiences): rock 'n' roll is music that is heard through the medium of the single record. This situation remained until the mid-1960s, when record buyers, often college age, began to dictate changes in rock 'n' roll, moving it away from being dance oriented and towards the dominance of long-playing albums.

SUMMARY

Rock 'n' roll did not dominate mainstream popular music in the 1950s, but if it originated as a regional music from a particular racial, class and urban context, it eventually became absorbed into the musical mainstream. Like other elements of US popular culture a minority product became part of the national culture.

> Two processes helped in this: the increasing dominance of the major record companies in the production of hit records, and the marketing of records targeted at the affluent teenager after the mid-1950s.

12   WHAT WAS ROCK 'N' ROLL?

Where did the term rock 'n' roll come from and why is it later called rock? Rock 'n' roll existed as a term long before the 1950s and was initially a sexual term, with perhaps a milder connotation of dancing. Tosches (1985, 1991) makes it clear that the term rock 'n' roll was used frequently either in songs or in song titles. In the early 1950s — and credit is given to disc jockey Alan Freed — the term began to be used to describe a certain type of music. At first it was used to describe what was then called rhythm and blues, a music that both *Billboard* and *Variety* in 1954 and 1955 cautioned was the 'one to watch' as popular music charts started witnessing cross over hits from the rhythm and blues charts (although rhythm and blues in 1953 still only accounted for about 6 per cent of total record sales). The reason for a change of name is obvious given the times: rhythm and blues suggested black music and the use of rock 'n' roll to conceal this was the beginning of popular music's tendency to view success through the medium of white youth.

Quite quickly, rock 'n' roll began to be used to describe and classify all music that appealed to teenagers. Once this began to occur it became increasingly difficult to distinguish the various elements of youth music. This was complicated even more by the emphasis placed on best selling records. Since the early 1920s the music industry had given labels to the types of music that appealed to Southerners, both black and white. 'Hillbilly' became 'folk' became 'country and western' (and for a time 'hillbilly and foreign records of the month'). 'Race' became 'Harlem hit parade' became 'rhythm and blues' and both this latter term and country and western were adopted in 1949 by *Billboard* to identify best selling records in these fields. In addition there were also charts that listed not only records that sold in stores but also records that were 'most played on the juke-boxes'. However, since the introduction of *Billboard*'s first popular music chart in 1940 the only real measure of commercial success was how high a record appeared in this, and other popular music charts. Records might sell a million copies over a period of time to blues and hillbilly fans but if they did not appear in the pop charts it signified almost nothing. The importance of the popular music charts helps in understanding the excitement when blues and hillbilly records did begin appearing in the early 1950s and it is in this decade that Southern based music becomes a significant presence in the charts. Hillbilly and rhythm and blues charts continued as separate entities; but it was the popular music charts that became the standard by which popularity was measured. As such rock 'n' roll singers lined up next to folk singers, popular music singers, instrumental bands, etc. Unfortunately the term rock 'n' roll began to be applied to much that was found in these other categories. To call music rock 'n' roll meant that it might appeal to teenagers: how else to explain Tony Bennett, Perry Como and Pat Boone being described as rock and rollers? The use of a musical term to increase sales has clouded the fact that rock 'n' roll was only one of many musical styles that appeared in the best selling charts. While rock 'n' roll was a purely American product, rock was not, incorporating, as it did, British musicians of the 1960s.

It is hard to identify rock 'n' roll within this larger field. There is no doubt that rock 'n' roll, as a collection of styles, was co-opted by the music industry who continue to use the term as a means of selling records. There is a parallel between rock 'n' roll in the mid-1950s and jazz in the early 1920s, swing music in the mid- to late 1930s and the Beatles led group boom in the mid-1960s; all occurred at a time of declining record sales and all these 'crazes' helped pull the record industry out of a recession. In doing so the music is made presentable to a larger number of consumers. What makes rock 'n' roll different, and difficult to define and articulate, is that whereas with jazz, rural blues, gospel, hillbilly, bluegrass, western swing, and bebop it is possible to say when the first recorded example of the music was made, it is impossible to do this with rock 'n' roll. Recently *Life* magazine proposed that we look for the start of rock 'n' roll not with a record or with an artist, but with an event. Alan Freed's *Moondog Coronation Ball* in Cleveland on 21 March 1952 — an integrated show starring artists such as Tony Grimes, Varetta Dillard and the Dominoes — gave the first signals to the north that young whites found rhythm and blues appealing and, incidentally, ended in a riot of sorts. This lack of consensus about a starting date is important in that it suggests rather than there being anything called rock 'n' roll we are

Moondog Coronation Ball, *Cleveland, 21 March 1952*

dealing with a term imposed upon various styles of music, imposed in order to identify a new sales opportunity and perhaps to describe something that was somewhat incomprehensible to Eisenhower's America.

SUMMARY

Rock 'n' roll was perhaps not one style of music, it was also a label used to sell records, and to try and make sense of a variety of musical styles.

13   CONCLUSION

Rock 'n' roll happened because of changes in black music and identification with and utilization of these changes by white artists and record buyers. Beneath the surface the changes in black music (e.g. urban blues, soul, rap) reflect the changing conditions and life-styles of African-Americans, becoming more urban and adapting to changing economic circumstances. In the 1950s this was also true of Southern white immigrants to the cities; it has been less so after 1960. Even the developments in American rock in the late 1960s had their origins in black music, co-opted and developed by British groups. But it is important to place the music in context, for without doing so it is possible to miss its significance. The context is the radical change in society in the years under discussion, as expressed by Richard Wright:

> millions in this our twentieth century have danced with abandonment and serious joy to jigs that had their birth in suffering ... [alluding to] the blues, those ... songs created by millions of nameless ... American Negroes in their confused wanderings over the American southland and in their intrusion into the northern American industrial cities.

(quoted in Oliver, 1990, p.xiii)

It is this 'rhythm of the soil', as *Grand Ole Op'ry* announcer George Hay termed it, and its urbanization that makes the period under discussion important. Sanjek and Sanjek (1991) have commented on two parallel themes. First, that each technological development in the music industry has been used by commercial interests to profit from the work of artists; moreover 'the progress of the twentieth century has shown that the control of the entertainment marketplace increasingly rests in a small body of conglomerates', a situation certainly true in the more recent history of rock music. Second, they also acknowledge that 'the musical canvas has become richer and more diverse as the work of marginalized members of American society has entered the mainstream', providing ongoing interest in rock 'n' roll and insight into the current discussion of the US as a pluralistic, multicultural nation. For the first time rock 'n' roll brought into the music industry styles and forms that no matter how much they were adopted and adapted, reflected this 'vast democratization' that Carl Haverlin spoke of, and in so doing, influenced both US and world culture. That this process continued after the mid-1960s, and continues today, is evidenced by the *Billboard* announcement that opened this part of the chapter. In other words listening to rock 'n' roll music is a way of listening to changing social conditions in the US. The changes might not always be in the lyrics but they are echoed in the sounds.

SUMMARY

Rock 'n' roll reflects the impact of change on black music, and its adaptation by and to white concerns. Changes in the music and the lyrics reflect the radical social changes of the period after 1945.

The success of rock 'n' roll reflects both the diversity of American popular music, and it is also in part the result of more general commercial processes in the music industry.

REFERENCES

Barlow, W. (1989) *Looking Up at Down*, Philadelphia, Temple University Press.

Chilton, J. (1987) *Sidney Bechet: the Wizard of Jazz*, London, Macmillan.

Chilton, J. (1989) *Who's Who of Jazz*, London, Macmillan (5th edn).

Daniel, P. (1990) *Standing at the Crossroads: Southern Life Since 1900*, New York, Hill & Wang.

Ennis, P.H. (1992) *The Seventh Stream: the Emergence of Rock 'n' Roll in American Popular Music*, Hanover, Wesleyan University Press.

Frith, S. (1981) *Sound Effects, Youth Leisure and the Politics of Rock and Roll*, New York, Pantheon.

Giddins, G. (1990) 'The evolution of jazz' in Baker, D.N. (ed.) *New Perspectives on Jazz*, Washington, Smithsonian Institute, pp.33–44.

Gillett, C. (1972) *The Sound of the City: the Rise of Rock and Roll*, New York, Outerbridge & Dienstfrey.

Harvey, M. (1991) 'Jazz and modernism: changing conceptions of innovation and tradition' in Buckner, R.T. and Welland, S. (eds) *Essays on the History and Meanings of Jazz*, Detroit, Wayne State University Press, pp.128–47.

Hill, T. (1991) 'The enemy within: censorship in rock music in the 1950s', *South Atlantic Quarterly*, vol.90, no.4, pp.675–707.

Hurst, J. (1989) *Nashville's Grand Ole Op'ry: the First Fifty Years 1925–1975*, New York, Abradale Press.

Jones, L. (1963) *Blues People*, New York, Morrow Quill.

Leonard, N. (1987) *Jazz: Myth and Religion*, Oxford, Oxford University Press.

Lewis, T. (1991) *Empire of the Air*, New York, HarperCollins.

Morganstern, D. (1977) 'Jazz as urban music' in McCabe, G. (ed.) *Music in American Society*, New Brunswick, Transaction Books, pp.133–43.

The New Grove Dictionary of Jazz (1988), London, Macmillan.

Ogren, K.J. (1989) *The Jazz Revolution: Twenties America and the Meaning of Jazz*, Oxford, Oxford University Press.

Oliver, P. (1982) *The Story of the Blues*, Radnor, Chilton Books.

Oliver, P. (1984) *Songsters and Saints, Vocal Traditions on Race Records*, Cambridge, Cambridge University Press.

Oliver, P. (1990) *Blues Fell This Morning: Meaning in the Blues*, Cambridge, Cambridge University Press.

Palmer, R. (1991) 'The church of the sonic guitar', *South Atlantic Quarterly*, vol.90, no.4, pp.649–73.

Passman, A. (1971) *The Deejays*, New York, Macmillan.

Peretti, B.W. (1992) *The Creation of Jazz: Music, Race and Culture in Urban America*, Urbana, University of Illinois Press.

Placksin, S. (1985) *Jazz Women 1900 to the Present*, London, Pluto Press.

Sanjek, R. and Sanjek, D. (1991) *American Popular Music Business in the 20th Century*, New York, Oxford University Press.

Schuller, G. (1968, 1989) *The History of Jazz, vol.1, Early Jazz: its Roots and Musical Development. The History of Jazz, vol.2, The Swing Era: the Development of Jazz 1930–1945*, New York, Oxford University Press.

Shaw, A. (1978) *Honkers and Shouters*, New York, Macmillan.

Shaw, A. (1987) *The Jazz Age: Popular Music in the 1920s*, Oxford, Oxford University Press.

Shepherd, J. (1992) 'Music as cultural text' in Paynter, J., Howell, T., Orton, R. and Seymour, D. (eds) *Companion to Contemporary Musical Thought, vol.1*, London, Routledge, pp.128–55.

Shumway, D. (1991) 'Rock and roll as a cultural practice', *South Atlantic Quarterly*, vol.90, no.4, pp.753–69.

Sosna, M. (1987) 'More important than the Civil War? The impact of World War Two on the South' in Cobb, J.C. and Wilson, C.R. (eds) *Perspectives on the American South, vol.4*, New York, Gordon & Breach.

Tosches, N. (1985) *Country*, London, Secker & Warburg.

Tosches, N. (1991) *Unsung Heroes of Rock and Roll*, New York, Harmony Books.

Tucker, M. (1991) *Ellington: the Early Years*, Oxford, Bayou Press.

Tucker, S. (1989) 'Rock and roll' in Wilson, C. and Ferris, W. (eds) *Encyclopedia of Southern Culture*, Chapel Hill, University of North Carolina Press.

FURTHER READING

JAZZ

Gioia, T. (1988) *The Imperfect Art: Reflections on Jazz and Modern Culture*, New York, Oxford University Press.

Sales, G. (1992) *Jazz: America's Classical Music*, New York, Da Capo Press (first published by Prentice-Hall in 1984).

Shaw, A. (1986) *Black Popular Music in America*, London, Collier Macmillan.

Shaw (1986) is a survey of black music from the late nineteenth century onwards; jazz is discussed in Chapters 5 and 6. There are several general one volume introductions to the history of jazz, among the most accessible is Sales (1992). The most authoritative studies of the music of jazz up to 1945 are the two volumes by Schuller (1968, 1989) given in the references; a third volume on later developments is promised. The social context of the development of jazz is discussed in Ogren (1989) and Peretti (1992). The book by Gioia (1988) is an interesting set of essays about the nature of jazz by a practising musician.

ROCK 'N' ROLL

George, N. (1989) *The Death of Rhythm and Blues*, New York, E.P. Dutton.

Jackson, J. (1991) *Big Beat Heat: Alan Freed and the Early Years of Rock and Roll*, New York, Schirmer Books.

Malone, B.C. (1968) *Country Music USA*, Austin, University of Texas.

Marcus, G. (1991) *Mystery Train, Images of America in Rock and Roll*, London, Penguin.

Martin, L. and Segrave, K. (1993) *Anti-Rock: the Opposition to Rock 'n' Roll*, New York, Da Capo Press.

Shaw, A. (1987) *The Rockin' Fifties*, New York, Da Capo Press.

Ward, E., Stokes, G. and Tucker, K. (1982) *Rock of Ages, The Rolling Stone History of Rock and Roll*, New York, Summit Books, Simon & Schuster.

Plate 3.1
' … a sculpting of the original body into a cultural form' (Butler, 1987).
Marilyn Monroe is but one of the many personae Madonna adopts in her performance as all the blondes in all the world.

Plate 4.1   Hollywood's utopian re-creation of America is expressed in *The Wizard of Oz* (1939), where the magical land of Oz turns out to be Kansas after all, only in Technicolor.

Plate 4.2   Fan magazines carried archetypal stories of the stars, combined with beauty and lifestyle advice. Clara Bow (right) represented an ideal type for young working-class women in the 1920s, but it was a type that created anxiety among the middle-class guardians of American cultural values.

Plate 4.3   Shirley Temple and Bill Robinson in *Rebecca of Sunnybrook Farm* (1938). Temple, the most popular box-office star of the mid-1930s, projected an idealized version of childhood that appealed primarily to adults. In Hollywood's system of racially segregated representations, the only white female permitted to have this intimate a relationship with a black man, even on the dance floor, was a child.

Plate 4.4   Robert Mitchum as the maladjusted hero trying to escape from *Out of the Past* (1947). 1940s *films noir* often trapped their characters in surroundings that were cramped and dramatically lit, and closely examined their faces for expressions of paranoia and self-doubt.

Plate 4.5 ▲ 'Capitalism at its finest': Michael Douglas expressing the corporate ethic of the 1980s in *Wall Street* (1987), 'Greed is good'.

Plate 4.6 ▶ Henry Fonda, icon of American decency, as Wyatt Earp in *My Darling Clementine* (1946). As a vow to his murdered brother, he undertakes his civilizing mission, to 'clean up the country so kids like you can grow up safe'.

★ ★

Plate 9.1   View of Rockefeller Center and adjacent area, *c.* 1960.

★ ★

Plate 9.2   William Van Alen, Chrysler Building,
New York, 1930.

Plate 9.3   Frank Lloyd Wright, Frederick C. Robie House, Chicago, 1908–9.

★ ★

Plate 9.4   Andy Warhol, *100 Cans*, 1962, oil on canvas, 72 × 52 in. (182.9 × 132.1 cm). Albright-Knox Art Gallery, Buffalo, New York. Gift of Seymour H. Knox, 1963. © 1993 The Andy Warhol Foundation for the Visual Arts, Inc.

★ ★

Plate 9.5   John Steuart Curry, *Baptism in Kansas*, 1928, oil on canvas, 40 × 50 in. (101.6 × 127 cm). Collection of Whitney Museum of American Art. Gift of Gertrude Vanderbilt Whitney 31.159.

Plate 9.6   John Marin, *Woolworth Building No. 31*, 1912, water colour over graphite, $18\frac{1}{2} \times 15\frac{3}{4}$ in. (47 × 39.8 cm). Gift of Eugene and Agnes E. Meyer © 1993 National Gallery of Art, Washington.

★ ★

Plate 9.7 ◄
Cass Gilbert,
Woolworth
Building, New
York, 1911–13.

Plate 9.8 ►
Daniel Burnham
and John Root,
Monadnock
Building,
Chicago,
1889–91.

Plate 9.9 ◄
Dankmar
Adler and
Louis
Sullivan,
Guaranty
Building,
Buffalo, NY,
1894–5.

Plate 9.10 ►
D.H. Burnham
and Company,
Reliance
Building,
Chicago,
1894–5.

Plate 9.11 ◄ Ludwig Mies van der Rohe and Philip Johnson, Seagram Building, New York, 1956–8.

Plate 9.12 ▼ Charles Moore (with Allen Eskew and Malcolm Heard Jr. of Perez & Associates and Ron Filson), Piazza d'Italia, New Orleans, 1976–9. © 1978 Norman McGrath.

Plate 9.13   Max Weber, *Rush Hour, New York*, 1915, canvas, $36\frac{1}{4} \times 30\frac{1}{4}$ in. (92×76.9 cm). Gift of the Avalon Foundation, © 1993 National Gallery of Art, Washington.

★ ★

Plate 9.14   Charles Sheeler, *American Landscape*, 1930, oil on canvas, 24 × 31 in. (61 × 78.8 cm).   The Museum of Modern Art, New York. Gift of Abby Aldrich Rockefeller.

Plate 9.15 Thomas Hart Benton, *City Activities with Dance Hall* from the *America Today* Series, 1930, distemper and egg tempera with oil glaze on gessoed linen, 92 × 134¼ in. (233.7 × 341.6 cm). © The Equitable Life Assurance Society of the United States. Collection, The Equitable Life Assurance Society.

Plate 9.16   Edward Hopper, *Compartment C, Car 293*, 1938, oil on canvas, 20 × 18 in. (50.8 × 45.7 cm). Collection IBM Corporation, Armonk, New York.

Plate 9.17   Eric Fischl, *Bad Boy*, 1981, oil on canvas, 66 × 96 in. (167.5 × 244 cm). Courtesy Thomas Ammann, Zurich.

Plate 10.1 The British artist Richard Hamilton's *Just what is it that makes today's homes so different, so appealing?* illustrates the international impact of the 'American Way' of life. 1956, collage, $10\frac{1}{4} \times 9\frac{3}{4}$ in. (26 × 25 cm). Kunsthalle Tübingen.

Plate 10.2 Roy Lichtenstein, *Whaam!*, 1963, acrylic on canvas, 68 × 160 in. (172.7 × 406.4 cm). Tate Gallery, London. © Roy Lichtenstein/DACS 1993.

★ ★

SPORT

John Wilson ★

Although highly-organized games were known in antiquity, specialized sports roles and organizations, guided by autonomous values and measured by rational criteria of performance, are associated only with modern societies, of which the United States is widely regarded as the most advanced. In the US thoroughly modern beliefs in equality of opportunity, individual achievement, and the benefits of the application of rational methods to all aspects of life, also reveal themselves in a highly developed sports complex ranging from organized play for young children through to the bureaucratic management of scholastic and professional athletics. But it is not the relative modernity of the United States this chapter chooses to emphasize. Sports are not different in the US simply because Americans are more modern. The US is exceptional in ways that cannot be reduced to relative stages of modernization, and this exceptionalism reveals itself in how Americans approach sport.

The argument for exceptionalism is that each society is distinct in ways that no amount of convergence in terms of technological or economic development can obliterate. Societies develop unique cultures that modify economic forces. Culture is comprised largely of beliefs and values. These beliefs and values influence the manner in which the processes of rationalization and commercialization that account for sport's development occur. In the limited space available, it is not possible to examine all the ways in which values and sport are related in the US. Instead, attention focuses on the values that most distinguish the US from other countries at approximately the same level of modernization; values that seem to have influenced most powerfully the way sports are played.

When sociologists write about values they have in mind ideas of what is desirable: they are guides to conduct. But the role of values in social action should not be misunderstood. They need not be thought of as preceding social action. Indeed, it is just as plausible to imagine that people think as they act as it is to imagine that they act as they think. If this much is admitted, then values take on a different appearance, less reasons for action than excuses for action, less the cause of what is done than a legitimation for it. In short, values become ideologies. One of the characteristics of ideologies is that from a position 'outside' it is possible to see ideologies as partial and selective, favouring the activities of some groups of people but not others.

Their selectivity is hidden, however, by the emphasis on 'common' values: seen from 'inside' they seem 'natural' and appropriate. The relevance of this argument for the study of sport is plain, for while sport might be said to reflect values all Americans share, looked at from the outside, the interests these values serve might not be shared by all.

The first of the values to be discussed in this chapter is patriotism. To some, this is not so much a value as the result of adhering to values; a patriotic American is one who believes in, and acts in accordance with, other values, such as freedom, equality and democracy. But it is precisely Americans' inclination to elevate patriotism itself to the level of an absolute value that makes them distinctive. For reasons to be outlined below, Americans place a premium on demonstrating one's allegiance to the flag and attachment to one's country. In few other countries is patriotism so exalted. Although this value is expressed as nationalism — taking pride in being an American — it reaches down also to the level of community, where one is expected to take pride in one's town, city, or community as an expression of American achievement. The second value is individualism. The pursuit of personal freedom and personal control over the natural and social environment is 'probably the most widely shared ideology in the US' (Gans, 1988, p.1). These two values, patriotism and individualism, are not in conflict. Patriotism means helping to build the kind of community in which personal freedoms are guaranteed. Nor is individualism opposed to conformity: while Americans seek to 'do their own thing', they do not mind if others do exactly the same (ibid., p.3).

1   A SPORTING PEOPLE

Americans like to think of themselves as a sporting people. This no doubt has something to do with their self-image as competitive, risk-taking, 'doers', and most at home in a world of action and rapid change. Americans are not alone in thinking of themselves as 'sports mad', but the rates of participation and spectating do seem to be unusually high in the US. Half of all Americans classify their interest in watching a sporting event as either 'very high' or 'somewhat high'. Three out of every four watch sports on television at least once a week, and 58 per cent read the sports pages weekly (Miller Brewing Co., 1983, p.17). Every day, 70 per cent of Americans engage in at least one of the following: watch sports on television or listen on the radio, read the sports pages of a newspaper or magazine, or talk about sports with friends. Fewer actually attend sporting events, but the numbers are still high: one quarter of Americans attend sporting events more than 20 times a year. The sports they most like to watch are football, baseball, basketball and boxing.

When high levels of interest and frequent attendance are combined in a measure of the 'ardent fan', roughly a fifth of the population, 35 million people, qualify. Most ardent fans are male, high school graduates and live in larger cities (ibid., p.20). American sports crowds are on the whole more affluent and more mixed in terms of gender and class than European soccer crowds: outside of sports like automobile racing, American crowds contain fewer of the 'rough working class' people found in such large numbers in European soccer stadiums (Elias and Dunning, 1986).

Seventy-one per cent of all Americans participate in at least one athletic activity on a weekly basis, while almost half (44 per cent) do so every day, or almost every day (Miller Brewing Co., 1983, p.29). The most frequently reported activities are callisthenics (29 per cent), swimming (33 per cent), cycling (28 per cent) and jogging (29 per cent). Participation in team sports, which involves an element of competition, requires more social organization and is less common. The most popular team sport is softball or baseball, in which about a fifth of Americans engage on a weekly basis. As might be expected, those most likely to participate frequently in a sport are younger, male city-dwellers. In the US, as elsewhere, it is normative for younger people, and especially males, to be more interested in and spend time in sports. City living also means more opportunities for sport participation.

These attendance and participation rates are higher than for the United Kingdom. Americans not only spend more time attending sporting events (the difference is especially marked among women) but also more time playing sports than the British (Robinson, 1980). In an annual survey British people were asked if they had participated in any sport sometime within the last month. Since this allows for a more casual participation, one might expect the figures to be higher than for the US, where the data cited above records weekly participation rates. But the opposite is true. Data from 1987 for the UK show that only 9 per cent report participation in callisthenics, 13 per cent in swimming, and 8 per cent in cycling (jogging is not separately mentioned in the survey). Participation in team sports is also lower: 5 per cent for soccer, the same figure as for rugby, and only 1 per cent play cricket regularly (Griffin, 1992, p.183).

There are a number of reasons why Americans are a more sporting people than the British. The climate undoubtedly makes a difference, as does income, which is higher in the US. But these material conditions alone are not sufficient to account for the difference observed, particularly in rate of participation. Americans attach considerable significance to the value of 'instrumental activism', broadly interpreted as the goal of active mastery over one's environment. The emphasis on activism leads to a corresponding accent on youth and youthful looks. The most popular sports in the US, and those in which America seems to be most distinctive, are chiefly health-oriented, individually conducted body-image activities: more Americans say they play sport to improve their health (56 per cent) than for the 'thrill of victory' (31 per cent) or 'sport competition' (17 per cent) (Miller Brewing Co., 1983, p.30). This enthusiasm for 'working out' also reflects the lingering effects of the Protestant work ethic, which took a much stronger hold in the US than in other Protestant countries (Snowman, 1977, p.50).

SUMMARY

In the US beliefs in equality of opportunity and individual achievement are revealed in a highly developed sports complex.

While the US shares many sports features with other modern nations, there are qualitative differences in the way Americans approach sport, differences created by the American system of values such as patriotism and individualism.

Participation and attendance rates in the US are perhaps the highest in any capitalist country; a difference to be explained, in part, by climate, greater affluence, and an emphasis on health.

2   SPORT AND COMMUNITY-BUILDING

All nations need to define their identity and purpose. However, this has been a problem for Americans since winning the War of Independence and becoming the 'first new nation' without a feudal past. A subsequent high rate of geographical and social mobility fuelled by rapid economic growth have not made dealing with this problem any easier. Nor has assimilating millions of new immigrants each year. Without an established church or landed aristocracy to impose standards from above, no group or community has an established past or fixed advantage. Where all claims deserve to be heard, none can be guaranteed acceptance, and the more urgent becomes the need to define who belongs and who does not. The result is that national identity in the US becomes an affirmation, an ideological commitment. This contrasts with other older and more settled nations of Europe, where nationality is largely a matter of birth, related to community and place. While those who reject American values are not simply non-conformists but unAmerican: 'one can not become un-English, or un-Swedish' (Lipset, 1990, p.19). Europeans can take their community largely for granted while Americans must constantly assert theirs.

The ideological commitment to Americanism provides a 'framing' device for sport in the US not found in any other society. Sports, like other institutions, must be scrutinized for the quality of their Americanness — they must express national 'spirit'. Americans see nothing wrong in playing the national anthem and saluting the flag before all but the most casual of sports events. Sports bring people together and ritually affirm the values they hold in common. This is why sports have long been a favoured instrument of assimilation. They cost the state little, they attracted mass audiences, they encountered little serious opposition, and athletic achievement appeared to be independent of language, culture or national origin. Voluntary associations like the Playground Movement and the Young Men's and Women's Christian Associations (YMCA and YWCA) were among the first to tie sports participation to citizenship. They were joined later by the

American Legion (a war veteran's organization), which integrated junior baseball leagues and tournaments in an 'Americanization programme' that included calls for restrictions on immigration (Seymour, 1990, p.85), and by Little League Baseball whose mission statement reads, in part: 'To help ... boys in developing qualities of citizenship, sportsmanship and manhood ... Using the discipline of the native American game of baseball ... '. Little League, which operates in almost every American community, requires its youthful participants to pledge to 'love my country and respect its laws'.

Even commercialized sports, which operate on more market-based principles, become patriotic statements in the United States. The first President of baseball's National League, Morgan Bulkeley, believed 'there is nothing which will help quicker and better to amalgamate the foreign born, and those born of foreign parents in this country, than to give them a little good bringing up in the good old-fashioned game of Baseball' (Seymour, 1971, p.4). He did not add that, to qualify as the 'national pastime', baseball's history had to be re-written by a quasi-official 'commission' to distance its origins from the British children's game of rounders. But this fact is worth noting because it is a reminder that the relation between sport and Americanism is hermetic — each defines the other. 'America *means* baseball because baseball *means* America' (Brown, 1991, p.67). Sport stands for America because it is re-interpreted to fit that role. At the same time, sport helps Americans understand themselves better, or at least more satisfyingly. In the process, each is transformed. Political culture is athleticized by the use of sports metaphors: Presidents become quarterbacks, cabinets become teams, and elections become races. National politics consequently appear more contested and more populist than they really are: the winners deserve their good fortune, while losers cannot complain, for they had their fair chance. Conversely, professional sports, when linked to patriotic values, seem less commercial, less profane, and more open — more of the people — than they really are.

What is true at the national level is also true at the level of the local community. While Americans are not alone in using sports teams to cement attachment to place, the need to affirm this attachment and to define community is especially strong in the US, where every year a fifth of the population changes residence, and where a community is considered well-established if it is more than 100 years old. Europeans tend to take their communities for granted. Americans are constantly building and re-building theirs. The competition to be the most attractive and progressive community, fuelled by the desire for more business activity, jobs and tax revenues, never ends.

Sport plays a role in this community-building, but it is structured in a uniquely American way. Europeans also identify sport with place: most amateur sports teams are associated with a village or town. But in Europe, these sports teams will be voluntary associations using facilities provided by local governments. What is unusual about the United States is how much local sport is administered by schools. Many private voluntary organizations in the US do provide sports opportunities outside the school, just as it is true that, in Europe, all schools administer some sports activities: the difference is not absolute but one of degree. School sports in Europe bear nothing like the community significance they have in the US, while Americans' strong voluntary spirit gives clear priority to school sports over more private initiatives.

Sociologists have long been aware of how much 'civic loyalty' centres around sport, and how much of that sport is centred in the local high school (Lynd and Lynd, 1929, p.485; Vidich and Bensman, 1960, p.28). To understand why it is necessary to know something about how Americans view their schools. While European schools tend to be somewhat closed institutions with relatively narrow curricula, American schools, because of the relative classlessness of the society, are more open; hence the uniquely American idea of the 'common school' which all should attend regardless of origins, status, or wealth. The 'common school' is expected to be a part of the community that supports it, and to make an effort to influence all aspects of its pupils' lives rather than confine itself to academic instruction. As a result, the American school is 'a kind of department store of constructive activities' (Kirschner, 1986, p.46). Sports are an attractive element in this mix of activities. Not only are they highly popular and accessible to most students, also teachers and parents believe they encourage good study habits, and they transcend a community's racial, economic and social differences.

Even so, high school sports would not loom so large were it not for the fact that Americans regard their high schools as measures of community achievement. In the absence of an established church, the local high school is the integrative focus for most American communities. If there is a single measure of what the community can do by pooling its resources and pulling together, it is the high school. Many a small town lacking all but the most minimal street lighting boasts proudly of its floodlit school sports stadium. The integrative function of high school sports is clearly demonstrated by the ritual of 'Friday night football'. Friday is the night set aside in the autumn for the game of the week, scheduled to avoid conflict with college and professional games at the weekend. Most schools anticipate the game by releasing students from classwork early for a 'pep rally' in the school's gymnasium, during which members of the team are paraded forth accompanied by fanfares from the school band and applause orchestrated by cheerleaders, with earnest speeches by team captains and coaches. While the major focus is on the players, other students contribute — cheerleaders, members of the marching band and the 'pep squads'. The importance of sport to the school is reflected in the superior social status of the athletes, cheerleaders and band members of whom even teachers are especially solicitous.

Friday night games are attended by most students and many of their parents, and in many communities supporting the local school team is considered a civic duty of all the community's inhabitants. A 'booster club', partly consisting of former students, forms a connection between school and community. Its purpose is to raise funds and mobilize support, but being removed from the academic context and placing heavy emphasis on winning its impact is to 'professionalize' school sports in the interest of community pride. Boosters encourage students to specialize in their best sport, and

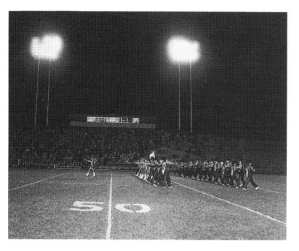

High school football's game of the week

to train all year round, honing their skills in the off season by attending sports camps and playing for local sports leagues. Boosters are influential in the hiring and firing of high school coaches, and exercise considerable influence over the school by virtue of their fund raising. Under pressure from boosters, high school coaches compete for players, while parents have been known to transfer their children from school to school to improve their chance of making the team. The contrast of the role of high school sports with a society like the UK's is striking: 'Nowhere in Britain can one see roadside signs cataloguing past glories of children's teams, usually named after a predator; the appointment of a games master (coach) is not noted in the local newspaper nor are his coaching skills publicly discussed, and school matches are not broadcast' (Chandler, 1988, p.79).

Sports provide a focus for civic effort and are considered a measure of community achievement and in this fashion help integrate the community. However, they do not achieve this goal by making everybody seem the same. School sports symbolize the community by reproducing and legitimating its social structure in miniature form. The division of labour between players and cheerleaders replicates gender divisions, whilst team selection usually replicates class divisions within the community. In many high schools the opportunity to participate or attend is limited for working-class students who lack transportation or whose time is needed at home, in the workplace, or on the farm. Where schools are racially mixed, team selection and coaching assignments will replicate these divisions also. Similarly, booster clubs are not a cross-section of the community but an organized expression of its power structure. Those who lead in business affairs are expected to take the lead in the voluntary effort. Booster clubs tend to be dominated by local merchants, farmers and civic leaders (Foley, 1990).

College sports teams perform many of the same symbolic functions as high school teams. This is because colleges in the United States are much more likely than those in Europe to be regarded as local products, since they are supported by local tax revenues and attended mainly by people drawn from the local area. Graduates (known as alumni) follow the fortunes of their college's teams with intense interest, and many of them will make annual donations to the athletic programme. Cross-town and inter-state rivalries are fierce and enduring. Successful football teams can expect sell-out crowds, some as many as 100,000. The local newspapers, radio and television stations make college athletes household names. The contrast with college sports in other countries is striking. For example, in Germany 'universities devote themselves to education (including physical education and the scientific study of sports), while private clubs provide both participant and spectator sports ... the intense interest in sport has been institutionalized in the private club rather than in the public university' (Guttmann, 1982, p.77).

College sports are credible emblems of community identity and well-being because they are believed to be the result of local civic effort. On the face of it, professional sports are ill-suited to perform this role. A professional sports club is less an outgrowth of a community's spirit and solidarity than a business venture. It is undeniable that professional sports management and marketing is much more sophisticated in the US than in Europe. In Europe, professional sports clubs retain such strong roots in neighbourhoods and factories that they are more likely to go bankrupt than move; in the US, the club is a moveable asset. American sports leagues have a long history of carefully managing the location of their teams. It is not without significance that Americans refer to sports teams as 'franchises'. This would appear to make a team's attachment to a location tenuous, but it does not, because the goal is to allocate teams where the league as a whole can make the most profit. The attachment to location is not totally severed by franchising. Club owners realize that the commodity they sell is not merely a diversion but loyalty, that their best customers are regular fans, and that this kind of relationship is forged by trading on, rather than destroying, the link between club and community. In short, they commodify the relation between community and club: a club sells itself as part of a city, while the city purchases the glamour of a major league team. It is no accident that baseball has a rule stipulating teams should be 'locally owned and operated'.

American club owners have thus secured the best of both worlds. Without denying the importance of attachment to *some* community they have preserved a free market for the precise location of each club in the league. This enables them to offer their team to the highest bidding city, demanding loyalty (and tax subsidies) from its citizens, while reserving for themselves the freedom to move should market trends dictate. It is their good fortune that they operate in a seller's market. Much more than is the case in Europe, American cities compete for business, to attract jobs and tax revenues. One method of attracting new business is to create an image of the city as being an attractive place to work, live and spend money, and sports franchises are considered an essential part of this image. Beginning in the 1960s pro-development cities in the south, southwest and west which were anxious to expand, such as Atlanta, Houston, Dallas, San Antonio, Phoenix, Los Angeles, Miami and San Diego, aggressively pursued major league teams, luring them away from older cities like New York, Baltimore and St. Louis. These older well-established cities were dominated by local Democratic Party officials, labour unions and urban planners and were reluctant to spend public money on building new stadiums, especially at the expense of housing for the poor. This 'trade' in sports franchises is quite unknown in Europe.

The theme that sports mean community thus repeats itself. From high school to major league team, from amateur to professional, Americans look to sport to articulate a sense of belonging. Unlike Europeans, Americans are not automatically involved in social relationships not of their own choosing. 'Leaving home', is not something done once and for all; it might happen many times. Geographical and social mobility create a need for ready sources of attachment, a quick way to put down roots. Many other associations, especially churches, do perform this function, but, as this section has shown, sports in America cannot be understood unless this need is appreciated, for it frames how Americans approach their sport.

SUMMARY

As the 'first new nation', and subject to inflows of immigrants from other cultures, the US still faces problems of self-determination and consensus-building. These problems have elevated patriotism and conformity to the level of a value — demonstrating allegiance is important.

The socialization of immigrants, civic boosterism, fiercely competitive high school and college athletic programmes, and municipal rivalry to host professional sports teams are some of the ways the value of patriotism is expressed in and through sport.

Sports provide a focus for community pride and achievement, they perform an integrative function and are a measure of the community's resources.

3   SPORT AND INDIVIDUAL FREEDOM

The United States is popularly regarded as 'the land of opportunity'. Whether or not upward mobility really is easier in the US, the desire to better one's self is undoubtedly an American value, something to believe in. The 'failure' in America is not the person who falls short of a target, but the person who sets no target at all, not the person who is second, but the person who settles for second best, not the person who has faults and shortcomings, but the person who blames others for his or her failure. This section will show what difference this value has made to the way Americans think about sports, and the way they play them.

Americans are fond of quoting a famous coach of the National Football League's Green Bay Packers, Vince Lombardi, who said 'Winning is not the most important thing: it is the only thing'. This attitude is a natural out-growth of the value of individual achievement. Americans are impatient with contests in which the focus is not clearly on the outcome or, worse, which have no outcome at all (a tie). While some other cultures might think that, in the event of a draw, both contestants are first, Americans think both contestants are second. Being willing to settle for second best is unAmerican. Intolerant of drawn games, Americans have devised all kinds of modifi-cations to make this outcome less likely: drawn games are impossible in basketball and baseball and extremely rare in football and ice hockey, both of which provide for 'overtime'. While some might regard this single-minded pursuit of victory as selfish — since one person's victory is another's defeat — Americans do not share this view. They are well aware that for one team to win another must lose. In this case, coming second takes on its own significance: if you cannot win, you must at least try as hard as possible.

Above all the emphasis is on the individual's responsibility to make it on his or her own: 'every man is the architect of his own destiny' (Potter, 1954, p.97). Mobility thus means something different for an American. Unlike the British system of 'sponsored' mobility, in which members of the élite ident-ify likely prospects in the classes below and consciously recruit them into higher levels of society, Americans regard high status as a prize to be won by the worthiest individual (Turner, 1960). Social life is a contest, in which the fittest will survive, where fitness is measured by such qualities as deter-mination, pluck, aggression, daring, risk-taking and the like.

In a perceptive analysis, Chandler (1988, pp.86–7) traces the impact of this view of mobility on American sport. The first thing to notice is Americans' approach to the rules of the game. Americans are careful to distinguish between breaking the rules and manipulating them, between cheating and trickery. It is acknowledged that rules are necessary to structure competition, but much more than in the UK, Americans treat the rules as potential resources for winning games, much as a lawyer might exploit a technicality in the law to clear a client. 'To play to the rules of any particular sport is … in America by definition to play fairly, … [but] creative manipulation of those rules must therefore be a sign not of unsporting behavior but of intel-ligence', with victory going to the person 'who takes the time and trouble to understand the rules of the game thoroughly, and who perceives where and how they can be manipulated' (ibid., p.85). Americans have thus translated sportsmanship, the scrupulous adherence to rules (at the possible expense of victory), into gamesmanship: 'bending the rules or finding loopholes in the rules that would give one side the advantage' is considered smart play (Ori-ard, 1991, p.17). Markovits (1988) notes that 'trick plays', basically unknown in soccer, cricket and rugby, have become woven into the fabric of American football and basketball.

Individualism has another effect on Americans' attitude toward sport. It encourages the view that each person's opinions and interest are as good as another's, that all are equal before the law, that no institution is the preserve of an élite or exclusive group, that authority is not permanent. It is an old maxim of political science that where the state is weak, the law is sovereign. This helps account for Americans' highly legalistic approach to sport, an intolerance of ambiguity, and reluctance to admit that many things happen in sport which are neither clearly right nor wrong. To eliminate ambiguity, games are closely policed: there are seven officials in football, four in baseball and three in basketball. 'Judgement calls, where the referee's own opinion must be taken on faith, must be made as few as possible … ' (Chandler, 1988, p.92). And Americans find it perfectly acceptable to question those calls that are made: 'indeed, coaches are expected to do it loudly, obviously, and energetically' (ibid., p.88). To help them, most sports arenas have giant television screens on which the game's events can be replayed so that the crowd can second-guess referees. As if this were not enough, football experimented with 'instant replay review' of officials' on-the-field-decisions, adding yet another layer of adjudication to calls with an official in a booth high up in the stadium, watching the questioned play in slow motion. Even the matter of time cannot be trusted to experts. While in Europe, soccer referees are trusted to keep time themselves, in the US highly-visible time clocks are used, so that all can judge for themselves how much time remains and exactly when the game has finished.

This more democratic approach to sports — the idea that it is an open institution, not the preserve of a knowledgeable few — helps account for the fact that commercial sports in the US have successfully marketed themselves as attractive to the ardent fan and the casual spectator alike. To make them family events, they are 'packaged' with music, cheerleading, contests, banners, displays, mascots and the like. What transpires on the field is just one among a number of attractions. Chandler (1988, p.89) likens the typical American baseball park to 'a disturbed anthill, as spectators roam in search of refreshments or programs or just to move … '. The desire to promote the event to an audience so wide it might extend beyond the knowledgeable fan also explains the American practice of instructing spectators about referees' calls, players, plays, time remaining, etc., a difference of approach reflected both in live attendance (where a continuous flow of information issues from the public address system, particularly in football) and in television commentary, where producers are 'constrained to act as if their audiences may not understand what they see' (ibid., p.90).

In summary, Americans organize and play sports in distinctive ways, despite the many resemblances created by common origins and similar socio-economic conditions. Americans are more likely than Europeans to expect sports to contribute to the task of nation-building, to see in sports a measure of civic strength and dynamism, to see sport as legitimation of the values of individualism, a place where the virtues of hard work and resourcefulness clearly pay off and, if sports seem to impugn these values, to change the way they are played. At the beginning of the chapter, however, the point was made that value systems are not simply abstractions of what everybody believes in. The dominant values of a society are those of the 'mainstream': they are the values most likely to be held by those in positions of influence and power. The question thus arises as to how accurately these values represent the beliefs, and practical realities, of ordinary Americans. For example, the 'civic virtues' promoted by high school sports and touted by the booster club benefit those who own property in, and make money from the economic development of communities rather than those for whom such benefits can only 'trickle down'. High school and college sports 'bring people together', but they do not so much overcome as legitimize gender, race and social class differences between them. The next section will address this issue of the relationship between values and practice explicitly. Its purpose is not to discredit the view that sport functions to affirm values and that, in turn, sport is shaped by those values. At this level sport is partly mythologized, its purity and wholesomeness exaggerated because this is what people want to believe. The reality is somewhat different.

SUMMARY

The American creed and the sports creed overlap at the point of exalting individual freedoms. The impact of the value of individual freedom on sport is evident from the stress on competitiveness and winning.

The US emphasis on contested, rather than sponsored, mobility is reflected in sport, where rules are there to be manipulated, authority to be questioned, and sportsmanship becomes gamesmanship.

Exaltation of individual freedom renders US sport more democratic, more accessible, less tolerant of hierarchy and experts, and more disputatious.

4   BEHIND THE MYTH: GENDER, RACE AND CLASS IN SPORT

Sports are popularly distinguished from games by their partial reliance on *physical* accomplishment, hence the exclusion of card and board games from sports studies. Physical differences in grace, strength, speed, and endurance, discriminate winners from losers. Despite the emphasis on biological differences, opportunities and rewards are also affected by social factors. The body, far from being a 'pure' expression of physical accomplishment, is a symbol of the individual's social worth. The appearance and performance of the body indicates a person's social standing: it is 'better' to be young than old, thin than fat, strong than weak. To the extent that this is true, sporting performance is read as an indication of a person's social standing. Gender and race furnish two, contrasting, examples of this tendency to associate body and status. In the case of gender, athleticism is used as a mark of masculinity, its absence being a mark of femininity. In the case of race, athleticism is a mark of mental inferiority, its absence a mark of civilization and refinement. These contrasting cases indicate that the relation between body and status is a social construct, for the relation changes depending on the power structure within which it is embedded. For women, lack of athleticism is read as another sign of inferiority; for black people, athleticism is read as another sign of reliance on 'instinct' rather than reasoning.

4.1 GENDER

Men are taught to find competition with women in sport threatening, not merely because they might experience defeat, but because their ideas of femininity, and therefore their ideas of masculinity, might be undermined. Women on the other hand, are expected to 'come to terms' with the possible masculinizing effects of sports participation, with the homophobia it often generates among both men and women, and take counter measures to assert their essential femininity. Because of the similarities in patriarchy in the advanced, capitalist countries, the problem becomes that of explaining the precise form the patriarchal system has assumed in the sports world in each country. Although no comparative studies of gender differences in sports participation have been conducted, it is probably true to say that American women enjoy considerably more freedom than women in Western European countries. Feminism has secured more equality of opportunity in employment and education in the US and this has improved women's chances of athletic participation.

American feminists were slow to turn their attention to gender discrimination in sport. When in the 1970s they did so, they found little Congressional support for reform legislation, and were forced to turn, instead, to the more costly and time-consuming strategy of legal action where public facilities were used for sport. Little League Baseball was the largest of the organizations forced to drop its ban on female participants. Legal suits also produced reforms in high school sports. Resources for girls' teams — usually inferior to those provided for boys — were improved, and most states amended their education laws to permit girls to play on boys' teams (while 'protecting' girls' teams from having boys try out for them).

At the collegiate level, women used the fact that many colleges and universities (unlike high schools) rely heavily on federal funding to pressure them into complying with federal civil rights laws. These laws did not actually require that men and women have identical sports programmes. Rather, they expected equality of opportunity in accommodation of interests and abilities, athletic scholarships, and other benefits and opportunities (Wong and Ensor, 1986, p.361). Nor did the law promise equality of condition, for it protected 'contact' sports from equal opportunity statutes: boxing, wrestling, rugby, ice hockey — but most importantly — football and basketball, were defined as contact sports. Nor, until 1988, was it established that *all* programmes run by an institution (including athletics) would have to comply with civil rights statutes, even if federal aid went to only part of the institution.

Despite the 1988 Civil Rights Restoration Act, gender discrimination in college athletics persists. Most colleges claim to fund their women's programmes from revenues generated by men's football and basketball teams.

To preserve this source of revenue, 'equality' has to be defined as splitting funds equally between men and women athletes *after* the men's football and basketball programmes had been removed from the budget. The economic imperatives of college athletics thus condemn the female athlete to secondary status. At the field management level, early gains have been lost. As women's athletic programmes began to receive more funding and offer higher salaries and more security, men began to elbow women out of the jobs of coaching women's teams that women had formerly monopolized. In turn this led to a change at the top: in 1972, women headed more than 90 per cent of women's programmes; by 1990, this proportion had fallen to 30 per cent.

Apart from a few brief experiments, and with the relatively minor exceptions of sports like tennis and golf, American women have not succeeded thus far in opening up the labour market for professional careers in sports. Most gains have been made at the high school level, where principles governing equality of opportunity in education have been used as leverage for more sports opportunities for women. At the same time, however, women have been displaced from positions of authority in sports which were formerly their own precisely because of gender segregation. Women continue fighting for equality of opportunity in management as well as in playing positions, but in order to do so they have been forced to abandon ideals of reforming sports to better suit feminist values.

4.2 RACE

The emancipation of slaves after the Civil War did not put an end to racial discrimination in the US: by the end of the nineteenth century a powerful caste system had replaced legalized slavery as a means of subordinating black people. Racist's beliefs in the 'natural' inferiority of black people were used to justify racial exclusion and deprivation. Laws designed to separate the social life of blacks and whites also segregated black and white people's sports. Black people were forced to organize their own teams and leagues, and, with the exception of boxing, inter-racial competition was rare until after the Second World War.

By 1964 when the Civil Rights Act was passed outlawing employment discrimination, racial segregation in sports was already largely a thing of the past. However, the desegregation of American sport owed relatively little to moral pressure, and much less to political or legal pressure from civil liberties groups. The major reason for the breakdown of racial barriers was business competition for players. Opportunities for black people improved after the Second World War when an abundance of factory jobs lured whites away from the athletic job market; and again in the 1960s when rival leagues were founded in both football and basketball, doubling the number of athletic jobs available. It is noteworthy that racial integration in baseball conformed to this pattern, even though no rival leagues were involved: the hungrier, poorer clubs were the first to sign black players in any numbers while clubs owned by wealthy individuals — the Boston Red Sox, Detroit

This short-lived magazine was launched in 1934 with a strongly pro-integration stance

Tigers, St. Louis Cardinals, Philadelphia Phillies, Chicago Cubs, and New York Yankees — were among the last.

The issue today is no longer the under-representation of black people in sport but their over-representation in the lower ranks. Black people are rarely appointed coaches or managers. Here, they would appear to have less to gain from economic competition for their services. Unlike on the field of play, which is thought to be easily measured and therefore difficult to marginalize minority groups, management is thought to demand interpersonal skills and the co-operation of others. Whenever performance is measured by such intangibles, room is created for discrimination, for it is more difficult to prove bias. The 'natural gifts' of black people can easily be represented as non-transferable to the management level. The abundance of blacks in the ranks of professional athletes, including the highest paid, should not be allowed to obscure the fact that most African-Americans are still treated as second-class citizens. Black people have fewer opportunities to watch or play sport than whites. Racial barriers in the private sphere, in the world of golf, swimming and tennis clubs, where the sports involve informal, personal and sexually mixed social interaction both on and off the field, have been slow to crumble. Low income means less money for sporting goods or tickets to sporting events. Inferior neighbourhood schools mean dilapidated and inadequate athletic facilities which, in any case, are placed out of bounds by large drop-out and truancy rates. Black people are less likely to attend college, or remain in college, and are thus prevented from enjoying scholarships and facilities. Black people are more likely to live in inner-city neighbourhoods or rural areas, where public provision of sports facilities is least adequate. The effects of race are so pervasive, in short, that the world of professional athletics has become a distorted mirror, no more representative of everyday life than it was in the days when it was all white.

4.3 CLASS

In the United States, as in other countries, 'taste' in sports varies by social class. Middle-class people enjoy 'traditional' sports like tennis and golf that carry a 'country club' image and can be combined with work or social networking. Working-class people gravitate toward sports that promise thrills, action and excitement (e.g. automobile racing), or can be a vehicle for casual socializing and are cheap to play, such as indoor bowling, playground basketball, and softball in city parks. However, the relative openness of American society is undeniable. Social barriers are more surmountable than in Europe, and a number of consequences follow.

First, the belief that the US is a classless society creates the impression that sport is where people from all kinds of social background can meet on an equal basis. In particular, 'the national game', baseball, is believed to be a classless sport, and baseball grounds democratic places. In truth, the image Americans have of sports as being classless is misleading. For many years, major league baseball games were played during working hours in order to exclude blue-collar workers. Baseball crowds, even today, are disproportionately middle class. Even once blue-collar sports, with their origins in industrial leagues, have been socially mobile. Spectators at professional football and basketball games today are even more middle class than those for baseball.

A second consequence of the reluctance to think in terms of social class is that Americans are more likely to see blocked opportunities to participate in sport as the result of individual failing rather than class barriers. Americans show little enthusiasm for government policies that, under the same banner of 'sport for all', try to redistribute sports opportunities from rich to poor. Even trade unions give priority to gaining more spending power and job security for their members over more free time. Sport for all in America means sport for all who can afford it. This is true of Americans in general. There is a preference for goods over services because the former preserve and promote individuals' freedom (Gans, 1988, p.33). Americans prefer cars over buses, private swimming pools and tennis courts over public parks and playgrounds. Public amenities lack the freedom of choice that more commercial amusements and goods provide. Public parks suffer in comparison to 'attractions', where amusements can be custom-built by the individual, or at least give that impression. Besides, having one's leisure administered places one in the position of inferiority, to the administrator, who is typically a professional and an 'expert'. Americans prefer not to be placed in such a position if it can be avoided. Purchasing one's leisure through goods maintains one's independence; should the goods prove to be unsatisfactory, one can always shop elsewhere. At most, Americans will support a kind of 'reluctant collectivism': for those who can afford it, leisure is privately provided; a minimum level of leisure is publicly provided for those who lack the means.

The only exception to this pattern, and it is an important one, is the provision of sports opportunities through schools. Schools are funded from state and local taxes, they are controlled locally, and their facilities are available for all pupils to enjoy. Under the mandate of providing physical education, which is easily broadened to the idea of supervised recreation, public policy designed to improve the nation's health and education smuggles in publicly-administered sport by the back door. While schools and colleges do not explicitly embrace the European notion of 'sport for all', their mandate of providing sport as part of the curriculum does achieve a measure of redistribution of sport opportunities tempering the effects of social class on the chances to 'play ball'.

A third consequence of the way class and sport are related in the US is that Americans attach less significance to the distinction between amateur and professional. In the nineteenth century, this could not have been said. As in Britain, amateur sports were considered the pursuit of gentlemen and voluntary organizations were formed to protect the ideal. The Amateur Athletic Union (AAU, founded 1889) espoused the ideal that sports should be pursued for their own sake rather than for extrinsic reward, it vigorously rejected the notion that sport should be harnessed to pedagogical goals or subordinated to the demands of the academic curriculum, and clung to the voluntaristic principle by which participation in, and particularly the organizing and financing of sport should be entirely voluntary and not for profit.

Why has the distinction between professional and amateur proved to be less durable in the United States? One reason was the greater permeability of social boundaries in the US, which made all status markers less permanent. Amateurism also had to struggle against the popular belief in freedom of opportunity, which legitimizes all kinds of careerism, including the pursuit of professional advancement in entertainment and sports. Another reason is that there is less stigma attached to professionalism. Americans do not share the British élite's horror of making money. They are more tolerant of the professional athlete who, having made it to the top, should be paid what he or she deserves.

A more complex reason why amateurism does not hold a higher status in the US has to do with the absorption of so much sports activity by schools and colleges. There are many opportunities for sport in private associations, such as tennis and golf clubs, that preserve some of the old British status distinctions, and innumerable voluntary associations where social distinctions, such as that between salmon fishing (high status) and bass fishing (low status), are preserved. But for the bulk of the population and especially its youth, sport means schools athletics. Ironically, schools assumed responsibility for the administration of sports in order to preserve the amateur ideal. In practice, however, schools and colleges have all but destroyed it. The explanation is to be found in the function of higher education in the US.

The typical American college, unlike its European counterpart, is extremely flexible with regard to goals and means, restrained only by the popular demand that education be above all practical. This leaves plenty of room for the absorption of physical education and interscholastic athletics as part of the school's purpose. Without assured government funding, American colleges must also compete vigorously for students and financial support. A winning sports team is thought to be an excellent method of boosting enrolments and donations to a college. American colleges also have to deal with a much more heterogeneous student population: a wide variety of aptitudes and interests must be catered for. Especially when students entering a college are relatively young, as is the case in the US, and are living far from home, the college becomes a surrogate parent, responsible for social as well as educational welfare.

Once absorbed into educational institutions and harnessed to the work of student recruitment and fund-raising, amateur sports change their character. They become hierarchically organized, with athletic directors at the top and 'student' athletes at the bottom. The student athletes are amateurs in name only, for they owe their scholarship or grant to their athletic prowess. Athletic departments, often legally separated from the rest of the college, become more commercialized, with ever-higher revenues needed to meet the escalating cost created by intense competition. Oversight is provided by the

National Collegiate Athletic Association, whose main task is to see that colleges compete fairly. This means that amateurism — in the old sense of 'playing for the fun of it' rather than some extrinsic reward — no longer exists, instead it means being a *bona fide* student. Amateurism is redefined to mean that the student meets some minimal academic standards, not in order to keep alive a certain spirit or approach to play, but to make sure that competition between business ventures does not get ruinously expensive.

The anomaly of the 'amateur' college athlete is one of those things that middle-class Americans, who comprise the bulk of the audience for college football and basketball games, choose 'to wink at', ignoring or downplaying the obvious professionalism and corruption. The anomaly is disregarded because Americans are attracted by the administered 'hustle' and orchestrated enthusiasm of college sports, besides which professional sports appear jaded. Americans are drawn to the amateur and ambivalent about the professional, attracted to the athlete who tries hard regardless of individual reward, whose play is still 'pure', and repulsed by the athlete who is 'only in it for the money' and is only 'going through the motions'. The line drawn between amateur and professional has therefore not lost all meaning, but a new cynicism has replaced the old. Now the category 'amateur' is used to legitimize the exploitation of the college-age athlete and to legalize the 'charitable' (and tax-deductible) donations alumni make to ensure the survival of the expensive athletic programmes that provide them with their weekly entertainment.

SUMMARY

Despite formal subscription to ideals of meritocracy, sports opportunities in the US are determined in large part by gender, race and class.

Compared to other modern societies, American women have made progress in securing equality of opportunity in the sports world, particularly at the collegiate level.

Black people, after many years of exclusion, are now well-represented in the sports world, except at managerial and ownership levels, where stereotypes about racial inferiority remain powerful.

The American sports creed portrays the sports world as an open and democratic place, despite the fact that access to many sports is determined by social class: working-class people are under-represented among the crowds at most sporting events.

There are few government programmes to provide leisure opportunities for the under-privileged.

Class boundaries are not marked in the US by the distinction between amateur and professional, in large part because amateur sports have been taken over by high schools and colleges which have broken down the barriers between amateur and professional.

5 AMERICAN SPORTS AND THE GLOBAL ORDER

The final substantive section of this chapter will deal with the role of the United States in the emerging global order of sports. What role has the US chosen to play in this global order? How has this choice been affected by American values and Americans' desire to promote those values globally? Performance in sport on the international stage has become an important symbol of national prowess. Many people believe that a nation's sporting achievement, indeed, its worth as a nation, can be gauged quite accurately by its performance in international competition. Americans share this view but only up to a point. In fact, when its size is considered, the question is not so much why a great power like the US has assumed such a large role on the world's sporting stage, but why its role has been so small.

The first reason why this role is smaller than expected is insularity. The second has to do with how Americans have chosen to organize their intervention into the global order of sport, a subject to be discussed below. The inhabitants of most countries regard domestic issues as more salient than foreign affairs. People will care more about, and know more of, the events and people of their own country. This will certainly be true of sporting events and participants, where the news is fleeting and ephemeral. Americans share this attitude: they are not so much ignorant of other societies as indifferent to them, the kind of neglect that comes from a feeling of natural superiority and leadership, in which the important events of the world are those that concern the US and where performance is measured solely against standards set by Americans. The reasons for this attitude are easily found. The United States is a huge and heterogeneous country, almost a world unto itself. It is far from Europe or South-East Asia, and such places can seem even more distant if one lives in the Midwest. It has been the preeminent economic power throughout most of the twentieth century, and Americans are taught from the cradle to think of the country as exceptional, as above or ahead of the rest, the model for others to follow.

These attitudes provide a frame for American sports:

> few aspects of American culture seem more peculiar, incomprehensible and irritating to European sports fans than calling the contest between two domestic teams for what essentially is the United States championship 'the world series' as in baseball, and — following that sport — 'world championship' in both professional football and basketball. What better reflects America's self-contained, parochial yet at the same time self-assured, even smug, culture than equating itself with the world, at least as far as sports are concerned?

> (Markovits, 1988, p.150)

Actually, Americans display a remarkable openness to imported goods, so long as they can be easily integrated into mainstream values and practices. There is a thriving international market for athletes, in which Americans participate at both the college and professional level, and favourite sports have been exported from the US to other countries and become enormously popular. Nevertheless, American sports are largely segmented in their own world: national teams are rarely pitted against foreigners and club teams rarely play teams from other countries. Professional football is uniquely American, as much a cultural marker as Gaelic sports in Ireland. Basketball is popular world-wide but American clubs play exclusively amongst themselves. Baseball has expanded across the open border with Canada, but club competition remains an exclusively North American affair, as is true of ice hockey, imported from Canada.

The one great exception to American sports isolation is the Olympic games, and here the US has tried to take the lead, assuming the mantle of defender of the amateur ideal in the global sports order. Preserving the spirit of amateurism is also preserving 'American' ideals of democracy, freedom and competitiveness. As the world began to divide after the Second World War into capitalist and socialist camps, the amateur ideal became associated with the former because it connoted individual freedom, while professionalism became associated with the latter because it connoted expediency. The conflict was sharpened after 1952 when the Soviets were admitted to the Olympic games and other Soviet bloc countries began promoting Olympic performance as a weapon in the Cold War. The Americans responded by redoubling their efforts to provide an alternative to the professionalism of the Soviet bloc.

The question arises — if Americans have identified so strongly with the Olympic ideal — why has their performance in the Olympic games so often given cause for disappointment and frustration? To some degree, how a nation prepares itself for Olympic competition is a measure of the significance attached to sport in the country. Americans are keen to do well in Olympic competition and have been more successful than most, but given the country's population and level of affluence, achievements fall far short of what is possible. The reasons are twofold: the US has relied heavily on voluntary efforts, with a minimum of government aid; and the voluntary efforts have been badly divided, suffering from a long-standing struggle for control over amateur athletics between the AAU and the National Collegiate Athletic Association (NCAA). No understanding of sport in America is complete without some knowledge of these two organizations and of their relation to each other.

The rivalry began in the nineteenth century. On one side were athletic programmes administered by colleges (and therefore confined to academically-eligible 18–21 year olds), staffed by professional athletic directors and coaches (whose interests were local and short-term), and dominated by the sport of football (which did little to prepare athletes for international competition). On the other side was the AAU, run by gentlemen volunteers, established as a co-ordinating organization of club-affiliated athletes long before collegiate conferences became an effective political force, and with its principal strength in the administration of the track and field events that were so important for the Olympic games, but which had limited spectator appeal on college campuses.

American Olympic organizers were caught in the middle of this rivalry, although they tended to favour the AAU because of its historical association with the International Olympic Committee. The effect of the rivalry on the American Olympic effort was devastating, for it separated the organization responsible for preparing the US for the Olympic games (the AAU) from the organization with most of the coaches and facilities necessary to accomplish this task. The formation of the NCAA in 1910 only made the situation worse because it gave the colleges an organizational coherence they had previously lacked. Incessant squabbling between the AAU and the NCAA in the inter-war period and into the 1950s, on top of some humiliating defeats at the hands of Soviet bloc teams, caused the federal government to change its 'hands off' policy with respect to sports and consider means of better co-ordinating the American Olympic effort. This change of policy was important. Not only did it modify long-established American policy toward amateur athletics, but it made it more difficult for the US to defend the principle that politics does not belong in sport.

Federal intervention took the form of a Commission on Olympic Sports, appointed by President Ford in 1975. In its 1977 report, the Commission described the US Olympic Committee as 'a maddening complex of organizations'. It recommended that a federally-chartered central sports organization be set up, with federal funding for 'the long-term improvement of the American sports effort' (US President's Commission on Olympic Sports, 1977, p.24). These proposals were highly unpopular, not least among traditionalists in the international Olympic movement, who saw the US as one of the few upholders of the 'free enterprise' basis of amateur sports. As a result the Amateur Sports Act, passed on the basis of the recommendations of the Commission, said nothing about a government agency and reduced the funding authorizations to a token sum.

The US Olympic campaign continues to rely on voluntary contributions and corporate sponsorship. Even the national governing bodies of individual sports in the US, chronically short of funds, are ambivalent about government support because they fear strings might be attached: funding for athletes and facilities might be granted, but only in exchange for gender equity in the hiring of coaches, regional dispersal of funds to suit Congressional interests, and a 'bill of rights' to facilitate representation of rank-and-file athletes. Americans, true to the spirit of freedom and choice, prefer not to have government directly involved in the regulation and administration of funding of sport, whether professional or amateur, and they are willing to pay the price of unsatisfying international competition to keep this spirit alive.

SUMMARY

The size, location, and power of the US leads to a certain level of insularity, resulting in limited participation in sport's global order by club teams and Americans displaying little interest in international sport outside of the Olympic games.

The US has enjoyed much success in international sports competition, yet achievements are less than might be expected. Under achievement is largely due to crippling rivalry between the AAU and the NCAA for control over amateur athletics, and to Americans' reluctance to involve the government in the administration of sports.

6   CONCLUSION

This chapter describes some of the distinctive ways in which Americans approach sport, paying particular attention to the impact of value differences on behaviour in sport. Little has been said here about some of the economic differences between American and European sports. For instance, the labour market for professional athletes in the US is more internalized than in European countries, with players only recently gaining much freedom to move from club to club. Another difference is the closer relationship between professional sports and television in the US, with TV coming to rely heavily on the revenues gained from selling advertising time on sports broadcasts and professional leagues living and dying by their ability to sign lucrative television contracts. These differences reflect the greater penetration of capitalist principles into sport in the US. Americans are ambivalent about the extent of this penetration. Many would prefer to think of sport as not really a business, but they also warm to and admire the more spectacular side of sports promotion, which heavy reliance on televised sport does little to diminish. This ambivalence is explained, in turn, by the values which this chapter has highlighted. Americans would like to think of sport as part of the national heritage, a sacred sphere in which ideals of nationhood and community are preserved. Americans would also like to think of sport, however, as an opportunity for individual advancement, self-expression and entrepreneurial genius. This ambivalence runs through all levels of sports activity, from the organized play of young children to the leagues of professional sports. And it reflects a tension that exists in the American system as a whole, which tries to combine the ideals of equality, openness and sharing with the ideals of personal freedom, private property and individual gain.

The distinctiveness of American sport should not be exaggerated. The end of the twentieth century could see sport's global order undergoing tremendous change, as the edifice on which the Olympic games was constructed, amateurism, crumbles. This is bound to affect the administration of amateur sport in the US, where so much energy has been devoted to defending the ideal. In the new global order of sport, winning athletes are global media stars who can earn huge sums of money, whatever their national origin or 'amateur' status. Individual sports are global 'products', desired emblems of modernity, competing with other global sports in a thriving international market. Powerful transnational, non-governmental organizations control the flow of sporting events and resources across national borders, with little regard for governments and national Olympic committees. And a global sports culture provides a common lexicon of phrases, images and rituals by which athletes and fans in different countries can communicate despite barriers of language. So universal has the language and practice of sport become that it is questionable whether or not national differences in sport remain. Rules are standardized by international sports federations; technological developments spread rapidly through international networks of coaches and trainers, boosted by the marketing efforts of sporting goods firms; and increasingly the global mass media diffuse knowledge of unfamiliar games and players, and educate fans in appropriate ways of spectating and crowd behaviour. The result is that individual sports determine their own destiny, and look more and more alike, wherever they are played.

REFERENCES

Brown, B. (1991) 'The meaning of baseball', *Public Culture*, vol.4, pp.43–70.

Chandler, J. (1988) *Television and National Sport*, Urbana, University of Illinois Press.

Elias, N. and Dunning, E. (1986) *The Quest for Excitement*, Oxford, Blackwell.

Foley, D. (1990) *Learning Capitalist Culture: Deep in the Heart of Tejas*, Philadelphia, University of Pennsylvania Press.

Gans, H. (1988) *Middle American Individualism: the Future of Liberal Democracy*, New York, Oxford University Press.

Griffin, T. (ed.) (1992) *Social Trends: 20*, London, HMSO.

Guttmann, A. (1982) 'The tiger devours the literary magazine: on intercollegiate athletes in America' in Frey, J. (ed.) *The Government of Intercollegiate Athletics*, West Point, Leisure Press, pp.71–9.

Kirschner, D. (1986) *The Paradox of Professionalism: Reform and Public Service in Urban America 1900–1940*, Westport, Greenwood Press.

Lipset, S.M. (1990) *Continental Divide: the Values and Institutions of the United States and Canada*, New York, Routledge.

Lynd, R.S. and Lynd, H.M. (1929) *Middletown: a Study in Modern American Culture*, New York, Harcourt, Brace & World.

Markovits, A. (1988) 'The other American exceptionalism: why is there no soccer in the United States?', *Praxis International*, vol.8, pp.125–50.

Miller Brewing Co. (1983) *The Miller Lite Report on American Attitudes Towards Sport*, Milwaukee.

Oriard, M. (1991) *Sporting With the Gods*, Cambridge, Cambridge University Press.

Potter, D. (1954) *People of Plenty: Economic Abundance and the American Character*, Chicago, University of Chicago Press.

Robinson, J. (1980) 'British–American differences in the use of time', *Society and Leisure*, vol.3, pp.281–97.

Seymour, H. (1971) *Baseball: the Golden Age*, New York, Oxford University Press.

Seymour H. (1990) *Baseball: the People's Game*, New York, Oxford University Press.

Snowman, D. (1977) *Britain and America: an Interpretation of Their Culture 1945–1975*, New York, New York University Press.

Turner, R. (1960) 'Sponsored and contest mobility and the school system', *American Sociological Review*, vol.25, pp.855–67.

United States President's Commission on Olympic Sports (1977) *Final Report*, Washington DC, Government Printing Office.

Vidich, A. and Bensman, J. (1960) *Small Town in Mass Society*, New York, Doubleday Anchor.

Wong, G. and Ensor, R. (1986) 'Sex discrimination in athletics', *Gonzaga Law Review*, vol.21, pp.345–94.

FURTHER READING

Adler, P. and Adler, P. (1991) *Backboards and Blackboards: College Athletes and Role Engulfment*, New York, Columbia University Press.

Fine, G. (1987) *With the Boys: Little League Baseball*, Chicago, University of Chicago Press.

Mrozek, D. (1983) *Sport and American Mentality, 1880–1910*, Nashville, University of Tennessee Press.

Sammons, J. (1987) *Beyond the Ring: the Role of Boxing in American Society*, Urbana, University of Illinois Press.

Scully, G. (1989) *The Business of Major League Baseball*, Chicago, University of Chicago Press.

Smith, R. (1988) *Sports and Freedom: the Rise of the Big-Time College Athletics*, New York, Oxford University Press.

Tygiel, J. (1983) *Baseball's Great Experiment: Jackie Robinson and His Legacy*, New York, Oxford University Press.

Jackson Pollock painting No. 32 *(1950), photographed by Rudolph Burckhardt*

ARCHITECTURE AND ART

Douglas Tallack ★

1 INTRODUCTION

The skyscrapers of Manhattan (Plates 9.1 and 9.2) or Frank Lloyd Wright's low-slung Prairie Houses (Plate 9.3); the paint-spattered surface of *No. 32* by Jackson Pollock (see facing page) or Andy Warhol's Pop Art (Plate 9.4): each of these have been taken as quintessentially American and as evidence that art and architecture provide us with very direct — because visual — representations of American society. But there are differences even among these famous examples: skyscrapers are urban and primarily vertical, but suburban ranch-houses express their 'Americanness' by spreading out into horizontal space and evoking an alternative to the city as the centre of American life, while still being demonstrably modern in their design. Frank Lloyd Wright claimed that a truly democratic architecture was best realized in the individual home, whereas his mentor, Louis Sullivan, promoted the democratic characteristics of 'the tall office building'. The relationship between painting and society is also more complicated than it first appears. Jackson Pollock's work has been called '"American-type" painting' (Greenberg, 1961, p.208) in part because there is *no* obvious American subject matter. It is abstract art — and bewilderingly so for many people. In contrast, there seems to be no such confusion about the subject matter or the 'Americanness' of Andy Warhol's art, but the fact that we recognize commodities on a supermarket shelf by a similar process makes us wonder what it is that we are seeing when we look at *100 Cans*.

It may be, then, that the relationship between American art and architecture and its society has to be approached more indirectly. We need to be aware of persistent tensions in American culture, notably between the country and the city. Frank Lloyd Wright's work would make little sense outside of this tension; nor would the self-conscious return to regional painting in the 1930s by John Steuart Curry and others (Plate 9.5). And we must also be aware of the specificity of the medium. What this means is that a painting of a New York skyscraper by an early American Modernist such as John Marin (Plate 9.6) is not just about that building. It is also about the process of representation in paint and new ways of seeing that differ from earlier, more traditional ways of seeing. Even the building which Marin paints — it is Cass

Gilbert's Woolworth Building (1911–13) (Plate 9.7) — is part of debates within architecture about how the external form relates to the function and structure of the building. We shall come back to all of these examples but the point to emphasize here is that when we ask how twentieth-century America has been represented in architecture and painting, we are also asking what *representation* means in those art forms? Other questions follow: has the relationship between American society — so often regarded as the epitome of modernity — and its art and architecture produced a different kind of *Modernism* from that in Europe? And is Modernism a unified movement or are there variations within it and also differences between Modernist art and Modernist architecture? A similar set of questions crops up when we consider the *Postmodernist* reaction against Modernism from the 1960s onwards.

Although these are difficult questions, they can be examined by detailed reference to a number of examples and within a chronological framework, so that the relationship between American society and its art and architecture is seen to be a developing one. We need to deal with art and architecture separately in order to respect the specificity of the medium and the debates surrounding the medium which Modernism and then Postmodernism precipitate. However, a good many cross-references can be explored and, hopefully, coming at Modernism and Postmodernism from the different, but related, perspectives offered by art and architecture will help to explain these concepts.

ARCHITECTURE

2   THE CHICAGO SCHOOL, 1880s–1920s

American Modernist architecture begins in Chicago with the skyscraper. A close analysis of selected buildings coming out of the Chicago School of architecture will allow us to identify the skyscraper form and, more importantly, to show that its emergence is intimately connected with material factors: demographic movements, technology, economics, and geography.

Although the idea of starting from scratch is an American myth, after the Great Fire of 1871 Chicago did just that. Its population rose from 325,000 in 1870 to 1 million in 1890, and doubled again by 1910. Louis Sullivan, the most celebrated of the Chicago architects, explains how aesthetics and pressing material changes intersected: 'The tall commercial building arose from the pressure of land prices, the land prices from pressure of population, the pressure of population from external pressure'. Sullivan acknowledges the contribution of the safety elevator, invented by Elisha Otis in 1857, and goes on to observe that 'it was inherent in the nature of masonry construction to fix a new limit of height. … its ever-thickening walls ate up ground and floor space of ever-increasing price, as the pressure of population rapidly increased'. This crucial point is marked by the completion, in 1891, of Daniel Burnham and John Root's Monadnock Building (Plate 9.8). Although the

Monadnock exhibited an unusually slim end-on profile to passers by, without the use of steel-frame technology its sixteen storeys was near to the limit for masonry skyscrapers. Once the load could be transferred from the walls to the steel frame the possibilities for building tall increased exponentially. Sullivan praises inventive American engineers and concludes that 'The architects of Chicago welcomed the steel frame and did something with it. The architects of the East were appalled by it and could make no contribution to it' (Sullivan, 1956, p.313).

Sullivan was more than an engineer and envisioned himself as the heir of the poet, Walt Whitman, who, in the Preface to *Leaves of Grass* (1855), had called for a distinctively American culture: individualistic but democratic, practical but idealistic, and able to make art out of unartistic materials and circumstances. This democratizing of architecture was no easy task. Nevertheless, in the years after the Civil War, when Whitman grew pessimistic at the prospect of Americans becoming more and more materialistic, he pinned some of his hopes on architects to revive the culture of democracy. Architecture, he felt, was more closely in tune with the realities of American life, though this proximity could equally endanger an architectural expression of democratic ideals if the utilitarian requirements of commercial clients became too dominant. And so, as if responding to Whitman's fears, Sullivan caps a catalogue of material determinants in his 1896 essay, 'The Tall Office Building Artistically Considered', with this poetic celebration of height: 'The tall office building … must be every inch a proud and soaring thing, rising in sheer exultation that from bottom to top it is a unit without a single dissenting line' (Sullivan, 1947, p.206). Whitman, writing in New York in the mid-1850s before anything approaching a skyscraper had been built, had only been able to emphasize the geographical dimension of American space.

Sullivan and Dankmar Adler's Guaranty Building (Buffalo, NY, 1894–5) exemplifies the Chicago School's new idealist-materialist theory of architecture (Plate 9.9). At thirteen storeys, the Guaranty is not startlingly tall for a steel-frame building. However, the arches over just the twelfth-storey windows link the windows down to the third storey into a single elongated window. While above the remarkably light and open base, false piers alternate with true piers to attenuate verticality. At the top of the piers we come across a further feature of Sullivan's architecture: a pronounced ornamental terracotta, which gushes over into the more elaborate filigree of the top floor band, just beneath the row of circular windows. When describing Sullivan's often profuse ornamentation, for instance on the Carson Pirie Scott Store (Chicago, 1899, 1903–4, 1906), we find ourselves using verbs like 'gushes', 'winds', and 'flows', which derive from the natural world, rather than the world of steel and concrete. Sullivan, despite his proclaimed functional aesthetics, could not wholly resist the legacy of Whitman and the Transcendentalist thinkers, Ralph Waldo Emerson and Henry David Thoreau. Ornament threatened the central Modernist relationship between form and function, which Sullivan himself propounded, but ornament was also one of the conduits through which architecture could become organic. Ornament is the site, then, of a tension in Sullivan: between the heroic individualism, inherited from Whitman and then Henry Hobson Richardson, the unofficial founder of the Chicago School, and the impersonal, machine world which the new rationalized technology and the new corporations exemplified, but which, equally, provided the vital impetus for Modern architecture.

The new possibilities which came with the steel frame went beyond mere height. Non-load-bearing walls could be just a skin and, increasingly, the skin could be transparent. The 'Chicago window', in evidence in Sullivan's Carson Pirie Scott Store and D.H. Burnham and Company's Reliance Building (Chicago, 1894–5) (Plate 9.10), was an intermediate stage between the masonry skyscraper and the fully-developed curtain wall of the 'glass box' skyscraper. The amount of glass on the Reliance Building is increased (to more than two-thirds of the street-front surface) by the use of bay windows, while the 'lightness' of the building also comes from the use of glazed terracotta. The Reliance never achieved the fame of such New York skyscrapers as the Woolworth or Chrysler buildings (which we shall come to shortly) and, not surprisingly, at fourteen storeys, it has been physically diminished by subsequent Chicago skyscrapers. Still, we can understand why Carl Condit, author of the standard study, *The Chicago School*, should see the Reliance as a forerunner of the rigorous Modernist skyscraper of Mies van der Rohe and praise it as

> the triumph of the structuralist and functionalist approach of the Chicago school. In its grace and airiness, in the purity and exactitude of its proportions and details, in the brilliant perfection of its transparent elevations, it stands today as an exciting exhibition of the potential kinesthetic expressiveness of the structural art.
>
> (Condit, 1964, p.111)

Structuralist, in this context, simply means that the constructive principles are not hidden but, instead, have a determining effect upon the overall 'look' of the building. Structure also has an aesthetic dimension (sometimes the term form is used instead of 'structural art'); thus, in the Monadnock, Burnham and Root resist the temptation to decorate or ornament the surface of their building, but, instead, allow the bay windows to create an undulating effect over the full extent of the longer side of the building. This suggests a distinction between ornament, which is added, usually at corners, doorways, windows and cornices, and pattern, which is integrated into the structure of the whole. The undulation of the Monadnock is functional, however, because bay windows introduce as much light into the offices as is possible with a thick-walled masonry building.

At stake, in the Monadnock, the Reliance and the Guaranty buildings, is the meaning of 'architecture', and, arguably, the Chicago School architects did as much as anyone to contest the nineteenth-century view that 'architecture' did not include factories and offices. By the 1920s, European Modernists had joined the early American Modernists in rejecting this definition of architecture on behalf of public housing, as well as other unfashionable buildings.

SUMMARY

Modern skyscrapers, which are central to Modernist American architecture, were first built in Chicago. Sullivan saw them as an embodiment of the democratic ideal in part because they developed out of both structural and functional imperatives. They were a response to technological developments — the use of steel-frame technology made it possible to build higher with a transparent skin — and also to the pressures caused by urban growth.

3   HISTORICIST AND MODERNISTIC SKYSCRAPERS, 1910s–1930s

In his 1925 novel, *Manhattan Transfer*, John Dos Passos opts for the skyscraper as a distinctive cultural symbol of the United States in the twentieth century: 'Steel, glass, tile, concrete will be the materials of the skyscrapers. Crammed on the narrow island the million-windowed buildings will jut glittering, pyramid on pyramid like the white cloudhead above a thunderstorm.' (Dos Passos, 1969, p.16.)

Skyscrapers populate the novel almost like characters. They shimmer in the New York morning and loom menacingly over the night streets; they metamorphose into dense mountains or cardboard cut-outs; and they house the latest instalment of the American dream, tempting the upwardly mobile but repulsing the unemployed. Where representative eighteenth- and nineteenth-century Americans were pictured in relation to scenes of nature or the modest buildings of frontier or small-town life, Jimmy Herf, the hero of *Manhattan Transfer* stands on a New York sidewalk 'looking up the glistening shaft of the Woolworth. ... He turned north and began to walk uptown. As he got away from it the Woolworth pulled out like a telescope' (ibid., p.305).

If there was ever an image of American modernity, this must be it. And yet it is difficult to match the 'glistening shaft' of Dos Passos's Woolworth Building with the building itself, designed by Cass Gilbert and completed in 1913 (Plate 9.7). This is not simply because we, unlike Dos Passos in 1925, have seen innumerable slimmer, taller skyscrapers with glass and mirrored surfaces. Even in its time, the modernity of an 800 foot building was in tension with its Neo-Gothic detail. The Woolworth exemplifies a general tension in American architecture between, on the one hand, a determinedly Modernist vision which looked to technology, function and materials (Dos Passos's 'steel, glass, tile, concrete') as guides to style and form and, on the other hand, a more representationalist architecture. Cass Gilbert was happy to follow an established historicist practice in American architecture which, well before the 1893 World's Fair, had encouraged a succession of revivals (Jacobean, Classical and

Renaissance, as well as Gothic). In genuflecting towards the Gothic, Gilbert endows the head office of the Woolworth Corporation with due cultural weight: it becomes a 'cathedral of commerce' which towers over City Hall, while literally depending upon the still revolutionary steel-frame technology which Chicago School architects had first exploited around the turn of the century. The attempt to marry form and function in Chicago School architecture was not wholly abandoned in the Woolworth Building. The choice of a grooved Neo-Gothic style at least acknowledged the inappropriateness of Neo-Classicism. Nevertheless, the Woolworth clearly represented an alternative to the truth-to-materials-and-structure Modernism of the Chicago School, and when a historicist design by Raymond Hood and John Mead Howells defeated an extraordinary panoply of nearly 300 entries to the 1922 *Chicago Tribune* competition, the Neo-Gothic revival, superimposed upon the newest technology, seemed to have colonized the skyscraper — and in Chicago, as well (see photograph, page 267).

In defence of the Gothic skyscraper, it may be said that Gilbert, Hood and Howells and others found in past styles a form of architectural representation which offered more scope than did a pared-down Modernism, which, so its detractors objected, could only represent its own technology and materials. During the post-First World War economic boom, this search for an architectural language looked to the future rather than the past. This is apparent in William Van Alen's Chrysler Building (New York, 1928–30) (Plate 9.2); Raymond Hood's black bricks and gold trim American Radiator Building (New York, 1924), which glowed in the dark in recognition of a machine civilization; and Hood's McGraw-Hill Building (New York, 1928–9), whose streamlined top anticipated a slightly later phase in what is sometimes called American Moderne or American Art Deco, but which can be more comprehensively labelled *Modernistic* architecture. The term *Modernistic* is very similar to *Modernist* but they denote different views of architecture and its relation to, and role in, society. The popularity of Modernistic architecture, especially for the head offices of such new industries as automobile manufacturing, the media and communications, suggests that architects may have been asserting the irrelevance of European historicist styles to a rampant *laissez-faire* economy. Alternatively, the successes of Modernistic skyscrapers may suggest that architects like Raymond Hood, who switched from Neo-Gothic, to Art Deco, to a more severe Modernist style in the space of just a few years, epitomized the American architect: aesthetically and politically non-programmatic in comparison with the European avant-garde purist.

In trying to understand the meaning of these representational additions to the structure, it is revealing that Van Alen's plans for the skyscraper which eventually became the Chrysler Building did not include the hub-capped spire (which raised the building some 50 feet higher than the Woolworth); the images of (more) hub-caps, wheels, and fenders on the brick friezes; and the extravagantly lit and furnished lobby. All were added when the site was bought by the Chrysler Company and confirm a modification of the Modernist tenet, form follows function, the function being generic (a warehouse or railroad terminus, for instance). Instead, the Chrysler Building seeks directly to represent the specific business of the company, as does Hood's design for the Queens showroom of New York General Electric: a white ice-box-like building with a penthouse in the shape of a General Electric fridge compressor. The building-as-advertisement suggests that Modernistic architecture is explained, in part at least, by the product-differentiation which marked the automobile industry in the mid-1920s, when Henry Ford's utilitarian designs, notably the relatively inexpensive Model T, had to give way under competition from General Motors' annual model change. The look of the Chevrolet, for instance, came to represent an *image* of travel and stylish living, which bore only a tangential relationship to the mechanics of the car. Arguably, then, the Modernistic style actually represented the operations of a specific phase of the consumer market. That there were some doubts about a consumer ethic is implied by the coexistence of the images of modernity with an icon of an older individualistic, craft ethic: Walter Chrysler's first set of tools, encased in glass just beneath the spire but later removed. That other doubts also found a stylistic resolution is evident from the years of the Depression when the Modernistic style metamorphosed once again, this time into the streamlined style. Shiny surfaces and elongated shapes on skyscrapers, but also on locomotives (the Burlington Zephyr) and even pencil sharpeners (the Loewy), symbolized a society speeding forward, free of the economic crisis.

In his essays of the 1890s, Louis Sullivan had asked about the cultural meaning of the individual skyscraper, and had concluded that the tall building was intimately connected with a democratic American society. Were there limits to its (and the society's) growth and was there an authentic shape to the skyscraper? Sullivan's immediate response, that the skyscraper ought to be a tripartite structure, was less important than his more considered view that the skyscraper could be conceived organically, rather than merely stylistically, and in the context of the social organism. Unfortunately, these questions were not seriously explored in the inter-war years, even though there was a general concern about the effect of the skyscraper, in the context of accelerated urban growth and rampant competition between individual companies and corporations within the economy (symbolized by the startling individuality of skyscrapers). The 1916 New York Zoning Law tried to ensure that more light reached street level by specifying that buildings could only rise if they were 'stepped back' from the street. Unfortunately, the city authorities' concern for the spaces between skyscrapers was too localized to make much of a contribution to the city conceived as an organism. There was, however, one limited architectural response to the increasing fragmentation of the city.

A skyscraper complex, consisting of the RCA Building, Radio City, office blocks, shopping areas, restaurants, and a square which became a public ice rink, Rockefeller Center (New York, 1931–40) would have been ambitious even in stable economic times, but in the Depression it was, in many respects, a remarkable achievement (Plate 9.1). The interconnecting high-level walkways did not get built, but the idea of public spaces in a downtown area, including the roof-top gardens (somewhat exaggeratedly called an urban park), was an important concept. Rockefeller Center eschewed the utopianism of the European avant-garde. Civic amenities, it was argued, made good commercial sense and much thought was given to architectural means for attracting the public as potential shoppers. Perhaps one point may be made to conclude this section on highly representational sky-scrapers: for all its commercial pragmatism, Rockefeller Center offered enough civic amenities for it not to need to rely on surface images. Though Rockefeller Center is distantly indebted to the verticality of the Neo-Gothic, and is stone, and not glass-clad, it is quite purist in its style and anticipates the triumph in America of the most pure kind of Modernism — the so-called International Style. More importantly, however, it remains a symbol of a less fragmented view of city architecture than either the eclecticism which we have been discussing or the uniformity of the 'glass box' which we can now consider.

SUMMARY

In the inter-war years there is a tension in architecture between Mod-ernist and more representational styles. In some buildings there was an attempt to indicate the specific business of the company involved. There was, however, little concern about controlling the urban effects of building skyscrapers through zoning or planning laws. In general commercial pressures produced an increasingly fragmented urban landscape but Rockefeller Center was a significant planned exception to these developments.

4   THE INTERNATIONAL STYLE, 1930s–1970s

Dos Passos's reference to 'the glistening shaft' of the Woolworth Building sounds more like the *Project for a Glass Skyscraper* and some others which remained on the drawing board of the German architect, Mies van der Rohe. Yet thinking about the skyscraper amongst the European Modernist avant-garde in the 1910s and 1920s could hardly have been more different from that which produced the historicist Woolworth Building and the Modernistic Chrysler Building; hence the spectacularly unsuccessful entries for the *Chicago Tribune* competition by the Bauhaus architects, Walter Gropius and Adolf Meyer (see illustration opposite), and Ludwig Hilberseimer, which only came into their own with the International Style 20 years later. How-ever, the stylistic development towards the glass box which, as we have noted, undoubtedly benefited from the examples of the Reliance Building in Chicago and American industrial architecture, was accompanied, in Euro-pean Modernism, by a desire to theorize the context of the individual build-ing. That context was sometimes the housing estate and sometimes the city

(Left) Raymond Hood and John Mead Howells, the Chicago Tribune *Building (Chicago, 1922–4). (Right) Design for the* Chicago Tribune *competition (1922) by Walter Gropius and Adolf Meyer*

as a whole. The word 'planning' has a bad press these days but for the European avant-garde, planning was inseparable from architecture. In this section, we can look at what happened to the social project of Modernist architecture in the very different context of post-1945 America.

In 1937 Gropius and Mies arrived in the United States, having escaped from the Nazis who, in 1933, had closed the Bauhaus. These émigré architects virtually took over American architecture but, by the late 1960s, it was apparent that the potential for an alliance between architecture and planning had not been realized. Instead, the skyscraper seemed to have even less to offer the city than at the time of the earlier zoning laws. The reasons were complicated but before outlining them, it should be said that in the work of Mies van der Rohe and his American followers — Philip Johnson, who was Mies' partner for the Seagram Building (Plate 9.11), and the firm of Skidmore, Owings & Merrill in their Lever House and the Chicago Civic Center (1963–8) — developments begun in Chicago in the 1880s reached a remarkable culmination. Ada Louise Huxtable is eloquent on the Seagram Building and other glass boxes in her 1982 book, *The Tall Building Artistically Reconsidered*: 'The Miesian aesthetic has produced an eminently suitable twentieth-century vernacular style for this century's unique and overpowering scale' (Huxtable, 1984, p.52). She admits, though, that

> the minimalism of the modernist aesthetic lends itself to a subtle, ascetic beauty or to the cheapest corner-cutting; and since the latter has been the easiest and most profitable route for the builder, an elegant reductive vocabulary was quickly reduced to a bottom-line banality that its creators never dreamed of.
>
> (Huxtable, 1984, pp.48–9)

We can begin to understand what happened to Modernism by noting the division between 'architecture' and 'housing' at the 1932 International Style Exhibition at the Museum of Modern Art, New York, through which Henry-Russell Hitchcock and Philip Johnson introduced European Modernist architecture (plus the neglected Frank Lloyd Wright) to the United States. Ironically, a celebration of Modernist architecture publicly overlooked the relationship between a building and its society which was so central to Modernism; in so doing the exhibition symbolically prepared for the transformation of the Modern Movement into the International Style, though there were more tangible reasons for the decline of the social perspective in architecture which Gropius and Mies brought with them but could not sustain. Initially, the rational planning, functional architecture and admiration for mass production methods which the Modern Movement stood for coincided with the post-Second World War desire by most Western governments to rebuild the world and provide homes and jobs for the people. In the US, more than anywhere else, however, Modernist tenets of technical practice were harnessed by corporate capital and stripped of their social ideology to perpetuate the narrow, wholly individualistic vision of the skyscraper which we have been tracing. The symbols of a triumphant new world were the sleek skyscrapers, free to rise in the absence of strong planning initiatives and laws.

The progress of the skyscraper considered only as an isolated block was taken to its ultimate conclusion in the super-skyscrapers of the late 1960s and beyond: Bruce Graham's and Skidmore, Owings & Merrill's 1,450 foot Sears Tower (Chicago, 1970–4) and John Hancock Building (Chicago, 1965–70), the 1,350 foot twin towers of Minoru Yamasaki's World Trade Center (New York, 1972), and a cluster of monster buildings on the new skyscraper frontier of Texas, where restrictions on zoning were virtually non-existent. These super-skyscrapers effectively signalled the end of the enlightenment tradition of rationality which underpinned the skyscraper strand of architectural Modernism. The social failure of skyscraper architecture — or at least the failure to develop the more socially orientated views of some members of the Chicago School and some European Modernists and to learn from the example of Rockefeller Center — leaves the fate of American Modernism resting largely upon the work of Frank Lloyd Wright.

SUMMARY

Under the influence of émigré architects from Europe, particularly from the Bauhaus, American architecture was increasingly dominated by the International Style after the 1930s. Modernism had initially suggested a particular relationship between a building and society, but in the US it was the technical and functional aspects of building which were accentuated during the post-war economic boom. Capitalist competition stressed the individualistic idea of the skyscraper and resulted in building ever higher isolated blocks.

5   FRANK LLOYD WRIGHT

Frank Lloyd Wright is known for offices (the Larkin Administration Building, Buffalo, NY, 1904, and the Johnson Wax Administration Building, 1936, and Research Tower, 1944, both Racine, Wis.); churches (Unity Temple, Oak Park, Ill., 1906); leisure amenities (Midway Gardens, Chicago, 1914, and the Imperial Hotel, Tokyo, 1916–22); and museums (the Guggenheim, New York, 1944–57); as well as for the Robie House (Oak Park, Ill., 1908–9) and Fallingwater (Edgar J. Kaufmann House) (Bear Run, Pa., 1936). Perhaps, thinking back to Sullivan's 'The Tall Office Building Artistically Considered', the most useful category to have in mind is height, or, rather, a reaction against it. Because although Wright built the Price Tower (Bartlesville, Okla., 1952–5) and speculated, on paper, about a 'mile high' skyscraper, his architecture is orientated towards horizontal space and a relationship to landscape.

Wright, like Sullivan, railed against revivalist styles: 'English … "manors" cut open and embellished inside to suit the ignorant "taste"' (Wright, 1960, p.94). In the Robie House (Plate 9.3), one of many houses designed for the well-off middle-classes in Oak Park, River Forest, and other Chicago suburbs, strong, straight, clean lines predominate. Load-bearing walls are kept to a minimum, Wright explains, 'to reduce the number of necessary parts of the house and the separate rooms … and make all come together as enclosed space — so divided that light, air and vista permeated the whole with a sense of unity' (quoted in Curtis, 1987, p.80). The fireplace is only a partial divide between living and dining room, but the resulting large space is unified by Wright's meticulous attention to carpet design, the straight lines of the furniture (oak is used throughout), and even the wooden ceiling grilles, which conceal utilities (lighting, pipes, wires), while creating abstract patterns when the lights shine through them.

Oak Park was open to the south of the Robie plot and the house was constructed to pick up the flatness of the landscape — the so-called prairie style. In his earlier suburban houses (for example, the Goodrich House, 1896, and the Winslow House, 1893), we see Wright refining the horizontality of his design: roofs become lower-pitched and multi-levelled, at their lowest on garages or wings running out into the garden or in parallel with garden walls. The front elevation of the Winslow House relies on traditional symmetry but the rear marks Wright's break from symmetry and recourse to the 'support' offered by the environment. The roofs, balconies, and walls in the Robie House create an abstract geometric pattern but because Wright was so aware of the landscape, even in a suburb, the building does not stand out against its environment, as a skyscraper always threatens to do. In Wright's words, 'we should recognize and accentuate this natural beauty [of the Prairie], its quiet level' (quoted in Frampton, 1985, p.59). On the other hand, the low-slung roofs of the Robie House protect the inhabitants' privacy, this being one of Frederick C. Robie's requirements. It is as though the inside can only be opened up when the relations with the outside are carefully controlled. Wright, himself, calls attention to this tension between radical, Modernist design and dedication to 'a cause conservative'. The Prairie Houses show an acceptance of the shape of society and a desire to conserve family values and maintain the order of the surrounding environment. These traditional ideals were hardly endorsed in 1909 when he abandoned his family and suburban life-style and went to Europe with Mamah Borthwick Cheney, the wife of a neighbour and client. This contradiction is less significant, though, than the possible connection between Wright's domestic designs and the privatized existence so common in the distinctively American ranch-style suburban tract houses which dated from the post-Second World War flight from the cities.

Even when Wright worked outside the domestic sphere, similar preoccupations can be observed. The Larkin Administration Building can be usefully approached through Wright's 1901 lecture, 'The Art and Craft of the Machine'. Wright believed that the Larkin Building, which was aptly situated, not in a leafy suburb, but in a city near to a gasworks and railway line, was an architectural embodiment of the machine age, to which architecture, as the most public and in-touch of the arts, must respond. The machine had an egalitarian potential and, properly directed, could counter the disorder of an urban city built upon the misuse of machines during the industrial revolution. In both lecture and building, therefore, we can see Frank Lloyd Wright addressing the characteristic American tension between country and city rather than being defined by it. More particularly, we can see him using Modernist tenets of design to humanize the often dehumanizing modern environment.

The Larkin Building makes maximum use of space to house the utilities: the ventilation shafts and stairways are in the corner piers and so do not interrupt the central interior space (see photograph opposite). In Wright's summarizing words, written some 20 years later, 'To incorporate all heating, lighting, plumbing so that these systems became constituent parts of the building itself. These service features became architectural' (quoted in Curtis, 1987, p.81). Inside, there is none of the obsessive oriental ornamentation of Adler and Sullivan's Auditorium Building (Chicago, 1887–9). As in the living rooms of Wright's suburban homes, the Larkin Building maximizes light by being, in effect, a single, open-plan interior space. As he said of

Frank Lloyd Wright, Larkin Administration Building (interior) (Buffalo, NY, 1904)

Unity Temple, 'In every part of the building freedom is active. Space [is] the basic element in architectural design' (Wright, 1960, p.314). However, any architect closely in touch with the times — this being a basic element in Modernism — is liable to get drawn into the assumptions of those times. Thus, in the Larkin Building artificial, rather than natural light predominates, suggesting the desire to create the openness of the outside inside a building. This interest in a controlled environment is evident down to the furnishings and Wright was annoyed when prevented from designing the telephones. The Larkin Building is, therefore, a wonderful example of the doubleness of Modern architecture — its sense of controlled freedom is apparent in the top-lit, airy space which also facilitates surveillance of employees from the balconied atrium. Wright later called the Larkin Building 'the great protestant' in architecture (ibid.), a description that fits uncomfortably well with the managerial rationalization of the work ethic represented by Frederick Winslow Taylor's time-and-motion studies, conducted in the 1880s and published as *The Principles of Scientific Management* in 1911.

Wright's career lasted from 1887 to his death in 1959, and our final example comes from the second phase which dates from the mid-1910s. In the utopian scheme for Broadacre City (plans 1935), Wright was in reaction against the International Style but was seeking to adapt aspects of the European Modern Movement to American conditions. The machine-principle, which Wright had earlier associated, in part, with skyscrapers had gone too far and so he sought, in the individual components (Usonian Houses) and overall plan for Broadacre City, to reorientate machine technology. The Usonian House employed techniques of prefabrication to provide, small(ish), convenient but comfortable houses, which retained the open-planned quality of his first houses but with a more democratic orientation. The greater expanse of glass in a Usonian House, such as the Herbert Jacobs House (Madison, Wis., 1936), confirms that Wright wanted to encourage a less privatized existence than the clients of his Prairie Houses demanded. The environmentalism or contextualism of the Prairie Houses went only so far — usually only to the end of the plot upon which the house was built — and Wright had shown no interest at that time in moves to plan and re-plan the city. In the more socialized intellectual atmosphere of the Depression, when public housing received federal support and when not even Oak Park was immune from dole queues, Wright outlined a social (though not socialist) role for architecture in the US. In contrast to Le Corbusier's 'Ville Radieuse', also of the 1930s, Broadacre City was to be a dispersed city, made possible by widespread ownership of automobiles, radios and telephones. Modern technology would allow Americans to reclaim their rural heritage and make full use of space, without sacrificing the community which comes with proximity. Although the plan envisaged a few very tall buildings, the individual family home on at least an acre of land, and not the giant apartment blocks of the 'Ville Radieuse', would be the basic unit.

We concluded Section 3 with Rockefeller Center, which resisted the isolating and fragmenting effects of individual skyscraper construction while yet remaining resolutely urban. The social ethos engendered by the New Deal of the 1930s, together with 'depressed' real estate values, created the unusual conditions, in the US at least, in which a project like Rockefeller Center became possible. Frank Lloyd Wright's Broadacre City also came out of the Depression but was a more radical response. However, its combination of new technology and decentralization, and individualism and collectivism stopped at the city limits in the sense that Wright remained mired in traditional political thinking. He seemed to be oblivious of the necessity for a political programme capable of intervening in the market economy. 'America needs no help to build Broadacre City', he announced. 'It will build itself, haphazard' (quoted in Frampton, 1985, p.190).

SUMMARY

Frank Lloyd Wright rejected revivalist styles of architecture while stressing horizontality rather than the verticality of many other American architects. He was concerned to use Modernist tenets to humanize the increasingly dehumanized modern environment. His response to the Depression was to suggest that technology could make possible a rediscovery of community and freedom, that it was now possible to combine individualism and decentralization in a spatially planned environment.

6 POSTMODERN ARCHITECTURE, 1960s TO THE PRESENT

The word *Postmodernism* is heard just about everywhere but is easier to pin down when applied to architecture than to other cultural spheres. Indeed, Postmodernism was initially a direct reaction against some of the failings of architectural Modernism which we have noted. The architectural critic, Charles Jencks, has even identified an event — the dynamiting in July 1972 of Minoru Yamasaki's massive, award-winning but then badly vandalized high-rise Pruitt-Igoe Housing Estate in St. Louis (1952–5) — as the symbolic end of Modernism. There are Postmodern skyscrapers, but the AT&T in New York and Republic Bank in Houston, both by Philip Johnson in his Postmodernist phase, are not known for their height or for any technological innovation but for their historicist references: the New York building for its Chippendale top and the Houston building, as Johnson himself put it in a television interview, for its 'little pyramids on top, and all those little scoops and enormous gables' (BBC, 1986, *Architecture at the Crossroads*).

The first important text for architectural Postmodernism was Robert Venturi's *Complexity and Contradiction in Architecture* (1966), published in conjunction with an exhibition at the Museum of Modern Art. Unlike Hitchcock and Johnson's *The International Style* (1932), Venturi's intervention is deliberately anti-avant-gardist and personal: 'Architects can no longer afford to be intimidated by the puritanically moral language of orthodox Modern architecture. I like elements which are hybrid rather than pure ... accommodating rather than excluding ... vestigial as well as innovating, inconsistent and equivocal rather than direct and clear' (Venturi, 1988, p.16). Compared with later, extravagant Postmodernist buildings, Venturi's house for his mother in Chestnut Hill, Pa. (1963) and Guild House (Philadelphia, 1962–6) are fairly low-key, like his 1966 book. Charles Jencks is more forthright in the tone of *The Language of Post-Modern Architecture* (1977) and his illustrations of a Postmodern alternative to, as he sees them, the disasters of

Modernism. Jencks instances, among other buildings, Michael Graves' Portland Building (Portland, Oreg., 1979–82), Johnson and John Burgee's AT&T Building (New York, 1978–82), Charles Moore's Piazza d'Italia (New Orleans, 1975–9), and SITE's Notch Project (Sacramento, Calif., 1977).

The more openly representational style of Postmodernism, which was internationally articulated as 'The presence of the past' (the title of the architecture section at the Venice Biennale in 1980), is well exemplified in Moore's Piazza d'Italia (Plate 9.12). Moore acknowledges Modernism by picking up the black and white design of an adjacent skyscraper in the steps of the Piazza, but arches and columns, the latter decked out in neon and with stainless steel capitals, are the basic elements of this 'eclectic classicism'. This is Charles Jencks' designation and it suggests that the range and, often, the sheer randomness of Postmodern borrowings from the past is what distinguishes the movement from the use of historicist styles which has been common throughout architectural history. In the case of the Piazza d'Italia the results seem to be more eclectic than the intentions. One of Moore's associates, Donlyn Lyndon, asserted some ten years before that 'the first purpose of architecture is territorial, that the architect sets out the stimuli with which the observer creates an image of "place"' (quoted in Stern, 1977, p.70). Accordingly, working with local New Orleans architects, Allen Eskew and Malcolm Heard Jr., Moore sought in the Piazza to communicate with the Italian community and buttress ethnic identity. In a pluralist city, Moore is saying, diversity must be an architectural keynote. Interestingly, Jencks adopts a Modernist rationale for diversity, pointing out that computer-assisted design permits variety within mass-production technologies, including the production of the kind of building materials we might expect to find on eighteenth-century New England houses or nineteenth-century Chicago office blocks. Jencks calls this combination of new technology and an open, pluralistic attitude towards style 'double-coding'. The Modernist insight into the importance of technology is one reason why the diversity Jencks describes is *post*-Modern and not just a resumption of a pre-Modern eclecticism, as Jencks sometimes claims. However, two years after its completion, Charles Moore himself alerts us to another, more sceptical way of seeing the combination of elements in the Piazza d'Italia:

> I remembered that the architectural orders were Italian, with a little help from the Greeks, and so we thought we could put Tuscan, Doric, Ionic and Corinthian columns over the fountain, but they overshadowed it … So instead we added a 'Delicatessen Order' that we thought could resemble sausages hanging in a shop window, thus illustrating its transalpine location. But I now think there is going to be an Italian restaurant and no sausages. … there was a little bit of money left over so we thought we would bang up a temple out front to show that our piazza was behind it.
>
> (quoted in Frampton, 1985, p.293)

Robert Venturi's later book, *Learning from Las Vegas* (1972), written with Denise Scott Brown and Steven Izenour, is much more strident in its anti-avant-gardism than *Complexity and Contradiction in Architecture*. The book celebrates what Modernists have regularly criticized as mere signs of the market, namely 'ugly and ordinary architecture': hamburger stands, suburban sprawl, mobile homes, and billboards. But 'billboards are almost all right' Venturi *et al.* declare, and provide just as many possibilities for architectural re-cycling as the great architectural movements of the past (Venturi *et al.*, 1977, p.6). With Modernism widely discredited, there seems currently to be no authoritative answer to Postmodernism's disarming question, why not?, though Kenneth Frampton observes sharply that 'the cult of "the ugly and the ordinary" becomes indistinguishable from the environmental consequences of the market economy' (Frampton, 1985, p.291).

The populist, 'fun' character of much Postmodernism is certainly a relief after the stentorian, sometimes hectoring tones of Le Corbusier, though amidst all the playful architecture in many gentrified urban districts it is possible to feel nostalgic for the sheer lines and reductive aesthetic of a skyscraper by Mies van der Rohe and to appreciate something of what he meant by the gnomic pronouncement 'Less is more'. Modern architecture established itself in the US in a market context but, whether through Sullivan and Wright's claims for architecture as more than just building at the behest of a client, or through the cross-fertilization with more socially-inflected European Modernists, it sought to have its say in a language which was more than the market demanded, and it sought to intervene in ways that would contest the implicit economic philosophy of the grid-plan of American cities. With so much populist opprobrium still being heaped upon the Modern Movement, whether by Charles Jencks on behalf of Postmodernism, or by Prince Charles on behalf of tradition, it is worth insisting on the important, if somewhat abstract, point that in making use of the technology and the materials of its own age, Modernism provided a measure of the relationship between architecture and society. In a society such as the United States, which has typically favoured private initiative over public, institutional intervention, and in which tradition can be arbitrarily chosen and used rather than simply abided by, the question of legitimacy — the legitimacy of individual style and form and also the 'proper' relationship between the individual building and its context — boomerangs from one project to another between the unconnected extremes of conservatism and innovation. These extremes tend to be manifested as rapid changes of style (even within a single building), giving the impression of a great deal of architectural activity. Postmodernism is often locally critical and attentive to power relations as they pertain to a particular site; for this reason, it deserves a more discriminating discussion than is possible here. But Postmodernism is too close to the workings of the market and too reluctant (because of the failures of Modernism) to attempt the reintegration of architecture and planning on a large scale to offer wholly satisfying answers to architectural questions.

It has been one of the aims of this chapter to show that while we must begin by attending to the specificity of the medium, eventually we arrive at the recognition that by 'architectural questions', we mean questions which cannot be answered aside from the social, political, economic, and wider cultural concerns which are addressed elsewhere in this set of volumes. This approach can also be used to talk about American art, though the nature of the medium — paint — suggests that the relationship between art and society is likely to be even less direct. We can, at least, begin with a familiar example.

SUMMARY

Postmodernism in architecture is a label applied to a variety of styles. Postmodernism builds on technological possibilities available to Modernism but is both more diverse and more representational. It is in part a reaction to Modern architecture but specific buildings are very much influenced by their context, and in America usually result from private rather than public initiatives. But even if Postmodernism rejects the aesthetic of many Modern buildings it too is closely linked to Modern non-architectural, cultural concerns.

ART

7   EARLY AMERICAN MODERNIST ART, 1900s–1930s

In New York in the 1910s and 1920s the tallest skyscraper of the age, Cass Gilbert's Woolworth Building, was painted by the early American Modernist, John Marin (Plate 9.6). But when we look at Marin's paintings of this, and other skyscrapers, we begin to see that painterly Modernism may be rather different from architectural Modernism. *Woolworth Building No. 31* (1912) or *Lower Manhattan* (1920), in which we see the Woolworth through the uprights of Brooklyn Bridge, count as Modernist precisely because the solidity and great height of the Woolworth are undermined by the mixture of water colours and crayon and by the perspective adopted, which angles the building, making its walls tilt alarmingly. Marin sees the building in what, from the point of view of any architect, is an irrational and dysfunctional way, so that the paintings of the completed skyscraper hardly differ from his earlier painting of the Woolworth under construction. If we look at the painting's internal relations, however, seeing it as a composition more than as a representation of an existing building, a different principle of unity becomes apparent from that which we have discussed in the sections on architectural Modernism. When we examine the more obviously abstract paintings of Jackson Pollock, for example, we will be able to differentiate more clearly between representation and composition, between seeing a painting such as *Woolworth Building No. 31* as a window into a different world (downtown New York in 1912, for instance) and, on the other hand, seeing the painting as an object on a wall in a room or as a surface beyond which we cannot easily see.

Four of Marin's Woolworth paintings were exhibited at the Armory Show in New York in 1913, along with the works of Joseph Stella, Marsden Hartley, Stanton Macdonald-Wright, Edward Hopper, Stuart Davis, Charles Sheeler and other up-and-coming American Modernists. More importantly, though, around 400 paintings by European Modernists were also exhibited. It was this concentrated burst of Impressionism, Post-Impressionism, Fauvism, and Cubism (the Futurists were not exhibited) which made the Armory Show so significant, and while visitors had little difficulty accepting Impressionism, later movements, particularly Cubism, were genuinely shocking or incomprehensible — perhaps in the way that we can be shocked by some performance art or find a completely white canvas or a pile of bricks in the Tate Gallery incomprehensible. Out of the interaction with European art, a number of strands of early American Modernism emerged: Cubist–Futurist painting, New York Dada, Synchronism, and Precisionism, though these labels often fail to do justice to an art scene which included such different painters as those mentioned above, plus Max Weber, Georgia O'Keeffe, Charles Demuth, and Man Ray. The diversity of early American Modernism can be overwhelming but our discussion of architecture suggests a way to assimilate two of the strands, at least: Cubist–Futurism and Precisionism, both of which engage very directly with urban-industrial America, *the* site of modernity.

Rush Hour, New York (1915) (Plate 9.13) shows that Max Weber is more wholeheartedly Cubist than Marin, though both are interested in intersecting planes and in turning objects around, including objects as large as skyscrapers, so that, against all the common sense of traditional representational art (against what is called one-point perspective), we see more than one side of a building at once, or we see through solid walls. Through the Cubist reduction to geometric shapes, Weber seeks to abstract some essence of city life, but, far from producing something static, the introduction of Futurist images of movement (wheels, intersecting lines and what we might now call 'go-fast' designs) conveys a dynamic quality, consonant with a prevailing view of New York as a city of movement and angularity. Marin may have been expressing a similar desire to represent urban processes, rather than simply urban scenes, when he chose to paint the Woolworth under construction, or when, in his painting *Lower Manhattan (Composing Derived from the Top of Woolworth Building)* (1922), he made use of a perspective which simply did not exist prior to the construction of the building. And Joseph Stella, the most Futurist of the early Modernists, raises the technological stakes by electrifying the diagonals that criss-cross his depiction of Brooklyn Bridge in *The Voice of the City: New York Interpreted* (1920–2). It can even be claimed that Weber's (or Marin's or Stella's) is the true representational art, whereas the more easily recognizable city scenes in the work of the slightly earlier Ash Can School painters lack the intensity of movement or sense of process that defined city life at that time. When we look at George Wesley Bellows' *Cliff Dwellers* (1913) we may adopt a critical attitude towards the tenements and the economic system which produced them, but we can imagine entering them. Weber's buildings in *Grand Central Terminal* (1915) or Marin's in *Movement, Fifth Avenue* (1912) provoke anxiety at the thought of being tilted and toppled over inside them. Just as there is a politics to the Ash Can School reformist paintings, so, in early American Modernism, the suggestion is that the excitement and dynamism of New York coexists with instability. When we put a number of Weber's city paintings together and add in Marin's *Lower Manhattan (Composing Derived from the Top of Woolworth Building)*, with its image of an explosion, and Joseph Stella's *Battle of Lights, Coney Island* (1913), with its electric signs and Tower of Light, we have the impression of a great power unleashed.

In the work of Charles Sheeler and other Precisionists we meet a much cooler response to modern America. *Church Street El* (1920), *Skyscrapers* (1922), *American Landscape* (1930), *Classic Landscape* (1931), *River Rouge Plant* (1932) and *City Interior* (1935) seem closer to architectural Modernism in their machine aesthetic and relentless photographic clarity of line than they do to painterly Modernism's partial reaction against rationality. One of Sheeler's photographs of the River Rouge Plant appeared in *Bauhausbusch* (1929) by Laszlo Moholy-Nagy, one of a number of Bauhaus architects and designers to be influenced by the anonymous American industrial buildings which Sheeler painted and photographed. Sheeler goes out of his way to maintain that anonymity or he opts for unexceptional buildings or the unexceptional bits of famous buildings, whether in the photograph *New York, Park Building* (1920), which is taken from the rear and formed the basis for *Skyscrapers*, or in the photograph, *New York, Towards the Woolworth Building* (1920), which renders Cass Gilbert's landmark unrecognizable.

The relationship between *New York, Park Building* and *Skyscrapers* is particularly interesting, given the challenge which the invention and development of photography issued to painting's claims to represent the world. There are less buildings in *Skyscrapers* and most of the distinguishing decorative features on the Park Row Building have been removed; all signs of activity have gone: the smoke from a factory chimney and the cranes on what is presumably the building site of a new skyscraper. And the painting is flatter. Both photograph and painting are literally flat, of course, but *New York, Park Building* has much more perspective depth: a blank wall on the right is nearer to us than the central building, the wedged indentations are deeper, and the source of the shadow of a smoking chimney is included in the photograph. In the painting, however, we are detained at the surface long enough to be made aware of compositional relationships, which barely allow for representational distinctions, even between a building and the shadow of a building. These observations apply more appositely, still, to *Church Street El*, in which it is possible to mistake the horizontal lines of an elevated railroad for the vertical lines of the buildings that tower above. In spite, then, of Sheeler's undoubted representationalism and the absence of distracting brush-strokes, we can see what the art critic, Clement Greenberg, is getting at in this important, if contested, definition of Modernist painting:

> Realistic, illusionistic art had dissembled the medium, using art to conceal art. Modernism used art to call attention to art. ...

It was the stressing, however, of the ineluctable flatness of the support that remained most fundamental in the processes by which pictorial art criticized and defined itself under Modernism ... Flatness, two-dimensionality, was the only condition painting shared with no other art, and so Modernist painting oriented itself to flatness as it did to nothing else.

(reproduced in Frascina and Harrison, 1982, p.6)

Greenberg's case becomes stronger with reference to later, more optical Modernists but weaker as the collage element in Modernism augmented the materiality of pigment and brush-strokes.

Sheeler's *American Landscape* (Plate 9.14) decisively puts aside the claims of such nineteenth-century nature painters as Thomas Cole and others in the Hudson River School, to be the definitive artists of the American landscape. Sheeler's painting deals primarily in straight lines: the river, the chimney, the reflection of the chimney in the river, the railway lines, and the cement works. The exciting but disconcertingly fragmented imagery used by European Cubist and Futurist painters to depict buildings and machinery is absent here and in the other five paintings which make up Sheeler's series on Henry Ford's River Rouge Plant and adjacent industries near Detroit. In a sense, Sheeler's techniques in *City Interior* represent not the plant, as such, but another set of techniques, those used on the Ford assembly line to eradicate human error and time-wasting, or in Ford's earlier Sociological Department's programme of Americanization, which sought to replace class divisions by a functionalist view of society as an interlocking whole. Sheeler was impressed when he spent six weeks at the River Rouge Plant in 1927 taking photographs as part of a publicity campaign for Ford's Model A. So it is perhaps not surprising that the untidy, the excessive, and the indistinct are mostly absent from the River Rouge series. One of the few examples of indistinctness is the small, blurred human figure in *American Landscape*. There are few signs of a *history* of production in these paintings about mass production. The geometric shapes are static and serene — history-less, endowed with 'the absolute beauty we are accustomed to associate with objects in a vacuum', to borrow Sheeler's words (quoted in Craven, 1923, p.71). What is surprising, though, is that two years after the initial photographs of the plant, when the economic crisis hit the US, Sheeler persisted with his unruffled portrayal, and utilized his own distinctive form of Modernism to do so.

One indistinct human figure in *American Landscape* is the sum total from the paintings discussed or cited in this section, and the number would be hardly any greater with three times as many examples. Buildings dominate the paintings and an analysis based simply upon subject matter would assume that they dominate people, too. However, what we have seen in our analysis is not so much modern subject matter as modern points of view. And they differ. It is true that human figures are largely absent from the Cubist–Futurists — Marin, Weber and Stella — as well as from Sheeler, Demuth and the other Precisionists. But the first group of painters seeks to be part of the process: the buildings tilt *from the artist's point of view* and none of these artists seeks to hide this subjective element amidst the intensity of external pressures exerted by the city — New York apparently above all other cities. Subjectivity is not pantheistic or overarching, as it can be in Romantic painting or literature. In his 1836 essay, *Nature*, the Transcendentalist, Ralph Waldo Emerson, recalls a revelatory moment: 'I am nothing; I see all; the currents of the Universal Being circulate through me; I am part or parcel of God' (Emerson, 1982, p.39). In Marin, Weber and Sheeler, however, subjectivity is part of a process in which points of view are created and destroyed by, for example, the construction of new buildings and new technologies of travel and perception. Writing about the experience of modernity in general, Marshall Berman catches something of what we can experience when looking at Stella's *Battle of Lights, Coney Island* or Weber's *Rush Hour, New York*: 'To be modern is to find ourselves in an environment that promises us adventure, power, joy, growth, transformation of ourselves and the world — and, at the same time, that threatens to destroy everything we have, everything we know, everything we are' (Berman, 1982, p.15).

In quite startling contrast, this is just what we do not get in *American Landscape*. Sheeler keeps himself at a distance, too: 'We are all confronted with social comment, but for myself I am keeping clear of all that. I am interested in intrinsic qualities in art not related to transitory things. I don't believe I could ever indulge in social comment. I could be disturbed by it' (quoted in Troyen and Hirshler, 1987, p.142).

By concentrating more on the compositional question of point of view, we have been able to appreciate that the *how* of a painting may be a better guide to the politics of art than the subject matter.

SUMMARY

Much American art is a dialogue with European Modernism. It can be characterized by diversity but we can isolate two strands in the art of the early part of this century: urban-industrial America is the site of Modernism and there is also a broad assumption that a painting is a composition, characterized by its own internal logic, rather than being just a representation.

8 AMERICAN PAINTING IN THE 1930s

No one could accuse Thomas Hart Benton of cool detachment, or of favouring a machine- and design-aesthetic over human concerns, and especially not during the Depression. Rather, the accusation is likely to be that sentiment is left to do the work of analysis that an economic crisis demands, even from artists. Something similar can be said of others, like John Steuart Curry and Grant Wood, who reacted to the growing insecurity of the 1920s and the economic disasters of the 1930s with a defiant return to representational art, allied to a desire to rediscover the real America, the 'Middle America', whether it was Wood's Iowa or Curry's Kansas. Whereas in the painters we have identified so far, the United States was a spur to Modernist art, for Benton, Curry and Wood returning to a folk idiom and regional focus after a decade or more of adolescent intellectualism was the answer to the excesses and decadence of Modernism. Benton was particularly extreme in his rejection of Modernism, probably because he was reacting against his own artistic youth when, in Paris and then New York, he had dallied with avant-garde art. Grant Wood insisted that he only appreciated Iowa after he had been to France.

Benton, Curry and Wood are of particular interest to us for reasons having to do with the label usually attached to them. As 'American Scene' artists they make claims about the representativeness of their paintings and, as we have noted, they reacted against the abstractions of Modernism in the name of representational art. They also stand for a different America from the urban-industrial one to which the early Modernists were attracted. The economic, but also moral, instability of the nation is patent in *City Activities with Dance Hall* (Plate 9.15), in which images of the stock exchange (the broker, the ticker-tape, the clock and the grabbing hands) are combined with images of a couple dancing, a still, a cinema, and a speak-easy. *The Engineer's Dream* (1931) and *The Wreck of the 'Ole 97'* (1943) depict the instability of an overly technological society. Yet, in a curiously Modernist gesture, which calls into question the supposedly neutral point of view of the representational artist intent upon not tinkering or experimenting with reality, Benton puts himself into *City Activities with Dance Hall*. In another panel a political poster hangs behind a representation of his wife and son, as if to indicate how radical politics intrudes into the family. In contrast, Benton presents a succession of agrarian images of order: the small town in *Chilmark* (1923), religion in *The Lord is My Shepherd* (1926), and family in the touching *Going Home* (1934). John Steuart Curry's *Baptism in Kansas* (1928) (Plate 9.5) is the centre-piece of the return to tradition and rural roots. There is no jarring of one-point perspective: the lane to the right of the house goes where it should go; the country people are not positive folk stereotypes, as they seem to be in Benton and Grant Wood; and Curry does not remove all contemporary signs in his evocation of tradition — a car is shown in the bottom left. But what are we to make of the explicitly religious symbolism of sunlight and clouds and a pair of doves? In American Scene paintings the seamlessness of commonsense representational art coexists awkwardly with polemic, as often occurs when artists and politicians alike purport to speak in populist tones.

In this connection, it is worth noting that the return to representationalism was also the call from a section of the artistic left, which set itself against the experimentalism of Cubism or Dada: there was already enough fragmentation amongst the 13 million unemployed in 1933, the year when Herbert Hoover was replaced as President by Franklin Roosevelt. The 'Social Realism', of Jack Levine, William Gropper, Philip Evergood, Moses and Raphael Soyer, and Reginald Marsh, differed from the earlier Ash Can School Realism because of its directly political message. Yet, when we compare Levine's *The Feast of Pure Reason* (1937), which shows a capitalist, a gambler or gangster, and a policeman in conference, with the rumbustious figures in Thomas Hart Benton, coming from the political right, we observe a similar folkish influence, combined with the techniques of magazine caricature. The differences between the Social Realists and the American Scene painters — bearing in mind their common objection to Modernist experimentalism — tell us that 'the real' and attempts to represent it are political as well as aesthetic issues. It was Edward Hopper's great achievement to paint in a broadly representational manner and yet to defamiliarize the real by foregrounding the ways in which the real is brought to us. In *Night Windows* (1928) we, as viewers, are behind the artist who is observing a woman through a window; in *Compartment C, Car 293* (1938), (Plate 9.16) the woman passenger's hat shades her eyes which are, in any case, on her reading matter. Identification, and knowledge of her character, are made difficult, while the other traditional focus — the countryside seen through the window — is off-centre and two dimensional. In consequence, we find ourselves looking at the excessively large expanse of blank, green wall.

In retrospect, the expanses of paint in Hopper's work of the 1930s and early 1940s seem like a turning point in American art. A few years later, in the work of Barnett Newman, great canvases covered by uniform colour — colour-fields they are sometimes called — were one of the signals that American Modernism had achieved its own internationally recognized language. Faced by such a canvas, it became difficult if not impossible to look through the painted surface, and different ways of talking about art had to be devised, as we shall see in the next section. Hopper's work is far more disturbing, though. That green expanse in *Compartment C, Car 293* also denies us access to 'the real' but because we have been led to this point in the context of what seems to be a straightforward representation, we are asked to contemplate the possibility that there is something missing in the scene and — if we think of Hopper's paintings of cafés late at night, lonely gas and railroad stations, and innumerable sparse hotel rooms — in the society more generally. His work will not permit either the consolations of the stereotypically constructed communities of American Scene painters or the freedom to speculate which comes with the colour-fields of Barnett Newman or the spattered canvases of Jackson Pollock. But, as the analysis of *Compartment C, Car 293* tries to show, his work will not allow us the consolation of keeping our distance from what is being represented.

SUMMARY

One reaction to the economic problems of the 1930s was a return to representational art, together with a rejection of Modernism. In the case of some artists this included a discovery of the 'real America', often with a regional focus. The achievement of Edward Hopper, however, was to produce paintings which ask us to question their context, both socially and as paintings.

9   ABSTRACT EXPRESSIONISM, 1940s–1960s

American art up to the Second World War had seriously engaged with the subject matter of the United States but up until the advent of Abstract Expressionism in the 1940s, it had only learned from, but never openly rivalled, the formal developments of European Modernism. What, then, were the sources of Abstract Expressionism, a category which covers such different artists as Jackson Pollock, Barnett Newman, Mark Rothko, Willem de Kooning, Clyfford Still, Franz Kline, Arshile Gorky, Lee Krasner, Philip Guston, Adolph Gottlieb, and Robert Motherwell? What did Abstract Expressionism bring to the international Modernist canon? And did it maintain the earlier involvement with American subject matter?

The Depression of the 1930s was such an all-encompassing disaster that Modernism gave ground to a more socially-relevant art. Indeed, many of the artists who were later labelled Abstract Expressionists or the New York School were themselves grateful for work on the Federal Art Project, which was just a part of the huge New Deal relief plan which gave employment to over 8 million people. As one of Thomas Hart Benton's students, Jackson Pollock was still more in the mainstream of an accessible populist art. However, from within the official progressive optimism of Roosevelt's New Deal, which sought to rebuild confidence as well as the infrastructure of roads, waterways, and power stations, Pollock began to fashion an art which tapped doubts, anxieties and other emotions missed or downplayed by the sentimental Realism of the American Scene or the explicitly political art of the Social Realists. Pollock's *Going West* (1934–8), as its title indicates, shares the American thematic orientation of Benton, and his bold, almost naïve, paint strokes as well. But where Benton's figures happily inhabit three dimensions and his curves (as in *Cradling Wheat*, 1938) come round to envelop and protect the figures and their activities, Pollock's paint strokes create unease, sweeping off to the top right or threatening to up-end the wagon train below. So much so, that it is hard to talk about the activity depicted — a scene from the frontier movement — without according a greater sense of activity to the movement of paint across the canvas. Perhaps it is hindsight but when we look back at the 1930s' work of Pollock, Clyfford Still, Philip Guston, and Franz Kline, we see in the representations of industrial architecture, townships, and landscapes, and even in the portraits, the shapes and patterns that pile up, collide, and snake across their later canvasses. The boldness of those canvasses is part of the legacy of the 1930s; their size also derives from the mural tradition of the thirties, but minus its overt politics or social commentary.

When the United States came out of the Depression and then the Second World War, a re-engagement with European Modernism occurred, accompanied by a reaction against the politics and representationalist aesthetics of the 1930s. It is important *not* to overstress the specifics of the political reaction against left-wing politics as the Cold War set in and the US moved to the right. Because while it is true that in the later 1950s Abstract Expressionism was lauded as America's distinctive contribution to art in a society free from the extremes of fascism and communism — and the evidence of CIA funding for travelling exhibitions and institutions has been assembled by Serge Guilbaut in *How New York Stole the Idea of Modern Art* — the group of painters who began to talk about Modern art in and around Greenwich Village in New York in the late 1940s and early 1950s were often critical of Cold War/McCarthyite politics. To the extent that the Abstract Expressionists eschewed a directly political art, they fell in with an era in which many American intellectuals called for 'an end of ideology' (in Daniel Bell's famous phrase) in politics; but to interpret their intense concentration upon the medium of their art, the size of their canvasses — for example, Pollock's *Mural* of 1943 (97.25 × 238 inches) — and the energy of the painting — we think of Rudolph Burckhardt's photograph of Pollock drip-painting (see page 258) — as implicitly supportive of the one-dimensional, tough, anti-intellectual Americanism of the Cold War is, at best, to evince remarkable confidence in one's ability to read off a specific meaning from some bewildering paintings.

In the catalogue to the 1943 American Modern Artists Show, Barnett Newman is outspoken in his rejection of populist art, such as Grant Wood's and Thomas Hart Benton's:

> We who dedicated ourselves to art — to modern art — to modern art in America, at a time when men found easy success crying 'to hell with art, let's have pictures of the old oaken bucket' — we mean to make manifest by our work, in our studios and in our galleries the requirement for a culture in a new America.

> (quoted in Guilbaut, 1983, p.69)

Although Newman refers to an American art, he and his group of late Modernists believed this would come about through re-establishing connections with European Modernism. In seriously investigating the properties of paint and the flatness of painting, they forged the first significant avant-garde in American art. As the broad term Abstract Expressionism indicates, their work is a combination of the optical and formal, on the one hand, and, on the other, the emotional, perhaps deriving from an awareness of the darker, uncertain side of American life. The sheer extremity of Kline's *Painting No. 11* (1951) — its rough and ragged lines and angles that are so different from the precision of Mondrian's grid-paintings — and Pollock's *No. 32* (1950) chimed with an interest in American intellectual circles in existentialism; more colloquially, the feeling of living on the forward wave of experience. The catalogue of breakdowns, accidents and suicides among the Abstract Expressionists marks out a generation which knew of, though had not experienced, the terrors of the concentration camps, the human cost of war, and the crises of the Depression, and was assailed by the intensities of the Cold War, the escalation of the nuclear arms race and the contradictions of an affluent society. But, aside from biographical evidence, these artists also *painted* on the edge. The influence of Cubism, especially Picasso's harsh, angular women in *Les Demoiselles d'Avignon* (1907) is there in Willem de Kooning's *Woman 1* (1950–2): paint is hacked about, and technical decisions seem to have left their traces on the canvas rather than being smoothed away. There are no satisfying conclusions to Pollock's paintings either, and no stories or recognizably secure scenes (as in Thomas Hart Benton). Instead, even the most distinctive of the dark lines in *Eyes in the Heat* (1946) swirl around, turn back on themselves and get lost in the scrapings of thick, light paint or have to compete with the smearings of red. As if this was not enough, a year later, Pollock developed his 'drip' method in which paint is dripped, flung and spattered from different angles, using sticks or — a great affront to 'art' — stiff, caked brushes, onto a very large canvas (sometimes sanded) spread out on the floor. Here is Pollock's own explanation, which we can read alongside Rudolph Burckhardt's photograph of Pollock at work on *No. 32*:

> When I am in my painting, I'm not aware of what I'm doing. It is only after a sort of 'get acquainted' period that I see what I have been about. I have no fears about making changes, destroying the image, etc., because the painting has a life of its own. I try to let it come through.
>
> (quoted in Anfam, 1990, p.125)

And, now, the equally well-known explanation by art critic, Harold Rosenberg:

> At a certain moment the canvas began to appear to one American painter after another as an arena in which to act — rather than as a space in which to reproduce, re-design, analyze or 'express' an object, actual or imagined. What was to go on the canvas was not a picture but an event.
>
> (Rosenberg, 1959, p.125)

The extremity of the method and the 'all-over' quality of paintings which have dispensed as absolutely with analytical Cubism as with the distinction between figure and ground, make it curious that Pollock and his contemporaries should have been identified with an age of conformity.

Even the double-barrelled label, Abstract Expressionism, is imprecise and in the midst of Pollock's aggressive action painting we glimpse the transcendental aspirations which reach a pitch in the so-called 'theological' wing of Mark Rothko, Clyfford Still and Barnett Newman. In Rothko the pitch of aspiration is so extreme that the painting cannot be transcended: 'However you paint the larger picture, you are in it. It isn't something you command' (quoted in Hughes, 1991, p.320). All we have to go on when responding to paintings such as *Ochre and Red on Red* and *Untitled* (both 1954) are the classic abstract elements of space, shape, surface and colour. Moreover, these elements do not remain discrete to give us an abstract, rather than representational, language with which to talk about the painting. The surface is so stained that it seems to have a depth but not in the illusionist sense of a painting with figures, say, in the foreground set against an unmistakable background; all we have, as the determinants of space and shape are the four edges of the painting, since the rectangular shapes blur into each other and, in the paintings in the Rothko Chapel at Rice University, Houston, are even more indistinct. Colour, in Rothko's colour-field painting, is so modulated that internal relations are difficult to fix and, of course, colour cannot be attached to objects, whether in the representational manner or in the Fauvist manner in which colour and objects are mis-matched. Robert Hughes probably comes closest to articulating all of this when describing his response to the 'huge obscure paintings' in the Rothko Chapel: 'Subjectless, formless (except for the shape of their framing edges), and almost without internal relations (except for the merest whispers of tonal adjustment in the darkness), they represent an astonishing degree of self-banishment' (Hughes, 1991, p.323).

In the context of this chapter and book, perhaps what is most extraordinary about the Abstract Expressionists is the range of interpretive responses they have provoked. In addition to Hughes' formalist account (with its hints of religious significance), we are confronted with explanations which present Pollock, especially, as the refinement of the Modernist preoccupation with surface; with mythical interpretations deriving from Surrealist influences; with the view which associates the Abstract Expressionists with a post-war interest in existentialism and painting (and living) on the edge; and, most notoriously, with the thesis that the sudden and unexpected success of these artists was a subtle part of Cold War propaganda. The direct correlation between art and society in the last of these interpretations says virtually nothing about the paintings themselves, while the explanation which reaches us through the intricacies of the history of Modernist art seems to ignore the complexities of post-war America. At least it is easier to explain how Abstract Expressionism contributed to the American art which followed it.

SUMMARY

Abstract Expressionism is a label attached to a group of painters who came to the fore in the late 1940s. With them America first achieved an internationally recognized painting language. The success of Abstract Expressionism derived from several sources and it required a new way of thinking about art. It had roots in the 1930s, in the politics of the Cold War, and in a re-engagement with European Modernism. It combined both a formal and an emotional response to American life.

10 AFTER MODERNISM, 1960s TO THE PRESENT

There is no obvious way to summarize the American art which came after Abstract Expressionism, but, as a way of linking at least the work of Robert Rauschenberg and Jasper Johns, Pop Artists such as Andy Warhol and Roy Lichtenstein, and a broadly Postmodernist art, we can identify a reaction against the high seriousness of Pollock, Rothko and their contemporaries, and against the theory of Modernism as the purifying of the art form. However, Modernism has been so much the art of this century that some of the reactions against it have been less an abandonment of Modernism under the umbrella of Postmodernism and more the pursuing to an extreme of the central tenets of Modernism, or pausing — almost in Modernist vein — to inspect, once more, the problem of representation.

Just as the architect, Philip Johnson admired but tired of his mentor — 'Mies is such a genius! But I grow old! And bored!' (quoted in Jencks, 1985, p.198) — so Robert Rauschenberg dripped paint onto a bed (*Bed*, 1955), and, in 1953, persuaded Willem de Kooning to let him rub out a de Kooning drawing, which he then re-titled *Erased De Kooning Drawing*. He and Jasper Johns looked back to the collage strain in Modernism and especially to Marcel Duchamp's radical questioning of both Modernist and representational art when he offered a mass-produced urinal to the Independents Exhibition in New York in 1917. In 1960 Johns cast beer cans in bronze, while Rauschenberg, in his 'combines' of the years 1953–64, concentrated on the waste products of a modern society: signs, packaging, and miscellaneous junk. *Gift for Apollo* (1959) is a battered bucket which appears chained to a painted door on wheels. These hybrids, neither painting nor sculpture, comment on the relationship between mass production and art which Pop Art exploits, but they also continue the Modernist investigation into the space and surface of painting, questioning whether 'painting' is even an adequate description for a work which includes other materials besides paint. If a traditional painting of a room gives the illusion of depth — the room's furniture seems to be 'behind' the surface of the painting — so, with Rauschenberg furniture and junk come out into the room where the work is being exhibited. Clement Greenberg's views on the 'flatness' of Modern art remained influential but Rauschenberg and the cooler, more reflective Jasper Johns took the question of representation in new directions. Jackson Pollock's trajectory round the canvas was so hypnotic that the question of representation was displaced into talk of action and automatism. But Johns stuck to a few limited objects — beer cans, flags, targets, maps, and numbers — and in *Numbers in Color* (1959) for instance, asks about the meaning of repeated numbers or, rather, painted representations of what are already among the most abstract, and certainly arbitrary of representations. And while colour is nowhere more significant than in Rothko and Newman, Johns still finds room to ask what it means to paint the word 'RED' in blue.

The 'drip' paintings of Pollock may propose an attack upon the idea of a personal style but there is something intensely involved in what Pollock was doing. It is as though he could not do other than paint in that way. The same can be said for Barnett Newman's vast colour-fields, often marked only by a vertical 'zip'. But then Roy Lichtenstein substituted for the intense brush-strokes and spatterings of Modernists, from Manet to Pollock, the magnified Benday dots of graphic designers, and Andy Warhol, operating out of The Factory, his studio in New York, forced the recognition that art could be mechanically produced, reproduced and disseminated. In *100 Cans* (1962) (Plate 9.4) it is not even the object but the packaging that attracts Warhol. Where the American Modernist poet, William Carlos Williams, had

claimed that there are 'No ideas except in things', Warhol seems to be saying that there are no ideas except in signs and that the point about signs is
that in theory nothing can stop them being infinitely repeated. Interestingly,
the fact that silkscreened rows of identical two-dollar bills could be repeated
over and over, as Rauschenberg's manual assemblages of used products
could not, may indicate a difference, rather than a similarity between what
Warhol and the advertising industry are doing, since the latter must, at all
costs, avoid the boredom of repetition. In the section on Postmodernist
architecture, it was argued that the variety of styles is a false radicalism
which disguises the extent to which Postmodernism is driven by the logic of
commodity differentiation. Whereas in Warhol we encounter a repetition
which empties a commodity of the meaning with which advertising tries to
endow it. This may be an argument for Pop Art's subversiveness and there
is little doubt that Warhol's work offers an inside knowledge of consumerism and its sophisticated colonization of alternative positions. The risk
must be that such a close acquaintance makes the difference between accepting consumerism and formulating a critique all but invisible.

The work of Eric Fischl and Cindy Sherman will have to suffice as an indication of more obviously Postmodernist challenges to Modernist art. Fischl's
Bad Boy (1981) (Plate 9.17), for example, is formally quite straightforward. It
is not abstract; there is a single perspective; the painting gives the illusion of
not being flat; and the figures and objects are recognizable. Roughly speaking, we know what is going on and we know where it is going on: 'I'm
dealing with American culture, and that aspect of it that I'm most familiar
with — the suburban middle classes' (quoted in Nairne, 1987, p.146). But
Bad Boy and *Pizza Eater* (1982) — in which two men look at a naked young
girl walking past them on a beach — and *Daddy's Girl* — in which a man
cuddles his young daughter on a sun-lounger on the patio outside a suburban house — are disturbing in other ways. The unease is similar to that
provoked by David Lynch's television series, *Twin Peaks* (1990), or his film,
Blue Velvet (1986). If a painting by Jackson Pollock or Barnett Newman made
looking difficult, Fischl's paintings follow on from Edward Hopper in being
about looking — looking to the point of explicit voyeurism and looking at a
reality which has already been visually filtered by other media: 'What the
suburbs are about is a picture-book reality; the way houses are designed, the
way objects people surround themselves with are chosen, is through photographs. Advertising feeds the imagination, and feeds the desire, and so people try to make kitchens look like the kitchens they see in photographs'
(quoted in Nairne, 1987, p.146).

Bad Boy evinces a 'knowing' representationalism, a *return* to a way of seeing
rather than an assumption that we see in this way. Thus, Fischl plays upon
the genre of the still-life: 'That painting started off with me looking at a
blank canvas and deciding that one thing I knew I wanted to paint was a
bowl of fruit. I painted a bowl of fruit; and then I was sitting there looking
at it' (quoted in Nairne, 1987, p.144). When we look at a still-life, whether
Cézanne's *Apples and Oranges* (1895–1900) or the bowl of fruit in *Bad Boy*, we
simultaneously acknowledge the realness of the fruit and the fact that these

objects have been isolated, looked at carefully and then painted. But Fischl's still-life is in a room where other kinds of looking are going on: the boy looking at the woman; the boy looking at the woman as a cover for another theft, stealing money from her bag, which suggests that he knows that she knows he is looking at him and is sufficiently distracted to miss the theft of money. We see all of this but, in so doing, become implicated in the complicated process of looking. This may sound like an endorsement of the Modernist concentration upon the medium. However, Modernism, having questioned the link between representation and the real world through its move to exclude anything which interfered with the condition of painting — as flat, as pure surface — set loose a pictorial logic which could not be contained within the painting itself. The act of looking at the painting, together with other forms of looking (through photography, film, television, and computer-generated graphics), cannot but become part of the work.

Not surprisingly, the explicit, yet cold and detached, sexuality of Fischl's paintings has been controversial:

> Fischl insists that these paintings are not pornographic or misogynistic and that he is not promoting these attitudes but simply revealing them. But the representation of images and experiences does not by itself encourage critical evaluation. Many of Fischl's paintings simply restate the attitude towards women that is so prevalent in the commercial patriarchal culture he denounces.
>
> (Borsa, 1985, p.23)

This is a cue to conclude this chapter with Cindy Sherman. Her work has been exhibited with Fischl's in New York's Artists' Space and she, too, represents women and engages with a 'commercial patriarchal culture'. Moreover, Sherman is a photographer and so her work permits us directly to confront the loss of painting's exclusivity in the face of mechanized reproduction while, at the same time, allowing us to see how artistic production or intervention persists.

The 'strength' of a painting by Jackson Pollock consists in its standing out against being used for non-artistic purposes; as we have seen, he and other Abstract Expressionists were in reaction against the overt politics of 1930s art. In contrast, Cindy Sherman's strengths lie in knowing that even a work of abstract art can be co-opted by a consumer system and used to sell a product. After all, images of women have been used, usually more subtly, by art itself, including during the ascendancy of late Modernism, as in Willem de Kooning's *Women* series. The works of Pop Artists (Lichtenstein's *Washing Machine*, 1961, James Rosenquist's *I Love You With My Ford*, 1961, and Warhol's *Marilyn*, 1964, for example) then introduced into the sphere of art a whole set of new images of women, derived from advertising and the media in general. Sherman's photographs have, at once, to represent this state of affairs and resist it.

In the 80 black and white *Untitled Film Stills* of the late 1970s and early 1980s Sherman photographs herself as a lone woman, often in an urban setting: against a backdrop of skyscrapers (*Number 21*, 1978) or hurrying along a dark street (*Number 54*, 1979). This series was a deliberately populist gesture for Sherman, who had been 'disgusted with the attitude of art being so religious and sacred, so I wanted to make something that people could relate to without having to read a book about it first' (quoted in Nairne, 1987, p.132). But there is also a subtle criticism of the media's representation of women. These are generic photographs, to the point that we can find it frustrating that we cannot quite recall the 1950s' and 1960s' Hollywood films from which they are supposedly taken. *Number 10* (1978) seems so familiar: it portrays a blond woman with a 1950s'-length skirt, white socks and sneakers, standing with her bag, seemingly waiting for a bus on a country road. Others more openly confront the construction of a feminine image. *Number 6* (1978) (see below) taken from above, is of a made-up young woman on a crumpled duvet, with her legs bare and her blouse open to reveal her underwear. Yet we can make out the cable for the delayed action shutter release. Sherman has re-constructed this and each scene; more particularly, she has re-constructed the character out of existing images. In her

Cindy Sherman, Untitled Film Still, *1978* (Number 6: black bra)*, black and white photograph, 10 × 8 in. (25.4 × 20.3 cm). The Eli and Edythe L. Broad Collection, Los Angeles/Metro Pictures*

studio colour photography of the 1980s, Sherman concentrates upon this 're-' in 're-construction'. To put it more straightforwardly, in putting herself on display in front of her own camera — for instance in a series commissioned by *Vogue* magazine in 1984 — she puts on show a type of display. Similarly, in her *Pink Robe* series (1982), she draws our attention to what intervenes in the process of representation:

> I was trying to make a content that would be alluring, but then as soon as you looked at it, it would kind of bite you back like something that would make you feel guilty for feeling that way, you would feel sorry for this person because they're victimised, or that you were victimising them by looking at them like that.

> (quoted in Nairne, 1987, p.133)

Although Sherman is describing her own project, her words have a general relevance to the second half of this chapter. She is working near the end of a century in which looking has become highly self-conscious; in part, this self-consciousness about looking and about the medium through which what we see is represented is what we mean by Modernism. And, as we have noticed, Modernism in art differs from Modernism in architecture in introducing a greater degree of subjectivity. Here, we can recall John Marin and Max Weber's paintings of New York skyscrapers, though what is interesting and important about both of these artists (and also Edward Hopper) is the extent to which a subjective point of view arises from, rather than detaches itself from, the objective changes which mark off the twentieth century and which we often associate with the growth of the city. Other Modernists — the Abstract Expressionists are perhaps the best example — have forced us to become more and more aware of painting as composition, rather than as representation. But as representation has become more detached from a recognizable subject matter (a painting might just as well be given a numerical title or called 'Untitled') so paintings became (or were openly recognized as) objects and, indeed, commodities to be accorded value within the art market. Some Modernist art — again the work of the Abstract Expressionists comes to mind — seeks to resist the co-opting of art by the market by its sheer focus upon the medium. But another body of art, going under the broad umbrella of Postmodernism, acknowledges commodification and the inevitable blurring of the line between art and non-art, between the specificity of a medium such as painting and the lack of discrimination implied by the idea of the *mass media*. This process dates back to Marcel Duchamp's 'readymades' and achieves full recognition with Warhol and Pop Art. In different ways, Robert Rauschenberg, Jasper Johns, Eric Fischl, and Cindy Sherman have tried to respond to this disturbing situation — have tried to respond to the consequences of Modernism.

Sherman's work is an especially appropriate point at which to conclude in so far as she concentrates upon the acts of looking and representing as they occur within a consumer culture. She reminds us that what intervenes in any kind of looking and representing is, precisely a culture with its dictionary of definitions of women; in the more recent *History Portraits* (1988–90),

Sherman also reminds us that art has played its part in stereotyping women. She, through the women she becomes, resists definition by *almost* occupying stereotyped positions. But, besides culture, what also intervenes in the process of representation, as we have seen throughout this chapter, is the driving motor force of the market and here there are more limited chances of effecting change.

SUMMARY

Much of the art which followed Abstract Expressionism, from about 1960, was characterized by a reaction against high seriousness. For example Pop Art is a reflection on consumerism as well as a comment on the arbitrariness of representation. More recently, Postmodern art, like Postmodern architecture, accepts some of the premises of Modernism whilst also seeking to extend them. It accepts that there is no obvious boundary between art and non-art but, as in the work of Cindy Sherman, this is a source of strength in the effort to comment critically on the commercial context in which 'artistic' representation takes place.

REFERENCES

Anfam, D. (1990) *Abstract Expressionism*, London, Thames & Hudson.

Berman, M. (1982) *All that is Solid Melts into Air: the Experience of Modernity*, London, Verso.

Borsa, J. (1985) 'Eric Fischl: representations of culture and sexuality', *Vanguard*, April, pp.18–25.

Condit, C.W. (1964) *The Chicago School of Architecture: a History of Commercial and Public Buildings in the Chicago Area, 1875–1925*, Chicago, University of Chicago Press.

Craven, T. (1923) 'Charles Sheeler', *Shadowland*, vol.8, pp.11, 71.

Curtis, W.J.R. (1987) *Modern Architecture Since 1900*, London, Phaidon Press.

Dos Passos, J. (1969) *Manhattan Transfer*, London, Sphere.

Emerson, R.W. (1982) *Selected Essays*, Ziff, L. (ed.), Harmondsworth, Penguin.

Frampton, K. (1985) *Modern Architecture: a Critical History*, London, Thames & Hudson (rev. edn).

Frascina, F. and Harrison, C. (eds) (1982) *Modern Art and Modernism: a Critical Anthology*, London, Harper & Row.

Greenberg, C. (1961) *Art and Culture: Critical Essays*, Boston, Beacon Press.

Guilbaut, S. (1983) *How New York Stole the Idea of Modern Art: Abstract Expressionism, Freedom, and the Cold War*, Goldhammer, A. (trans.), Chicago, University of Chicago Press.

Hughes, R. (1991) *The Shock of the New: Art and the Century of Change*, London, Thames & Hudson (rev. edn).

Huxtable, A.L. (1984) *The Tall Building Artistically Reconsidered: the Search for a Sky-scraper Style*, New York, Pantheon.

Jencks, C. (1985) *Modern Movements in Architecture*, Harmondsworth, Penguin (2nd edn).

Nairne, S. (1987) *State of the Art: Ideas and Images in the 1980s*, London, Chatto & Windus.

Rosenberg, H. (1959) *The Tradition of the New*, Chicago, University of Chicago Press.

Stern, R.A.M. (1977) *New Directions in American Architecture*, New York, George Braziller (rev. edn).

Sullivan, L. (1947) *Kindergarten Chats (Revised 1918) and Other Writings*, New York, Wittenborn Art Books.

Sullivan, L. (1956) *The Autobiography of an Idea*, New York, Dover.

Troyen, C. and Hirshler, E.E. (1987) *Charles Sheeler: Paintings and Drawings*, Boston, Museum of Fine Arts.

Venturi, R. (1988) *Complexity and Contradiction in Architecture*, London, Butterworth Architecture.

Venturi, R., Scott Brown, D. and Izenour, S. (1977) *Learning from Las Vegas: the Forgotten Symbolism of Architectural Form*, Cambridge, Mass., MIT Press (rev. edn).

Wright, F.L. (1960) *Frank Lloyd Wright: Writings and Buildings*, Kaufmann, E. and Raeburn, B. (eds), New York, Horizon Press.

FURTHER READING

ARCHITECTURE

See Curtis (1987) and Frampton (1985) in the references.

Handlin, D. (1985) *American Architecture*, London, Thames & Hudson.

Roth, L.M. (1980) *A Concise History of American Architecture*, New York, Icon Books.

Wolfe, T. (1982) *From Bauhaus to Our House*, London, Cape.

ART

See Anfam (1990) and Hughes (1991) in the references.

Ashton, D. (1982) *American Art Since 1945*, London, Thames & Hudson.

Davidson, A.A. (1981) *Early American Modernist Painting, 1910–1935*, New York, Harper & Row.

Rose, B. (1980) *American Painting: the Twentieth Century*, Geneva, Skira.

IS THERE AN AMERICAN CULTURE?

Allan Lloyd Smith ★

The continental size and the diversity of regional and ethnic circumstances of the United States, together with its differing settlement patterns over time, means that many cultures coexist. The ever present possibility of political fragmentation has led to an assertive dominant culture which organizes loyalty to abstract ideals of 'America' around the spectacular iconography of patriotic symbols and encourages a consensus politics adjusted by political and judicial compromise. A competitive social philosophy accompanies an economics of individualism, and to some extent conceals structures of economic co-operation and control. The effects of 'late capitalism' on culture also have to be considered; it has been argued that one effect is to turn the past into an exploitable 'heritage' of images, and to translate independent cultural expressions into commodities for consumption by tourism and the media, so that diversity becomes an imitation of itself or, like Disneyland, an imitation of an original that never existed, the culture of the simulacrum. Whether or not this formulation is accurate, the homogeneity of the dominant national culture, and its expression through the media, has produced an Americanism that is recognizable world-wide.

1 THE CULTURE EVERYBODY KNOWS

When thinking about American culture the first images that come to mind are likely to be of skyscraper cities filled with a busy, and possibly violent, street life, and immigrants from all over the world. Outside the cities are multi-lane highways, and huge landscapes populated by factories, fast-food outlets and Holiday Inns, mountains and prairies, and ocean shores. What holds it all together? What are the informing ideas or ideologies that keep this vast and impossibly various federation of places and peoples from flying apart under the centrifugal forces of conflicting interests and traditions? Yet American life is, for all its variety, oddly homogeneous, a shared culture that crosses ethnic and class divisions, as well as the historical schisms between north and south, east and west, and the gulfs between deeply felt but deeply differing religious affiliations. Without obvious communities of place and racial derivation, Americans have developed instead a set of shared abstractions, including beliefs in democracy, religious tolerance, and egalitarianism (of opportunity, at least), centring around an iconography of the Flag, the Capitol, the White House, the anthems, and the charismatic notion of 'America' itself, the 'United States' of a new human order, a New World.

At the mythic centre of these abstractions is an ideal place, the warm and rewarding community of the small town where, as the credits of the television show *Cheers* would have it, 'everybody knows your name'. This small town, the product of countless novels, movies, musicals, radio and TV shows, and even memoirs, has often enough been laid open to critical scrutiny, whether by Sherwood Anderson's *Winesburg, Ohio*, Sinclair Lewis's *Main Street*, John Dollard's *Caste and Class in a Southern Town*, or Robert and Helen Lynd's *Middletown*. Yet the mystique of the small town persists, as a model for the ideal organization of the larger community: the President lives not in a palace but in 'the White House' and may address the nation, like Roosevelt, in folksy 'fireside' conversation, or even join in TV chat shows; the shopping malls approximate the old form of a village street (and often take the name 'village' too); the mass media assume a communality of values and even *tone*, across the nation; and the private lives of film stars supply the gossip that might once have circulated across the garden fence. The notion of the small town as the mythic heart of America is worth close scrutiny because in its insistent centripetal pressure and in its contradictions it embodies the aspirations and difficulties of the culture and at least approximates a stable basis for an assumed American identity.

In Thornton Wilder's play, *Our Town*, which opened in January 1938, we find an only slightly ironic representation of the idyllic American town of the early twentieth century. Grover's Corners, New Hampshire, in 1901, has all the features you would expect to find in the America that has been endlessly re-created in movies, magazines and fiction until it has almost become believable. When the play opens the stage manager talks to the audience, describing the main features of his town: its railway station, its Polish town and associated Canuck families, its combined town hall/post office, with the jail in the basement, its school and its drugstores (where everyone drops in once or twice a day); and above all, its many churches, including Presbyterian, Methodist, Unitarian, Baptist, and Catholic varieties of the dominant Christian faith. He concludes that it's a 'nice' town, and equally, that nobody very remarkable ever came out of it, which seems itself almost a mark of virtue in his down-home unpretentious discourse

Our Town presents a harmonious community with its doctor, its newspaper editor (and single twice-weekly newspaper, Editor Webb's presumably ever-vigilant *Sentinel*); its grocery store and drug store; its flower gardens and frame houses; its egalitarian public schools; all working together in a rhythmic score. In this kindly, unchanging community people talk to one another; they even talk to each other when they are dead, as Emily discovers after she dies young in childbirth and arrives among them at the cemetery, to find the buried townspeople still chatting on about her 'right smart farm'.

But there is also an underscore here: after Main Street the first thing the narrator mentions is the railroad, that great force for change, movement and the impact of the outside world; and across the tracks — significantly — is Polish town, the immigrant ghetto community, and some 'Canuck' families. The list of churches suggests a community that practices an almost excessive freedom of choice in religion; and again, the Catholic church is over *beyond* the tracks. That is the church of the immigrants, the non-Americans or the not-yet-Americans; the others are all Protestant sects. The first automobile — that other great force for change in twentieth-century America — has not yet arrived; when it does, it will belong to the town's richest citizen, the banker, who lives in the big white house up on the hill. So the apparent homogeneity of this peaceful town, the American Dream itself as it would seem, actually disguises deep ethnic, financial, and social divisions.

The stage manager's overt narrative and the open manipulation of scenery — for those who think they have to have scenery — as well as the tricksy time scheme, in which he says that the first automobile's *going to* come along but immediately contrasts this with his use of the past tense, the first car belong*ed* to Banker Cartwright, who he says — reverting to the present tense — liv*es* in the house up on the hill, foregrounds not only the artificiality of the play as a staged performance, but better, for our purposes, the artificiality of the small town as itself a construct, a piece of nostalgia, a mystification of the American reality. The play looks back to 1901 from 1938, from an America deep in the Great Depression and confronting an increasingly fascist and war-bound Europe, to a world of apparent certainty and security, in which the only real conundrum is how to make sense of an individual's death, and how to fully realize the wonder of being alive. Today, nostalgia isn't what it used to be, the stage scenery of the American Dream has fallen apart, Coke is 'the real thing', and it becomes possible to seriously ask, 'is there an American culture?'

With that question, inevitably, come others. Was there ever an American culture? Weren't there — and aren't there now — *many* American cultures? And what is a *culture* anyway?

SUMMARY

The continental size and great diversity of the US has led to an assertive dominant culture involving ideas of 'Americanness' and represented in such images as the idealized small-town America of *Our Town* which omit or suppress divisive elements of class or racial difference.

2   WHAT IS A CULTURE?

The simplest way to describe what a *culture* is would be to offer some formal definition, perhaps: *a culture is the set of practices and thought that distinguishes one group of people from another.* Such a description obviously leaves out of the account practices that are common to all groups of people, such as breathing or eating. However, we should be aware that even these are culturally marked; the Japanese and the British eat fish, but the fish may be prepared very differently. With a simple formulation like this, it is immediately evident, first, that there *is* an American culture and, secondly, that there are *many* American cultures. First we will examine the dominant American culture, and to do so we will have to complicate somewhat the initial definition.

Raymond Williams describes in *Culture and Society 1780–1950* how the word 'culture' has changed its meanings over time, from the tending of natural growth, or human development, the culture *of* something, to *culture* as such, a thing in itself, first the state of general intellectual development in a society, next the general body of the arts, and finally 'a whole way of life, material, intellectual and spiritual' (Williams, 1971, p.16). Its development is itself a reaction to great historical changes in industry, democracy and class, and if so, we may add, how much more must we look to a difference in *American* culture where such upheavals are arguably more raw, more roughly experienced, less moderated by the resistance of tradition or established interests? Williams discusses the emergence of the idea of *culture* as involving:

> two general responses — first, the recognition of the practical separation of certain moral and intellectual activities from the driven impetus of a new kind of society; second, the emphasis of these activities, as a court of human appeal, to be set over the processes of practical social judgement and yet to offer itself as a mitigating and rallying alternative.
>
> (Williams, 1971, p.17)

Williams's separation of certain activities from the 'driven', or apparently simply necessary, direction of the society and the appeal to these activities in mitigation of, or sometimes to propose an alternative to, the existing social conditions, gives a workable complexity in thinking about what a culture might be. It is not without problems of its own, however. What, exactly, should we decide is the 'driven' impetus of a society? The assumption of what is necessary and not open to choice in a particular culture may itself be a variable feature. The need for economic growth, for example, or for 'full' employment, has no place in some societies. And what about deviance? Is culturally disapproved or prohibited behaviour part of a culture, or something other than it? Some theorists have argued that crime shadows the legitimate activities of a society, so that organized crime in America offers an alternative ladder of opportunity to the socially deprived. One could certainly argue that some kinds of deviance, such as sexual offences, are closely linked to the culture's dominant values. But Williams's model will at least provide a starting point for further thought and argument. Certainly the American culture has been internationally visible, the cause of much emulation and dissension in other countries. It does clearly exist, and with knowable features, some of which will be identified in the following sections. And if culture is to be described thus, as a whole way of life, it might be useful to remember that the American way of life, or simply the 'American Way', has sometimes seemed more visible from outside the US in its impact on other countries (see Plate 10.1).

SUMMARY

The definition of 'culture' is complex. There is not simply one American culture, nor simply many competing cultures: there is an internationally recognizable *dominant* culture and there are also several subcultures.

3   SOME DESCRIPTIONS OF AMERICAN CULTURE

Just as Raymond Williams needed to return to the history of the eighteenth century to explain what culture might mean in contemporary British society, to properly understand the US in the twentieth century it really would be necessary to describe its development from a much earlier period. Brief reference will be made where appropriate to these determining conditions, and some possible further reading is suggested at the end of this chapter. But it is essential to remember that although America is, in Gertrude Stein's witty recognition, *older* than Europe, because it has experienced the twentieth century longer than other countries, much of that post-1900 experience was directed by the formative circumstances of an earlier period. To give one brief example: studies of the geographical distribution of voting for and against Prohibition of alcohol up to 1919, when the Eighteenth Amendment was passed, show a remarkably close correlation with the earlier voting patterns of 1892–4 when farmers and small-towners in the 'Populist revolt' rebelled against high interest rates and the monetary squeeze caused by the gold standard, big city financiers, and what seemed to them unfairly high railroad freight rates (Gusfield, 1966, pp.102–3). In less obviously measurable ways, too, the American culture only makes sense if it is seen in relation to its earlier history. Ideas of individualism and equality of opportunity (rather than of wealth or right to benefit) have deep roots in the Enlightenment rationalism principles with which the Republic was founded, and also in the 'transcendentalism' of Ralph Waldo Emerson and Henry David Thoreau (author of *Walden* and *Civil Disobedience*) in the mid-nineteenth century, which extended Romantic concepts into a celebration of the supremacy of the individual spirit. Ideas may have no force on their own, but where they provide a useful legitimation for, say, the concentration of great wealth and power in the hands of an Andrew Carnegie or a William Randolph Hearst they can become powerful agents of social cohesion. Emerson's motto 'trust thyself' was founded on a notion of cosmic beneficence; in the philosophy of the robber barons, as late nineteenth-century entrepreneurs were often called, the appeal to such views was founded on self-interest, but could still serve well enough to disguise rapacity in an argument for the public good involved in the creation of wealth.

The social theory that dominated American life at the opening of the twentieth century has, despite the revisions of New Deal thought and welfare concerns, maintained a powerful hold on the culture. Based loosely on an application of Darwin's ideas to the evolution of society rather than the strictly biological realm, it held that all compete in the struggle for wealth and are rewarded according to their ability and energy. The highest 'types' discover new ways to organize resources and create wealth, and in building up their own structures provide leadership and increased wealth for all. The mediocre majority divide a fund determined by the resources of land and capital; while the weakest few simply disappear in the struggle. At its most extreme, Social Darwinist theory suggested that charity or philanthropy was not just ineffectual, it was positively damaging, an artificial restriction on the forces that would lead society onwards and upwards to riches and higher stages of social evolution. In this formulation, the proper role of government would be to keep out of the way as far as possible, maintaining public order and minimal public services, so that the beneficial effects of free competition could be felt. As William Graham Sumner, a rigorous prophet of this school of thought, put it: 'The law of survival of the fittest was not made by man, and cannot be abrogated by man. We can only, by interfering with it, produce the survival of the unfittest.' (Quoted in Miller, 1965, p.80.) Such arguments might have seemed refuted by the experience of the Depression and the economics of the New Deal, but their re-emergence in the late twentieth century suggests that they retain a significant place in the dominant culture.

Although these beliefs have persisted in American life, and have produced a powerfully individualist and entrepreneurial dominant culture, the actuality is (and always was) rather different. Bureaucratic control, strategic manipulation of advantage, the development of monopoly and the subversion of regulative structures have been another 'American Way'. So among the features of the majority culture we have to acknowledge a capacity for living with the contradiction between the apparent and the actual processes of the society. In the twentieth century, scientific management, bureaucratic government, philosophical pragmatism, and vast, integrated structures of financial control have often underpinned the slogans of independence, individualism and the free market that continue to dominate public discourse in the United States.

Theorists of American life have not been slow to point this out. In 1950 for example, David Reisman explained how the pressures of corporate existence had conspired to create a change in the supposed American character, from 'inner-directed', i.e. self-motivated, driven by principles, independent of the opinions of others (the archetypal Protestant personality), to 'other-directed' people; actuated by considerations of expediency and the approval of others, largely indifferent to questions of principle but with skills in minimizing conflict and getting along with people, in short, members of *The Lonely Crowd*, as his book named these new Americans. This was not a startling insight; after all, Sinclair Lewis had described the very person in his novel *Babbitt*, as early as 1922. What was merely a trend in 1922, however, had become the established norm by mid-century, in Reisman's view at least, and it spelled an end to the rugged individualist so often portrayed as an ideal in the contemporary mythology and sanctified in popular films like *Shane* or *High Noon*. William H. Whyte's *The Organisation Man* followed on in 1956 and alongside these came popular criticisms of the advertising industry in Vance Packard's *The Hidden Persuaders* (1960), *The Status Seekers* (1961) and *The Waste Makers* (1963), and Daniel Boorstin's analysis of the substitution of the spectacle for the real in *The Image, or, Whatever Happened to the American Dream?* (1961). These essentially liberal critiques amassed convincing evidence to show that whatever the official ideology of America at mid-century, the reality was of a corporately structured and managerially co-opted society of time-serving employees. The political pressures of the Cold War period with its 'witch hunts' of supposed communists and fellow travellers by Joe McCarthy and the House Committee on Un-American Activities had done much to subdue possible dissent in the early 1950s, when 'guilt by association' ruined many careers, of schoolteachers as well as film scriptwriters; and some of the observations of the sociologists might be seen as reflecting the consequences of this repressive political atmosphere. The same period also saw the development of the 'Beat' counter-culture, of Jack Kerouac, Allen Ginsberg, William Burroughs, Lawrence Ferlinghetti, Paul Bowles, and Gregory Corso, who felt the need to explore opposition to the conformity, business values and Cold War thinking of the dominant culture. Movies were produced that can be read either way, either as pro or anti conformity, as they deal with the dilemmas of individuals facing up to group threats: the melodramas of Douglas Sirk, the politically informed science fiction of the *Invasion of the Body Snatchers*, and even *High Noon* itself.

Some analysts argued that the observable contradictions between American ideas and actualities were less a question of specifically *American* conditions, and more an inevitable consequence of other social and psychological forces. Norman O. Brown, for example, held that repression was an unavoidable circumstance, if Freud's theories were properly understood (*Life Against Death*, 1959), and Herbert Marcuse in *Eros and Civilization* (1955) attempted to find a way past Freud's formulations to demonstrate 'the possibility of a non-repressive development' of the self under the conditions of mature capitalism. But the optimism of this hoped-for transformation of work into play became subdued by the time of his *One Dimensional Man* (1964) into the despairing recognition of a mere 'pacified existence' under capitalist technology. Marcuse's indictment, which was popular in the Vietnam years of opposition to the state's military-industrial complex, included the notion of repressive tolerance, in which acceptance of the individual's freedom by society simply facilitates a further reach of control: the 'loss of conscience due to the satisfactory liberties granted by an unfree society makes for a happy consciousness which facilitates acceptance of the misdeeds of this society' (Marcuse, 1968, p.76). The citizen is seen as free to protest, but not free to make any effective difference to the policies of the benevolent dictatorship of the organized military-industrial state.

The onslaught on the failings of the American culture continued. In fiction the novels of Norman Mailer offered a progressive indictment of the culture's many derelictions, especially its sacrifice of the individual's independence and integrity, and subduing of impulse; and the liberal anguish of Saul Bellow, Philip Roth and John Updike at the impossibility of living a meaningful life in American urban or suburban conditions has also made a consistent refrain. Joseph Heller and Ken Kesey wrote black comic perspectives on the inconsistency of the culture in *Catch-22, Something Happened*, and *One Flew Over the Cuckoo's Nest*; and Kurt Vonnegut has unfailingly satirized its violence and hypocrisy in a series of novels from *Player Piano* and *Cat's Cradle* to *Mother Night, Slaughterhouse-5* and *Jailbird*. A quieter but no more optimistic report on the state of the nation has come in the subdued sense of powerlessness and frustration purveyed by the 'dirty realists', like Raymond Carver, Richard Ford, and Jayne Ann Philips, who have been satirized as the 'K-Mart Realists' or the 'rural septic tank' school of minimalists. But the most powerful assaults on the dominant culture have recently come from black writers like Toni Morrison and Alice Walker who, instead of criticizing the majority in a direct assault, like Ralph Ellison, James Baldwin, Eldridge Cleaver and LeRoi Jones before them, develop instead a perception of the *value* of minority group culture, however threatened and damaged by the history of black life in America.

One of the more spectacular criticisms came in Christopher Lasch's *The Culture of Narcissism: American Life in an Age of Diminishing Expectations*.

> The new narcissist is haunted not by guilt but by anxiety. He seeks not to inflict his own certainties on others but to find a meaning of life. Liberated from the superstitions of the past, he doubts even the reality of his own existence. Superficially relaxed and tolerant, he finds little use for dogmas of racial and ethnic purity but at the same time forfeits the security of group loyalties and regards everyone as a rival for the favors conferred by a paternalistic state. His sexual attitudes are permissive rather than puritanical, even though his emancipation from ancient taboos brings him no sexual peace. Fiercely competitive in his demand for approval and acclaim he distrusts competition because he associates it unconsciously with an unbridled urge to destroy. Hence he repudiates the competitive ideologies that flourished at an earlier stage of capitalist development and distrusts even their limited expression in sports and games. He extols cooperation and teamwork while harboring deeply antisocial impulses. He praises respect for rules and regulations in the secret belief that they do not apply to himself. Acquisitive in the sense that his cravings have no limits, he does not accumulate goods and provisions against the future, in the manner of the acquisitive

individualist of nineteenth-century political economy, but demands immediate gratification and lives in a state of restless, perpetually unsatisfied desire.

(Lasch, 1978, p.xvi)

'The narcissist has no interest in the future', Lasch added, 'because, in part, he has so little interest in the past.' Charming as this uncertain and eager-to-please individual may seem to those of us who like Woody Allen's movies, he has, we are told, a vicious amorality about him that Lasch deplores. However, to suggest that this is the new norm for the American personality is to leave aside such important issues as the *variety* of different personality types encountered in a continental society and, indeed, the number of different American *cultures* that coexist, sometimes uncomfortably, within the huge and loose association of the United States.

SUMMARY

To understand twentieth-century American culture it is necessary to take some account of social and political theories from an earlier period, the founding principles of the new nation, its westward expansion and ideology of competitive individualism; and the somewhat contradictory experience of large-scale corporate management and governmental bureaucracy. Theorists since the 1950s have discussed these contradictions, and the extent to which they should be seen as specifically American or more generally true of the industrialized countries. Novelists have offered similar criticisms. A new 'narcissistic' (self-regarding) personality has been diagnosed as representative.

4 *E PLURIBUS UNUM*: MANY AMERICAN CULTURES

The common language of the Republic is English. But it may be a surprise to hear of the legend that at one stage in its history, the US debated whether the language should not be changed to German, and only one vote prevented that extraordinary move. In actual fact the vote was a little different. Seven years after the adoption of the Constitution a proposal to print sets of federal laws in German as well as in English was only narrowly defeated in the House of Representatives (Schlesinger, 1992, p.107). Given the Anglo dominance we have seen since, such a story might be thought frivolous. But it dramatically reflects the situation of a country made up of immigrants, who came in vast and varying numbers, from northern and then southern and eastern Europe, and who continue to come, especially now from Asia and the countries of Latin America. As the population of Spanish-speaking Americans grows to approach one in three, perhaps another vote on the national language would be in order?

The foundations of American culture were largely British: in 1790 it has been estimated almost 80 per cent of the white population originated from the British Isles, whereas less than 10 per cent came from Germany and less than 4 per cent from the Netherlands. The French made up under 2 per cent and Swedes less than 1 per cent; the origin of 6.6 per cent was unknown (figures based on analysis of surnames, *The Harvard Encyclopedia of American Ethnic Groups*, 1980, p.479). After 1820 the numbers of Germans and Scandinavians greatly increased, and for most of the nineteenth century northwestern Europe still accounted for more than two-thirds of US immigration; with Ireland progressively more important than UK sources. Towards the end of the nineteenth century came a shift towards southern Europe, leading to agitation for restriction of immigration and ultimately the quota laws of the 1920s. These checked the 'New Immigration' until new and more liberal legislation in the 1960s reversed the pattern. In the 1980s and 1990s much the largest group of immigrants have come from Asia or Central and South America, and Puerto Rico which has increased racial tension, especially in such states as California and Texas, or cities like New York.

The effects of large-scale immigration on the culture of the US went very deep, and profoundly altered the development of public life at critical stages. Most of the great westward expansion of the 'frontier' was a migration of native-born white people; whereas immigrants conversely played a disproportionate part in the growth of urban centres. In 1890, for example, although the foreign born and their children only amounted to a third of the US population, they made up 53 per cent of the urban population (ibid., p.481). Black Americans remained concentrated in Southern agriculture until large numbers moved to northern cities after the Second World War. In the legends of the West we can see a propaganda for a certain sort of ethnic affiliation (a particularly good example would be Owen Wister's famous novel, *The Virginian*); and in the late nineteenth and early twentieth century agitation against alleged urban immoralities demonstrated a profound status anxiety on the part of the originally dominant groups. The different cultural practices of immigrants — drinking habits, gambling, the street crime of young males which could give a whole ethnic group like Italians a bad reputation — focused attention on urban conditions as problematic to the point of crisis, and ultimately, together with the effects of tax-rating bands, encouraged a flight from the cities which left inner-city areas ravaged by loss of work opportunities, under-skilled populations and under-financed government.

Because of difficulties in assimilation, whether due to language barriers (most ethnic groups maintained newspapers in their native language, for example) or other differences in cultural practices, immigrants tended to settle together, and formed enclaves in states and cities. Such immigrant groups were an open invitation to a certain kind of political organization; one which rewarded unquestioning loyalties by the manipulation of public funds and public offices. This was the origin of the big city machine, or government by 'bossism', which has dominated American urban and regional government and in part at least accounts for the fervour with which Americans distrust the processes of government. Mayor Daly's 'machine' in Chicago up to the 1960s would be an example, although now ostensibly cleaned up. Anyone following urban life in Philadelphia would recognize exactly the same systems at work in the contemporary setting. Ethnic politics is still an extremely powerful force in American public life — perhaps *the* most powerful force — in its creation of group identities, the perception of issues, and the distribution of resources. Its persistence, in fact, has surprised social scientists since it was assumed that ethnicity as a factor would decrease in second- and third-generation immigrants, or with the increasing integration of black and Hispanic groups, and with urbanization and other 'modernizing' social changes which tend to break down traditional loyalties (Litt, 1970, p.17).

The popular background to immigration-restriction legislation needs to be understood in reaching a sense of how the American culture came to be what we know it as today. During 1919 and 1920 over 20 states passed laws to require increased night school provision for foreigners. This was not thoughtfulness on their part, but a fearful response to foreignness. Idaho and Utah actually required attendance in Americanization classes. In 1919 fifteen states mandated English to be the only language of instruction in all primary schools. New York insisted that all schoolteachers be citizens, and other states followed that lead. Oregon even required all foreign-language publications to display a full English translation of their contents. And California in 1920 demanded that every adult alien must register and pay a poll tax of $10 (Higham, 1968, p.260). That was the polite face of nativism and racism. The other, that of the Ku-Klux-Klan, was engaged in carrying on the large-scale vigilante tradition of the nineteenth century in vicious physical attacks on black people, who were lynched and tortured, and also against Catholics and Jews. By 1924 membership of the Klan had swelled to 4.5 million. Foreigners were also particularly singled out as victims in the 'Red Raids' of the 1920s (Graham and Gurr, 1969).

The nativism and racism implied in these events emerged in many other areas, and with long-lasting consequences. However, at a less violent level we can see how Americans have constantly struggled to find unifying images around which to rally the disparate citizenry: the flag, the Declaration of Independence, the Liberty Bell, Lincoln's Emancipation speech, 'The Star-Spangled Banner', and so on. The intensity of the 1950s' purges and loyalty crusades depended perhaps as much on the fear of centrifugal disintegration as the actual likelihood of communist subversion. And we might, therefore, speculate here on the deeper reasons for the extreme homogeneity of culture that is often remarked upon by visitors to the US: those endless and indistinguishable Holiday Inns, Howard Johnsons or Crown Motels; the preference for McDonald's or Burger King hamburgers, expressed through consumer choice; the apparent sameness of television programming, even across 30 channels. These are powerful cohesive statements that help to organize an enormous continent made up of evacuees from other countries, other cultures.

SUMMARY

The people of the US are ethnically diverse, reflecting shifts in large-scale immigration patterns from northern Europe, then from southern Europe and, more recently, from the Far East and South America. Tensions resulting from this ethnic diversity have shaped the American culture, affecting the history of the cities as well as the nature of American politics. The homogeneous national culture may be a response to considerable local diversity; a unifying and stabilizing set of cultural assumptions.

5 AMERICAN POLITICS: THE MAINSTREAM

Considering the diversity we have been discussing, American politics at the national level is perhaps surprisingly a politics of *consensus*, in which two major parties ritually contest their minimally differentiated programmes. Neither the Democratic Party nor the Republican Party have an interest in radical policies, nor even in such less than radical measures as the invention of a reasonably egalitarian national health care policy. They both agree that the capitalist structure delivers the goods, taxation is inherently bad, the budget should be balanced (but not just yet, please), that to increase the cost of gasoline by more than a few cents would be ruinous, and so on. In this (liberal) context, liberalism is regarded as a politically suicidal posture, and left to maverick politicians like Governor Brown of California, or pressure groups like the Rainbow Coalition. There is a long tradition of third party entrants to this essentially two-horse race; they rarely get anywhere in the Presidential and Congressional elections but they do serve to put particular issues more clearly on the agenda. Sometimes, as in Perot's 1992 candidacy, they merely express a dissatisfaction with current political practice, but without any definite sense of how it should be changed.

American politics is much more openly addressed to local or regional interests than the politics of the UK; if an American congressman or senator fails to deliver the new industries, the contracts and farm prices, or even the legislation, that affects his (or more rarely her) constituency's interests, he or she is unlikely to be re-elected. This makes for some nice adjustments in party management by the party leaders. Lyndon Johnson was thought to be especially effective in this aspect of his presidency — he knew so much about the representatives and senators that he could push through the legislation Kennedy was unable to achieve, even more effectively than might have been expected given his congressional majority, which was then temporarily with the presidency. Because of local and regional pressures American voters frequently choose their presidents, representatives and senators from different parties. This paralyses government and is inconvenient to politicians, but it does have some beneficial effects from the ordinary voter's point of view. First, the intractable conflicts of interest have to be addressed rather than simply ignored, as they can be in a system like the British parliament. And secondly, the enormous *inertia* of the political behemoth helps to generate a consensus that persists over time, avoiding abrupt changes in political and economic policy. Americans long held the belief that 'that government is best that governs least', and they certainly invented a structure that made government almost impossible. Capping off the system of 'checks and balances' is the independent judiciary, the Supreme Court, whose members are appointed for life and adjudicate the constitutional legality of legislation, as well as serving as the ultimate court of appeal in civil and criminal cases. It has, in theory, enormous power to shape the American culture by judgements on such matters as state laws on abortion, the rights of criminal suspects, the constitutionality of educational practices (like the 'separate but equal' school segregation it ended in a famous 1954 ruling). But the Supreme Court has no power to enforce its opinions and effectively, therefore, governs by consent only; this makes it normally responsive to a sense of public opinion. Its remoteness from ordinary voters, however, and the often sophisticated constitutional interpretations on which it bases its decisions, can make it seem an Olympian body which is not answerable to the citizens' desire either for stability or change. The very existence of a *written* constitution to be interpreted increases the quality of abstraction that is inherent in the notion of America and Americanism: the culture is predicated on the *idea* of America; it is on the one hand highly materialistic and practical, on the other idealistic and abstract. The American political system is home to the crudest of interest trading and 'pork barrel' legislation, and yet at the same time a forum for high-flown rhetoric about noble intentions, shared by conservatives and radicals alike. Martin Luther King's 'I Have a Dream' speech has everything in common with John F. Kennedy's inauguration appeal; and neither, arguably, had much to do with the actualities of American life.

What most strikes foreign observers of the American political scene is the element of *spectacle* involved: American politics seems to outsiders — and to many insiders — to have a show business ethos. The political conventions are stage managed, the candidates fine-tune their election addresses and perfect the 'sound-bite' technique; Presidents carefully time announcements and press conferences so that they will meet the news deadlines. The *content* of politics itself seems often to have disappeared, what matters is not the policy *per se*, but its relation to voter preferences as reflected in opinion polls. In the 1980s commentators were struck by Ronald Reagan's unique fitness for his task. He could say the lines as if he meant them. Subsequently the Bush victory of 1988 was perceived to be a continuation of style over substance or the medium over the message. Taking this to an arguably hysterical extreme, the French sociologist Jean Baudrillard argues that Watergate was not a scandal, it was rather a scenario manipulated to make it appear that politics is generally ethical: 'The denunciation of scandal always pays homage to the law. And Watergate above all succeeded in imposing the idea that Watergate was a scandal ... ' (Baudrillard, 1981, p.173). This kind of formulation, which sees American politics as itself a Disneyland, gains substance when informed journalists claim that the President actively sought further military confrontation with Iraq in the 1992 election period, to distract attention from the failings of the economy. In such circumstances it makes sense to talk of the *scenario* of power, the *scenario* of ideology, substituting for the thing itself.

Nevertheless, to analyse the American political scene only in such terms is certainly a mistake: voting does follow the lines of genuine issues, particularly the perception of economic advantage; the 'ecstasy of communication' (described in the next section) should not be allowed to obscure the realities of class, race, gender and economic status, as the main determinants of the political process.

SUMMARY

A national politics based on consensus and the trading of interest groups manages to address local and regional issues. It is possible that the system of checks and balances of the government — which often results in an inactive 'stalemate' — helps to hold together a community that tends to fragment. In the same way, the use of a written constitution and an idealized version of 'America' helps to regulate conflict. But it also makes the political agenda manipulable through the politics of 'spectacle'.

6 CONSUMER CULTURE AND THE POSTMODERN CONDITION

One of the first on the scene, or scenario, of the *new* New World, was the Canadian academic, Marshall McCluhan, with his 1964 study *Understanding Media*. His claims, which seemed hyperbolical at the time, have since lost all power to astonish. Saying that 'our private lives have become information processes because we have put our central nervous systems outside us in electric technology' (McCluhan, 1964, p.61), he took seriously the interactions of the media, both between each other and in terms of their effect on us, the users or consumers of televisions, telephones, movies and, increasingly, interactive electronics. 'When electric speed takes over from mechanical movie sequences, then lines of force in structures and in media become loud and clear. We return to the inclusive form of the icon' (ibid., p.27). McCluhan diagnosed a new 'tribal' TV consciousness. As Tom Wolfe described it: 'the TV children, a whole generation of Americans … they are the new tribesmen. They have tribal sensory balances. They have the tribal habit of responding emotionally to the spoken word, they are "hot", they want to participate, to *touch*, to be involved.' (Stearn, 1968, p.44.) McCluhan's idea of TV couch-potatoes as 'hot', 'participatory' and so on, proved implausible. In fact Thomas Pynchon offered a more recognizable description of the effects of TV on the culture in his novel *Vineland* (1990), which describes a 'National Endowment for Video Education and Rehabilitation', with 'tubal detox' units to treat 'tubal abuse and other video-related disorders' (Pynchon, 1990, p.33). McCluhan's enthusiastic assumption that the new electronic integration spelled the end of print-oriented culture was equally unfounded, as electronic information systems proved instead to intensify the accessibility, the ready manipulability, and even the necessity of print. Similarly, the supposed freedom of the new medias turned out to be preprogrammed: the forms of organization that structure such choices are themselves organized according to certain implicit hierarchies, and organize their users' thought accordingly. As with the freedom to change channels on a TV set, limits are built in. The new culture may be more democratic and anti-canonical, but critics often point out that its freedom may be more in theory than in fact, an increase in mystification rather than a decrease in the controlling pressures of the 'real'.

Thinkers about the new American culture — and its echoes or parallels in the international culture of late capitalism — have seen the coming to an end of the explanatory structures of modernism, the name given to the dominant tendency in the arts and social thought in the twentieth century. Whereas modernism engaged in a profound questioning of the assumptions of the nineteenth century, and endorsed the significance of the individual's perspective in experiencing and understanding the vast incoherence of recent history, it remained an essentially serious search for coherence and meaning. Thus it resulted in new forms of aesthetic organization such as the stress on functionality of design in architecture ('form follows function'); the endorsement of technology (whether in 'Futurism', city planning, or social engineering); or the use of structures from myth or psychoanalysis or spatial metaphors in shaping literary works, or the fullest possible representation of the twists and turns of the mind in 'stream of consciousness' fiction. Modernism was marked by a series of manifestos about the true understanding of art and society, and has been described as basically *epistemological*, that is, concerned with the exploration of the process of knowledge and interpretation. In literature William Faulkner, for example, explored the way that experience is interpreted out of a flux of consciousness (in *The Sound and the Fury*, 1929), and is reinvented by the historical imagination (in *Absalom, Absalom!*, 1936). John Dos Passos interweaved fact and fiction, newsreels and newspaper items, biography, popular song lyrics, and the demoralized lives of multiple characters into his epic trilogy *USA* (1937); Ernest Hemingway stripped his language of subjective modifiers and experimented with the effects of repetition, a technique he learned from Gertrude Stein, whose essays into new consciousness threatened legibility itself. In art and architecture modernism similarly asked profound questions and answered them with a high seriousness.

However, more recently the scepticism inherent in the modernist project has resulted in a further shift, into what has been described as an *ontological* focus, involving questions of being and feeling, and incorporating a tendency to disintegration and indiscriminateness, inclusiveness rather than exclusiveness, and random happenstance instead of elaborate formal patterning (McHale, 1987, p.7). Features of what is often called *post*modernism, include experiment, fragmentation, the end of theory, a loss of historical or spatial orientation, of originality and the self; and a new poetics of collage, intertextuality and pastiche. In these terms Fredric Jameson talks of a new *depthlessness*; a weakening of the sense of history; and a new technology which figures a multinational late capitalist world order (Jameson, 1991, p.6). 'Postmodernism', he says, 'is what you have when the modernization process is complete and nature is gone for good' (ibid., p.ix). He notes the importance of popular culture in the new order, a rhetoric of *inclusion* which effaces the old frontier between high and low culture once described by commentators like Dwight McDonald. According to Jameson, 'the post-modernisms have in fact been fascinated precisely by this whole "degraded" landscape of schlock and kitsch, of TV series and *Reader's Digest* culture, of advertising and motels, of the late show and the grade-B Hollywood film ... ' (ibid., p.2) which they incorporate into their structure, rather than just quote, as modernist art did. Jameson and McHale see postmodernism as a new *cultural dominant*, which allows for the co-presence of other features. The extent of the shift is seen by its absorption without qualm by the establishment, however offensive or squalid its features. This is not entirely true, of course, since artists strive to discover what the boundaries might be and manage to create a reaction by, for example, violating the American flag, or producing works like the infamous 'Piss Christ'. Aesthetic production has been integrated into commodity production. Those cultural theorists and others like Jean Baudrillard see the development of the new 'depthlessness' in the culture of the image or the *simulacrum*, the exact imitation of something. This involves a fascination with the machinery of *reproduction* of the image, the TV and the computer. Art like Andy Warhol's or Roy Lichtenstein's (Plates 9.4 and 10.2) is based on a commodification of the image, whether of soup tins or film stars, equally reproducible and without depth, as objects or persons 'commodified and transformed into their own images' (Jameson, 1991, p.11).

According to this argument, it can be seen that contemporary culture repudiates the older models of significant *depth* (of the inside versus the outside; of essence against appearance; the Freudian models of latent and manifest elements of consciousness and of repression; the existential modes of authenticity and inauthenticity; and finally, even the opposition between signifier and signified, the sign for something and the thing itself). Depth is replaced by multiple surfaces and a sense of 'intertextuality', the positioning of one text (or piece of writing, image or speech act) in relation to others. Therefore concepts such as alienation and anxiety become inappropriate in the postmodern world, where, according to Jameson, 'the alienation of the subject is displaced by the latter's fragmentation', the 'death of the subject' itself (ibid., pp.14–15). Feelings are supposedly replaced by more free floating 'intensities' and euphorias, and with this goes a 'waning of affect' in postmodern culture. To quote an instance from the novelist Donald Barthelme; one of his hilariously reimagined Seven Dwarfs says of Snow White, who allows them only to shower with her, 'And yet ... I am fond of her. Yes, I am. For when sexual pleasure is had, it makes you fond, in a strange way, of the other one, the one with whom you are having it.' (Barthelme, 1980, p.36.)

With the decentralizing of the old subject comes the loss of the idea of style, along with any collective ideals of an artistic or political vanguard or avant-garde, style is displaced by mechanical reproduction and replication, to give way to the simulacrum: 'the identical copy for which no original has ever existed'. Jean Baudrillard and Umberto Eco have read American culture as this brave new world of the simulacra, in which the image has replaced the thing, and reality is replicated as 'better than the real thing', in theme parks, museums offering improved versions of the *Mona Lisa*, three-dimensional realizations of *The Last Supper*; and the overwhelmingly significatory land-scape of the road, or the emptiness of the desert, the postmodern sublime. As Baudrillard says, in a typically postmodernist formulation, 'Illusion is no longer possible, because the real is no longer possible' (Baudrillard, 1981, p.177). Western culture now apparently exists in a state of 'hyperreality' which puts into question familiar assumptions about the real. Thus, he claims, 'Disneyland is there to conceal the fact that it is the "real" country, all of "real" America, which is Disneyland ... Disneyland is presented as imaginary in order to make us believe that the rest is real, when in fact Los Angeles and the America surrounding it are no longer real, but of the order of the hyperreal and simulation.' Similarly, the modernist thematics of time are displaced: in Baudrillard's terms, 'when the real is no longer what it used to be, nostalgia assumes its full meaning' (ibid., pp.172, 171). The pro-ducers of American culture turn to pillaging the styles of the past 'stored up in the imaginary museum of a now global culture' (Jameson, 1991, p.18) in random cannibalization, whether in architecture, literature or film. The com-modified past then becomes, instead of a history, simply 'a vast collection of images, a multitudinous photographic simulacrum'. Nostalgia films like George Lucas's *American Graffiti,* and the whole heritage culture itself, now 'approach the past through stylistic connotation, conveying pastness by the glossy quality of the image' (ibid., pp.18, 19).

Particularly interesting, however, are the new attempts through such dis-course to understand the immediate American past, in, for example, Oliver Stone's *Born on the Fourth of July* and *JFK,* the British director Alan Parker's *Mississippi Burning,* or in literature, Thomas Pynchon's *V, Gravity's Rainbow* and *Vineland,* Don DeLillo's *Libra,* and E.L. Doctorow's *Ragtime.* In such texts another aspect of the 'weakening of historicity' can be seen, the urge to pro-vide an alternative or secret history, in opposition to the official version. They may be criticized for their imaginative free play or even wilful distor-tion, as in Parker's version of the FBI's role in Mississippi, and as products of the paranoia generated by the new global order, but they are nevertheless perhaps making an effort to do what William Burroughs once called for: 'retake the reality studio, play back the film'.

Much of the argument about contemporary American culture can be exem-plified in films and fictions, as when Jameson discusses how 'image-addition' by 'transforming the past into visual mirages, stereotypes, or texts, effectively abolishes any practical sense of the future and of the collective project, thereby abandoning the thinking of future change to fantasies of sheer catastrophe and inexplicable cataclysm, from visions of "terrorism" on the social level to those of cancer on the personal' (Jameson, 1991, p.46). Don DeLillo's *White Noise* (1984) is a text obsessed by exactly this kind of meaningless catastrophism: the arrival of a cloud of poisonous gas, which upsets, among others, the disaster agencies who have always before had the advantage of orderly (because imaginary) bodies to count and dispose of.

'How is it going?' I said.

'The insertion curve isn't as smooth as we would like. There's a probability excess. Plus which we don't have our victims laid out where we'd want them if this was an actual simulation ... You have to make allowances for the fact that everything we see tonight is real. There's a lot of polishing still to do. But that's what this exercise is all about.'

(DeLillo, 1986, p.136)

White Noise is also obsessed by the problem of personal death, in fact the term 'white noise' is code for our awareness of this, an ever-present static that can not be understood. The film *Terminator 2: Judgement Day* similarly *plays with* visions of an appropriately terroristic response to the coming apocalypse, and the destabilizing of the personal through future cyber-technology. The same could be said of Ridley Scott's *Blade Runner* or even Terry Gilliam's *Brazil*. But the disparaging term 'plays with' seems almost unavoidable, since effective critical thought is made impossible by the image culture, which actually 'does more than merely replicate the logic of late capitalism; it reinforces and intensifies it' (Jameson, 1991, p.46).

In movies, such accommodations seem most evident in the artificial resolutions. In *Pretty Woman, Wall Street,* and *Working Girl,* for instance, the contradictions of society are made apparent but then circumvented through rhetoric, the use of the spectacle and the surface. 'Have a nice day', these films suggest, as society's defects are noted but supposedly rectified, or at least given a human face, much as postmodern architecture provides a humanized façade to the quite incomprehensible (and ultimately inhuman) structure it disguises. *Robocop, Terminator 2,* and *Total Recall* each make an approach to that formless 'other' of the new corporatist world-state, with its passion for control, but then leak away their criticisms in a recourse to the personal, despite the complication that the personal 'self' they appeal to is actually robotic. These texts, like *Blade Runner,* deal with the potential breakdown of all explanatory structures by attaching a falsifying ending. Similar features appear in, for example, David Lynch's *Blue Velvet,* or his *Twin Peaks.* Here the narrative conventions are subverted, much in the same way that contemporary writers draw attention to the fictionality of their work, through fragmentation, unusual and unexplained focusing on the image, or pastiche, the imitation of a style without any clear indication of whether the intention is satirical or respectful. The beginning and ending sequences of *Blue Velvet* are significant: the film opens with an evocation of *Our Town* with its friendly waving firemen passing by on the firetruck, it then moves to a domestic garden where a man waters his lawn, then coolly watches his heart attack, before panning to the world of insect competition in the grass beneath. Finally, after scenes of sexually perverse mayhem, the film's ending celebrates a robin eating a beetle outside the kitchen window (but although these birds have been especially meaningful symbols of happiness and innocence to the girl in the film, this robin is clearly a mechanical imitation). It seems characteristic of recent American culture that such 'alienation devices' can be incorporated without comment: there is, especially perhaps in *Twin Peaks*, no apparent *point* to them. But it also seems quite possible that, as some critics have argued, such 'play' serves to support the economic and political status quo, by diverting and preventing criticism or change.

One way in which some critical pressure may be applied to this playful surface of contemporary culture is to ask how it deals with the issue of gender. From the birth control movement in the early years of the century; through the struggle for the vote for women which was won in 1920, and the large-scale movement of women into the work-force during the Second World War (which was *not* reversed by propaganda in favour of a return to the kitchen after 1945); to the theorizing of feminism, beginning in the 1950s with Betty Friedan's *The Feminine Mystique* (Friedan also founded NOW, the National Organization of Women), gaining strength in the 1960s and 1970s with Kate Millett's *Sexual Politics*, and eventually becoming a resource for academic analysis with the work of Juliet Mitchell, Elaine Showalter, Annette Kolodny, Susan Faludi, Tania Modleski, Susan Gubar and Sandra Gilbert in recent years — after such powerful and articulate advocacy we might expect to find a culture sensitized to questions of gender. And we do. But the nature of that sensitivity suggests that the new culture finds ever more ingenious ways to reprise the same old stories. To consider just some recent films: there is the prostitute with a heart of gold in *Pretty Woman*, the boss's subservient ideal 'daughter' in *Working Girl*, the frozenly-delayed but inevitable death of *Thelma and Louise* (who may be entering the Imaginary, but are certainly punished for their crimes against the patriarchy), the reassertion of the power of marriage and the family in *Fatal Attraction*, the treachery of sexually independent women in *Basic Instinct* and *Single White Female* ... the list seems potentially endless. But critic Robin Wood is hard put to find even a few alternatives. After all, as he puts it, 'why should major studios, which are patriarchal capitalist structures from top to bottom, be expected to finance films that call into question their very premises? It is surprising enough that they agree to distribute them' (Wood, 1986, pp.211–12). This is similarly true of films concerned (however indirectly) with homosexuality. We can also see a tendency for the film business to attempt the ideal (and yet contradictory) compromise of the 'blockbuster' with something-for-everybody: the film that can be read as empowering for lesbians and at the same time seen as a moral fable against the danger of homosexuality (*Basic Instinct*); the film that endorses a women's desire to succeed in a man's world, and shows her how to employ conventional feminity to win that success (*Working Girl*); and the film that offers audiences the excitement of extramarital sexuality, and shows the strength of the single woman, only to damn her unbridled sexual aggression (*Fatal Attraction*). Much the same can be argued of the media's treatment of capitalism (*Wall Street*), Vietnam (*The Deer Hunter, Born on the Fourth of July*), recent American politics (*JFK*), or racial intolerance (*Mississippi Burning*). There are a few films by black film makers like Spike Lee, whose *Do the Right Thing* or *Malcolm X* do pose something of a challenge to the mainstream, as do such films as *Boyz n the Hood*, but the treatment of Alice Walker's *The Color Purple* by director Steven Spielberg, which omitted the lesbian sexuality at the centre of the novel, is arguably more representative. If the cinema has now replaced the theatre and the novel as the popular forum for staging the issues that animate public life we would have to note that its conditions of production prevent rather than enable any significant debate.

SUMMARY

The new American culture has been seen as a proving ground for postmodernism; that is, a culture in which the image has replaced the authentic reality, the 'scenario' has replaced the genuine action, and the individual has been 'decentred' to the point of aimless consumerism. 'Hyperreality' is supposed to have overtaken the real, and nostalgia has overcome any sense of history. Catastrophism on the one hand, and a playful sense of imitation on the other, reduce the possible meanings of literature, film, or other cultural productions. But examination of any given area, such as the treatment of gender in fiction and films, reveals the way that contemporary culture covers over some difficult and contradictory assumptions.

7   WHAT HAPPENED TO *OUR TOWN*?

The ideal American town celebrated by Thornton Wilder is — and arguably always was — a necessary fiction, as a glance back to Sherwood Anderson's *Winesburg, Ohio* (1919) or Sinclair Lewis's *Main Street* (1920), will confirm. The great cities remain, where urban life is carried on in ever more difficult circumstances, the 'golden ghettos' with armed guards at the gates and apartment blocks with doormen and security systems at one end of the social spectrum, the lawless no-go areas of the Bronx or Los Angeles at the other. Life in these cities was a major theme of American fiction from Theodore Dreiser's *Sister Carrie* of 1900 through Sinclair Lewis's *Babbitt* (1922), James T. Farrell's *Studs Lonigan* trilogy (1932–5), Richard Wright's *Native Son* (1940), and so on into Saul Bellow's *The Adventures of Augie March* (1953), *Herzog* (1964) and *Mr Sammler's Planet* (1970), or Hubert Selby's *Last Exit to Brooklyn* (1957). But in 1987 Tom Wolfe, the new-journalist-cum-novelist, launched a sharp attack on what he saw as the novelists' recent turning away from such realist fictions, on the assumption that American culture had shifted into some kind of unknowability that could only be approached by way of paradox and the absurd. In 'Stalking the Billion-footed Beast' (in *Harper's Magazine*) he argued that American writers had shirked their responsibility to respond to the actual conditions around them, specifically New York as exemplary of things-as-they-are. Wolfe quoted a famous remark of Philip Roth, who wrote in 1961 of the writer's despair of inventing a believable American reality because 'the actuality is continually outdoing our talents, and the culture tosses up figures daily that are the envy of any novelist.' Wolfe agreed:

> What novelist would dare concoct a plot in which, say, a southern television evangelist has a tryst in a motel with a church secretary from Babylon, New York — did you have to make it *Babylon*? — and is ruined to the point where he has to sell all his worldly goods at auction, including his air-conditioned doghouse — *air-conditioned doghouse*? — whereupon he is termed a 'decadent pompadour boy' by a second television evangelist, who, we soon learn, has been combing his own rather well-teased blond hair forward over his forehead and wearing headbands in order to disguise himself as he goes into Louisiana waterbed motels with combat-zone prostitutes — *Oh, come on* — prompting a third television evangelist, who is under serious consideration for the Republican presidential nomination, to charge that the damning evidence has been leaked to the press by the Vice President of the United States ... while, meantime, the aforesaid church secretary has now bared her chest to the photographers and has thereby become an international celebrity and has gone to live happily ever after in a castle known as the Playboy mansion ... and her erstwhile tryst mate, evangelist number one, was last seen hiding in the fetal position under his lawyer's couch in Charlotte, North Carolina ... What novelist would dare dream up such crazy stuff and then ask you to suspend your disbelief?
>
> (Wolfe, 1987, p.282)

Wolfe argued for the need to get to grips with such a culture and do it justice in realistic terms, while acknowledging the changes that had been making American life almost unrecognizable. His own writing exemplifies the 'new journalism' that has emerged since the 1960s, a committed, engaged, involved, amused, and often scurrilous writing that puts the observer breathlessly in the thick of it all. Norman Mailer's *The Armies of the Night* (1968), a documentary novel about the Vietnam protests, Hunter Thompson's *Fear and Loathing in Las Vegas* (1972), and Wolfe's own many essays on the contemporary scene offer comparable forays into the penetralia of the American culture. That their powerfully hostile writing has been so complacently received by the political and economic establishment is seen by some as a measure of the culture's ability to absorb criticism, render it harmless, and then financially profit from it. Nevertheless it is a culture that the erstwhile majority believes to be seriously at risk. In the novel Wolfe wrote in reply to his own strictures, *The Bonfire of the Vanities* (1987), the mayor of New York raves to himself as he is hustled away from a disastrous meeting in Harlem, that the Italians, the Irish, and the WASPs —

the old masters of the city — will be watching his humiliation on TV, and probably enjoying the show. He silently harangues them:

> You don't even know, do you? Do you really think this is *your* city any longer? Open your eyes! The greatest city of the twentieth century! Do you think *money* will keep it yours? Come down from your swell co-ops, you general partners and merger lawyers! It's the Third World down there! Puerto Ricans, West Indians, Haitians, Dominicans, Cubans, Columbians, Hondurans, Koreans, Chinese, Thais, Vietnamese, Ecuadorians, Panamanians, Filipinos, Albanians, Senegalese, and Afro-Americans! Go visit the frontiers, you gutless wonders! Morningside Heights, St. Nicholas Park, Washington Heights, Fort Tryon — *por qué pagar más*! The Bronx — the Bronx is finished for you!
>
> You think the future doesn't know how to cross a *bridge*?

>   (Wolfe, 1988, p.13)

Wolfe's perspective is not racist (although some have argued that his book is offensively Eurocentric) so much as an awed recognition of fundamental change, whereby whole enclaves of the American scene cease to be interpretable by the dominant culture. Along with the confusion of language and cultural practices is an uncontrollable drug-related crime epidemic, which creates no-go areas even for the police.

In response to the new urban condition many of the previous inhabitants of the city, those Italians, Irish, and WASPs, have fled, not just to the suburbs but further, out to the 'edge cities', the almost invisible conurbations linked by highways and enacting a make-believe rural existence, sometimes identifiable only by the interstates that surround them, and the clusters of tentative 'village' centres and shopping malls they support. These 'villages' are united only in their shopping and TV watching, with perhaps some involvement with the local high school basketball or baseball teams. The agrarian impulse was always a powerful force in American life, and we could reasonably describe these edge cities as participants in some new form of pastoral; a life lived as though in the country, but painlessly serviced by automobiles, electronics, and elaborate shopping and entertainment facilities in 'the Mall'.

There are some signs, too, that the electronic village Marshall McCluhan so prematurely hailed *is* beginning to take form, as even a city like Cleveland generates its invisible ghostly twin in computer networks (see Figure 10.1).

This is not some distant future, it is the present. The great old cities are thus made obsolete and left to crumble under their load of welfare and health needs, with only impressive financial centres and occasional urban renewal projects to suggest that they still have a future. But in the 'edge cities' attempts to build new local communities, whether for political or social reasons, are made difficult by distance and the absence of a clear central focus. And the inner-city crime, which these outer-suburban dwellers fled, is now following them to their leafy retreats.

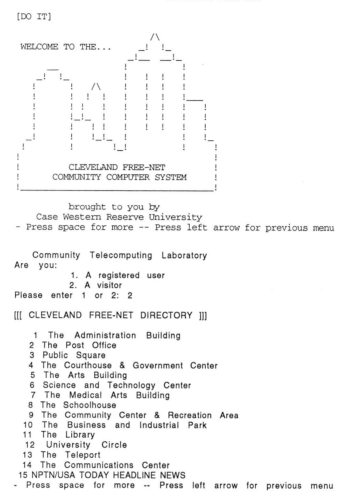

Figure 10.1 *Is this what* Our Town *looks like today? The usual places and functions are replicated electronically, and made instantly accessible via 'telnet' from your own desk (even from the UK)*

There *is* a dominant American culture, expressed through Hollywood, TV and radio, newspapers and magazines, organized and amateur sport, patterns of consumption, leisure, and political consensus; and it shows every sign of eventually absorbing and remaking all the various different cultures that make up American society. Black, Hispanic and Chinese-American writers have recently become prominent, and very substantial changes have occurred, both in the intellectual agenda (in education and in the media) and in the further development of equal opportunities programmes — as signalled by the 'pc' or 'political correctness' furore — despite the backlash against feminism, and despite Reaganomic's reduction in benefit for what is newly diagnosed as the 'underclass'. Proposals have emerged for a radical rethinking of *what* is studied in universities, producing new 'canons' of important texts and knowledge, as in the University of Berkeley, California, where a long-lived controversy over what is culturally significant in 'civilization' has rumbled on for some years. And just as important, *how* it is studied has been addressed. These changes, however, are unlikely very much to ruffle the surface of the culture, driven as it is by the increasingly multinational forces of consumption and commodification processes.

The old 'melting-pot' metaphor, with its suggestion of *enforced* and inevitable cultural assimilation, has been abandoned and replaced by a more differentiated version of American society, the 'salad bowl'. But the metaphor of a salad, however mixed, is still suggestive of an ultimate fate, the incorporation of all its variety in a larger body, the 'American Way'.

SUMMARY

Returning to the idea of *Our Town* we find that the ideal American community was merely a useful fiction and that the chaos and violence of the great cities has resulted in signals of alarm from cultural commentators, and a retreat by urban and suburban Americans into the mock-rural TV communities (or 'edge cities') of outer suburbia.

REFERENCES

Barthelme, D. (1980) *Snow White*, New York, Atheneum (first published in 1965).

Baudrillard, J. (1981) 'Simulcra and simulations' in Poster, M. (ed. and trans.) (1990) *Jean Baudrillard: Selected Writings*, London, Blackwell.

DeLillo, D. (1986) *White Noise*, London, Picador (first published in 1984).

Graham, H.D. and Gurr, T.R. (eds) (1969) *Violence in America: Historical and Comparative Perspectives*, New York, Bantam.

Gusfield, J. (1966) *Symbolic Crusade: Status Politics and the American Temperance Movement*, Urbana, University of Illinois Press.

The Harvard Encyclopedia of American Ethnic Groups (1980), Thernstrom, S. (ed.), New Haven, Harvard University Press.

Higham, J. (1968) *Strangers in the Land: Patterns of American Nativism 1860–1925*, New York, Atheneum.

Jameson, F. (1991) *Postmodernism: or, the Cultural Logic of Late Capitalism*, London, Verso (first published in *New Left Review*, vol.146, in 1984).

Lasch, C. (1978) *The Culture of Narcissism: American Life in an Age of Diminishing Expectations*, New York, Norton.

Litt, E. (1970) *Beyond Pluralism: Ethnic Politics in America*, New York, Scott Foresman.

McCluhan, M. (1964) *Understanding Media*, New York, Signet.

McHale, B. (1987) *Postmodernist Fiction*, London, Methuen.

Marcuse, H. (1968) *One Dimensional Man*, Boston, Beacon Press (first published in 1964).

Miller, P. (1965) *American Thought*, New York, Holt, Rinehart & Winston (first published in 1954).

Pynchon, T. (1990) *Vineland*, London, Secker & Warburg.

Schlesinger Jr, A. (1992) *The Disuniting of America: Reflections on a Multicultural Society*, New York, Norton.

Stearn, G. (ed.) (1968) *McCluhan Hot and Cool*, Harmondsworth, Penguin.

Wilder, T. (1964) *Our Town*, Harmondsworth, Penguin (first published in 1938).

Williams, R. (1971) *Culture and Society 1780–1950*, Harmondsworth, Penguin (first published in 1958).

Wolfe, T. (1987) 'Stalking the billion-footed beast', *Harper's Magazine* (reprinted as an introduction to *The Bonfire of the Vanities*, London, Picador in 1992).

Wolfe, T. (1988) *The Bonfire of the Vanities*, London, Picador (first published in 1987).

Wood, R. (1986) *Hollywood From Vietnam to Reagan*, New York, Columbia University Press.

FURTHER READING

Corrigan, T. (1991) *A Cinema Without Walls: Movies and Culture After Vietnam*, London, Routledge.

Degler, C. (1984) *Out of Our Past: the Forces that Shaped Modern America*, New York, Harper (first published in 1959).

Denzin, N.K. (1991) *Images of Postmodern Society: Social Theory and Contemporary Cinema*, London, Sage.

Tallack, D. (1991) *Twentieth-Century America: the Cultural and Intellectual Context*, London, Longman.

Zinn, H. (1980) *A People's History of the United States*, London, Longman.

INDEX

References to illustrations on unnumbered pages are shown in the index by the number of the plate, for example Plate 3.1.

ACKNOWLEDGEMENTS

Grateful acknowledgement is made to the following sources for permission to reproduce material in this book.

TEXT

Friedan, B. (1963) *The Feminine Mystique,* by permission of Victor Gollancz. Also by permission of W.W. Norton and Co.

TABLE

Table 1.1: Sowell, T. (1981) *Ethnic America: a History,* Basic Books.

FIGURES

Figure 5.1: Reprinted with permission from *TV Guide* ® Magazine. Copyright © 1993 by News America Publications Inc.; Figure 5.2: *Media Systems in Society: Understanding Industries, Strategies and Power,* by Joseph Turow. Copyright © 1992 by Longman Publishing Group; Figure 5.3: Courtesy of A.C. Nielsen Co. Inc.; Figure 10.1: 'Community computer system: title page and main index print out', *Cleveland Free-Net Computer System,* Case Western Reserve University.

ILLUSTRATIONS

Plate 3.1 (both): London Features International (right) photograph by Nick Elgar; Plates 4.1–4.6: Kobal Collection; Plates 9.1, 9.3, 9.7–9.10: Chicago Architectural Photographing Company; Plate 9.2: J. Allan Cash; Plate 9.11: Seagram Building, 1956–8. Architects: Ludwig Mies van der Rohe and Philip Johnson. Photograph by Ezra Stoller 1958. Lent by Joseph E. Seagram & Sons, Inc.

p.80 (left): Copyright Rollie McKenna and Faber and Faber Ltd; p.80 (right): Copyright Robert Shapiro/The Womens Press; p.89 (left): Copyright Jean Weisinger/The Womens Press; p.89 (right): Copyright Chatto and Windus; pp.104, 113, 119, 120, 123, 125, 131: Kobal Collection; p.109: Hulton Deutsch Collection/UPI-Bettmann; p.169: Culver Pictures; p.173: Mander & Mitchenson Collection; pp.200, 202: Frank Driggs Collection; p.204: Copyright Duncan P. Schiedt; p.205: Ken Whitten Collection; pp.213, 216 (bottom): Colin Escott/Showtime Archives (Toronto); p.216 (top left): Courtesy of Capitol Records; p.216 (top right): Redferns; pp.221, 228: National Television Archives; p.239: Copyright Geoff Winningham Photography; p.247: Photographs and Prints Division; Schomburg Center for Research in Black Culture; The New York Public Library; Astor, Lenox and Tilden Foundations; p.267 (left): Chicago Architectural Photographing Company; p.267 (right): *Chicago Tribune* Archives, The First Division Museum at Cantigny; p.271: Buffalo and Erie County Historical Society.